Gulf War Air Power Survey

Gulf War Air Power Survey

Weapons, Tactics, and Training
and
Space Operation

Volume 4

GOVERNMENT REPRINTS PRESS
Washington, D.C.

Printed in The United States of America
Ross & Perry, Inc. Publishers
216 G St., N.E.,
Washington, D.C. 20002
Telephone (202) 675-8300
Facsimile (801)459-7535
info@RossPerry.com

SAN 253-8555

Government Reprints Press Edition 2002

Government Reprints Press is an Imprint of Ross & Perry, Inc.

Library of Congress Control Number: 2001092251
http://www.GPOreprints.com

ISBN 1-931641-08-0

Book Cover designed by Sapna. sapna@rossperry.com

Image on cover is a U. S. Air Force Photo provided by www.af.mil

⊗ The paper used in this publication meets the requirements for permanence established by the American National Standard for Information Sciences "Permanence of Paper for Printed Library Materials" (ANSI Z39.48-1984).

Gulf War Air Power Survey

Staff

Dr. Eliot A. Cohen, *Director*

Col. Emery M. Kiraly	*Executive Director*
Lt. Gen. Robert E. Kelley (Retired, USAF)	*Senior Military Advisor*
Dr. Wayne W. Thompson	*Senior Historical Advisor*
Mr. Ernest D. Cruea	*ANSER Program Manager*
Maj. Joseph W. Patterson	*Executive Officer*
Mr. Lawrence J. Paszek	*Publishing Manager*
Lt. Col. Daniel T. Kuehl	*Chief, Statistics*
Lt. Col. Robert C. Owen	*Chief, Chronology*
Dr. John F. Guilmartin	*Chief, Weapons, Tactics and Training*
Mr. Richard A. Gunkel	*Chief, Logistics, Space, and Support*
Dr. Thomas C. Hone	*Chief, Command, Control, and Organization*
Dr. Alexander S. Cochran	*Chief, Strategy and Plans*
Mr. Barry D. Watts	*Chief, Operations and Effects*
Dr. Thomas A. Keaney	*Chief, Summary Report*

Gulf War Air Power Survey

Review Committee

Foreword

From 16 January through 28 February 1991, the United States and its allies conducted one of the most operationally successful wars in history, a conflict in which air operations played a preeminent role. The Gulf War Air Power Survey was commissioned on 22 August 1991 to review all aspects of air warfare in the Persian Gulf for use by the United States Air Force, but it was not to confine itself to discussion of that institution. The Survey has produced reports on planning, the conduct of operations, the effects of the air campaign, command and control, logistics, air base support, space, weapons and tactics, as well as a chronology and a compendium of statistics on the war. It has prepared as well a summary report and some shorter papers and assembled an archive composed of paper, microfilm, and electronic records, all of which have been deposited at the Air Force Historical Research Agency at Maxwell Air Force Base, Alabama. The Survey was just that, an attempt to provide a comprehensive and documented account of the war. It is not a definitive history: that will await the passage of time and the opening of sources (Iraqi records, for example) that were not available to Survey researchers. Nor is it a summary of lessons learned: other organizations, including many within the Air Force have already done that. Rather, the Survey provides an analytical and evidentiary point of departure for future studies of the air campaign. It concentrates on an analysis of the operational level of war in the belief that this level of warfare is at once one of the most difficult to characterize and one of the most important to understand.

The Survey was directed by Dr. Eliot Cohen of Johns Hopkins University's School of Advanced International Studies and was staffed by a mixture of civilian and military analysts, including retired officers from the Army, Navy, and Marine Corps. It was divided into task forces, most of which were run by civilians working temporarily for the Air Force. The work produced by the Survey was examined by a distinguished review committee, that included scholars, retired general officers from the Air Force, Navy, and Army, as well as former and current senior government officials. Throughout, the Survey strived to conduct its research in a spirit of impartiality and scholarly rigor. Its members had as their standard the observation of Mr. Franklin D'Olier, chairman of the United States Strategic Bombing Survey during and after the second World War: "We wanted to burn into everybody's souls that fact that the survey's responsibility . . . was to ascertain facts and to seek truth, eliminating completely any preconceived theories or dogmas."

The Survey attempted to create a body of data common to all of the reports. Because one group of researchers compiled this core material while other task forces were researching and drafting other, more narrowly focused studies, it is possible that discrepancies exist among the reports with regard to points of detail. More importantly, authors were given discretion, within the bounds of evidence and plausibility, to interpret events as they saw them. In some cases, task forces came to differing conclusions about particular aspects of this war. Such divergences of view were expected and even desired: the Survey was intended to serve as a point of departure for those who read its reports, and not their analytical terminus.

In the classified version, this volume consists of two reports: *Weapons, Tactics, and Training*, which focuses on Coalition as well as Iraqi air forces and Iraqi surface-based air defenses in the Gulf War, and *Space Operations*, which examines the use of space systems, mobilization of equipment for space operations, and the role of commercial space systems within a military context. However, because the Space report contains such an excessive amount of classified detail that the balance would be incomprehensible, the report is not published in the unclassified volume.

Acknowledgments

The Survey's members owe a great debt of gratitude to Secretary of the Air Force Donald B. Rice, who conceived of the project, provided it with resources, and set for it the highest standards of independence and objectivity. Many organizations and individuals gave generously of their resources and time to support this effort. Various branches and commands of the Air Force were particularly helpful in providing material for and, in some cases, personnel to conduct the study. The United States Navy, Marine Corps, and Army aided with this study in different ways, including the sharing of data pertaining to the air war. A number of the United States' Coalition partners also made available individuals and records that were vital to the Survey's work. Many participants in the war, including senior political officials and officers from all of the Services were willing to speak with the Survey and share their recollections of Desert Shield and Desert Storm. Private students of the Gulf War also made available their knowledge of the crisis and conflict. Wherever possible and appropriate such assistance has been acknowledged in the text.

The Survey's independence was its reason for being. Each report is the product of the authors who wrote it and does not necessarily represent the views of the Review Committee, the Air Force or the Department of Defense.

Security Review

The Gulf War Air Power Survey reports were submitted to the Department of Defense for policy and security review. In accordance with this review, certain information has been removed from the original text. These areas have been annotated as [DELETED].

Gulf War Air Power Survey
Reports

Summary Report

Volume I:

Part I:	Planning Report
Part II:	Command and Control Report

Volume II:

Part I:	Operations Report
Part II:	Effectiveness Report

Volume III:

Part I:	Logistics Report
Part II:	Support Report

Volume IV:

Part I:	Weapons, Tactics, and Training Report
Part II:	Space Report

Volume V:

Part I:	A Statistical Compendium
Part II:	Chronology

Contents

Part I

Weapons, Tactics, and Training

Part I

Weapons, Tactics, and Training

Task Force Chief

Dr. John F. Guilmartin, Jr.

Principal Authors

Mr. Richard J. Blanchfield
Mr. Paul Bloch
Mr. Jon Dunham
Lt. Col. Robert D. Eskridge
Col. Frank L. Goldstein
Dr. John F. Guilmartin, Jr.
Capt. Jeffrey A. Hodgdon
Col. Daniel W. Jacobowitz
Lt. Col. Charles P. Marshall
Col. Mark L. Tarpley

Principal Contributors

MSgt. Richard Blair
Mr. Donald Kellum
MSgt. Linda Morrison
Mr. Dewey Nash
Maj. Theron L. Severance

Contents

Figures

Tables

Report Acknowledgements

The Task Force for this report surveyed a mass of highly technical material in considerable detail. The experience and professional background of several members was directly relevant to the project, and the principal authors reviewed the entire report for completeness, accuracy, and objectivity. Authorship was therefore a shared endeavor. The task force's leader, Dr. John F. Guilmartin, Jr., was editor-in-chief and primary author of the report. Other principal contributions came from Col. Daniel W. Jacobowitz, who as an associate editor wrote, organized, and structured this report; retired Navy captain Paul Bloch, who became the associate editor to finalize this report and authored chapter one; Col. Frank Goldstein, Air Force professional psychologist, who authored sections in chapter four; retired Marine Corps Col. Rich Blanchfield, who helped to edit final versions and authored a section in chapter four; Col. Mark Tarpley, who provided final technical editing and authored sections on air refueling, B-52s, and electronic warfare; Lt. Col. Charles Marshall, who provided expertise, research, and inputs for the report and authored the chapter on training; Lt. Col. Robert Eskridge, who provided expertise, research, and inputs on Iraqi air defenses; Capt. Jeff Hodgdon, who provided final technical editing, expertise, research, and input and wrote most sections on aircraft, weapons, and tactics; and Mr. Jon Dunham, who authored the section on tactical deception.

MSgt. Richard Blair and MSgt. Linda Morrison were responsible for archival research; Mr. Dewey Nash for artwork, with several illustrations prepared by Maj. Randall Marbury. Editors Ms. Anne H. Predzin and Mr. Chris Pankow deserve credit for enhancing the quality of the report. Finally, Ms. Kathy Glahe was responsible for data input, word processing, and administrative support during the entire project, without which the timely completion of the report would have been impossible.

Introduction

This report brings together analyses of three crucial determinants of an armed force's overall capability:

- weapons–the tools used by the soldier, sailor, and airman,
- tactics–the ways in which the tools are used to produce desired effects and,
- training–the way in which the individual soldier, sailor, and airman acquires the skills required to combine weapons and tactics into the operational art of warfare.

The report focuses on the impact of these three elements on the application of air power projected by the U.S. and Coalition forces in the Gulf War. The information and conclusions presented provide background essential to a more complete understanding of the facts, principles, and precepts developed and discussed in other volumes of this study.

The research to support this report was drawn from several sources. First and foremost, the extensive operational and technical expertise of the principal authors and contributors served as a reservoir of knowledge and background. Their primary search for information focused on intelligence estimates, unit reports, flight data bases, and earlier studies pertinent to the task. Additionally, the authors interviewed Gulf War participants from the United States and Coalition countries and obtained volumes of supporting documents and information now resting within the GWAPS archive. Because of time constraints and the ambitious scope of the task, some issues and topics within this report are either addressed only at the surface or not addressed at all. These issues are usually identified as areas for future study.

To frame ensuing discussions and to establish a basis for comparison, the report begins with an overview of weapons, tactics, and training within the Iraqi armed forces. Quantitative indices and past performance indicated that Iraq possessed a formidable military organization–a battle-hardened force that could test the capabilities of any military power thrown against it. Chapter one looks beyond numbers and Iraqi propaganda to examine the full range of Iraq's weapon systems and its tactics for employing them. The chapter continues by describing Iraqi tactics and performance during the Iran-Iraq war and concludes with a discussion of Iraqi actions and responses to Coalition air power during the Gulf War.

Chapter two begins an in-depth look at U.S. and Coalition aircraft and weapons used during the Gulf War. To aid the analysis, the weapons and aircraft are grouped by mission: air-to-ground, electronic warfare and reconnaissance, and air-to-air. This study of equipment and systems yields an understanding of the decided advantage that the Coalition forces possessed by virtue of their technological superiority.

Chapters three and four are a comprehensive examination of the tactics employed by U.S. and to a lesser extent Coalition air forces. Chapter three begins by discussing the fundamental aerial employment tactics used in the war, with U.S. Air Force tactics as the central focus. The chapter then addresses the capabilities required to accomplish representative Gulf War missions ranging from ordnance delivery to air-to-air engagements to electronic warfare. To illustrate these capabilities, a typical mission and associated planning considerations and special requirements are analyzed in detail. Next, the focus shifts to the tactics employed to achieve specific objectives. First is a study of the way in which Coalition aircraft attacked the core of Iraqi power. The study discusses the opening attacks designed to not only achieve air superiority but to strike directly at Iraq's strategic core, paralyzing the national leadership and neutralizing its major offensive threats. This discussion is followed by a look at Coalition air operations designed to gain and maintain air superiority by neutralizing the Iraqi air defense network and eliminating the Iraqi air force as a factor in the war. The chapter concludes by examining the tactics used by Coalition air forces to attack Iraqi ground and naval forces, with particular emphasis on close air support/battlefield air interdiction missions.

While chapter three examines the tactics that contributed to the Coalition victory, chapter four highlights special systems, tactics, and issues that made the Gulf War different from previous conflicts. Stealth and low-observable technology, which played a key role in the outcome of

Desert Storm, is the initial topic of discussion. Three systems used in the Gulf War—the F-117 stealth fighter, the Tomahawk Land Attack Missile, and the Conventional Air-Launched Cruise Missile—are discussed in detail. The next section assesses the relative merits of mass bombing versus those of precision-guided munitions. The capability to conduct a twenty-four hour air war is addressed next. This analysis reveals both improved capabilities and remaining significant limitations. The next section of the chapter details efforts used to neutralize the threat of Iraqi Scud missiles and describes the campaign against Scuds, from the early effort to destroy fixed-launch sites and storage facilities to later attempts to search out and destroy mobile Scud launchers. Chapter four concludes by examining special operations, air refueling, tactical deception, and psychological operations from the airpower perspective.

The weapons of Desert Storm and the tactics for using them were only part of the story. This war, like all of its predecessors, was fought by people. For people to succeed in war, they must be well trained in the tactics, techniques, and procedures required to use the tools of their trade effectively. Chapter five examines training, the means through which U.S. and, to a lesser extent, Coalition airmen learned their craft and maintained their proficiency. The chapter addresses three essential questions: Did the U.S. and Coalition air forces fight the way they had been trained? Were some kinds of training more useful than others? Were combat skills continually honed in preparing for the war, or did they deteriorate during the five months of Desert Shield? The chapter begins with a look at the pre-August 1990 training of combat ready forces before deployment to Southwest Asia. It then addresses the training accomplished during the next five months during Desert Shield. The analysis takes into account the conflicting demands of training and combat readiness. It concludes by discussing the training initiatives advanced and implemented during Desert Storm to modify procedures as the war unfolded. Appendices provide further information on aerial definitions, psyops leaflets, and basic flight training by the Services; recurring exercises designed to maintain combat readiness; and particular training problems experienced by aircrews from B-52 units, Special Operations Forces, and the Navy and Marine Corps.

The authors of this report attempted to provide an understandable frame of reference for analyzing the air campaign in the Gulf War. The enormity of this task was complicated by the highly technical developments of recent decades that produced exceptionally capable weapons and systems, which, in many cases, were being employed in combat for the first time. These seemingly revolutionary technical advancements produced the best equipped, most highly trained air power forces in the history of the United States and perhaps the world. It is hoped that the ensuing pages will impart to the reader a basic understanding of the weapons, tactics, and training responsible for the airpower successes in Desert Storm.

1

Iraqi Weapons, Tactics, And Training

Overall Defense Capabilities

In the summer of 1990, the Iraqi armed forces looked very impressive on paper. Iraq had over a million men in its regular army, fourth largest in the world. It had a substantial inventory of reliable, technologically sophisticated, relatively modern instruments of war. Its Army had over 5,000 tanks, 8,000 other armored vehicles, and 3,300 artillery pieces. It had a multilayered air defense system and an air force with over 700 tactical aircraft, including some of the latest Soviet designs such as the MIG-29 Fulcrum and SU-25 Frogfoot. Iraq had used chemical weapons in the Iran-Iraq War and against the Kurds, and was believed to be developing nuclear weapons and the long-range missiles to deliver them.

If the Iraqis performed up to the standards of their equipment, they had the potential to give any opponent a tough fight. However, the impressive numbers and capabilities disguised serious deficiencies. The highly centralized command and control system needed to support the political structure also acted to stifle the initiative of lower ranking personnel. The few pieces of new equipment overshadowed the fact that most of the rest were old and technologically inferior to the best Western systems. The large number of personnel under arms hid the fact that most were poorly trained conscripts.

This chapter discusses Iraqi weapons systems and tactics. It is meant to support the discussion of Coalition tactics and weapon systems that follows. The chapter then describes and analyzes the Iraqi air command and control structure, including equipment. Ground-based systems such as surface-to-air (SAM) missiles and antiaircraft artillery will be discussed first, followed by a discussion of aircraft and related systems. To provide some feel for Iraqi ideas on tactical employment, the chapter discusses Iraqi performance in the Iran-Iraq War. It concludes with a look at Iraqi tactics and behavior in response to the onslaught of the Coalition air assault.

Military and Air Defense Command and Control

Two key factors drove the organization of the Iraqi armed forces. First, it had to be centralized. As with everything else in the Iraqi Government, supreme military authority rested solely in the hands of Saddam Hussein. Though he had no military experience, he assumed the rank of Marshal and wore military uniforms to underscore the fact that he was the Commander-in-Chief. To reinforce his control of the military, Saddam installed relatives and kinsmen in key positions and established a parallel reporting system through Ba'ath party officers in the military units.[1] Survival of the regime was the first priority of the government and the armed forces. Iraqi's relations with its Middle Eastern neighbors was the second factor having an impact on its military equipment and tactics. The Israeli attack on the Osirak nuclear reactor in 1981 caused Iraq to disperse and harden its weapons research facilities and concern itself with attacks from the west. Similarly, the performance of its forces in the eight-year war with Iran had precipitated major developments in its air defense and air forces in an attempt to address that threat from the east. In effect, Iraq faced a "two front" threat.

At the time of the Gulf War, the highly centralized military command and control systems all led to Saddam Hussein. In order for these systems to operate properly, Saddam needed to receive an immense amount of accurate information. Among the systems that provided this information was a mainframe computer installed in the Iraqi Ministry of Defense computer center. Information ran up to the Presidential Palace and General Headquarters and down to the brigade level and improved Iraq's ability to plan large scale operations.[2] The Iraqis purchased the system

---

[1]Samir al-Khalil, *Republic of Fear*, Pantheon Books, 1989, p 26. For a list of Saddam Hussein's associates in the government and military of Iraq see also Appendices 1 and 2 of *Instant Empire* by Simon Henderson, Mercury House, 1991.

[2](S/NF/WN/NC) *Iraqi Threat to U.S. Forces*, Navy SPEAR, NIC 26605-018-90, 10 Dec 1990, p 1-5. This document was the source of much of the material in this section. It was, in fact, compiled from a variety of sources, including CIA, DIA, Defense Attaches, and Army, Navy, and Air Force weapons research facilities. It was a primary source of information about Iraq before the Gulf War.

to correct deficiencies noted during the Iran-Iraq war and the Iraqi intelligence system was a vital element.

Iraq's air defense system was formidable. It was optimized against two threat axes, east against Iran, and west against Israel.[3] Since the country's material assets were so widely dispersed, no attempt was made to defend them all; instead, defense of the capital was considered foremost.[4]

The Iraqi Army and the Iraqi Air and Air Defense Forces (IAADF) shared responsibility for air defense. The Iraqi Army was responsible for tactical air defense of the ground force headquarters, maneuver units, and logistics facilities. The IAADF was in charge of strategic air defense, which included control of Iraqi airspace, defense of key areas, protection of important installations and most important of all, protection of Baghdad.[5] IAADF organizational structure is shown below (Figure 1). Army air defense was organized as shown in Figure 2.

The highly centralized air defense structure relied on extensive, redundant connectivity. The Iraqi Air Defense Forces (IADF) headquarters was at Rasheed Air Base, near Baghdad. The IADF's Air Defense Operations Center assigned air defense priorities, but did not directly control operations within the air defense sectors. Each air defense sector had a sector operations center (SOC), which controlled and was responsible for all air defense within its area. Each SOC was supported by several intercept operations centers (IOCs). Each IOC was in turn fed by a network of visual and radar reporting posts. In theory, the SOCs made all combat engagement decisions for their respective sectors, while the

---

[3](S/NF/WN) Navy SPEAR Office briefing to GWAPS, 15 May 1992.

[4](S/NF/WN/NC) "Iraq as a Military Adversary (C/NF)," Central Intelligence Agency, SNIE 2-5-90, Oct 1990.

[5](S/NF/WN/NC) Iraqi Threat to U.S. Forces, p 3-7.

Figure 1
IAADF Organizational Structure[6]

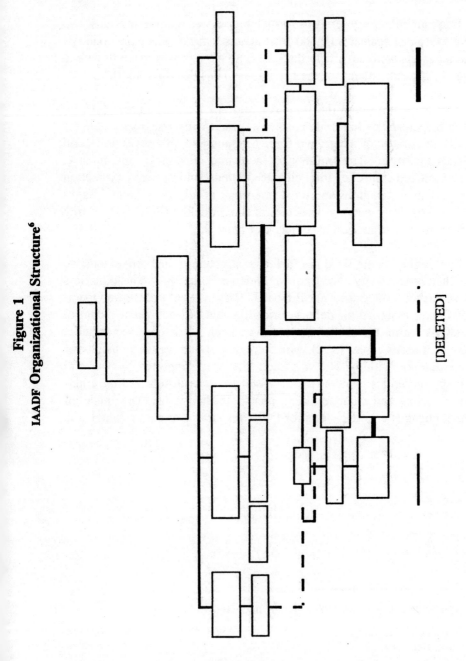

[DELETED]

[6](S/NF/WN/NC) *Ibid*, p 3-8.

Figure 2
Army Organizational Structure[7]

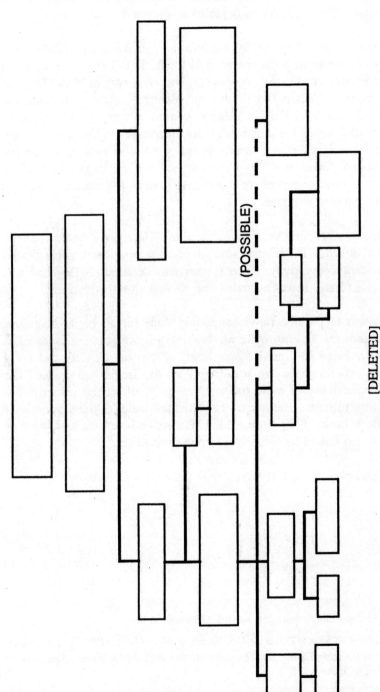

(POSSIBLE)

[DELETED]

[7] (S//NF/WN/NC) *Ibid*, p 3-9.

respective IOC controlled the use of SAMs or interceptors to carry out the engagement. This structure is depicted in Figure 3.

Utilizing Soviet doctrine, the air defense system was designed around KARI,[8] a computerized Command and Control (C^2) system purchased from the French. KARI was the spine and nervous system of the Iraqi air defense system. When functioning as advertised, KARI combined the disparate elements of the air defense system–including early warning radars, ground controlled intercept radars, interceptor fighters, surface-to-air missiles, and anti-aircraft artillery–into a cohesive system responsive to centralized direction. The technical and tactical capabilities of its individual system components made this system a potentially serious threat to Coalition airpower.

Initial contracts for KARI were initiated in 1974 and the system became operational in 1987. The primary strength of the system was its sophisticated and redundant connectivity. The system was centered in Baghdad and covered all of Iraq. It was extended into Kuwait after the invasion.[9]

KARI was to provide rapid communications for air battle diagnosis and management. To ensure the survivability of KARI, the Iraqis installed multiple hardened communications links. From the Soviets and from their own experience in the Iran-Iraq War, the Iraqis had learned the tactical vulnerability of radio transmissions. To offset the vulnerability of radio transmissions, the Iraqis connected the nodes of the system with a network of buried fiber optic cables. For redundancy, each element of KARI was also linked by microwave communications.[10]

[DELETED]

---

[8]The acronym comes from Iraq spelled backwards in French.

[9](S/NF/WN/NC) *Iraqi Threat To U.S. Forces*, p 3-15. Also see (S/NF) *Iraq Ground and Air Force Doctrine, Tactics, and Operations* (C/NF), *Defense Intelligence Agency DDB-2600-6123-90*, Feb 1990, p 115.

[10](S/NF/WN/NC) *Iraqi Threat To U.S. Forces*, pp 3-15, 3-17.

Figure 3
Iraqi Air Defense Command and Control Chart[11]

FIGURE DELETED

---

[11](S/NF/WN/NC) *Ibid*, p 3-16.

[DELETED]¹²

[DELETED]¹³

[DELETED]¹⁴ [DELETED]¹⁵

[DELETED]¹⁶ [DELETED].¹⁷

Battle management was done at the SOCs. These nodes had engagement authority and held sufficient information to enable the controllers to understand the overall air situation within their sectors. The SOCs were the critical element of the integrated battle management system.¹⁸ [DELETED]. The SOC personnel determined the best systems to engage the targets, even the type of intercept or the number of missiles to be fired at the intruder. [DELETED] Once decisions were made, they were immediately passed to the affected IOCs for ground-controlled intercept by manned aircraft, missile or gun engagement.¹⁹

Each IOC developed the air situation for its area, using input from as many as six radar reporting posts along with voice or data reports from observation and command posts. [DELETED]²⁰

Information, the life blood of the IOCs, came to them from their radar reporting posts (RP). [DELETED] Skilled radar operators, crucial to the operation of the RPs, had to view tracks and select likely targets.²¹

---

¹²(S/NF/WN/NC) *Ibid*, p 3-17.

¹³(S/NF/WN/NC) *Ibid*, p 3-19.

¹⁴(S/NF/WN/NC) *Ibid*, p 3-20.

¹⁵(S/NF/WN) SPEAR Briefing.

¹⁶(S/NF) *Iraqi Ground and Air Force Doctrine, Tactics, and Operations* (C/NF), p 115.

¹⁷(S/NF/WN/NC) *Iraqi Threat to U.S. Forces*, p 3-20.

¹⁸(S/NF) *Iraqi Ground and Air Forces Doctrine, Tactics, and Operations* (C/NF), p 115.

¹⁹(S/NF/WN/NC) *Iraqi Threat to U.S. Forces*, p 3-20.

²⁰(S/NF/WN/NC) *Ibid*, p 3-22.

²¹(S/NF/WN/NC) *Ibid*, pp 3-22, 3-24.

Another older method of tracking aircraft was also an important part of the KARI system. Observation posts (OPs) provided aural and, presumably, visual tracking to the KARI system, filling in voids in radar coverage.[22] [DELETED][23]

Although the IOC sub-system was efficient within its design limitations, it was vulnerable to saturation. [DELETED][24] [DELETED]

In summation, while the KARI system was designed to be operated by personnel with roughly the western equivalent of a sixth grade education, training for operators at the lower levels was still crucial. The level and extent of initial and follow-on training programs for operators was unknown.[25] Also unknown was how much effort the Iraqis invested in live ground controlled intercept (GCI) training. [DELETED] Like other aspects of the Iraqi defense forces the KARI system looked much better on paper than in combat.

SAM and AAA Systems

KARI was probably the most advanced aspect of the Iraqi air defense system. It was able to integrate the wide variety of air defense weapons Iraq had obtained from numerous sources around the world. The variety of sources was a weakness in the system. Table 1 lists the Surface-to-Air Missile (SAM) Order of Battle for Iraq in December 1990. While the number of launchers (see Table 1) was large, it was not sufficient to protect all of Iraq. As a result, Iraq effectively established a point defense system. Figure 4 illustrates SAM and radar coverage. Priority was given to the areas critical to the survival of the regime. Figure 5 shows the deployment of SAM systems around Baghdad, the seat of Saddam's power, and the site of the most critical military installations.

These SAMs were assigned to the Iraqi Air and Air Defense Force (IAADF) and were grouped into battalions and regiments to defend priority

---

[22](S/NF) *Iraq Ground and Air Force Doctrine, Tactics, and Operations* (C/NF), p 115.

[23](S/NF/WN/NC) *Iraqi Threat to U.S. Forces*, pp 3-24 and 3-38, 39.

[24](S/NF/WN) CDR Fitzgerald, SPEAR Briefing, and (S/NF/WN/NC) *Iraqi Threat to U.S. Forces*, p 3-20.

[25](S/NF/WN/NC) *Iraqi Threat to U.S. Forces*, p 3-25.

Table 1
SAM Order of Battle For Iraq[26]

Type	Origin	Batteries	[DELETED]
SA-2	Soviet		
SA-3	Soviet		
SA-6	Soviet		
SA-8	Soviet	[DELETED]	[DELETED]
SA-9	Soviet		
SA-13	Soviet		
SA-14[27]	Soviet		
Roland	French		
		120	

areas. A senior air defense officer was charged with coordinating defense of the area. [DELETED].[28]

A problem with the Iraqi SAM systems was the mix of older and newer equipment. In some cases, the more modern SA-6 system had to be withdrawn from the frontline army units it was designed to protect, to replace or supplement aging SA-2 or SA-3 missile systems. Table 1 also reveals that most of the Iraqi SAM systems were of Soviet origin. This meant that the tactical employment, firing doctrine, and crew training were heavily influenced by Soviet doctrine. Large numbers of antiaircraft artillery (AAA) weapons supported the surface-to-air missile systems in certain areas.

[DELETED]

---

[26](S/NF/WN/NC) *Ibid*, p U-1; GWAPS *Statistical Compendium*, Table 3, "Iraqi Order of Battle", Page 19.

[27](S/NF) SA-14s, shoulder-fired, infrared homing missiles, and mobile Roland systems were not organized into batteries. They were normally employed individually or in teams.

[28](S/NF/WN/NC) *Ibid*, p 3-71.

Figure 4
Radar-Guided SAM and EW Radar Coverage[29]

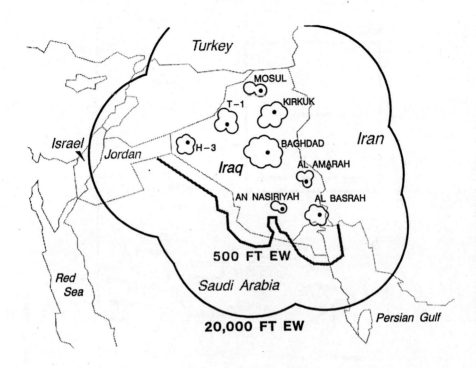

Iraqi SAM Systems

SA-2 Guideline/SA-3 GOA

The SA-2 and SA-3 systems formed the backbone of the Iraqi air defense system. These older systems were usually supplemented by an SA-6 battery.[30] The SA-2, while updated somewhat, was originally designed to go against the B-52 and presented few problems to modern,

---

[29](S/NF) Briefing Slide, CENTAF presentation to GWAPS Team, Shaw AFB, 9 Mar 1992. U.S. CAP and AWACs positions have been removed.

[30](S/NF) *Iraqi Ground and Air Forces Doctrine, Tactics, and Operations* (C/NF), p 115.

Figure 5
Radar-Guided SAM Locations In The Baghdad Area[31]

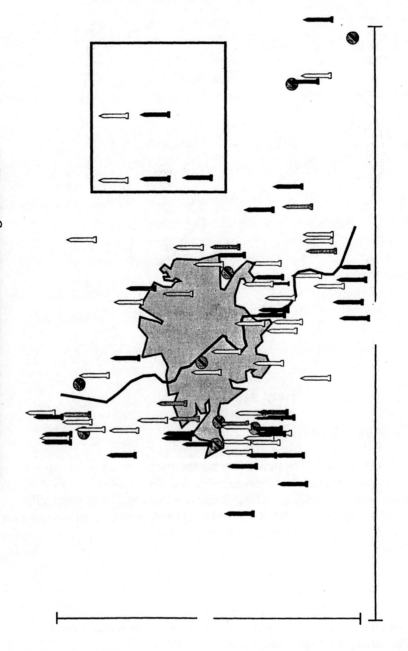

[31](S) *52d Fighter Wing Desert Storm, A Success Story*, Briefing, GWAPS files.

12

fast moving, maneuverable fighter aircraft. It had a range of twenty seven nautical miles and was designed for high-altitude targets.[32] The SA-3, developed shortly after the SA-2, had a range of fourteen miles and was designed to defeat low- to medium-altitude aircraft.[33]

[DELETED][34] [DELETED][35]

[DELETED][36] [DELETED][37]

SA-6 Gainful

The SA-6 was developed in the 1960s to protect maneuvering ground units. Originally employed by the Iraqis in that capacity, it was withdrawn from frontline units during the Iran-Iraq War to protect key strategic sites. The SA-6 had a range of thirteen miles and was designed to be used mainly against very-low- to medium-altitude threats.[38] After the Iran-Iraq War, many of the SA-6 batteries were returned to their ground units, particularly the Republican Guards.

During Desert Shield, SA-6s were again placed at fixed sites defending airfields, key logistics centers, and command and control positions. [DELETED][39] SA-6 systems were also concentrated around Baghdad and the H3 areas. [DELETED][40]

---

[32](S/NF) *Multi-Command Manual (MCM) 3-1*, Vol II, *"Threat Reference Guide and Counter Tactics,"* U.S. Air Force, 1991, pp 5-2 to 5-10. Henceforth referred to as *MCM 3-1, Vol II*. According to this manual, the maximum range is based on a target at 500 knots.

[33](S/NF) *Ibid*, pp 5-9 to 5-14.

[34](S/NF) *Ibid*, p 5-14.

[35](S/NF/WN/NC) *Iraqi Threat to U.S. Forces*, pp 3-72, 3-73.

[36](S/NF/WN/NC) *Ibid*, p 3-72.

[37](S/NF/WN/NC) GWAPS *Statistical Compendium*, Table 217, "Desert Storm Coalition Aircraft Attrition."

[38](S/NF) *MCM 3-1, Vol II*, pp 5-26 to 5-37.

[39](S/NF/WN/NC) *Iraqi Threat to U.S. Forces*, p 3-73.

[40](S/NF/WN/NC) GWAPS *Statistical Compendium*, Table 204, "Desert Storm Coalition Aircraft Attrition."

SA-8 Gecko

The SA-8 was another tactical SAM designed to protect maneuver units. However, most SA-8s had been incorporated into the joint defense of strategically important areas, as had the SA-6s. The SA-8 had a maximum range of six nautical miles. [DELETED][41]

Roland

The French Roland was another short-range missile designed to protect tactical ground units. It had a range of approximately three and one half miles.[42] Approximately thirteen Roland I (clear weather) systems and one hundred Roland II (all weather) systems had been sold to Iraq. By the beginning of the Gulf War, it appeared that most Rolands had been incorporated into the strategic air defense system protecting high-value targets.[43]

[DELETED][44] [DELETED],[45] [DELETED];[46] [DELETED].

SA-9 Gaskin/SA-13 Gopher

As Desert Storm approached, the only mounted systems organic to Army Air Defense units apparently were the SA-9 and SA-13s. These short-range systems used infrared seekers and could be foiled by flare countermeasures. However, fired against an unaware target, they could be quite effective. The SA-9 and SA-13s were usually used in conjunction with the highly capable ZSU-23/4 AAA weapon system with its Gun Dish radar. The ZSU-23/4 was generally considered the most lethal threat to low-flying aircraft. [DELETED].[47]

---

[41](S/NF) MCM 3-1, Vol II, pp 5-33 to 5-37.

[42](S/NF) Ibid, pp 5-134 to 5-137.

[43](S/NF/WN/NC) Iraqi Threat to U.S. Forces, p 3-75.

[44](S/NF/WN/NC) Ibid.

[45](S/NF/WN/NC) GWAPS Statistical Compendium, Table 204, "Desert Storm Coalition Aircraft Attrition."

[46](S) Robert F. Dorr, Desert Storm Air War (Motor Book Intl: Osceola, NY, 1991), p 48. [DELETED].

[47](S/NF/WN/NC) Iraqi Threat to U.S. Forces, pp 3-80, 3-81.

Man Portable Air Defense SAMs (Man PADS)

The Iraqis had SA-14s and over 3,000 SA-7s. Both were small, shoulder-fired, heat-seeking missiles used for close-in defense. The SA-7 (Grail) was believed to be a copy of the U.S. Redeye infrared surface-to-air missile. The SA-7 had a range of about two-and-one-half nautical miles and had to be fired at the heat created by an aircraft's exhaust.[48] The SA-14 had a range of about three nautical miles and had an improved all-aspect seeker. SA-7s and SA-14s were distributed throughout the Iraqi Army and Air Defense Forces. Overall, infrared surface-to-air missiles were credited with downing or damaging several Coalition aircraft.[49]

Hawk

Iraqi forces captured a number of U.S.-made Hawk SAM batteries from the Kuwaitis. Hawk was a highly capable missile with excellent low-altitude and ECM capabilities. Since the Iraqis proved unable to operate the Hawk, it was not a factor in Desert Storm, although there was initial concern that it might be used.[50]

AntiAircraft Artillery (AAA)

Numerically, the most important element of the Iraqi Air Defense system was the antiaircraft artillery. Table 2 is a list of the number and country of origin of the various AAA weapons. These 7,500 or more AAA weapons proved to be the most effective Iraqi antiaircraft systems in both the Iran-Iraq War and in Desert Storm. As with other Iraqi air defense weapon systems, AAA was deployed to protect the most important strategic locations. AAA systems used with co-located SAM systems presented a formidable threat to Coalition aircraft. Some post-war evaluations of Iraqi tactics indicated that the purpose of SAMs was not to destroy attacking aircraft as much as to force Coalition aircraft to maneuver into the AAA envelope.

---

[48](S/NF) *MCM 3-1, Vol II*, pp 5-79 to 5-80.

[49](S/NF/WN/NC) GWAPS, *Statistical Compendium*, Table 204, "Desert Storm Coalition Aircraft Attrition."

[50](S/NF/WN/NC) *Iraqi Threat to U.S. Forces*, p 3-76. Also see (S/NF) *MCM 3-1, Vol II*, pp 5-106 to 5-111.

Table 2
AntiAircraft Artillery[51]

Nomenclature	Country of Origin	A/O 1 FEB 91
Self-Propelled		
57mm, ZSU-57-2	USSR	[DELETED]
30mm, M53/59, M53/70	Czechoslovakia	
23mm, ZSU-23/4	USSR	
(Subtotal)		————
Towed		
130mm, KS-30	USSR	
100mm, KS-19	USSR	
85mm, KS-12/12A/18	USSR	
57mm, Type 59	China	
57mm, S-60	USSR	
40mm, Bofors L-70	Switzerland	[DELETED]
37mm, Type 55	China	
37mm, M1939	USSR	
35mm, Oerlikon	Switzerland	
23mm, ZU-23/2	USSR	
20mm, M55 Single	Yugoslavia	
14.5mm, ZPU-4	USSR	
14.5mm, MR-4	Romania	
14.5mm, Type 56	China	
14.5mm, ZPU-2	USSR/Bulgaria	
(Subtotal)		7600
Total Air Defense		

Most Iraqi AAA fell into two categories: (1) the ZSU-23/2, 23mm cannon systems, and 14.5mm heavy machine guns firing contact-fuzed or kinetic energy rounds; and (2) larger guns firing rounds with time-delay fuzes. Guns in the first category had high rates of fire, and relatively short effective ranges, and had to achieve a direct hit to inflict damage. As a general rule, they were used for barrage fire. Guns in the second category fired longer range exploding shells at a slower rate of fire. The primary damage mechanism was the collision of the fragments from the exploding shells with the aircraft. These larger weapons were used mainly in aimed and sector fire. The ZSU-23/4 falls into a separate

---

[51](S/NF/WN/NC) *Iraqi Threat To U.S. Forces*, p V-1; GWAPS *Statistical Compendium*, Table 3, "Iraqi Order of Battle" p 18.

category. A self-propelled, four-barrelled system with an integral Gun Dish fire control radar, it was capable of delivering a high volume of accurate fire against individual high-speed targets.[52]

As with surface-to-air missiles, most of the AAA systems were older but were still potentially dangerous. While relatively unsophisticated, many of the AAA weapons posed a significant threat by virtue of the numbers in which they were employed. AAA batteries were frequently located on specially constructed ten-to-thirteen-foot berms for better coverage of low-flying aircraft. Many were located on the roofs of buildings in cities, notably Baghdad and Kuwait City. AAA batteries in important areas like Baghdad were connected with simple command and control systems to receive barrage and cease fire orders. They could also receive information about impending attacks from early warning radars.

Figure 6 shows the distribution of infrared SAM and AAA guns in Iraq. The numbers tell the story. Even considering the age of the systems, AAA remained a threat to Coalition aircraft flying below 15,000 feet. It was implicated in the loss of several aircraft during the Gulf War and was second only to infrared surface-to-air missiles in suspected downings.

The Iraqi Air Force

Another key element of the Iraqi air defense structure was the Iraqi Air Force, which had two primary missions. First, to defend Iraq against hostile attack, it provided interceptors to the air defense system. Second, it performed this strategic role of conducting offensive air operations. The Iraqi Air Force was an elite force, with the best personnel available and some first-rate equipment, but it had problems reaching its potential. Table 3 lists aircraft in the Iraqi Air Force.

The over 700 plus combat aircraft do not present an accurate measure of Iraqi capability vis-a-vis their Coalition counterparts. Table 4 roughly compares Iraqi aircraft with their approximate Coalition equivalents.

---

[52] The ZSU-23/4 was first used in numbers in the 1973 Arab-Israeli War and proved highly effective against low-flying jets.

Figure 6
Iraqi SAMs and AAA[53]

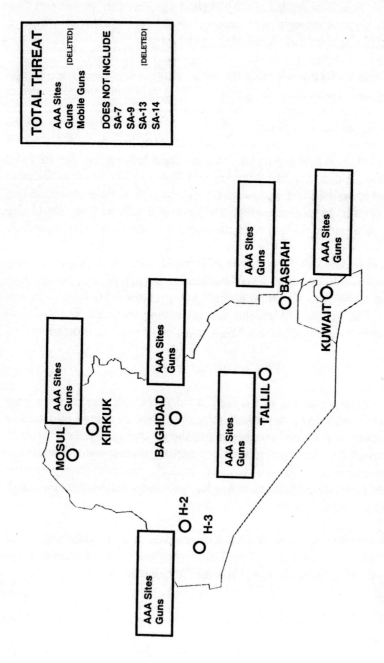

TOTAL THREAT

AAA Sites
Guns   [DELETED]
Mobile Guns

DOES NOT INCLUDE
SA-7
SA-9
SA-13
SA-14   [DELETED]

AAA Sites
Guns

MOSUL ○
KIRKUK ○

AAA Sites
Guns

BAGHDAD ○

○ H-2
○ H-3

AAA Sites
Guns

AAA Sites
Guns

TALLIL ○

AAA Sites
Guns

BASRAH ○

KUWAIT ○

AAA Sites
Guns

[53](S) Chart taken from CENTAF briefing to GWAPS Team, Shaw AFB, SC, 9 Mar 1992. The data reflect Coalition information and do not correlate with totals in table 2.

Table 3
Combat Aircraft[54]

Fighters/Interceptors	[DELETED]
MIG-29 Fulcrum	
MIG-25 Foxbat	[DELETED]
MIG-21/F-7 Fishbed	
MIG-17/F-6 Fresco/Fantan	
Subtotal	————
Ground Attack	
SU-25 Frogfoot	
Mirage F-1E	
SU-24 Fencer	[DELETED]
MIG-23 Flogger	
SU-7/20/22 Fitter	————
Subtotal	
Total Tactical Combat	728

As with other branches of the Iraqi armed forces, the Air Force consisted of a small number of relatively new aircraft and a larger quantity of older, less capable systems. Of the interceptors, only the MIG-29 Fulcrum was fourth generation, roughly the technological equivalent of the U.S. F-15. The MIG-25 was third generation and approximately equivalent to the U.S. F-4. Of the ground-attack aircraft, the Su-25 Frogfoot was fourth generation; however, the most highly regarded aircraft was the French Mirage F-1, a third-generation aircraft introduced in the 1970s. The status of the Mirage was due less to the aircraft itself and more to the quality of the training and the employment doctrine that accompanied it.

Table 5 lists Iraqi fighter interceptor aircraft according to their night/all weather capabilities.

Less than half (thirty-nine percent) of the Iraqi air defense interceptors were night, all-weather capable. This percentage includes the

---

[54](S/NF/WN/NC) GWAPS *Statistical Compendium*, Table 3, "Iraqi Air Order of Battle." Information reflecting numbers as of Jan 1991.

Table 4
Aircraft Modernization[55]

Coalition	[DELETED]	Year IOC or Latest Model	Iraq	[DELETED]
F-15E		Mid to Late 1980s	MIG-29/Fulcrum	
F-16			SU-25/Frogfoot	
F-14			SU-22/Fitter H/J/K	
F-4G			SU-24/Fencer	
F-15C				
F-117				
F/A-18				
A-6E				
Tornado F3	[DELETED]			
Tornado GR1				
F-111F		1980	MIG-23/Flogger F/H	
Mirage 2000			MIG-23/Flogger G	
A-10			MIG-25/Foxbat E	
Mirage F-1			MIG-23/Flogger E	
			SU-20/Fitter C/D/F	
			Mirage F-1E	
Jaguar		1970	MIG-21/F-7/Fishbed	
		1960	SU-7/Fitter A	
			MIG-17/Fresco	

---

[55]Michael J. H. Taylor, *Jane's World Combat Aircraft* (JANE'S Information Group, Coulsdon: Surrey, UK), 1988. This book describes the latest modifications, on which the ordering of this table is based. The priorities on this graph were determined by either the aircraft's initial operational capability (IOC) or the latest update to its weapons system. The numbers came from the GWAPS *Statistical Compendium*, Order of Battle Tables, for the U.S. Coalition and Iraqi aircraft, and from various other sources for some Coalition aircraft. The information reflects numbers as of 1 Jan 1991.

Table 5
Iraqi Fighter Aircraft By Capability[56]

Night/All-Weather Capable		Day/Visual Only Capable	
Aircraft	[DELETED]	Aircraft	[DELETED]
MIG-29 Fulcrum		MIG-21 Fishbed	
Mirage F-1E		MIG-23 Flogger	
MIG-23 Flogger G	[DELETED]		[DELETED]
MIG-25 Foxbat			

Note: The number of Floggers listed above differs from that in Table 3 because the Iraqis flew their Flogger F/H variant as an attack aircraft instead of in a fighter/interceptor role.

Mirage F-1EQ aircraft, which normally served in an attack role but could have been highly capable in the interceptor role. The Iraqi all-weather fighter force was not impressive in terms of its size or hardware capabilities, particularly when compared to the over 800 all-weather Coalition fighters.

At the beginning of the Gulf War, the structure and capabilities of the Iraqi Air Force were very much a product of their experiences in the Iran-Iraq War. During that conflict, they had recognized their deficiencies and had attempted to rectify them by purchasing new systems. When they attempted to destroy the Iranian Air Force on the ground at the start of the War, the Iraqi Air Force found that the Iranians had positioned most of their aircraft in hardened shelters.[57] One result of this experience was that Iraq instituted a massive air base construction and modernization program involving twenty-four primary operating bases and thirty dispersal fields. These new bases included nearly six-hundred hardened aircraft shelters built to defend against a crippling first strike. The Iraqis obtained enough state-of-the-art shelters to protect virtually their entire tactical air force.[58]

---

[56](S/NF/WN/NC) GWAPS *Statistical Compendium*, Table 3, "Iraqi Air Order of Battle."

[57]Ephraim Karsh, "The Iran-Iraq War: A Military Analysis," IISS Adelphi Papers, Spring 1987, p 37.

[58](S/NF/WN/NC) *Iraqi Threat to U.S. Force*, p 3-49.

In addition to the hardened aircraft shelters, Iraqi airfields themselves were constructed to present a major challenge to any attacking force. Multiple runways and taxiways stressed for takeoffs and landings meant that disabling an airfield would require more than a few runway cuts. In addition, the Iraqis invested heavily in rapid runway repair equipment, acquiring the latest technologies in graders and quick drying cement. At the time of the invasion of Kuwait, the Iraqis had a total of 96 airfields, 65 of which were permanently surfaced. Of the total, over half had a longest runway of over 2,440 meters, and seven had longest runways of over 3,659 meters. Figure 7 shows the location of the major Iraqi air bases and deployment/dispersal fields as of December 1991.

Iraqi air defense was anchored by approximately 300 mostly Soviet-built interceptors, with some French and Chinese aircraft among the inventory. Although interceptors were stationed throughout the country, the majority were in hardened shelters at airfields in central and western Iraq to facilitate the protection of Baghdad.[59]

The best aircraft in the inventory was the MIG-29 Fulcrum; it was the only Iraqi fighter with a look-down, shoot-down radar. [DELETED] An all-weather fighter, the Fulcrum first entered service with Soviet forces in 1984. [DELETED]. This highly capable aircraft was significantly limited by its small internal fuel load [DELETED]. Able to reach a speed of Mach 2.35 and an altitude of 60,000 feet, the aircraft was potentially capable of taking on Coalition fighters one-on-one. Aircraft strengths included its turn rate, acceleration; rate of climb; all-aspect, look-down, shoot-down radar; antiair ordnance, and its electronic counter-countermeasures (ECCM) capability.

---

[59](S/NF/WN/NC) *Ibid*, pp 3-53 - 3-59.

Figure 7
Air Defense Fighter Bases and
Probable Deployment Fields as of December 1991[60]

FIGURE DELETED

[DELETED].[61]

---

[60](S/NF/WN/NC) *Ibid*, p 3-50

[61](S/NF) *MCM 3-1*, Vol II, p 6-18.

The MIG-25 Foxbat was a third-generation Soviet aircraft capable of speeds up to Mach 2.5 and able to carry four air-to-air missiles. It became operational in 1966. Designed to intercept high-flying bombers, the MIG-25 had little capability against low flyers. The MIG-19 Fresco and MIG-21 Fishbed were both day, clear-weather-only fighters. They were operational in Vietnam twenty years ago. The F-6 and F-7 were Chinese-built versions of the MIG-19 and MIG-21 with Western avionics.[62] Their main contribution to an aerial engagement would have been to add mass to the Iraqi side. It appears they were planned to be used for point defense of strategic sites.

The quality of the pilots assigned to the Fulcrum and other air defense fighters were considered second rate, even by Iraqi standards, since the best Iraqi pilots were assigned to the Mirage F-1s. [DELETED].[63]

Of course, training in a Soviet air-to-air aircraft was much different than training in its Western counterpart. Aircraft such as the F/A-18 or F-15 are optimized for independent pilot decision making. Soviet air-to-air fighter aircraft, on the other hand, were virtually inoperable without the Integrated Air Defense System (IADS) supporting them. While the Soviet system enabled the weapons to work, and work well under optimum conditions, it also fundamentally shaped and ultimately limited their capabilities in combat. A full-blown Soviet-style system relied on ground control for identifying enemy aircraft, vectoring of friendly aircraft, and placing friendly aircraft in position to complete the intercept. In the Soviet system, triggering the weapon was the pilot's most important role. Soviet aircraft themselves were not designed for pilot visibility, long range, loiter, or independent detection, identification, and tracking of enemy aircraft. These were not required or desirable characteristics under the tightly centralized Soviet system. All of these deficiencies were present in the Iraqi air defense and air force structures.

Since ground attack was considered the most important mission of the Iraqi Air Force, they purchased the French-built (Dassault Aviation) Mirage F-1 and considered it to be their most effective aircraft. Although having somewhat limited capabilities, the Mirage F-1 was an all-weather aircraft that could perform the interceptor or ground attack role. Standard

---

[62]Frank Chadwick, "Gulf War Fact Book," 1992, p 49.

[63](S/NF/WN/NC) *Iraqi Threat to U.S. Forces*, p 3-63

armament included two 30-mm DEFA 553 cannon with 135 rounds per gun. The maximum practical external combat load was 8,188 pounds mounted on various external racks. Possible weapons loads included Matra Super 530 air-to-air missiles, Armat antiradar ground-attack missiles, the AM 39 Exocet antiship missile, 500-pound bombs, or Thomson-Brandt rockets. The Iraqi versions were capable of carrying laser-guided weapons such as the AS.30L missile and Matra 400-kilogram guided bomb. Maximum speed of the Mirage was Mach 2.2, and its service ceiling was 65,600 feet. Combat radius was 265 statute miles with maximum internal fuel, a high-low-high mission profile, and fourteen 500-pound bombs. Carrying just one Exocet missile, the aircraft could strike at a radius of 435 miles without refueling. In addition, the Iraqi Air Force could configure some of its Mirage F-1s to accomplish buddy refueling.[64]

[DELETED].[65] [DELETED].[66] [DELETED].

With the F-1, the Iraqis appeared to have acquired more than just an aircraft; they were also exposed to the Western attitude towards offensive air power. While the F-1 was not among the most modern aircraft, only the best Iraqi pilots were selected to fly it. [DELETED].[67] [DELETED].[68] [DELETED].[69]

As the Gulf War approached, the status of Iraq's Air Force was very much like that of the rest of the Iraqi defense structure. The large number of aircraft and some of the pilot training showed potential for a formidable force. However, full potential was not realized because of old equipment, overall inadequate training, and unrealistic exercises. Once the Coalition assembled its force, Iraq was simply not in the same league.

---

[64] *Jane's All the World's Aircraft*, pp 68-69.

[65] (S/NF/WN/NC) *Iraqi Threat to U.S. Forces*, p 2-7.

[66] (S/NF) *MCM 3-1*, Vol II, p 6-88.

[67] (S/NF/WN/NC) *Iraqi Threat to U.S. Forces*, p 3-63.

[68] (S/NF/WN) SPEAR Briefing.

[69] (S/NF/WN/NC) *Iraqi Threat to U.S. Forces*, p 3-64.

An understanding of the Iraqi attitude towards tactics and the employment of its air force and air defense systems can be gained by examining Iraqi behavior against a more equal opponent, Iran in the Iran-Iraq War. This is the subject of the next section.

Iraqi Tactics

A study of Iraqi behavior in the Iran-Iraq War of 1980-1988 can foster a better understanding of the tactical employment of the equipment discussed in the previous sections. Two overall lessons become apparent from such a study. First, the Iraqis did poorly early in that conflict, learned from their mistakes, and as a result, improved their tactics. Second, even the improved tactics employed against the Iranians were not good preparation for war with the Coalition.

While the Iran-Iraq War could hardly be termed an absolute success, at its close Iraqi forces, particularly the air forces, had demonstrated greatly improved operational and tactical competence. The Iraqi order of battle had increased significantly, and maintenance and ancillary services had improved. The Iraqi Air Force could often maintain a rate of 150 sorties per day, and, during the final stages of the war, were known to have averaged as many as 240 sorties per day.[70] Iraq had also moved away from systems purchased from the Soviet Union to those purchased from various Western suppliers.

It must be understood that even with improved equipment and tactics, the Iraqi Air Force and air defense network had an entirely different orientation than Western forces. For the Iraqi Air Force, deterrence, not offensive combat, was the purpose of existence. During the Iran-Iraq War, a primary function of the air forces of both countries was to prevent strategic attacks. This was accomplished not through defensive capabilities, but rather by deterrence–by their ability to threaten similar or greater destruction on the enemy.[71] An air force built to be a deterrent force behaves quite differently than one organized and trained for offensive air superiority.

---

[70]Ephraim Karsh, p 39.

[71]Maj Ronald E. Bergquist, *The Role of Air Power in the Iran-Iraq War*, (Maxwell AFB, AL: Air University Press, 1988), p 46.

26

The first requirement of a deterrent force is existence; a deterrent air force must remain a force in being. The Iraqis did this by hardening airfields, sheltering aircraft, building a robust air defense based on means other than offensive counter air, and in the extreme, seeking a safe haven for aircraft in times of threat. The Iraqi Air Force placed a constant command emphasis on preserving aircraft, regardless of the cost to effectiveness. During the Iran-Iraq War, commanders were punished for losing aircraft, regardless of the tactical success of the mission.[72]

The air-to-air battles in the Iran-Iraq War were described by one observer, who said, "In practice, the two Air Forces proved to be equally incompetent."[73] Both sides seemed to overestimate the capability of their adversary and had an exaggerated fear of radar-guided missiles. Iraqi pilots generally avoided air-to-air engagements. Any engagements that did occur were noteworthy for their lack of aggressive maneuvering. The Iraqis would normally conduct high-speed, maximum range, air-to-air missile launches, then break off and return to their airfields.[74]

Iraq had conducted the initial attacks of the Iran-Iraq War and, for a short period, retained the offensive. But, after gaining what appeared to be Saddam Hussein's initial goals, Iraq went on the defensive and attempted to negotiate for its war aims. Iran responded with its own series of offensives against Iraqi positions.[75]

In an attempt to convince Iran to negotiate, Iraq initiated a strategic bombing campaign against Iranian population centers and economic targets with an emphasis on Iran's oil exporting capability. However, to minimize aircraft losses, the Iraqis used mostly high-altitude attacks. While this was in keeping with their survival doctrine, it resulted in reduced effectiveness. Occasionally, the Iraqis demonstrated some innovation. [DELETED].[76] [DELETED].

---

[72] Anthony H. Cordesman and Abraham R. Wagner, *The Lessons of Modern War, Volume II: The Iran-Iraq War* (Boulder, CO: Westview Press, 1990), p 495.

[73] Ephraim Karsh, p 37.

[74] (S/NF/WN/NC) *Iraqi Threat to U.S. Forces*, p 3-63.

[75] Ephraim Karsh, p 37.

[76] Cordesman and Wagner, p 209.

During the early phases of the war, the Iraqis never mastered combined arms techniques. In conducting battlefield support, they generally used available air power in small packages without coordination with other attacks. Similarly, they established free-fire zones for surface-to-air missiles and anti-aircraft artillery over important strategic zones such as Baghdad because of the difficulty they had coordinating interceptor aircraft and ground-based air defense systems. [DELETED].[77]

In July 1986, a conference was held and the Iraqi leadership decided to build forces that could seize the initiative. The group chose to expand the Republican Guards, escalate the strategic war against Iranian oil exports, use more poison gas, and prepare military forces capable of attacking.[78] Key to these changes were efforts to improve Iraq's air force. Aircraft inventories were upgraded with the acquisition of better airframes, avionics, and armaments. Fifteen new air bases with aircraft shelters and support equipment were built. Reconnaissance capabilities were upgraded. Modern Soviet aircraft, such as the SU-22, SU-25, MIG-25R and MIG-29, were obtained.

Apparently spurred on by the French-trained Mirage pilots, tactical changes accompanied the upgrading of equipment. On bombing missions the Iraqis started to use low-altitude attacks. Precision-guided munitions such as laser-guided bombs were used with increased accuracy. [DELETED].

[DELETED]

---

[77](S/NF/WN/NC) *Iraqi Threat to U.S. Forces*, p 3-52.

[78]Cordesman and Wagner, pp 259-260.

Figure 8
14 May 1988 Larak Island Strike[79]

FIGURE DELETED

[DELETED].[80]

[DELETED].[81]

---

[79](S/NF/WN/NC) *Ibid*, p D-2.

[80](S/NF/WN/NC) *Iraqi Threat to U.S. Forces*, p D-1.

[81](S/NF/WN/NC) *Ibid*, p 3-64.

A weapon that did not involve tactics was considered instrumental in ending the war. This was the Scud missile, used during the so-called "War of the Cities." There were actually two distinct periods; the first "War of the Cities," which involved only aircraft, ended in June 1985. The second "War of the Cities" began in February 1988, once again started by Iraq. On 27 February, after an initial exchange, Iraq used a new weapon, the modified Scud-B called Al-Husayn. The new weapon's salient feature was its ability to reach Tehran; the range had been increased to 370 miles.[82] The second War of the Cities continued until 20 April 1988. By the end, Iraq had fired perhaps 200 Al-Husayns, causing as many as 2,000 civilian casualties.[83] Most importantly, for the first time Scuds had a measurable political effect on the conduct of a war.

Overall, the air portion of the Iran-Iraq War was less intense, by an order of magnitude in mass, tempo, and tactics, than previous air combat in the Middle East. The Iraqi air defense system was a particular disappointment.[84] Despite a large inventory of radars, interceptors, surface-to-air missiles, and antiaircraft artillery, the Iraqis displayed little ability to coordinate these air defense elements into a coherent system. Even though faced with a large amount of Iraqi air defense equipment, the Iranians penetrated the system virtually at will throughout the war. The Iranians normally used the low-level techniques learned from their one-time American mentors. Iranian air attacks were more severely constrained by logistic difficulties and other internal problems than by the effectiveness of the Iraqi air defense network.[85]

---

[82]Seth Carus and Joseph S. Bermudez, Jr., "Iraq's Al-Husayn Missile Program," *Jane's Soviet Intelligence Review*, May 1990, p 204.

[83]Dilip Hiro, *The Longest War: The Iran-Iraq Military Conflict*, (New York: Routledge, 1991), p 200.

[84]Cordesman and Wagner, p 457.

[85]The Iranians had removed many of their best pilots from their air force because they had been trained in the Unites States. Also, parts for their U.S. equipment were hard to obtain.

Air-to-air engagements were virtually nonexistent; neither side had anything to gain by risking precious aircraft to deflect an insignificant individual attack. In addition, the Iraqi Air Force appeared to be underutilized. It claimed to have flown a total of about 400,000 sorties during the eight year war. While surge sortie generation rates sometimes reached one sortie per day, the wartime average equalled only about one sortie per aircraft every three days.

The tactics employed by the Iraqi Air Defense and Air Force during the Iran-Iraq War failed to prepare them for war with the Coalition forces. While Iraq dominated the skies for most of the Iran-Iraq War and demonstrated a decided improvement after their reforms of 1986, it never developed a coherent strategy for employing its air forces or the ability to bring the entire force up to the standards displayed by the French-trained Mirage pilots. If anything, the Iran-Iraq War may have taught the Iraqis the wrong lesson, convincing them that they had capabilities they did not in fact possess.

Desert Storm

The strategy and tactics developed for the Iran-Iraq War did not prepare Iraq for war with the Coalition. The fury of the Coalition attack destroyed not only structures and equipment but also Iraqi assumptions about air power. Stealth aircraft and cruise missiles penetrated Baghdad's defenses virtually unscathed. Precision-guided munitions struck targets with standards of accuracy not previously experienced by the Iraqis. The Coalition's untested pilots were victorious over the presumably battle-hardened Iraqi Air Force. As Coalition air attacks continued, Saddam Hussein's stated hope for a short air war followed by an early entry into the real war on the ground faded. Iraqi tactics against the Coalition air campaign fell into three areas. First were efforts to counter Coalition air by modifying tactics, equipment use, and operational procedures. Second were efforts to protect high-value forces and material; and third were efforts to move the battle into the public relations arena in hopes of fracturing the Coalition or causing it to modify its plan.

The Coalition's efforts to blind the Iraqi air defense network were very effective. However, the Iraqis developed workarounds, utilized undamaged equipment and nodes, and maintained some air defense capability. [DELETED]. As discussed earlier, the KARI system had a capability to expand the responsibilities of various nodes. Iraqi technicians appeared to have been able to develop local networks using this expansion capability. They tied the various networks together by stringing combat phone lines and wire between the stations.[86]

[DELETED].[87]

Other inputs to this backup system were from ground observers. It appears that they had both phone lines and a simple data reporting system at each site. The information system used by observers was very rudimentary. Basically, the observer/operator passed only the information they were capable of sending with no special training. As a Coalition air raid proceeded inbound, other systems were used to gain additional information. Radars associated with the Roland or SA-8 would be brought online for short fifteen-second bursts. The intention was apparently to use the radars as height-finders, to determine the altitude of inbound aircraft. Antiaircraft artillery sites used this information to set the fuzes on their ammunition.[88]

Enough information seems to have been gained through these means to permit the Iraqis to shoot missile systems at Coalition aircraft with little or no illumination by target-tracking radars. [DELETED].[89] There is also a possibility that Iraq used optical trackers for some of these firings. [DELETED].

---

[86](S/NF/WN) SPEAR Briefing.

[87](S/NF/WN) *Ibid.*

[88](S/NF/WN) *Ibid.*

[89](S/NF/WN) *Ibid.*

A weakness in the Iraqi air defense system was the apparent lack of coordination between AAA sites. The Iraqis appeared unable to organize several sites into aimed or barrage fire. While firing was random and indiscriminate, there were still enough AAA sites in the Baghdad area to make even this random fire dangerous.

The Iraqis used other techniques to gain tracking information. At night, battlefield illumination flares were used to light up an area. With this artificial light, attacking aircraft could be tracked either visually or with optical trackers. [DELETED].[90]

After the war began, the Iraqis used decoys and simulations to deceive and foil Coalition attacks. [DELETED].[91] [DELETED].[92] [DELETED].

Another weapon system the Iraqis protected by deception was the Scud and its variants. One method they used was to park the missile system under a highway viaduct. They could pull the missile out, launch it, and then return the transporter-erector-launcher (TEL) to the safety of the viaduct in less than five minutes–less time than Coalition aircraft needed to target the position.[93]

The Iraqis seemed to believe that U.S. intelligence collection was almost perfect. [DELETED].[94] [DELETED].[95] [DELETED].[96]

The Iraqis used several techniques in an effort to preserve assets from destruction. After the Iraqis realized that their sector operation centers were not as impregnable as thought, they removed the equipment from

---

[90](S/NF/WN) *Ibid.*

[91]Mohammed Heikal, *Illusions of Triumph*, (Harper Collins: London, 1991), p 303.

[92](S/NF) MSG 312200Z Dec 90, AFSAC Det 21, Iraq Air Force Issues– Desert Shield.

[93](S/NF/WN) SPEAR Briefing.

[94](S/REL UK) "The Gulf War: An Iraqi General Perspective," Joint Debriefing Center MFR, 11 Mar 1991, GWAPS Files, CHST 32-2, pp 5, 6.

[95](S/NF/WN) SPEAR Briefing.

[96](S/REL UK) "The Gulf War: An Iraqi General Perspective," p 5.

the centers to areas thought to be safe from targeting. In some cases, ammunition and weapons stocks were moved from known storage areas to holes dug in the middle of empty fields for burial or covering with nets. In the Kuwait Theater of Operations, tanks were dispersed, but as the air strikes continued, more and more Iraqi tanks were camouflaged, buried with sandbags, or covered with camouflage nets.[97]

While the overall performance of the Iraqi Air Force in air-to-air combat was abysmal, certain procedures were noteworthy. Aircrews seemed very conscious of electronic warfare, and particularly, of communications security. [DELETED].[98]

Although Iraqi pilots sometimes started encounters with decent setups, the consistent and overriding tactical pattern evident in debriefs of kills by U.S. F-15 pilots indicates a startling lack of situational awareness by their Iraqi adversaries. In general, the Iraqi pilots shot down did not react to radar lock-ons by Coalition fighters. They attempted very little maneuvering, either offensive or defensive, between the time when the air intercept radar locked on to them and the time when they were hit by air-to-air missiles (or, in two cases, before running into the ground).[99]

There is little evidence that the Iraqis believed they could go head to head with the Coalition air forces, either tactically or operationally. As in the Iran-Iraq War, their over-arching goal appeared to be the survival of their more modern advanced aircraft. [DELETED].[100] Initially, aircraft were ordered stowed in hardened aircraft shelters when not actually flying. However, the shelter-busting campaign quickly inflicted unacceptable loss rates. The Iraqis then used two alternatives to preserve the aircraft. They moved aircraft away from airfields, in some cases parking them in seemingly unsuspected places such as alongside roads, in gullies

---

[97](S/NF/WN) SPEAR Briefing.

[98](S/NF/WN) *Ibid.*

[99](S) "33rd TFW Air-to-Air Engagements Through 21 Feb 1991."

[100]Heikal, p 304.

covered with camouflage nets, and in known safe areas such as residential neighborhoods. [DELETED].[101] During the Iran-Iraq War, the Iraqis had flown their most valuable aircraft to northern Iraq beyond the reach of Iranian air strikes. Coalition operations from Turkey in this war denied them that option. Flying valuable aircraft to another country had to then be considered. Iraq decided to take the chance and fly aircraft that could avoid the Coalition fighters to Iran. [DELETED].[102]

Having learned their political value during the Iran-Iraq War, the Iraqis employed Scud missiles from the very onset of hostilities. Since the missiles were not capable of destroying high-value targets, they were instead used to attack Coalition cohesion and national will. The most obvious Iraqi effort, and probably Iraq's greatest hope, was firing missiles at Israel in hopes of drawing an Israeli reaction. If the Iraqis could portray the war as an Arab-Israel conflict, it was thought that countries not directly threatened by the war such as Egypt or Syria might leave the Coalition. There were reports that a group of Egyptian and Syrian soldiers in Saudi Arabia cheered when they heard that Iraq had launched its first Scuds against Israel.[103] To address the Scud problem, the United States replied with adroit diplomacy and a heavy application of force. They concentrated military force to find the Scuds on the firing end and to destroy them with Patriot Missiles on the receiving end. Israel was persuaded not to retaliate, and Coalition cohesion was maintained. President Mubarak of Egypt went so far as to publicly declare that it was the inherent right of every nation to defend itself.[104]

---

[101](S/NF/WN) SPEAR Briefing.

[102]Heikal, p 304.

[103]Ibid, p 13.

[104]bid, p 307.

In an apparent attempt to attack a Navy ship and produce a large number of casualties, the Iraqi Air Force launched two Mirage aircraft armed with Exocet missiles towards the Persian Gulf. In this case, the Iraqis were not successful. With six sections of combat air patrol aircraft in the area to choose from, two Saudi F-15's were vectored for the attack. One Saudi F-15 aircraft downed both Mirages.

In another attempt to attack a Navy ship, Iraq fired two Silkworm missiles at the USS *Wisconsin*. One missile fell into the water, and the other was downed by a missile from HMS *Gloucester*, the *Wisconsin's* British escort.

The potential threat posed by the Iraqi Air Force never went away. Throughout the war, there remained a concern that the Iraqis could launch a large-scale air raid at a major U.S. facility. Since they did not sacrifice their air force in this manner, some contend they husbanded these assets to retain a strategic capability for after the war.[105]

This chapter presented a cursory overview of Iraqi weapons, training, and tactics. In the beginning, it stated that Iraq could have been a formidable opponent. Closer examination, however, revealed significant deficiencies in organization, training, and tactics, which rendered the Iraqi force vulnerable. Specifically, defense of Iraqi airspace heavily depended on the survival and smooth functioning of the KARI system. When Coalition air attacks removed this central pillar, the tactical competence of Iraqi aircrews, gunners, and commanders could not overcome the deficiency. In simple terms, the Iraqi integrated air defense system crumbled.

Developed in a large part to face the Israelis after the Osirak raid of 1980, and honed against the Iranians in the Eight Year War, Iraqi air power was no match for the Coalition force arrayed against it. The question that remains is whether the Iraqis realized such a large disparity existed, and if they did, what other course of action could they have followed? The probable conclusion is that they were simply overwhelmed before they came to realize the disparity fully. Regardless of the disparity, the remnants of the Iraqi air defense posed a threat to Coalition air power to the bitter end.

---

[105](S) CIA Brief to GWAPS, Aug 1992.

(Above) Iraqi ZSU-23/4 (Below) Iraqi T-54/55 Tank

2

Aircraft and Weapons

The overwhelming tactical dominance demonstrated by Coalition air forces in the Gulf War can be attributed in large part to superior equipment. Stealth strike platforms, laser-guided bombs, advanced sensors, and electronic countermeasures represent but a few areas in which the Coalition enjoyed overwhelming advantages over Iraqi forces. This chapter describes Coalition equipment, particularly aircraft and weapons, and highlights their employment in the Gulf War. For convenience, aircraft and weapons are grouped according to mission: air-to-ground, electronic warfare and reconnaissance, air-to-air, and special aircraft. Transport and refueling aircraft are described in the *Logistics* Report. Aircraft that performed in more than one area will be addressed under their primary mission. The chapter concludes with a selective discussion of systems available but not used in the Gulf War. (See also Appendix A, Definition of Aerial Missions.)

Air-to-Ground Aircraft Systems

Air-To-Ground Aircraft

F-117 Stealth Fighter: the first operational strike platform (aircraft) designed from the outset to depend on low observability for penetrating enemy defenses. It was designed to passively defeat radar detection as it penetrates dense threat environments and delivers precision munitions from medium altitude at night. Target identification and designation is accomplished by means of forward-looking infrared (FLIR) and downward-looking infrared (DLIR) systems integrated with a laser designator. This single-seat aircraft, with its primary offensive load of two 2,000-pound GBU-27 laser-guided bombs, proved to be an exceptionally accurate bombing platform in Operation Desert Storm. Its unrefueled radius of action with a full offensive ordnance load was approximately 550 nautical miles. The F-117 achieved initial operational capability in October 1983. The last of 59 F-117s were delivered in July 1990.

Forty-two F-117s flew 1,299 combat sorties in Desert Storm.[1] They scored 1,664 direct hits with laser-guided bombs (LGBs) without suffering battle damage.[2] Throughout Desert Storm, the F-117 was the weapon system of choice for attacks on hard targets in high-threat areas, particularly the heavily defended Baghdad area.[3] In the early morning hours of 17 January 1991, F-117s initiated attacks on Iraqi leadership, command and control installations, and strategic air defense targets, notably air defense sector operations centers (SOCs). During Desert Storm, F-117s recorded 1,788 strikes covering virtually all 12 target categories in the Automated Intelligence Installation File (AIF), and participated in the following types of missions:[4]

- Suppression of Enemy Air Defense. In addition to attacking Iraqi SOCs, interceptor operation centers (IOCs), and the Air Defense Operations Center (ADOC), F-117s bombed SAM sites to clear a path for B-52 strikes on the Taji industrial complex. They also struck SAM sites interfering with F-15 and Scud combat air patrol (CAP) missions in eastern and western Iraq.[5]

- Night attacks against high-value targets. The F-117 flew 1,112 strikes against key leadership, communications, and strategic air defense assets; and nuclear, biological, and chemical warfare storage and production facilities.[6] The F-117 also flew 219 strikes against hardened aircraft shelters and 120 strikes against bridges.[7]

---

[1] The 37th TFW, based at Tonopah Test Range Air Field, Nevada, was the only unit to operate the F-117. First used operationally during Operation Just Cause, the F-117 had only recently emerged from the "black" world when Iraq invaded Kuwait.

[2] (U) GWAPS *Statistical Compendium*, Table 94, "F-117: USAF Sorties by Mission Type"; and (S/NF/WN/NC) GWAPS F-117 Missions Database.

[3] The F-117's bombing accuracy minimized the risk of collateral damage in densely populated areas, an important consideration.

[4] (U) GWAPS *Statistical Compendium*, Table 177, "Strikes by AIF Categories."

[5] (S/NF/WN/NC) GWAPS F-117 Missions Database: One hundred and twelve strikes were flown against Strategic Air Defense (SAD) targets and forty-nine strikes against Surface-to-Air (SAM) targets.

[6] (U) GWAPS *Statistical Compendium*, Table 185, "Strikes by Master Target List Categories."

[7] (U) *Ibid.*

40

- <u>Scud hunting</u>. F-117s flew approximately 168 strikes against Scud-associated targets, notably storage and maintenance facilities, production facilities, rocket motor and rocket fuel test and production facilities, and suspected Scud hide-sites in western Iraq.[8]

- <u>Support of ground forces</u>. F-117s flew approximately 300 sorties to support ground forces in the Kuwait theater of operations (KTO), attacking Republican Guard headquarters and command posts, communications sites, logistics targets, supply chokepoints, and bridges.[9] On D+30, F-117s dropped 32 GBU-27 2,000-pound bombs on the Iraqi fire trench network facing the 1st Marine Division in preparation for Marine breaching operations.[10]

Because of the difficulty of flying formation at night without lights, all F-117 attacks were flown by single aircraft. During air refueling, F-117s flew two-ship formations, used air-to-air Tacan and aircraft lights to join with the tanker, and reverted to single-ship profiles after refueling. The size and hardness of many F-117 targets meant that more than one aircraft was required to achieve the desired effect. When this was the case, mission planners would plan for simultaneous bomb impacts from as many as six different aircraft, with each aircraft flying a separate run-in heading and altitude. F-117 attacks were delivered from medium altitudes.

The F-117 can carry the full range of air-to-ground weaponry, but used the following ordnance combinations in Desert Storm: two 2,000-pound GBU-27s, two 2,000-pound GBU-10s, or any combination of the two.[11]

---

[8](S/NF/WN/NC) *Ibid.*

[9](S/NF/WN/NC) Analysis of GWAPS F-117 Missions Database for ordnance delivered between 28.30° to 32° north latitude and 45° to 48.30° east longitude.

[10](S/NF/WN/NC) GWAPS F-117 Missions Database.

[11](S) *USCENTAF Combat Plans Handout*, "F-117 Standard Conventional Loads (SCLs)," p 7-2.

F-111 Aardvark: a twin-engine, tactical aircraft with a crew of two–a pilot and a weapons system operator (WSO). Designed for long range, heavy payloads, and low-altitude penetration in all weather conditions using inertial navigation and terrain-following radar, the F-111 is capable of radar bombing from all altitudes.

Two versions of the F-111 were used in the Gulf War: the F-111E with analog avionics and the F-111F with digital avionics. The F-111F has improved turbofan engines and was equipped with the Pave Tack infrared target acquisition and laser designation pod; the pod permitted precision attacks with laser-guided bombs (LGBs) from all altitudes, day or night. The F-111F is also equipped to deliver the infrared (IR) and electro-optical GBU-15, a glide bomb controlled by the WSO by a datalink hook-up between the delivery aircraft and the weapon.[12, 13] Range and logistic considerations dictated smaller than maximum bomb loads in Desert Storm.[14] [DELETED].[15]

The F-111 first flew on 20 December 1964 and achieved initial operational capability (IOC) in 1968. A total of 461 F-111s were built between 1967 and 1976; of these, approximately 325 were in service in 1991. Salient F-111 contributions to Desert Storm included the following:

- <u>All-weather night attacks against point and area targets</u> to support the strategic bombing campaign. F-111s flew 912 strikes against targets such as airfields, aircraft, and support facilities; hardened aircraft shelters; command, control, communications and intelligence facilities; bunkers; nuclear, biological, and chemical war-

---

[12](S) The F-111F was the only aircraft used in Desert Storm that could deliver the GBU-15. The GBU-15 came in two versions, electro-optical for daylight use and infrared for night. [DELETED].

[13]*Desert Score*, July 1991, p 37.

[14]As explained above, heavier bomb loads cut into range and fuel margins. [DELETED].

[15](S) USCENTAF *Combat Plans Handout,* "F-111 Standard Conventional Loads (SCLs)," p 10-1.

fare facilities; bridges; and air defense assets.[16] Many of these missions were conducted in adverse weather conditions; sortie lengths averaged 3 hours or more. The Pave Tack FLIR system proved particularly effective in night attacks with LGBs.

- Support of ground forces. The F-111F was used for battlefield preparation in the KTO; its significant antiarmor missions were known as "tank-plinking." It flew 1,804 antiarmor strikes using predominantly 500-pound laser-guided GBU-12s.[17]

- Scud hunting. F-111Fs flew sixty-nine strikes to support anti-Scud operations, dropping laser-guided bombs on road culverts and CBU-89 Gator mines around road culverts suspected of being Scud hide-sites.[18]

The F-111 force committed to Desert Storm flew over 2,881 sorties without loss and struck 3,225 targets.[19] F-111Fs were responsible for forty-six percent of the LGB precision strikes in the strategic air campaign.[20] The relatively long range of the F-111 was a significant source of tactical flexibility in the air campaign: Taif-based F-111Fs could be used in the KTO without air refueling and could attack targets in northern Iraq without exposing the tankers to Iraqi defenses. Incirlik-based F-111Es added flexibility by attacking targets in northern Iraq, thereby releasing other aircraft to concentrate on targets from Baghdad south to the KTO. On the last day of the war, two F-111Fs released 4,700-pound hard-target-penetrating, laser-guided GBU-28s against the

---

[16]F-111Fs flew 757 and F-111Es flew 155 strikes.   (U) GWAPS *Statistical Compendium*, Table 177, "Strikes by AIF Categories."

[17](S/NF/WN/NC) *Ibid.*

[18](S/NF/WN/NC) *Ibid.*

[19]The 64 F-111Fs based at Taif Air Base, Saudia Arabia, flew 2,423 sorties striking 2,802 targets, and the 26 F-111Es, based at Incirlik Air Base, Turkey, (part of EUCOM-supported Operation Proven Force) flew 458 sorties striking 423 targets. (U) GWAPS *Statistical Compendium*, Tables 92 and 93, "F-111E/F-111F: USAF Sorties by Mission Type," and Table 177, "Strikes by AIF Categories."

[20](U) GWAPS *Statistical Compendium*, Table 183, "Precision-Guided Munition (PGM) Strikes by AIF Categories."

North Taji command bunker with apparent success.[21] F-111Fs also destroyed the oil pumping manifold off the Kuwaiti coast with electro-optically guided GBU-15 standoff bombs.[22] Iraqi forces were using the manifold to pump oil into the Persian Gulf. During Desert Storm, the F-111 mission-capable rate rose eight percent above peacetime levels to eight-five percent.[23]

F-111s flew two-aircraft formations as the basic fighting element, combined with other elements to form flights of four aircraft. Attack formations (packages) against point and area targets varied in size up to thirty-two aircraft, and many missions were flown without suppression of enemy air defense (SEAD) assets for protection.[24] The aircraft used low-altitude tactics for the first three days of Desert Storm and released mostly precision-guided munitions against airfield complexes. After transitioning to medium-altitude tactics, the aircraft flew in large packages, used multiple attack headings, and employed altitude and time differences to avoid midair collisions; attack times were compressed to fifteen minutes or less.[25, 26]

Tank-plinking missions were flown at medium altitude. They were each armed with four GBU-12s. Tanks, hotter than the surrounding terrain immediately after sunset, were found by using the IR Pave Tack pod. [DELETED].[27] [DELETED].[28] [DELETED].

The F-111F carried 2 AIM-9s plus one of the following munition loads during Operation Desert Storm: eight to twelve 500-pound MK-82s, two to four 2,000-pound MK-84s, two to four 500-pound

---

[21]A description of the GBU-28 deep penetration bomb is discussed under the "Special Purpose One-of-a-Kind Munitions" section in this report.

[22]DOD, *Conduct of the Persian Gulf War*, Annex T, April 1992, p T-70.

[23]*Desert Score*, p 37.

[24](S/NF/WN/NC) *Tactical Analysis Bulletin*, Volume 91-2, Jul 1991, pp 7-2 and 7-9.

[25](S/NF/WN/NC) *Ibid.*

[26]Attacking aircraft deconflicted in the target area (i.e., avoided midair collisions and weapons effects of other aircraft in the attack group) by maintaining sufficient lateral or vertical distances from other attacking aircraft or flying at set time intervals.

[27](S/NF/WN/NC) *Tactical Analysis Bulletin*, Vol 91-2, p 7-11.

[28](S/NF/WN/NC) *Ibid.*

GBU-12s, two to four 2,000-pound GBU-10s, two to four 2,000-pound GBU-24s, one 4,700 lb GBU-28, eight CBU-87s, eight CBU-89 Gators; eight to twelve CBU-52s, eight to twelve CBU-58/71s; eight to twelve MK-20 Rockeyes; or one to two 2,000-pound GBU-15s.[29]

 **F-15E Strike Eagle**: a two-seat, high-performance, supersonic, all-weather, dual-role, air-to-air and air-to-surface fighter developed from the F-15C air-superiority fighter. Its air-to-air weapons are radar-guided missiles, infrared-homing missiles, and a 20-mm gun. In the air-to-surface role, the aircraft carries Low-Altitude Navigation and Targeting Infrared (system) for Night (LANTIRN) pods along with guided and unguided air-to-ground munitions. [DELETED].[30] During Desert Storm, the F-15E was used for the following missions:

- <u>All-weather night attacks against point and area targets</u> to support the strategic bombing campaign. F-15Es flew 595 strikes against targets such as airfields, NBC storage facilities, bridges, communications facilities, and ammunition storage areas.[31]

- <u>Scud Hunt</u>. F-15Es flew 391 anti-Scud sorties.[32] The aircraft worked with the Airborne Warning and Control System (AWACS), used FLIR to find suspected Scuds and launchers in the western Scud boxes (see "The Scud Hunt" section in Chapter 4 of this report), and launched primarily LGBs against Scud targets.

- <u>Support of ground forces</u>. F-15Es flew 949 strikes and primarily delivered GBU-12 LGBs during "tank-plinking" operations against armored vehicles in the KTO.[33]

---

[29](S) *USCENTAF Combat Plans Handout*, "F-111 Standard Conventional Loads (SCLs)," p 10-1.

[30](S) *USCENTAF Combat Plans Handout*, "F-15E Standard Conventional Loads (SCLs)," p 9-6.

[31](U) GWAPS *Statistical Compendium*, Table 177, "Strikes by AIF Categories."

[32](U) *Ibid.*

[33](U) *Ibid.*

The two F-15E squadrons that flew in Desert Shield and Desert Storm had attained operational readiness only shortly before deployment. LANTIRN operational test and evaluation was not completed and was continued in theater. Testing of the targeting pods, which were shipped after deployment, was also completed in theater. The targeting pods proved valuable for designating targets for LGBs, locating targets, and providing real-time bomb damage assessment. The Desert Storm Strike Eagle force consisted of forty-eight F-15Es based at Al-Kharj, Saudi Arabia.

F-15Es flew 2,172 sorties, striking 2,124 targets in Iraq and Kuwait as part of the air assaults of Operation Desert Storm.[34] Average sortie length was 3.27 hours. The two squadrons flew 40-60 sorties a night with a mission-capable rate of 85.9 percent. The aircraft proved reliable and flexible enough to carry out precision attacks, maritime surveillance, and close air support. In one case, an F-15E shot down an Iraqi helicopter with a GBU-10 laser-guided bomb. Low-level attacks were initially flown at approximately 540 knots (Mach 0.85), but later attacks were delivered from medium altitude. Two F-15E aircraft were lost during combat.[35]

Salient F-15E tactical issues include the following: Initially, aircraft used time intervals to deconflict in the target area and flew "pop-up" maneuvers against targets such as the H-2 Airfield in Iraq. The first night low-altitude ingress and air-interdiction missions had been practiced extensively before Desert Shield. For these missions, terrain-following radar (TFR) was set at an altitude of 200 feet. Aircrews flew with the navigation mode selected so that their radar altimeter would display current altitude. These procedures allowed the aircrews to fly manually at 500 to 1,000 feet above the ground but prepared for 200-foot operation if necessary.[36] Transitioning to medium altitude presented a problem in determining accurate weapon biases for unguided ordnance. F-15Es had only six

---

[34](U) GWAPS *Statistical Compendium*, Tables 97, "F-15E: USAF Sorties by Mission Type," and 177, "Strikes by AIF Categories."

[35]*Desert Score*, p 45.

[36](U) TFR was tied into the avionics and flight control system and flew the aircraft at a preset altitude (SCP) when placed in an auto mode. When aircraft flew below this preset altitude, a fly-up occurred until acknowledged by the pilot. By setting a SCP at an altitude below what was manually flown, aircrews gave themselves this fly-up protection, if needed. (S/NF/WN/NC) *Tactical Analysis Bulletin*, Vol 91-2, p 3-3.

operational laser targeting pods and used buddy lase tactics on many medium-altitude missions. F-15E aircrews also used their synthetic aperture radar to identify targets.[37] Once the target was identified on radar, the WSO would transition to the FLIR to find, track, lase the intended target, and record bomb damage assessment (BDA). The F-15E carried 500 rounds of 20-mm ammunition and four AIM-9s plus one of the following optional munitions loads during Desert Storm: six to twelve MK-82s, four MK-84s, eight GBU-12s, four GBU-10s, six CBU-87s, six CBU-89 Gators, six to twelve CBU-52s, six to twelve CBU-58/71s, or six MK-20 Rockeyes.[38]

 **F-16 Fighting Falcon**: a multirole, single-seat fighter. Highly maneuverable, the F-16 has both air-to-air and air-to-surface capability. [DELETED].[39] Newer models of the F-16 are equipped with LANTIRN and Global Positioning System (GPS) equipment. The first F-16 flight was in early 1974 and initial operational capability occurred in 1979. Over 3,000 had been ordered or produced at the time of Desert Storm, and the F-16 had been widely exported.

F-16s flew mostly daytime and some night missions against all types of targets. The following lists some of these missions:

- <u>Day visual attacks against point and area targets</u> to support the strategic bombing campaign. F-16s flew 2,912 sorties hitting targets such as NBC storage facilities, bridges, ammunition storage areas, communications facilities, surface-to-air sites, oil refineries, Republican Guard headquarters buildings, and airfield facilities.[40] Visual deliveries were the preferred mode of operation with nonprecision munitions from medium altitude.

---

[37][DELETED].

[38](S) USCENTAF *Combat Plans Handout*, "F-15E Standard Conventional Loads (SCLs)," p 9-1.

[39](S) USCENTAF *Combat Plans Handout*, "F-16 Standard conventional Load (SCLs)," p 8-1.

[40](U) GWAPS *Statistical Compendium*, Table 177, "Strikes by AIF Categories."

- Scud hunting. F-16s flew 421 strikes to support the Scud hunt in the eastern Scud kill boxes.[41] GPS/LANTIRN-equipped aircraft carrying cluster munitions were the optimum configuration for anti-Scud operations.

- Support of ground forces. Armed with AGM-65 Mavericks and non-precision munitions, F-16s flew 8,258 strikes against ground forces.[42]

- Killer Scouts. F-16s also flew daylight armed reconnaissance strikes in kill boxes and coordinated air strikes.[43] Killer Scouts, as they were called, provided target type and location updates as well as threat status and position information on friendly aircraft. The intent was to locate and identify assigned targets within an area of operations and coordinate incoming attacks against the targets before they could change position.

Since more F-16s (248) were deployed to Operation Desert Storm than any other U.S. fighter aircraft, they flew the most sorties.[44] Most of the F-16s were day-only attack aircraft, except for two squadrons equipped with LANTIRN navigational pods for flying night attack sorties. Also, 12 of the F-16s based in Turkey fired the high-speed antiradiation missile (HARM).

During Desert Storm, the F-16A/Cs flew 13,087 sorties, striking 11,698 targets in Iraq and Kuwait.[45, 46] Their principal weapons were nonprecision bombs and AGM-65 Maverick missiles. The average time for each sortie was 3.24 hours,[47] and mission-capable rates were high at

---

[41](U) *Ibid.*

[42](U) *Ibid.*

[43]For command and control of aircraft attacking ground targets, CENTAF had divided the Kuwait theater into 30- by 30-nautical mile zones, or "kill boxes."

[44]There were 212 F-16s in the CENTCOM AOR and 36 at Incirlik AB, Turkey, as part of the Proven Force.

[45](U) GWAPS *Statistical Compendium*, Tables 98, "F-16: USAF and Bahrain Sorties by Mission Type," and 177, "Strikes by AIF Categories."

[46](U) Bahrain also flew 166 F-16 OCA/DCA sorties during Desert Storm. GWAPS *Statistical Compendium*, Table 98, "F-16: USAF and Bahrain Sorties by Mission Type."

[47]*Desert Score*, p 48.

88.8 percent. Eight F-16s were lost during the 7-week war; 3 in combat and 5 in noncombat accidents.[48]

Salient F-16 tactical issues include the following: During the air campaign, F-16s used a two-aircraft formation as the basic fighting element. This element combined with other elements to form flights of four aircraft. The flights of four then joined other flights, and on one occasion, fifty-six F-16s were used in a single strike package.[49] In the early stages of the campaign, large packages were routine, but as air supremacy was gained and targeting priorities changed, F-16s flew smaller squadron-size (twenty-four aircraft) packages with better results. Air Force Reserve, Air National Guard, and Regular Air Force crews flew the F-16s in Desert Storm.

F-16s had an internal 20-mm M61 Vulcan cannon. Some Air National Guard F-16As had 30-mm, 4-barrel Gatling cannons. F-16s also had six wing pylons for external stores and two tip rails for air-to-air missiles. [DELETED].[50] The F-16 carried two AIM-9s and 500 rounds of 20-mm armor-piercing incendiary high explosives ammunition plus one of the following munitions loads during Operation Desert Storm: four to six MK-82s, two MK-84s, four CBU-52/58/71s, four CBU-87s, four CBU-89 Gators, or two to four AGM-65 Maverick.[51]

---

[48](U) GWAPS *Statistical Compendium*, Table 207, "Desert Storm Coalition Aircraft Attrition."

[49]On 19 January, 56 F-16s attacked the Baghdad Nuclear Research Center in the largest single raid of the war. *Conduct of the Persian Gulf War*, p T-65.

[50]*Desert Score*, p 48.

[51](S) USCENTAF *Combat Plans Handout*, "F-16 Standard Conventional Loads (SCLs)," p 8-1.

 **B-52 Stratofortress**: (nicknamed "BUFF" for Big, Ugly, Flying Fellow) a long-range, heavy bomber capable of flying at high subsonic speeds at altitudes up to 50,000 feet. The B-52 first flew on 15 April 1952 and attained initial operational capability in June 1955. Seven hundred and forty-four aircraft were produced through October 1962. Numerous modifications had been made to the B-52, including the new Offensive Avionics System[52] and improvements in electronic countermeasures. In all, 41 B-52Gs were modified with improved conventional capabilities. The aircraft carries a full range of conventional munitions internally and externally along with conventional air-launched cruise missiles (CALCMs) for standoff operations.

As the air campaign evolved, the B-52 force grew to 68 B-52Gs, which flew out of Barksdale in Louisiana, Wurtsmith in Michigan, Saudi Arabia, Diego Garcia in the Indian Ocean, RAF Fairford in Great Britain, and Moron de la Frontera in southern Spain.[53] In all, B-52s flew 1,741 sorties for 15,269 combat hours during Operation Desert Storm.[54] B-52s dropped ordnance on both strategic and tactical targets and were important for psychological operations. The following are representative examples of B-52 missions in Desert Storm:

- Seven B-52s from Barksdale AFB, Louisiana, carried CALCMs and launched before H-Hour. Aircraft carrying out these round-trip sorties flew a total distance of over 14,000 miles and remained aloft for over 35 hours–completing the longest combat missions in history and the first combat employment of CALCM. In the early hours of Desert Storm, the B-52s launched 35 CALCMs programmed to attack 8 targets, including military communications sites and power generation/transmission facilities.

---

[52] 264 B-52G and B-52H aircraft were refitted with the digital, solid-state Offensive Avionics System (OAS) from 1980 to 1986. *Desert Score*, p 54.

[53] Sorties flown from Wurtsmith AFB, MI.

[54] (U) GWAPS *Statistical Compendium*, Table 108, "B-52: USAF Sorties by Mission Type." Also, (S) Maj John Masotti, *Operations Desert Shield and Desert Storm Bomber Story*, Hq SAC/DOBX, 18 Sep 91, p 50.

- Night low-level operations against strategic targets continued through the third day of Operation Desert Storm. After striking the Uwayjah petroleum refineries during the air campaign's third night, a B-52G apparently was hit by a missile or antiaircraft artillery, but the aircraft returned safely to its base.[55] After the third night, all B-52 missions were conducted at high altitude.

- B-52s flew ninety-nine offensive counterair strikes against airfields, aircraft on the ground, and airfield-supporting infrastructure, using general-purpose bombs and cluster bomb units.[56] Thirteen B-52s launched in the opening attack, using mixed loads of weapons (UK-1000s, CBU-58s, and CBU-89s).[57] One B-52 sustained minor damage when it was hit leaving the target area, but there were no casualties.

- B-52s flew 303 strikes against strategic targets (industrial facilities, command, control, and communications (C^3) facilities, nuclear/chemical/biological facilities, and short-range ballistic missiles); interdiction targets including fixed installations such as petroleum, oil and lubricant storage facilities, and railroads.[58] Most raids were conducted at high altitude with weapons employed using radar deliveries.

- B-52s, using a variety of general-purpose bombs and cluster munitions, flew 1,175 strikes against Republican Guard, armor, and mechanized and infantry units in the KTO.[59] The B-52's large bomb load and area coverage rendered it most effective in this role.

B-52s generally flew in threes and were most useful for attacking area targets. Its outstanding characteristic was its ability to fly large bomb loads great distances without refueling, freeing tankers for other missions. B-52s were not sent into the highest threat areas and were always used in conjunction with Wild Weasels and/or CAP aircraft in

---

[55](S) Masotti, p 30.

[56](U) GWAPS *Statistical Compendium*, Table 177, "Strikes by AIF Categories."

[57](S) Masotti, pp 29, 30.

[58](U) GWAPS *Statistical Compendium*, Table 177, "Strikes by AIF Categories."

[59](S/NF/WN/NC) *Ibid.*

areas where a significant threat remained. Despite the B-52's advanced age, few of its missions had to be aborted, and its overall mission-capable rate averaged 86.2 percent.[60] The B-52 flew 1,741 sorties without a combat loss.

As in Vietnam, the effect of B-52s on Iraqi material and morale was debated in the absence of definitive evidence. Although B-52s only comprised 3 percent of the total combat aircraft, they dropped 72,000 bombs weighing a total of 27,000 tons, which amounted to approximately 30 percent of all U.S. tonnage dropped.[61] Because of a lack of precision capability, bombing was directed at area targets such as chemical storage sites, factories, and supply depots in northern Iraq. Raids against the Republican Guards began on Day 1 and continued throughout the campaign. The B-52 can carry approximately 70,000 pounds of ordnance internally and externally. Defensive armament included 4 50-caliber machine guns, chaff, and flares. [DELETED].[62]

 **A-10 Thunderbolt II (Warthog):** the first Air Force aircraft specifically designed for close air support (CAS) of ground forces. Designed around the GAU-8 gun, it is intended for use against tanks and other armored vehicles.[63] The A-10 has excellent maneuverability and better survivability in its CAS role than previous aircraft. Its weapons delivery system includes a heads-up display, a Pave Penny laser tracking pod, and the GAU-8/A Avenger 30-mm seven-barrel Gatling-type cannon. The gun fires inert-depleted-uranium armor-piercing projectiles capable of penetrating medium and heavy tanks. It can also fire high-explosive ammunition, which is extremely effective against trucks and other soft targets. The GAU-8/A has a cyclic rate of fire of 3,900 rounds per minute.

---

[60](S/NF/WN/RD) *History of the Strategic Air Command*, Volume I, 1 Jan-31 Dec 90, p 497.

[61]*Conduct of the Persian Gulf War*, p T-27.

[62](S) USCENTAF *Combat Plans Handout*, "B-52 Standard Conventional Loads (SCLs), p 12-1.

[63]The World War II-era Soviet II-2 Sturmovik ground-attack aircraft and the more recent SU-25 Frogfoot were designed for a similar mission.

The A-10 first flew on 10 May 1972 and achieved initial operational capability in 1977. Seven hundred and seven production and six preproduction aircraft were delivered before production ceased in 1984. [DELETED].[64]

Both regular Air Force and Air National Guard units operated A-10s in Desert Storm. A total of 132 A-10s and 12 OA-10s deployed to Saudi Arabia during Operation Desert Shield. All A-10s were based at King Fahd International Airport and used King Kahlid Military City (KKMC) as a forward operating location. In addition to its traditional CAS mission, the A-10 was used for the following missions in Desert Storm:

- A-10s flew 175 strikes during an offensive counterair (OCA) effort focused primarily on destroying electronic warfare and ground control intercept sites during the first few days of the air campaign.[65]

- A-10s flew forty-nine strikes during missions to suppress enemy air defenses; sometimes they were teamed with F-4Gs to attack fixed SA-2/3/6 sites.[66]

- A-10s flew 3,367 day and night strikes against Iraqi artillery and armor units.[67] The weapons of choice were AGM-65 Mavericks and its internal 30-mm cannon.

- A-10s flew 135 strikes on Scud CAP and anti-Scud armed reconnaissance missions.[68]

- Aircraft designated for CAS and search and rescue (SAR) missions were continuously on alert from the beginning of the war. In one case, A-10s escorted a Special Operations Forces (SOF) combat

---

[64](S) USCENTAF *Combat Plans Handout*, "A-10 Standard Conventional Loads (SCLs), pp 11-1, 11-2.

[65](U) GWAPS *Statistical Compendium*, Table 177, "Strikes by AIF Categories."

[66](U) *Ibid.*

[67](U) *Ibid.*

[68](U) *Ibid.*

search and rescue helicopter to retrieve a downed F-14 pilot and destroyed an Iraqi radio intercept truck searching for the pilot.[69]

- OA-10s flew 656 missions as dedicated forward air control (FAC) assets providing airborne control of CAS aircraft.[70]

The A-10 was used primarily as a day CAS/attack aircraft; it could carry a large weapons load and loiter for long periods in the target area. Its relatively long loiter time made the A-10 useful for "look and see" types of missions such as Scud hunting. But, its slower speed and long loiter time over the battlefield also made it susceptible to enemy fire. In fact, fifty-one aircraft were damaged during missions in Desert Storm; of these, fourteen apparently were damaged in combat.[71] Ten of the fourteen A-10s damaged were returned to action within a day, and all but one flew again during the war. Nevertheless, six aircraft were combat lost (four A-10s and two OA-10s).

One of the six A-10 squadrons deployed to the AOR operated exclusively at night using the infrared video of the AGM-65D Maverick missile as a "poor man's FLIR". The Maverick's infrared seeker became a search tool for targets not only for the missile but for other weapons. A-10s fired 4,801 Maverick missiles,[72] which was more than 90 percent of the Mavericks fired by Air Force aircraft. The 30-mm cannon also proved effective against a variety of targets, including two helicopters shot down over Kuwait. A-10s were also used extensively early in the war for taking out the border early-warning radars to deny as much information as possible to the Iraqis. If the Iraqi army had ever moved south, the A-10, along with the AV-8 and F/A-18, was considered the primary weapon system for stopping that advance. When preparation for the ground war began, most A-10 sorties were directed against Iraqi armored and unarmored vehicles. In all, A-10s flew 8,084 sorties, strik-

---

[69] *Conduct of the Persian Gulf War*, p T-10.

[70] (U) GWAPS *Statistical Compendium*, Table 129, "OA-10: USAF Sorties by Mission Type."

[71] (U) GWAPS *Statistical Compendium*, Table 207, "Desert Storm Coalition Aircraft Attrition."

[72] *Conduct of the Persian Gulf War*, p T-11.

ing 6,834 targets; 1,041 sorties were identified as CAS missions.[73] The aircraft averaged 2.37 hours per flight[74] and had a mission-capable rate of 87.7 percent.

Salient A-10 tactical issues include the following: Tactical employment tended to be two rather than four aircraft. Two-ship formations ingressed at altitudes between 15,000 and 20,000 feet in line-abreast, wedge, or trail formation. Some aircraft released their ordnance first to allow for greater maneuverability and to regain energy, and then used their gun against targets, threats permitting. Almost all two-ship formation tactics flew one flight member to maintain a high, cover position while the other released ordnance; then the aircraft reversed roles.[75]

The Iraqi army provided a tremendous target array. Pilots acquired targets easily, but target identification—discriminating a tank or self-propelled artillery piece from a truck—proved a constant challenge. When engaging an armored or mechanized position, some flights made medium-altitude gun and/or reconnaissance passes, dropping from 15,000 feet to 5,000-8,000 feet to attempt to distinguish revetted trucks from revetted armor. Photos, when provided, helped the pilot identify the position of his intended target. Some pilots used binoculars to assist in target identification; others remarked that the magnification was too little or that the plane vibrated excessively. The A-10 pilot almost always visually acquired the desired priority target and used either a precision munition or area weapon to destroy it.[76]

In addition to its GAU-8/A's 1,170 rounds of 30-mm high-explosive or armor-piercing ammunition, the A-10 could use 11 external points for carrying most conventional munitions.[77]

---

[73](U) GWAPS *Statistical Compendium*, Table 85, "A-10: USAF Sorties by Mission Type," and Table 177, "Strikes by AIF Categories."

[74]*Desert Score*, p 20.

[75](S/NF/WN/NC) *Tactical Analysis Bulletin*, Vol 91-2, p 6-8.

[76](S/NF/WN/NC) *Ibid*, p 6-9.

[77](S) USCENTAF *Combat Plans Handout*, "A-10 Standard conventional Loads (SCLs)," pp 11-1, 11-2.

AC-130A/H Spectre. Discussed later in a section entitled, "Special Aircraft."

 **A-6E Intruder:** a carrier- and land-based, long-range, subsonic attack aircraft capable of accurate weapon delivery during day, night, and all-weather conditions. First flown in 1963, the A-6 achieved initial operational capability in 1965. All A-6 aircraft used by the Navy and Marine Corps in the Gulf War were A-6Es with an improved radar and digital avionics. Additionally, all aircraft were equipped with a Target Recognition and Acquisition Multisensor (TRAM) System, which gave the aircraft a FLIR sensor, a combination laser designator/range finder, and a laser designation receiver. Two Navy A-6 squadrons were also equipped with the Systems Weapons Improvement Program (SWIP) upgrade, which in addition to bringing all avionics to state-of-the-art, allowed the aircraft to fire HARM, Standoff Land-Attack Missile (SLAM), and Maverick missiles.

A-6s flew 5,619 sorties striking 2,617 targets in Operation Desert Storm.[78] Their missions included:

- All-weather and night attacks using radar and FLIR deliveries against point and area targets to support the strategic bombing campaign. A-6's flew 156 strikes and hit targets such as ammunition storage, oil terminals, C^3 facilities, and power plants.[79]

- A-6s flew 221 strikes on suppression of enemy air defense (SEAD) missions against SOCs and airfields.[80] The SWIP Squadron fired HARM missiles to suppress enemy radars and also launched tactical air-launched decoys (TALDs) to further confuse Iraqi defensive measures.

---

[78](U) GWAPS *Statistical Compendium*, Tables 83, "A-6: USN and USMC sorties by Mission Type," and 177, "Strikes by AIF Categories."

[79](U) GWAPS *Statistical Compendium*, Table 177, "Strikes by AIF Categories."

[80](U) *Ibid.*

- Support of Ground Forces. The A-6 flew 1,610 strikes against targets such as bridges, ammo storage areas, railroad yards, and armor.[81]

- Directed by both the Joint Force Air Component Commander (JFACC) and the Anti-Surface Unit Warfare Commander (ASUWC) of the Naval Battle force, the A-6 flew 183 strikes against naval and coastal defense targets such as port facilities, individual ships and boats, and Silkworm shore-based antiship missile sites.[82] These missions often involved a weapons load of a 1,000-pound MK-83 laser-guided bomb and two Rockeyes.

- SWIP A-6s launched the first combat deliveries of the SLAM, and seven SLAMs were fired during the Gulf War.

Before the war, A-6 crews normally trained for low-level (below 1,000 feet) penetration and attack. After initial low-level strikes encountered intense antiaircraft defenses, most A-6s attacked from above 10,000 feet and used either a level or a shallow dive delivery. Initial target acquisition was accomplished with the radar with a handoff to the FLIR. About one-third of the strike missions were radar deliveries when weather, smoke, or haze precluded FLIR acquisition of the target.

The A-6 carried a wide range of weapon loads in Desert Storm, including the following; eight to twelve MK-82s, eight to twelve MK-20 Rockeye (APAMs), six MK-83's, two to four GBU-10s, two GBU-16s, or two to four MK-84s.[83]

 **F/A-18A/C Hornet:** a single-seat, twin-engine, high-performance, multimission tactical aircraft operated by the U.S. Navy and Marine Corps. Its first flight was in 1978 and initial operational capability was achieved in 1983. By Desert Storm, some 900 F/A-18s had been delivered to U.S. and international customers.

---

[81](U) *Ibid.*

[82](U) *Ibid.*

[83]*Conduct of the Persian Gulf War*, p T-6.

During the initial hours of Desert Storm, 89 Navy and 72 Marine Corps F/A-18s conducted both defense suppression and strike missions against Iraqi targets.[84] The Navy Hornets flew 4,449 sorties and the Marine Corps' F/A-18s flew 4,936 sorties resulting in a reported combined total of 4,551 strikes against targets during Operation Desert Storm.[85] [DELETED].[86]

Twenty-six Canadian CF-18s were deployed from Lahr in Germany to the Persian Gulf. The CF-18s conducted their first offensive mission, an antiradar sweep of hostile airspace ahead of U.S. attack aircraft, on 24 January 1991.[87] A majority of their 961 sorties were DCA missions, and they also struck targets during the 100-hour ground war.[88]

The Hornet performed air-to-air and air-to-surface missions. In its air-to-air role, the F/A-18 projected tactical air over land and sea and complemented fleet air defense. Its primary attack missions were interdiction, CAS, defense suppression, and attacks against land and seaborne targets. The following F/A-18 missions were flown in Desert Storm:

- Hornets flew 157 strikes during SEAD missions.[89] Normal mission load consisted of two AIM-9s, two AIM-7s, 20-mm cannon, and two AGM-88 HARMs.

- F/A-18s flew 217 strikes on airfields during OCA missions.[90] Typical loads for these missions were two AIM-9s, one AIM-7, 20-mm cannon, and either five MK-83s or two MK-84s, along with a FLIR pod. Typical target attacks were made from a 30-

---

[84]The Navy Hornets flew from carriers in the Persian Gulf and Red Sea, and the Marine Hornets were based at Shaikh Isa in Bahrain.

[85](U) GWAPS *Statistical Compendium*, Tables 89, "F/A-18: USN and USMC Sorties by Mission Type," and 177, "Strikes by AIF Categories."

[86]*Royal Saudi Air Force Systems Analysis*, "The Gulf War, A History and Summary of Events," p 179.

[87]*Desert Score*, p 33.

[88](U) GWAPS *Statistical Compendium*, Table 88, "CF-18: Canada Sorties by Mission Type."

[89](U) GWAPS *Statistical Compendium*, Table 177, "Strikes by AIF Categories."

[90](U) *Ibid.*

degree or greater dive angle beginning at an altitude of 30,000 to 35,000 feet, with release between 20,000 and 10,000 feet and airspeed around 480 to 540 knots.[91]

- F-18s also flew 2,129 defensive counterair (DCA) escort sorties.[92] The F/A-18's typical load for these missions comprised two AIM-9s, one AIM-7, a 20-mm cannon, and, occasionally, a HARM.

The F/A-18 Hornet dropped more than 17,500 tons of ordnance against a variety of targets. Its multimission capability was demonstrated on 17 January when a flight of four F/A-18s encountered two Iraqi MIG-21s about 35 miles from their target. The F/A-18s acquired, identified, and destroyed the two MIGs, then shifted to an air-to-ground role and dropped their MK-84s. This was the only such incident in the Gulf War. During Desert Storm, 3 Marine F/A-18s were damaged by surface-to-air missiles and 1 by antiaircraft artillery; all returned to base and flew again within 36 hours. One Navy F/A-18 was lost in combat.[93]

The F/A-18 carried ordnance on nine external stations including two wingtip stations for AIM-9 Sidewinders; two outboard wing stations for an assortment of air-to-air and air-to-ground weapons, including AIM-7s, AIM-9s, AGM-84 Harpoons, AGM-88 HARMs, and AGM-65 Mavericks; two inboard wing stations for external fuel tanks or air-to-ground weapons; two nacelle fuselage stations for either AIM-7s, a Laser Detector Tracker Strike Camera, a targeting FLIR, or a navigation FLIR; and a center station for a fuel tank or air-to-ground weapons. Air-to-ground weaponry included laser-guided GBU-10/12s, MK-80 series general-purpose bombs, cluster bombs, and a M61 20-mm six-barrel gun with 540 rounds of ammunition.[94]

---

[91]*Conduct of the Persian Gulf War*, p T-78.

[92]The U.S. Navy flew 1,436 and Canada 693 defensive counterair sorties. (U) GWAPS *Statistical Compendium, Tables 88*, "*CF-18: Canada Sorties by Mission Type*," *and 89*, "*F/A-18: USN and USMC Sorties by Mission Type.*"

[93]*Conduct of the Persian Gulf War*, p T-78.

[94]*Ibid.*

 **AV-8B Harrier:** a Marine Corps short-takeoff and vertical-landing attack aircraft. Its attack avionics system uses a nose-mounted angle-rate bombing set, which has a TV/laser target seeker and tracker, but can not self-designate for laser-guided munitions. Eighty-six AV-8Bs were deployed to support Operation Desert Storm.[95] They operated from an expeditionary airfield (King Abdul Aziz AB), from ships (LHA-1, USS *Tarawa* and LHA-4, USS *Nassau*), and from a forward-area rearming and refueling point at Tanajib.

As the Marine Corps' principal light attack aircraft, Harriers flew 3,359 sorties, striking 2,585 targets during Operation Desert Storm.[96] They flew 2,421 strikes against Iraq's Ground Order of Battle and attacked targets such as artillery, tanks, armored vehicles, ammunition storage bunkers, convoys, logistic sites, troop locations, and airfields.[97] AV-8Bs expended 7,175 MK-20 Rockeyes, 288 MK-83s, 4,167 MK-82s, and 83,373 rounds of 25-mm machine-gun ammunition.[98]

During the first two phases of the air war, AV-8Bs generally flew medium-altitude profiles between 10,000 to 20,000 feet. They would occasionally drop to a lower altitude to locate and engage targets at less than 8,000 feet. During the battlefield preparation and ground war phases, AV-8Bs flew at lower altitudes to ensure target acquisition and increase weapons effectiveness and accuracy. At these lower altitudes, five AV-8Bs were lost to enemy action.

 **A-7 Corsair:** a U.S. Navy, single-engine, single-seat, carrier-based strike aircraft. The A-7 first flew in 1965 and its initial operational capability was achieved in 1966. When Iraq invaded Kuwait, the A-7 was being withdrawn from service; the *John F. Kennedy* (CV 67) was the only

---

[95]HQMC Brief to SECDEF, APP-A/1160-7/JQ/91.

[96](U) GWAPS *Statistical Compendium*, Tables 86, "AV-8: USMC Sorties by Mission Type," and 177, "Strikes by AIF Categories."

[97](U) GWAPS *Statistical Compendium*, Table 177, "Strikes by AIF Categories."

[98]*Conduct of the Persian Gulf War*, p T-22.

carrier still flying A-7s. During Desert Storm, the *Kennedy's* 24 A-7s staged attacks from the Red Sea and also guided the first operational AGM-84E SLAMs into Iraqi missile storage facilities. A total of 737 A-7 sorties were flown in Desert Storm.[99]

Armament consisted of a M61 Gatling-type cannon with 500 rounds (1,000 rounds maximum) and up to 15,000 pounds of external stores. These stores included MK-80 series bombs, laser-guided bombs, AGM-65 Maverick missiles, AGM-45 Shrike and AGM-88 HARM antiradar missiles, and cluster bombs.

Forward Air Control Aircraft

OV-10 Bronco: an armed, light observation and reconnaissance aircraft with FLIR and laser designation capability. The Marine Corps deployed 20 of these aircraft to Southwest Asia. While praised by the Marine Division commanders, some delays associated with deploying the OV-10 to Southwest Asia occurred since it could not refuel in flight or be transported by strategic airlift.[100] Co-located with the AV-8Bs at King Abdul Aziz Naval Base, the OV-10s flew 482 sorties, of which 411 were logged as CAS missions.[101]

Salient points included a relatively long loiter time at low airspeeds, which allowed OV-10s to fly aerial reconnaissance, airborne forward air control and tactical air control, armed reconnaissance, helicopter escort, and command and control missions. The aircraft also used their FLIR sensors to provide laser designation, night observation, and reconnaissance.

---

[99](U) GWAPS *Statistical Compendium*, Table 84, "A-7: USN Sorties by Mission Type."

[100]HQMC Brief to SECDEF, APP-A/1160-7/JQ/91.

[101](U) GWAPS *Statistical Compendium*, Table 130, "OV-10: USMC Sorties by Mission Type."

 **F/A-18D Hornet:** a Marine, two-seat, all-weather, day/night attack aircraft. Its mission was to attack and destroy surface targets; conduct multisensor imagery reconnaissance; provide supporting arms coordination, including air, naval gunfire and artillery; and to intercept and engage enemy aircraft.

The Marines deployed twelve F/A-18D aircraft to Southwest Asia. The aircraft were used in tactical-air-coordinator and airborne-forward-air-control roles. They flew into target areas ahead of Coalition attacks to locate and identify high-value targets during tactical air missions. F/A-18s provided almost twenty-four-hour battlefield coverage for CAS missions.

The F/A-18D flew 557 sorties with a mission-capable rate of 85.9 percent in Operation Desert Storm. No F/A-18Ds were lost to enemy fire, and only two sustained battle damage. Armament capability was the same as for F/A-18A/C aircraft, and during Desert Storm, F/A-18Ds expended 2,325 rockets and 27,000 rounds of 20-mm cannon ammunition.[102]

Helicopters

 **AH-64A Apache:** the U.S. Army's principal attack helicopter. It was designed for antiarmor operations and for operations under field conditions in daytime, nighttime, and adverse weather. The Apache's primary armament is the Hellfire modular missile system, a laser-homing-guided, antiarmor weapon. It can designate targets itself or receive designations from remote sources. Hydra 70, 2.75-inch folding fin aerial rockets are carried in addition to, or instead of, Hellfires. A chin-turret-mounted 30-mm cannon is controlled by a sight in the pilot's helmet. The Apache is also equipped with electronic systems such as night vision sensors, infrared and radar jamming systems, and global positioning system equipment.

---

[102] *Conduct of the Persian Gulf War*, p T-81.

 **AH-1 Cobra:** an attack helicopter designed for close-in fire support and antitank missions. The initial version, the AH-1G, had a 1966 initial operational capability. The Army and Marine Corps deployed with 224 Cobras to Southwest Asia.[103] The Marine Corps Cobras flew 1,273 sorties and accumulated 3,014 hours, providing close-in fire support, helicopter escort, and antiarmor and armed reconnaissance missions.[104] The Army conducted daylight armed reconnaissance operations and security patrols with tube-launched, optically-tracked, wire guided (TOW) missiles, 2.75 inch rockets, and 20-mm guns.

Coalition Aircraft

 **Tornado:**[105] a two-seat all-weather bomber developed by the United Kingdom (UK), Germany, and Italy and also purchased by Saudi Arabia. Its initial operational capability was in 1982, and seventy-four ground attack versions served in the Gulf War.[106] The United Kingdom also flew Tornados modified for reconnaissance missions.

The Tornado flew a variety of missions during the war, including the following:

- The Tornado initially used its JP233 runway denial weapon, which was designed for low-level attacks on airfields in Europe. With JP233, Tornados flew level deliveries at extremely low altitudes and attacked runways and aircraft parking areas. Fifty-three sorties were flown in the first four days, expending 106

---

[103] *Ibid*, p T-13. The Army deployed with 145 and the Marine Corps with 79.

[104] HQMC Brief to SECDEF, APP-1/1160-7/JQ/91.

[105] This ground attack version had different designations according to country. The UK version was called GR1, the Saudi version IDS, and the Italians simply called it Tornado.

[106] (S) This total included the UK, Italy, and Saudi Arabia. (S) *Desert Shield, USCENTAF/RASF Combat Plans Handout,* Jan 1991, pp 17-4, 17-5.

JP233s.[107] Reduced enemy airfield activity negated the need to continue delivering JP233 from low-level, and the United Kingdom Tornados switched to medium-altitude tactics to fly above the antiaircraft artillery threat. During this timeframe, United Kingdom Tornados continued to target airfields using UK 1000-pound bombs to cut runways.

- With the arrival of Buccaneer aircraft equipped with the Pave Spike laser designating pod on day 17 of Desert Storm, Tornados dropped laser-guided bombs that were buddy-lased by Buccaneers. Tornados flew 488 strikes against targets such as bridges, hardened aircraft shelters, and other elements of air base infrastructure.[108] The arrival of two thermal imaging and laser designating pods in the last ten days of the air war allowed the Tornado to designate targets for its own laser-guided bombs.

- The Tornados also carried air-launched antiradiation missiles (ALARMs) on SEAD missions; they fired 113 ALARMs during the war.[109]

The United Kingdom Tornado ground attack force flew 2,535 sorties in Desert Storm, mostly in interdiction roles.[110] Its main weapons were JP233 and UK-1000s. The Tornado carried two JP233s, four to eight unguided UK 1,000-pound bombs, or two to three UK 1,000-pound bombs configured as laser-guided bombs. United Kingdom Tornados dropped 106 JP233s and 3,631 unguided bombs along with 1,079 laser-guided versions of the UK's 1,000-pound bomb.[111] In addition, RAF Reconnaissance Tornados flew 140 sorties.

---

[107](S) Operational Research Branch Headquarters RAF Strike Command, "Analysis of Attack and Reconnaissance Operations During Operation Granby," 26 July 91, p 8.

[108](U) GWAPS *Statistical Compendium*, Table 183, "Precision-Guided Munitions (PGM) Strikes by AIF Categories."

[109](S) Operational Research Branch Headquarters RAF Strike Command, p 8.

[110](U) GWAPS *Statistical Compendium*, Tables 104, 106, and 107, "Saudi Arabia, Italy and UK Sorties by Mission Type."

[111](S) Operational Research Branch Headquarters Strike Command, pp 7-8.

 **Buccaneer**: a dual-engined bomber originally built for the Royal Navy in the late 1950s, but transferred to the Royal Air Force with the retirement of that Navy's last conventional carrier. Updated in the 1980s with a new avionics suite, the aircraft carries a daytime-only Pave Spike laser designating pod. When the Tornados transitioned to medium-altitude, 12 Buccaneers were brought to the theater to laser-designate laser-guided bombs on day 17. The Buccaneers flew 226 sorties in Desert Storm, mostly as buddy laser designators without weapons.[112] After the arrival of the Tornado's thermal imaging and laser designating (TIALD) pod, they flew sixteen missions and designated their own weapons.

 **Jaguar**: an aircraft jointly developed by France and the United Kingdom in the late 1960s as a tactical support aircraft. In all, 12 United Kingdom and 24 French Jaguars flew 1,145 sorties striking targets in Kuwait and ships in the Persian Gulf. Those sorties included 26 reconnaissance missions.[113]

United Kingdom Jaguars expended 741 UK-1000 bombs, 387 CBU-87 cluster bombs, 608 rockets, and 8 BL-755 cluster bombs during the war.[114]

 **Mirage F1**: an all-weather intercepter with initial operational capability in 1973. It is also capable of visual attack missions and has an unrefueled radius of action of 230 nautical miles. One variant, the F-1CR, was developed for a reconnaissance role. The Coalition Mirage F1s did not fly in the first week of Desert Storm to avoid confusion with Iraq's F1s and the risk of being shot down by friendly aircraft.[115] The Kuwait and Qatari air forces flew 170 ground attack missions, while the French flew 44 recon-

---

[112](U) GWAPS *Statistical Compendium*, Table 81, "Total Sorties by U.S. Service/Allied Country by Aircraft Type."

[113](U) GWAPS *Statistical Compendium*, Table 101, "Jaguar: UK and France Sorties by Mission Type."

[114](S) Operational Research Branch Headquarters RAF Strike Command, pp 10-11.

[115]Royal Saudi Air Force Systems Analysis, pp 193, 194.

naissance missions.[116] The Fls flew only daytime sorties because they lacked night capability.

Air-to-Ground Weapons

A large selection of air-to-ground weapons were available to Coalition forces during the Gulf War. This section begins with a brief discussion of the basic characteristics of air-to-ground munitions and then describes the weapons used.

Bombs and Missiles

A bomb is an explosive filler enclosed in a casing. Bombs are generally classified according to the ratio of explosive material to total weight. The principal classes are general-purpose (GP), fragmentation, and penetration bombs. Approximately 50-percent of the GP bomb's weight is explosive material.[117] These bombs usually weigh between 500 and 2,000 pounds and produce a combination of blast and fragmentation effects.[118] The most common GP bombs are the MK-80 series weapons. Only ten to twenty percent of a fragmentation bomb's weight is explosive material;[119] the remainder include specially scored cases that break into predictably sized pieces. The fragments, which travel at high velocities, are the primary cause of damage. Cluster munitions are primarily fragmentation weapons. Penetration bombs have between twenty-five and thirty percent explosive filler.[120] The casings are designed to penetrate hardened targets such as bunkers before the explosives detonate.[121]

---

[116](U) GWAPS *Statistical Compendium*, Tables 90, "F-1: Kuwait and Qatar Sorties by Mission Type," and 91, "F-1CR: France Sorties by Mission Type."

[117] *Flight Manual, T.O. 1-1M-34, Aircrew Weapons Delivery Manual,* (Non-nuclear), 15 Feb 86, p 1-4.

[118] The approximately one-half-inch-thick casing creates a fragmentation effect at the moment of detonation, and the 50-percent explosive filler causes considerable damage from blast effect.

[119] *Flight Manual, T.O. 1-1M-34,* p 1-4.

[120] *Ibid.*

[121] Penetration was achieved by either kinetic energy of the entire projectile (BLU-109) or the effects of a shaped-charge (AGM-65G).

Free-fall bombs have three sections. The bomb body is the casing containing the explosive material. The fuze section can be located in the nose and/or the rear of the bomb and determines the timing of the explosion. The tail section, or fins, determines how the bomb flies through the air. Desired weapons effects are achieved by selecting a particular combination of bomb body, fuzing, and tail section.

Bomb Configurations

Bomb bodies vary in size, weight, and thickness of casing. GP bombs have a thinner case and more explosive filler than penetrating bombs, whereas cluster bombs generally come in dispensers that open to release bomblets at predetermined altitudes. The bomb body casing (except for cluster munitions) houses the explosive filler. Upon detonation, the high-explosive filler creates an explosive train to achieve the desired weapons effect; detonation is triggered by fuzing.

A **fuze** initiates bomb detonation at a predetermined time and under the desired circumstances. Fuzes are located in the nose or tail of the munition, or both. They are armed by one, or a combination, of the following methods:

- The *arming vane*, a small propeller, is rotated by airflow after weapon release. A specified number of rotations arms the fuse.

- The *arming pin* is ejected or withdrawn by a spring action releasing the arming mechanism and allowing the fuze to arm.

- The *inertia fuze* is armed by abrupt changes in the velocity of the bomb caused by the deployment of fins or ballutes.

- The *electric fuze* is armed by a time-delay circuit powered by a thermal battery activated by extraction of the arming lanyard upon bomb release.[122]

---

[122] *Flight Manual, T.O. 1-1M-34*, p 2-4.

FMU-113 Proximity Fuse Being Attached to a MK-82 Bomb.

Different effects are obtained by mating different bombs to different fuzes. A fuze functions in one of the following ways. An impact fuze is designed to function on or after impact. Detonation upon impact is selected for targets such as supply dumps when the main destructive energy desired is blast. For a building, a delayed detonation might be selected so the bomb can penetrate several floors before exploding. A proximity fuze contains a miniature doppler radar set that senses height above the ground. When the explosion occurs above the ground, most of the destructive effect is caused by the bomb casing fragments. Prox-imity-fuzed bombs are used against targets such as troops in trenches, radars, trucks, and other vehicles. In a timed fuze, the delay is normally initiated at bomb release rather than on impact. The timing element is a mechanical or electrical device. A hydrostatic fuze is employed in depth bombs used for underwater demolition work. The MK-36/40 Destructor is a special fuze with a sensor that can be mated to a bomb. It senses the presence of metallic objects such as trucks or ships, making it, in effect, a mine. These weapons can be used against either land or water targets.

In Southwest Asia, the MK-36 (500-pound) detonators were used to mine the waters in the vicinity of Umn Qasr naval facility.

The conical fin was the **tail section** type most often installed on GP bombs dropped in Southwest Asia. The conical fin assembly helped stabilize the bomb in flight, allowing the bomb to exhibit the best effects of low drag and stabilization after release. A conical fin mated with a GP bomb results in a low-drag general-purpose bomb. Two types of high-drag retarders were used in Desert Storm. The first was the air-inflatable retarder tail assembly containing a ballute (combination balloon and parachute) device that deployed shortly after bomb release. There were two types of ballutes, the BSU-49 mated to a 500-pound MK-82 bomb, and the BSU-50 mated to a 2,000-pound MK-84 bomb. The second type of retarding fin was the Snakeye, which had four metal vanes that opened into the windstream to slow the bomb after release. Snakeye fins were used by Navy aircraft to deliver mines into the waters around Iraqi naval bases. These high-drag retarder tail assemblies were used to slow the bomb quickly after a high-speed, low-level release, thereby reducing the chance of an aircraft being damaged by its own bomb fragments.

General-Purpose Bombs

General-purpose bombs were the type of ordnance most frequently employed in the Gulf War. According to Iraqi prisoners of war, formations of B-52s dropping general-purpose bombs were one of the most feared aircraft-weapon combinations of the war.[123] GP bombs served as the basic building blocks for many of the other munitions used during the Gulf War. GP bombs dropped during the Gulf War were as follows:

---

[123](S/REL UK) "The Gulf War: An Iraqi General's Perspective," Memorandum for Record - Joint Debriefing Center, 11 Mar 1991, p 7.

Bomb	Total weight (lb Class)	Weight of Explosives (lbs)[124]	# Dropped[125]
MK-82	500	192	77,653
MK-83	1,000	416	19,018
MK-84	2,000	945	12,189
M117	750	386	43,435

MK-80 Series: developed in the 1950s in response to the need for bombs producing less aerodynamic drag. MK-80 series bombs are cylindrical in shape and are equipped with conical fins or retarders for external high-speed carriage. They are fitted for both nose and tail fuzes to ensure reliability and produce effects of blast, cratering, or fragmentation. The MK-80 series of bombs were dropped from literally every fixed-wing

U.S. Marines assemble tail section to MK-82 Bombs.

---

[124] *Flight Manual, T.O. 1-1M-34*, pp 1-13, 1-14, and 1-21.

[125] Weapons utilization figures throughout this section from (U) GWAPS *Statistical Compendium*, Table 191, "Desert Shield/Storm: Total USAF, USN, and USMC Weapons Cost and Utilization (FY 90/91$)," unless otherwise specifically noted.

aircraft that supported the ground offensive. The bombs were used against a wide variety of targets, including artillery, trucks, bunkers, Scuds, surface-to-air missile sites, antiaircraft artillery sites, early warning radars, and supply points. All MK-80 series bombs are similar in construction.

MK-82: a free-fall, nonguided GP 500-pound bomb. The bomb is usually equipped with the mechanical M904 (nose) and M905 (tail) fuzes or the radar-proximity FMU-113 air-burst fuze. The MK-82, along with the M117, were the primary weapons used by B-52s. Air Force F-16s and Marine Corps F/A-18s and AV-8Bs also dropped MK-82s.

MK-83: a free-fall, nonguided GP 1,000-pound bomb. The bomb can be fitted either with mechanial nose and tail fuzes or with a proximity fuze. During Desert Storm, this bomb was dropped mainly by Marine aircraft conducting close air support/battlefield air interdiction (CAS/BAI) missions.

MK-84: a free-fall, nonguided GP 2,000-pound bomb. Normal fuzes are the mechanical M904 (nose) and the M905 (tail). Most of the over 12,000 MK-84s expended during Desert Storm were dropped by Air Force F-15Es, F-16s and F-111Fs; less than 1,000 of the total were dropped by Marine Corps tactical aircraft.

M117: a free-fall, unguided, GP 750-pound bomb. Its usual fuzes are the mechanical M904 (nose) and M905 (tail), or the mechanical FMU-54 (tail). The B-52s dropped virtually all of the M117 bombs.

BLU-109/B (I-2000): an improved 2,000-pound-class bomb designed as a penetrator without a forward fuze well. Its configuration is relatively slim, and its skin is much harder than that of the standard MK-84 bomb. The skin is a single-piece, forged warhead casing of one-inch, high-grade steel. The BLU-109/B was always mated with a laser guidance kit to form a laser-guided bomb in Desert Storm. Its usual tail fuze is a mechanical-electrical FMU-143. The 1,925-pound bomb has a 550-pound tritonal high-explosive blast warhead.[126]

---

[126]*Ibid*, p 1-20.

Cluster Bombs

Cluster bombs, like GP bombs, can feature mix and match components (submunitions, fuzes, etc.) to produce the desired effect.

CBU-52/58/71: The CBU-52, -58 and -71 all use SUU-30 dispensers, a metal cylinder divided longitudinally. One-half contains a strong back section that provides for forced ejection and sway-bracing. The two halves lock together. Four cast aluminum fins are attached at a 90-degree angle to the aft end of the dispenser and are canted 1.25 degrees to impart spin-stabilized flight. When released from the aircraft, the arming wire/lanyard initiates the fuze arming and delay cycle. At fuze function, the fuze booster ignites and unlocks the forward end of the dispenser. Ram air action on the dispenser forces the two halves apart, instantaneously dispensing the payload and allowing the bomblets to spin-arm and self-dispense. A total of 17,831 were expended during the Gulf War.

CBU-52: loaded with 220 antimaterial, antipersonnel bomblets.[127] The CBU-52 weighs 785 pounds and can be used with a variety of proximity fuzes or the mechanical MK-339 timed fuze. The submunition is a 3.5-inch spherical bomblet weighing 2.7 pounds with a 0.65-pound high-explosive warhead.[128]

CBU-58: loaded with 650 bomblets.[129] These bomblets contain 5-gram titanium pellets, making them incendiary and useful against flammable targets.

CBU-71: loaded with 650 bomblets.[130] It has two separate kill mechanisms, one fragmentation, the other incendiary. Both incorporate a time delay fuze, which detonates at random times after impact.

CBU-72: the 550-pound cluster bomb contains three submunitions known as fuel/air explosive (FAE). The submunitions weigh approximately

---

[127] *Ibid*, p 1-75.

[128] *Ibid*, p 1-82.

[129] *Ibid*, p 1-75.

[130] *Ibid*.

100 pounds and contain 75 pounds of ethylene oxide with air-burst fuzing set for 30 feet.[131] An aerosol cloud approximately 60 feet in diameter and 8 feet thick is created and later ignited. The main destructive force of FAE was very high overpressure, useful against soft targets. The Marine Corps dropped all 254 CBU-72s, primarily from A-6Es, against mine fields and personnel in trenches. Some secondary explosions were noted when it was used as a mine clearer; however, FAE was primarily useful as a psychological weapon.[132]

CBU-78 Gator: a tri-Service weapon featuring anti-vehicle and antipersonnel land mines used adjacent to enemy forces to disrupt or deny use of selected areas. The 500-pound CBU-78 contains 45 antitank and 15 antipersonnel mines. These mines can be detonated by target sensors (magnetic field for antitank and trip line for antipersonnel) or by a disturbance-antidisturbance device. They also have a backup self-destruct time set before aircraft launch. The Navy and the Marine Corps dropped 209 CBU-78s.[133]

CBU-87 Combined Effects Munition (CEM): a SUU-65 tactical munitions dispenser (TMD) with an optional FZU-39 proximity sensor and 202 bomblets.[134] The bomblet case is made of scored steel designed to break into approximately 300 preformed 30-grain fragments for defeating light armor and personnel.[135] The U.S. Air Force dropped 10,035 CBU-87s.[136]

CBU-89 Gator Mine: a SUU-64 tactical munitions dispenser with 72 antitank mines, 22 antipersonnel mines, and an optional FZU-39 proximity sensor.[137] Mine arming begins when the dispenser opens. Mine detonation

---

[131](S) IDA Document 1080, *Desert Storm: Fixed Wing BAI/CAS Operations and Lessons Learned*, Jan 1992, p A-5.

[132]HQMC Brief to SECDEF, USMC Aircraft and Munitions: Performance in Desert Storm, updated 9 Oct 91.

[133](U) GWAPS *Statistical Compendium*, Tables 189 and 190, "Desert Shield/Storm: USN, and USMC Weapons Cost and Utilization (FY 91$)."

[134]*Flight Manual, T.O. 1-1M-34*, p 1-85.

[135]*Ibid*, p 1-86.

[136](U) GWAPS *Statistical Compendium*, Table 188, "Desert Shield/Storm: USAF Weapons Cost and Utilization (FY 90$)."

[137]*Flight Manual, T.O. 1-1M-34*, p 1-86.1.

is initiated by target detection, mine disturbance, low battery voltage, and a self-destruct time-out. The antitank mine is a magnetic sensing submunition effective against tanks and armored vehicles. The antipersonnel mine has a fragmenting case warhead triggered by trip wires. The U.S. Air Force employed 1,105 CBU-89s during the Gulf War.[138]

MK-20 Rockeye: a free-fall, unguided cluster weapon designed to kill tanks and armored vehicles. The system consists of a clamshell dispenser, a mechanical MK-339 timed fuze, and 247 dual-purpose armor-piercing shaped-charge bomblets.[139] The bomblet weighs 1.32 pounds and has a 0.4-pound shaped-charge warhead of high explosives, which produces up to 250,000 psi at the point of impact, allowing penetration of approximately 7.5 inches of armor.[140] Rockeye is most efficiently used against area targets requiring penetration to kill. Marines used the weapon extensively, dropping 15,828 of the 27,987 total Rockeyes against armor, artillery, and antipersonnel targets. The remainder were dropped by Air Force (5,345) and Navy (6,814) aircraft.[141]

CBU-59 APAM: an antipersonnel, antimaterial weapon developed in the 1970s as a successor to Rockeye. It uses the same Rockeye dispenser, but has 717 smaller BLU-77 bomblets fitted into the case. In addition to its armor-piercing effect, it also has antipersonnel fragmentation and incendiary features. One hundred and eight-six were delivered during the war.

Laser-Guided Bombs

With the assistance of build-up guidance kits, general GP bombs are turned into laser-guided bombs (LGBs). The kits consist of a computer-control group (CCG), guidance canards attached to the front of the warhead to provide steering commands, and a wing assembly attached to the aft end to provide lift. LGBs are maneuverable, free-fall weapons requiring no electronic interconnect to the aircraft. They have an internal semiactive

---

[138](U) GWAPS *Statistical Compendium*, Table 188, "Desert Shield/Storm: USAF Weapons Cost and Utilization (FY 90$)."

[139] *Flight Manual, T.O. 1-1M-34*, p 1-88.

[140] *Ibid*, p 1-90.

[141](U) GWAPS *Statistical Compendium*, Tables 188, 189, 190, and 191 "Desert Shield/Storm: USAF, USN, USMC, and Total Weapons Cost and Utilization (FY 90/91$)."

guidance system that detects laser energy and guides the weapon to a target illuminated by an external laser source. The designator can be located in the delivery aircraft, another aircraft, or a ground source.

All LGB weapons have a CCG, a warhead (bomb body with fuze), and an airfoil group. The computer section transmits directional command signals to the appropriate pair(s) of canards. The guidance canards are attached to each quadrant of the control unit to change the flightpath of the weapon. The canard deflections are always full scale (referred to as "bang, bang" guidance).[142]

The LGB flightpath is divided into three phases: ballistic, transition, and terminal guidance. During the ballistic phase, the weapon continues on the unguided trajectory established by the flightpath of the delivery aircraft at the moment of release. In the ballistic phase, the delivery attitude takes on additional importance, since maneuverability of the LGB is related to the weapon velocity during terminal guidance. Therefore, airspeed lost during the ballistic phase equates to a proportional loss of maneuverability. The transition phase begins at acquisition. During the transition phase, the weapon attempts to align its velocity vector with the line-of-sight vector to the target. During terminal guidance, the LGB attempts to keep its velocity vector aligned with the instantaneous line-of-sight. At the instant alignment occurs, the reflected laser energy centers on the detector and commands the canards to a trail position, which causes the weapon to fly ballistically with gravity biasing towards the target.

GBU-10: an MK-84 2,000-pound bomb with an added laser guidance package.[143] The GBU-10I mates a BLU-109B weapon with a Paveway II laser guidance kit. This improved 2,000-pound bomb is used against targets requiring deeper penetration. In Operation Desert Storm, GBU-10/10Is were used extensively by F-15Es and F-111Fs mainly against bridges, Scuds, C³I (command, control, communications, intelligence) nodes, and bunkers. Of the 2,637 expended,[144] over one-

---

[142]Flight Manual, T.O. 1-1M-34, p 1-29.

[143]Ibid, p 1-25.

[144](U) GWAPS Statistical Compendium, Table 191, "Desert Shield/Desert Storm: Total USAF, USN, and USMC Weapons Cost and Utilization (FY 90/91$)."

third were dropped by F-111Fs, and the rest by F-117s, F-15Es, and Navy and Marine Corps aircraft.

GBU-12: a MK-82 500-pound bomb with an added laser guidance package. The GBU-12 was dropped by F-111Fs, F-15Es, and A-6s, mostly against fixed armor. It was the F-111F tank-busting weapon of choice. Of the 4,493 GBU-12s employed,[145] over half were dropped by the F-111F.

There are two generations of GBU-10/12 LGBs: Paveway I with fixed wings and Paveway II with folding wings. Paveway II models have the following improvements: detector optics and housing made of injection-molded plastic to reduce weight and cost; increased detector sensitivity; reduced thermal battery delay after release; increased maximum canard deflection; laser coding; folding wings for carriage, and increased detector field of view. (Paveway II's instantaneous field of view is thirty percent greater than that of the Paveway I's field of view).[146]

GBU-16: a MK-83 1,000-pound bomb modified with a common Paveway II laser guidance kit. Virtually all 219 GBU-16s were dropped by Navy A-6Es, which had the capability to lase the target themselves (self-designation).[147]

GBU-24: either a MK-84 or BLU-109 bomb modified with a Paveway III low-level laser-guided bomb kit to add the proportional guidance in place of the bang-bang type used in the Paveway II. Performance envelopes for all modes of delivery are improved because the larger wings of the GBU-24 increases maneuverability. Paveway III also has increased seeker sensitivity and a larger field of regard. All of the 1,181 GBU-24s were released by F-111Fs.[148]

GBU-27: a BLU-109 bomb with a low-level laser-guidance kit. It has a modified GBU-24 seeker head and a smaller GBU-10 tail assembly

---

[145](S/NF/WN/NC) *Ibid.*

[146]Flight Manual, *T.O. 1-1M-34*, p 1-27.

[147](U) GWAPS *Statistical Compendium*, Table 191, "Desert Shield/Desert Storm: Total USAF, USN, and USMC Weapons Cost and Utilization (FY 90/91$)."

[148](U) GWAPS *Statistical Compendium*, Table 188, "Desert Shield/Storm: USAF Weapons Cost and Utilization (FY 90$)."

necessary for internal carriage. All 739 GBU-27s expended were dropped by F-117s.[149]

Cruise Missiles

BGM-109 Tomahawk: a cruise missile carried by surface ships and submarines. It has a range of approximately 700 nautical miles, a weight of 3,200 pounds, an attached solid-propellant booster, an air-breathing

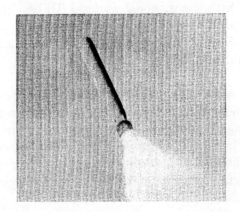

BGM-109 Tomahawk land-attack missile (TLAM) takes to the air after being launched from the battleship U.S.S. Wisconsin.

turbofan engine, and a guidance system that navigates by comparing stored digital ground images with actual ground points along its flight path. The solid-propellant rocket booster propels the missile until the small turbofan engine takes over for the cruise portion of the flight. Initial guidance is provided by a terrain-contour-matching system. The system compares a stored map reference with the actual terrain to determine the missile's position and then inputs course corrections. Final guidance is accomplished by digitized scene matching area correlation (DSMAC). This system compares views of the ground below the missile with digitized pictures in memory and directs appropriate course corrections. Tomahawk is highly survivable because of its small radar cross-section and its ability to fly at extremely low altitudes, making radar detection difficult. Infrared detection is also difficult because of the low

---

[149](U) *Ibid.*

level of heat emitted from its turbofan engine. Two types of Tomahawks were used in Desert Storm: the C model, which has a unitary 1,000-pound high-explosive blast and fragmentation warhead, and the D model, which has a cluster warhead containing 166 bomblets for attacking multiple targets.[150] The Navy fired 298 Tomahawks during Desert Storm.[151]

Conventional Air-Launched Cruise Missile (CALCM): a conventional derivative of the air-launched cruise missile (originally designed to carry a nuclear warhead), which was developed to give the B-52 standoff capability. The small, winged CALCM is powered by a turbofan jet engine and has a conventional warhead [DELETED].[152] [DELETED]. It flies to targets using an inertial navigation system aided by a Global Positioning System (GPS) receiver, and is programmed to fly at constant pressure altitude or constant AGL.

In the early stages of Desert Storm, seven B-52s flew round robin missions from Barksdale AFB in Louisiana, to the area of responsibility (AOR). These missions were time phased into the Strategic Air Campaign and lasted more than 35 hours. Two launch areas were established in northwest Saudi Arabia beyond the range of Iraq's early warning and ground control intercept radars. From these areas, the B-52s fired 35 CALCMs.[153]

Aircraft Air-to-Ground Missiles

AGM-62B Walleye: a guided bomb for daytime, clear-weather use only. Walleye is used against large targets. It is an electro-optical (2,000-pound class) weapon that uses proportional navigation to glide to the target. A two-way radio frequency datalink allows the pilot (in the release aircraft or another aircraft) to control the weapon by use of a small joystick. Wider fins can be attached to increase range for greater

---

[150]Stanley W. Kandebo, "U.S. Fires Over twenty-five percent of its Conventional Land Attack Tomahawks in First Week of War," *Aviation Week and Space Technology*, 28 Jan 91, p 29.

[151](U) GWAPS *Statistical Compendium*, Table 189, "Desert Shield/Storm: USN Weapons Cost and Utilization (FY 91$)."

[152](S) Maj Karns, "Background Paper on Conventional ALCM in Desert Storm," Hq SAC/DOOQ, 13 Feb 92, p 1.

[153](S) *Ibid*, p 2.

standoff distance. The weapon has a 2,015-pound warhead with a linearly shaped charge.[154] Only 133 Walleyes were expended in Desert Storm, virtually all of them by the U.S. Navy.[155]

AGM-65 Maverick (USAF): a 500-pound, rocket-propelled air-to-ground missile. Various modes of guidance can be used in the Maverick series. The Air Force has procured four models: the electro-optical AGM-65 models A and B and the infrared AGM-65 models D and G. The AGM-65A/B/D models have a 125-pound, shaped-charge warhead for use against armored vehicles, bunkers, boats, radar vans, and small hard targets.[156] The AGM-65G uses a larger kinetic-energy penetrator and a 300-pound blast and fragmentation warhead. The AGM-65G is effective against unusually shaped targets such as hangars, bridges, and ships and against small point targets such as tanks and bunkers. An additional force correlate mode allows this missile to strike a specific aimpoint that differs from the centroid of the target. (For example, a specific aimpoint would be a certain building in an industrial complex). A dual field of view capability was added to the infrared versions to provide wide fields of view for target acquisition and narrow fields of view for improved target identification and increased launch range. The infrared seeker expanded the missile launch environment to include night and degraded visual conditions. Targets must be acquired by all Maverick missiles before launch. All missiles are guided autonomously, providing a launch and leave capability. Infrared missiles can also be slaved to on-board aircraft sensors. Up to three AGM-65A/B/Ds are carried on LAU-88 launchers, whereas only one AGM-65G can be carried on a single-rail LAU-117 launcher. A total of 5,255 AGM-65 B/D/G Mavericks were fired in Desert Storm; of those, the A-10s fired over 4,000.[157] Mavericks were the primary "tank-plinking" weapons used by aircraft without a self-designation precision-guided munitions capability.

AGM-65E Maverick: a semiactive, laser-guided, solid-rocket-propelled air-to-ground standoff weapon. This missile is similar to the

---

[154]1990 Weapons File, MSD/XR, p 5-A-2.

[155](U) GWAPS *Statistical Compendium*, Tables 189 and 190, "Desert Shield/Storm: USN and USMC Weapons Cost and Utilization (FY 91$)."

[156]*Flight Manual, T.O. 1-1M-34*, p 1-46.

[157](S/NF/WN/NC) *Tactical Analysis Bulletin*, Vol 91-2, Jul 91, p 6-19.

Mavericks described above but has a heavy warhead and laser seeker. It is a day and night weapon primarily for close air support and homes on reflected laser energy. The AGM-65E is a modified AGM-65D, with a 300-pound penetrating blast and fragmentation warhead and a cockpit-selectable fuze. Only 36 "E" model Mavericks were used in Desert Storm, all by the Marine Corps.[158]

AGM-84E SLAM (Standoff Land-Attack Missile): a multimission Harpoon derivative designed for strikes against ships in harbors and high-value fixed targets. The weapon combines the airframe, turbojet power-plant, and warhead of the Harpoon missile with the imaging infrared terminal guidance unit of the AGM-65D Maverick missile, the datalink capability of the AGM-62 Walleye glide bomb, and a GPS receiver. After launch, midcourse guidance is aided by GPS. Seeker video is transmitted to the system operator, who recognizes, acquires, and selects the specific aimpoint on the target. The blast and fragmentation penetrating warhead has either a proximity or an impact-delay fuze and contains 488 pounds of high explosives.[159] The Navy dropped all 7 of the AGM-84Es expended during Desert Storm.[160]

AGM-123A Skipper: a day and night, medium-range, standoff glide weapon that is directed to the target by reflected laser energy. The AGM-123A was built around an AGM-45 Shrike solid-propellant rocket motor, a Paveway II seeker and airfoil group, and a MK-83 bomb body. The rocket motor doubles the range of current Paveway II series muni-tions. The Navy and the Marine Corps used a total of twelve during Desert Storm.[161]

Helicopter Air-to-Ground Missiles

BGM-71 TOW (Tube-Launched, Optically-Tracked, Wire-Guided): an antitank guided weapon. In 1974, the DOD directed the Marine Corps to

---

[158](U) GWAPS *Statistical Compendium*, Table 190, "Desert Shield/Storm: USMC Weapons Cost and Utilization (FY 91$)."

[159]Christopher Gant, *World Encyclopedia of Modern Air Weapons*, 1988, p 287.

[160](U) GWAPS *Statistical Compendium*, Table 189, "Desert Shield/Storm: USN Weapons Cost and Utilization (FY 91$)."

[161](U) GWAPS *Statistical Compendium*, Tables 189 and 190, "Desert Shield/Storm: USN and USMC Weapons Cost and Utilization (FY 91$)."

procure TOWs for helicopters. The shaped-charge warhead, used for armor penetration, contains 10 pounds of high explosives. Marine Corps' Cobras and Army helicopters operating from Navy ships fired 293 BGM-71 TOWs during Desert Storm; this figure does not include Marine Corps ground-launched TOWs or TOWs expended from U.S. Army stores.[162]

AGM-114 Hellfire (Heliborne-Launched Fire and Forget): an antiarmor, air-to-surface weapon. The Hellfire's semiactive seeker receives and homes in on reflected coded laser energy illuminated by a laser designator remote from the missile. Hellfire is not limited to direct line-of-sight attack, allowing launch without seeker lock-on, and thereby reducing exposure time and increasing survivability of the launch platform. The shaped-charge warhead contained 20 pounds of high explosives.[163] U.S. Army aircraft fired all but 189 of the over 3,000 Hellfires expended during combat.[164] Hellfire was the Army's biggest killer of armored vehicles during Desert Storm.

Rockets and Guns

Guns and unguided fin-stabilized rockets were used extensively for a wide variety of missions. They were primarily employed by Air Force and Marine Corps CAS aircraft and Army and Marine Corps helicopters during Desert Storm.

Rockets: a variety of rockets were used to both mark and destroy targets. Virtually all of the approximately 3,000 2.75-inch rockets expended by the Air Force were fired by OA-10 aircraft to mark targets. The Marine F/A-18D forward air controllers (Fast FACs) used 2.75-inch white phosphorous rockets to mark targets. In addition, Marine AH-1 Cobras expended almost 4,000 rockets: over half to mark targets and the remainder against vehicles and personnel.[165]

---

[162](U) *Ibid.*

[163]Gant, p 249.

[164](U) GWAPS *Statistical Compendium*, Tables 189 and 190, "Desert Shield/Storm: USN and USMC Weapons Cost and Utilization (FY 91$)." U.S. Army Aviation Center, Coordination Draft, Operation Desert Shield/Desert Storm After Action Report, 22 Nov 91.

[165]HQMC Brief to SECDEF, APP-A/1160-7/JQ/91.

Guns: used to mark and destroy a variety of targets, including armored vehicles and trucks. The biggest gun user was the Air Force A-10 aircraft. Its GAU-8 Avenger, a 30-mm 7-barrel, Gatling-type cannon, featured selectable rates of fire of 2,100 or 4,200 rounds per minute and a magazine holding 1,350 rounds. At a slant range of 4,000 feet, the GAU-8/A round has 14 times the kinetic energy of a 20-mm projectile fired from a M61 Vulcan cannon.[166] A-10s fired almost a million rounds of ammunition against all types of targets, especially armor and trucks; OA-10s fired an additional 16,000 plus rounds of 30-mm high explosive incendiary rounds to mark targets.[167]

AC-130 aircraft used their two 20-mm, single 40-mm, and single 105-mm guns to attack a variety of targets in and around the KTO. Marine AV-8 Harriers also used guns to conduct strafing missions and to hit enemy positions at the Battle of Khafji. AH-1 Cobras were equipped with a 20-mm gun, and the AH-64 Apaches were equipped with a 30-mm gun. Armed helicopters used guns as close-in fire-support weapons.

Coalition Munitions (United Kingdom)

JP233: a heavy-weight airfield attack and area-denial submunition dispenser with 30 concrete-penetrating and 215 area-denial bomblets.[168] The concrete-penetrating bomblets are parachute-retarded and fall to the ground in a nearly vertical trajectory. A contact fuze detonates on impact to open a hole through which a second charge is fired to penetrate and detonate, thus creating a large crater. The area-denial minelets are fitted with disturbance fuzes and variable self-destruct fuzes to slow enemy repair teams. Tornados used 106 JP233s for runway denial.[169]

BL-755: a medium-weight cluster bomb with 147 antitank frag-mentation bomblets.[170] The dispenser is armed when released and opens after a preselected time delay. The ejected bomblets, which detonate on impact, have shaped-charge warheads able to penetrate at least 9.84

---

[166]Gant, p 44.

[167](S) IDA Document 1080, p 27.

[168]Gant, p 115.

[169](S) Operational Research Branch Headquarters Strike Command, p 8.

[170]Gant, p 111.

inches of armor; they also scatter a cloud of at least 2,000 lethal frag-ments.[171] The submunitions are retarded to increase their angle of attack at impact and thus their armor penetrating capability. Jaguar aircraft used 8 BL-755s in strikes against Iraqi ground targets.[172]

UK-1000: a 1,000-pound bomb that can be carried by the B-52, Tornado, Buccaneer, or Jaguar aircraft. It is configured as either a free-fall weapon or as a laser-guided bomb. There were 4,372 UK-1000s delivered in the free-fall mode and 1,079 as LGBs.[173]

CRV-7: a weapon consisting of a pod containing 19 rockets. The rockets have a very flat trajectory and were designed to be used against naval targets. Carried only by the Jaguar, 32 CRV-7s (608 rockets) were used in the war, primarily against surface targets of the Iraqi Navy.[174]

Special Purpose One-of-a-Kind Munitions

GBU-15: an unpowered, standoff electro-optically or infrared-guided glide bomb. The GBU-15 provides the capability for accurate (automatic or manual) guided delivery of a MK-84 bomb at increased ranges. The weapon is built from modular elements consisting of various interchangeable guidance, fuzing, and control systems designed to meet specific mission requirements. The GBU-15's effective standoff range is greater than that of laser-guided munitions, since the GBU-15 does not need to have acquired the target before it is released. The weapon is remotely controlled by a datalink system, and the weapon systems opera-tor locates the target area and the specific aimpoint by observing the video transmitted from the weapon. The weapon's midcourse flight path can be adjusted either automatically or manually. Weapon video is either electro-optical (TV camera) or infrared, and generated in the nose of the weapon. During Desert Storm, all 71 GBU-15 modular glide bombs used

---

[171]*Ibid*, p 114.

[172](S) Operational Research Branch Headquarters Strike Command, p 11.

[173](S) *Ibid*, pp 10, 12. See also (S/NF/WN/RD) *History of the Strategic Air Command*, p 251.

[174](S) Operational Research Branch Headquarters Strike Command, p 11.

were dropped from F-111F aircraft.[175] Most notably, GBU-15s were the munitions used for destroying the oil manifolds on the storage tanks to stop oil from spilling into the Gulf.[176]

BLU-82: a 15,000-pound GP bomb originally designed to clear helicopter landing zones in Vietnam. The warhead contains 12,600 pounds of GSX slurry and is detonated just above ground level by a 38-inch fuze extender. The weapon produces an overpressure of 1,000 pounds per square inch.[177] Eleven BLU-82s were dropped during Desert Storm, all from Special Operations C-130s. The initial drops were intended to test the ability of the bomb to clear mines; no reliable bomb damage assessment exist on mine-clearing effectiveness. Later, bombs were dropped as much for their psychological effect as for their destructive power.

GBU-28: a special weapon developed for penetrating hardened Iraqi command centers located deep underground. The bombs are modified Army artillery tubes, weigh 4,637 pounds, and contain 630 pounds of high explosives. They are fitted with GBU-27 LGB kits, 14.5 inches in diameter and almost 19 feet long.[178] Only two of these weapons were dropped in Desert Storm, both by F-111Fs. One weapon hit its precise aimpoint, and the onboard aircraft video recorder displayed an outpouring of smoke from an entrance way approximately 6 seconds after impact.

MK-77: a napalm canister munition. The Marine Corps dropped all of the approximately 500 MK-77s used in the Gulf War.[179] They were delivered primarily by the AV-8 Harriers from relatively low altitudes. MK-77s were used to ignite the Iraqis oil-filled fire trenches, which were part of barriers constructed in southern Kuwait.

---

[175](U) GWAPS *Statistical Compendium*, Table 188, "Desert Shield/Storm: USAF Weapons Cost and Utilization (FY 90$)."

[176](S) IDA Document 1080, p 55.

[177]Gant, p 138

[178]GBU-28/B HTPM Description Briefing Slide, 57 FWW/DT PRO-111.

[179]HQMC, ASL-30, Point Paper, Desert Shield/Storm Expenditures, 16 Jul 92.

Air-To-Ground Issues

Tactical Bombing Accuracy Issues

Although laser-guided munitions constituted only 6.7 percent of bombs dropped from tactical aircraft during Desert Storm,[180] accurate bombing played a pivotal role in the exercise of air power by Coalition and particularly U.S. air forces. The relatively low percentage of precision-guided bombs reflects in part the fact that many of the unguided bombs were dropped from "smart" platforms (e.g., aircraft) that were, at least in principle, capable of achieving near precision-guided munitions accuracy with "dumb" bombs. Both capabilities reflect important advances in both platform and munitions technology, which began in earnest in the final stages of the Vietnam War. While those technological advances yielded unprecedented tactical capabilities, they also brought tactical and technical problems with them. The tactical capabilities are addressed elsewhere in this report. Here, we are concerned primarily with the factors that limited tactically obtainable accuracy.

One such factor stems from the fact that technological complexity has limited interchangeability. Although most aircraft can release virtually all munitions, only certain aircraft can both release and provide terminal guidance. Almost all aircraft participating in the Gulf War could drop LGBs, but only F-117s, F-111Fs, A-6s, and a small number of F-15Es could laser-designate their own targets. In addition, some munitions were developed for particular aircraft. For example, only the F-111F was equipped with the radio frequency datalink needed to control the GBU-15, a standoff electro-optical or infrared-guided 2,000-pound bomb; and only a limited number of B-52s could carry CALCMs along with the rocket-propelled Have Nap. These limitations tied certain aircraft to specific roles, which made planning 24-hour operations difficult.

---

[180](S) A total of 219,498 bombs were dropped by USAF, USN, and USMC aircraft, of which 9,494 were laser-guided, counting the AGM-123 Skipper, AGM-62 Walleye, and AGM-84 SLAM as guided bombs rather than missiles. The 6.7 percent figure is obtained by excluding the 77,299 bombs dropped by B-52s. Numbers derived from (U) GWAPS *Statistical Compendium*, Table 191, "Desert Shield/Storm: Total USAF, USN and USMC Weapons Cost and Utilization (FY 90/91$)," and (S) Masotti, p 53.

The appearance of digital electronic navigation, weapons guidance systems, and sensors afforded two basic options for improving bombing accuracy. One option was to make the weapon itself "smart," that is, capable of accurately guiding itself (autonomous) or of accepting precision guidance from the aircraft. The second option was to make the aircraft "smart." In the second case, an aircraft system must be able to identify a three-dimensional point in space from which a ballistic "dumb" bomb will fall accurately upon the intended target. For either option, bombing parameters and tactics were largely determined by the ability of the enemy to deny access to the critical point above the earth from which a weapon, dumb or smart, might be released to destroy the target.

Medium- and high-altitude bombing with unguided munitions posed problems, even with digital "smart platforms." First, the visual bombing pipper was 2 milliradians wide. At a slant range of 20,000 feet, typical for high-angle dive deliveries, the pipper blanked out an area on the ground 40 feet across, often hiding the target. To the resulting errors must be added bomb dispersion errors. For example, the MK-84 GP weapon dispersion was 5-6 milliradians.[181] The result of both of these kinds of errors was a worst-case 160-foot miss distance, even if the pilot did everything right and the system worked perfectly. Furthermore, aircraft systems played a key role in weapon delivery accuracy. For example, if the aircraft system altitude had a 200-foot error, the bomb could have hit 120 feet from the intended target, under the same circumstances as described above. Using "smart platforms" to deliver "dumb" bombs against point targets smaller than the circular error probable (CEP)[182] may well require redundant targeting.[183] Only weapons (e.g., cluster bomb units) with footprints larger than the CEP, could expect to hit such point targets in one shot, and their explosive effect may not be

---

[181]Capt John Fyfe, "Medium Altitude Ingress and Attack Considerations," FWS Student Paper, F-16 Class 91 BIF, 15 Aug 1991, p 11.

[182]CEP is defined as the radius of the smallest circle that will include the impact points of half of the bombs dropped against a given target. Note that CEP is a measure of precision, not accuracy, since the target is not necessarily the center of the circle.

[183]Multiple missions would have to be sent to achieve the destruction required, increasing risk, resource use, and chances of collateral damage. The Joint Munitions Employment Manual lays out mission planning redundancy requirements.

sufficient or of proper type to achieve the necessary functional destruction required for tactical effectiveness.

During Desert Storm, the effects of these basic sources of inaccuracy were magnified by preconflict training. 'Generally speaking, training was focused on a NATO Central Region conflict and emphasized low-altitude tactics. In addition, weapons systems, aircraft, and munitions had been designed to complement this thinking. By contrast, the tactical realities of Iraqi defenses in Desert Storm required Coalition aircraft to drop a wide variety of "dumb" bombs from medium and high altitudes. The Gulf War thus was a useful test case for highlighting the differences between low- and medium-altitude bombing accuracy and demonstrated a need for a more accurate way to deliver unguided ordnance from medium altitude.

Against point targets, laser-guided bombs offered distinct advantages over "dumb" bombs. The most obvious was that the guided bombs could correct for ballistic and release errors in flight. Explosive loads could also be more accurately tailored for the target, since the planner could assume most bombs would strike in the place and manner expected. Unlike "dumb" bombs, LGBs released from medium to high altitude were highly accurate. But as with pippers, forward-looking infrared (FLIR) sensors had design limitations. [DELETED].[184] [DELETED]. Weapon dispersions were overcome through laser guidance on reflected energy all the way to impact, which resulted in better accuracies against point targets. Risk, resulting from the aircraft's need to remain in the target area to provide terminal guidance after weapon release, was balanced by the likelihood that the target could be destroyed with a single strike. In addition, aircraft dropping Paveway III LGBs reduced this risk further by being able to stand off further from the target while effecting release.

Desert Storm reconfirmed that LGBs possessed a near single-bomb target-destruction capability, an unprecedented if not revolutionary development in aerial warfare. The magnitude of effort to destroy individual targets in previous wars illustrates the point. Were they so targeted during WW II, it would have taken 150 B-17 sorties dropping over 9,000 bombs to hit a particular building. Twenty-five years later, in

---

[184][DELETED].

1967-68, 177 F-105 sorties and 380 tons of bombs were required to destroy the Doumer bridge in Hanoi.

The Gulf War As A Live-Fire OT&E[185]

The LANTIRN targeting pods procured for the F-15E, were still undergoing OT&E when the Gulf War began. These targeting pods gave the F-15E night, all weather weapons delivery capability, plus self-designation for LGBs. Moreover, when Desert Shield began, the F-15E was not yet certified to deliver the full range of air-to-ground ordnance. LANTIRN was used operationally on F-15Es in Desert Storm with notable success. Undertaking the OT&E process under live-fire conditions signifi-cantly accelerated the bureaucratic process and produced results that called for further study.

Availability, Existing Plans, And Standoff Risk

The characteristics of the munitions available for Desert Storm were driven largely by Cold War plans emphasizing threat avoidance. The confluence of threat, weather, terrain, and existing technologies drove operational planners to procure weapons and aircraft delivery platforms designed for low-altitude deliveries. Another response was to move away from direct overflight of targets with conventional bombs and move towards standoff weapons for increased survivability. Unfortunately, these standoff weapons were more expensive and were relatively few in number.

The most readily available munitions, general-purpose (GP) bombs, were good low-altitude weapons, but miss distances increased when the weapons were released from higher altitudes. Even though these weapons could be dropped from high altitude, albeit with decreased accuracy, some munitions were designed for only low-altitude delivery. The British JP233 runway cratering area-denial munition was a prime example.

MK-20 Rockeye, an armor-penetrating munition, was another example of an excellent low-altitude weapon that was less effective when

---

[185]To some extent, all wars in the post-Industrial Revolution era have been used for OT&E (Operational Test and Evaluation) purposes. The classic example was the Spanish Civil War of 1936-39.

released from high altitude. Rockeye was fitted only with a timed delay fuze, which had to be preset on the ground. Conditions had to be perfect for the munition to detonate at the appropriate point in space. If release parameters and winds were not true, the ground-set timed fuze had little chance of achieving the desired results. The probability that a Rockeye clamshell dispenser would open at the appropriate altitude, on the basis of a preselected time, was not high. Dispensers opening at other than planned altitudes greatly affected bomblet density and decreased the probability of a kill.[186]

The desire to avoid exposing attack aircraft in heavily defended areas changed tactics for existing munitions and drove the desire for standoff weapons. Early versions of LGBs, notably Paveway I and II, increased accuracy, but did not offer any significant standoff benefit. The desire for greater standoff distances led to the development of munitions such as the AGM-65 Maverick missile, a launch-and-leave system designed for use against armor. This same desire sparked improvements to existing weapons. Laser-guided GBU-24s (that is, 2,000-pound Paveway III bombs) were developed with larger fins and proportional, rather than "bang-bang"[187] guidance, to extend their range. The Navy doubled Paveway II ranges by attaching a rocket motor to an existing MK-83 body, creating the AGM-123A Skipper. All of these latter weapons were used to reduce risk associated with attacking targets in high-threat areas.

The improved weapons, however, were expensive. In addition, relatively few aircraft could employ them. Cost limited the numbers procured and the assets available for training. While the high cost of these

---

[186]This problem was the father of the proximity fuze. Artillery and antiaircraft shells relying on timing to ensure detonation at precise altitudes were distinguished mostly by their ineffectiveness. For example, range, wind, trajectory, Coriolos effect, pressure altitude, and a multiple of other factors, including operator skill, determined success. The designers of proximity fuses eliminated this guesswork and operator-induced errors by putting a tiny radar set in the shell or bomb. The operator need choose only the optimum altitude above the target for maximum blast effect, set the fuze accordingly, and reduce the variables to the azimuth/range problem. Higher than desired dud rates with Rockeye were reported by A-10 and F-16 pilots during Desert Storm. (S/NF/WN/NC) *Tactical Analysis Bulletin*, Vol 91-2, pp 4-14, 6-5.

[187]Proportional guidance moved the aerodynamic control surfaces no more or less than required to achieve the desired change in direction. The more primitive "bang-bang" guidance briefly moved opposite control surfaces to their limit of travel for each required change.

weapons was offset by the benefits associated with risk avoidance and the probability of a first shot kill, the fact that many of them could be used only with certain platforms limited their utility.

Hard-Target-Penetrating Free-Fall Munitions (I-2000)

Lucrative targets such as C^2 bunkers and aircraft shelters were usually protected by some form of hardening that had to be penetrated to cause physical destruction. The requirement for a munition capable of penetrating such targets led to the development of the BLU-109 (I-2000) penetrating 2,000-pound bomb. The BLU-109 was built with a heavy forged steel case designed to reduce break-up and to achieve penetration through kinetic energy. Its greater penetrating ability offered increased flexibility against a wider variety of targets. An even greater degree of flexibility was achieved by mating laser-guided bomb (LGB) kits to BLU-109 bomb bodies. Paveway II (GBU-10) and Paveway III (GBU-24 A/B and GBU-27) effectively complemented the BLU-109. [DELETED].[188]

[DELETED].

Electronic/Reconnaissance Systems

Electronic warfare as displayed in the Gulf War was the product of decades of development and exploitation of the electromagnetic spectrum. This effort yielded dramatic results in three often-conflicting areas: the destruction of enemy radars; the disruption, through jamming, of enemy radar and communications; and surveillance and collection of electronic information. The effectiveness of the systems involved in these dimensions of warfare can best be gauged by the results of the air campaign. The degree to which the Coalition air forces achieved air supremacy reflects to a large extent the victories and advantages the Coalition forces had over Iraq in electronic warfare.

The elements of the synergistic electronic warfare effort can be simplistically grouped as (1) shooters–those systems that released weapons to destroy the enemy's electronic systems, (2) jammers–those that,

---

[188](S) GWAPS Microfilm Reel #23996, Frame #1030, Memorandum for TAC/DRA, "Dense Penetrating Weapon," 28 Jan 91.

through electronic pulse and frequency interference, disrupted or neutralized the enemy's electronic capabilities, and (3) collectors–those systems that exploited information about the enemy that could be obtained through electronic means. These elements of warfare cause very little damage to an enemy's infrastructure or hardware by themselves, but were incalculable force multipliers that increased the survivability of U.S. aircraft and rendered enemy forces more vulnerable to attack.

To amplify this concept, the following text presents a scenario involving the electronic warfare support generated and utilized during a hypothetical but typical F-111 mission against an Iraqi bunker. The target was selected on the basis of an analysis of intelligence, establishing that an Iraqi bunker was operational and actively engaged in command and control of Iraqi forces. Iraqi air defense systems posing a threat to the attack force are identified. Suppression of these threatening systems would have been achieved through escort or standoff jamming. F-4G Wild Weasels provided a still greater degree of survivability by firing high-speed antiradiation missiles (HARMs) to destroy any ground air defense radars attempting to detect the incoming F-111 flight. EC-130H Compass Call aircraft would stand by to neutralize Iraqi fighters by jamming their controller communications. Should Iraqi fighters approach the F-111s, E-3A AWACS surveillance aircraft would control the intercept of the hostile aircraft by U.S. fighters. With the attack mission completed, bomb damage assessment could be obtained either instantaneously through onboard aircraft video recorders or by RF-4C photo reconnaissance aircraft. Hence, this relatively small F-111 flight on a single mission revolved around the entire spectrum of electronic warfare–the collection of intelligence, the offensive jamming of enemy radars and communication frequencies, and finally the lethal destruction of air defense radars that posed a threat to the mission. Each system operated independently but linked through the integrated effort of the air campaign.

Electronic/Reconnaissance Aircraft

Shooters

F-4G Wild Weasel: an aircraft equipped to destroy, neutralize, or degrade enemy radar-directed surface-to-air threats. The F-4G Wild Weasel aircraft was specially modified to carry the AN/APR-47 Radar Attack and Warning System, which detects, identifies, and locates pulsed and continuous wave radar emitters. Although the F-4G could carry virtually every type of air-to-air and air-to-surface munition, the preferred SEAD ordnance in the Gulf War was the AGM-88 (HARM).

The U.S. Air Force committed 61 F-4Gs to support Operation Desert Storm. Most aircraft operated from Bahrain, and 12 F-4Gs deployed to Incirlik, Turkey.[189] The F-4Gs flew 2,683 sorties,[190] and were used to conduct autonomous operations, direct support, and area SEAD missions. During autonomous operations, F-4Gs attacked targets in a particular geographic area to reduce the enemy air defense threat or roll back the air defenses for upcoming Coalition air operations. During direct support missions, F-4Gs joined aircraft flying attack missions and suppressed enemy air defenses that could pose a threat to the attacking aircraft. On area suppression missions, F-4Gs were not tied to a particular attack force, but provided suppression of enemy defense support for numerous strikes against various targets. The majority of F-4G missions were in the direct-support role, and all F-4G missions during Desert Storm required in-flight refueling.

The F-4G was the weapon system of choice when it came to destroying Iraqi SAM sites.[191] Early in the war, the Weasels and jammers flew with specific attack packages to ensure maximum survivability. Jammers and BQM-74 drones complemented the Weasels by forcing the Iraqi radar

---

[189] *Conduct of the Persian Gulf War*, p T-49.

[190] (U) GWAPS *Statistical Compendium*, Table 81, "Total Sorties by U.S. Service/Allied Country by Aircraft Type."

[191] (S) USCENTAF Electronic Combat (EC) in Desert Shield and Desert Storm After Action Report, Oct 91, p 5-4.

operators to stay on the air longer, and therefore make the HARM more effective. As the war progressed and the perceived threat lessened, the Weasel and jammer packages were split to cover more packages and to provide a longer on-station time for Wild Weasels and more electronic warfare coverage.[192]

The Weasel was also the weapon of choice to provide lethal SEAD escort for high-value assets. The Weasel was valued for its ability to launch HARMs against mobile and/or specific targets. Weasels were in limited supply (as were all electronic warfare assets), so a concerted effort was made to maximize their use by piggybacking as many attack packages as possible into a given area at a specific time. [DELETED].[193] Later in the war, Weasels were sent into larger areas to cover attack packages in the KTO. Weasels would roam in the allotted airspace as "Weasel Police," and establish a nearly continuous presence so that all aircraft heading into the KTO did so under an electronic warfare umbrella.

Timely and accurate enemy electronic order-of-battle information was, in part, unavailable. Conversely, an overabundance of inaccurate information was available. However, the perceived threat of destruction reduced Iraqi propensity to operate their equipment. Indeed, the potential threat of physical destruction by antiradiation missiles in general (launched from any platform: F-4G, EA-6, A-6, F/A-18, and F-16) perhaps was the biggest single winning factor in the SEAD campaign, as evidenced by the dramatic decrease in emissions after Day 1 of Operation Desert Storm.

 EA-6B Prowler: a four-seat carrier- or land-based aircraft incorporating comprehensive electronic countermeasures (ECM) equipment to jam enemy radars and communications. It is a modified Intruder with an additional AN/ALQ-99 Tactical Jamming System. Information on specific enemy emitters likely to be encountered is fed into the ALQ-99 system by the Tactical EA-6B Mission Planning System before

---

[192]The standard Weasel configuration used in Desert Storm for long station times was two HARMS and three fuel tanks.

[193](S) USCENTAF EC After-Action Report, p 5-4.

launch.[194] It is equipped to deny the enemy the use of the electromagnetic spectrum. This electronic countermeasure support contributed substantially to Coalition effectiveness by denying early warning and tracking data to enemy integrated air defense system (IADS) operators and by disrupting the firing solutions of enemy antiaircraft weapons. EA-6B support was considered essential for every Navy and Marine strike. The aircraft also supported Coalition strikes involving aircraft of all types.

During Desert Storm, 15 Navy EA-6Bs operated from aircraft carriers in the Red Sea, and 12 from carriers in the Persian Gulf, while the Marines had 12 EA-6Bs at Shaikh Isa, Bahrain. On the first day of Desert Storm, Navy EA-6Bs used jammer pods and HARMs to support attacks on airfields in western Iraq while Marine EA-6Bs jammed Iraqi electronic warfare/ground controlled intercept (EW/GCI) radars to screen Coalition inflight refueling operations along with supporting a large F/A-18 strike on Tallil airfield. Throughout Desert Storm, EA-6B systems jammed Iraqi radar systems, and the perceived threat of destruction from EA-6B HARMs forced Iraqi radars off the air or into highly ineffective operating modes. EA-6Bs flew 1,630 combat sorties with no combat losses.[195] They successfully provided electronic countermeasures jamming and launched over 150 HARMs in support of Coalition forces.[196]

Jammers

EF-111A Raven: an aircraft equipped to provide electronic countermeasures support for tactical air forces. The Raven can detect, sort, and identify different enemy radars observing an attack force and make them ineffective, thereby preventing interception of the attack force by hostile air defenses. The forty-two EF-111As are modified F-111As. These modifications provide antennas for high-powered jamming transmitters and a processor to detect hostile radar emissions. The

---

[194][DELETED]

[195](U) GWAPS *Statistical Compendium*, Table 81, "Total Sorties by U.S. Service/Allied Country by Aircraft Type."

[196](S) Center for Naval Analyses (CNA), Desert Storm Reconstruction Report, Vol III, pp 3-53 - 3-59.

primary electronic countermeasures unit is the AN/ALQ-99E jamming subsystem, which scans across frequency bands under computer or manual control. When threats are identified, appropriate countermeasures are initiated, either automatically by computer or with the electronic warfare officer's assistance.

The EF-111 provided jamming support to Desert Storm tactical forces in three ways. In its standoff jammer role, the aircraft orbited outside enemy territory. From there, safely out of range of enemy ground-based weapons, EF-111 jamming systems screened the routes of friendly attack aircraft. In its penetration role, the EF-111 flew along with the attack force through critical phases of the mission, providing countermeasures as required to protect friendly aircraft from surveillance and acquisition radars. The close-in jamming role called for the EF-111 to neutralize enemy battlefield acquisition radars while the attack force delivered its weapons on enemy targets.[197]

EF-111s from the 390th Electronic Combat Squadron were based in Saudi Arabia as part of Operation Desert Shield. On 17 January 1991, EF-111s and EA-6Bs played an important role in the initial attacks against Iraqi targets, effectively jamming Iraq's air defense system.[198] EF-111s used their terrain-following ability to fly low enough to elude Iraqi defenses. In fact, the first day of Desert Storm saw some Iraqi interceptors launching to search for two Ravens supporting a F-15E attack mission. AWACS called bandits airborne, MIG-29s heading towards their area, and Mirage F-1s in the area. A single F-1, picked up visually, was locked-on to the trailing EF-111. This EF-111 countered by slicing down to the earth while expending chaff and flares. The F-1 followed, fired a missile to no avail, and then flew into the ground.[199]

---

[197] USAF EF-111A Fact Sheet.

[198] [DELETED]. Source: (S) *Air Force Electronic Warfare Center (AFEWC) Operation Desert Storm Electronic Combat (EC) Effectiveness Analysis,* Jan 1992, p 10-14.

[199] John M. Deur, "Wall of Eagles, Aerial Engagements and Victories in Operation Desert Storm," p 10.

The 24 EF-111s flew a total of 1,105 combat sorties in Desert Storm with no combat losses and only one noncombat loss during the conflict.[200] The overall results of the Raven's performance indicate that it was very effective in neutralizing Iraq's electronic warfare system. Coupled with the total electronic warfare capability brought to bear by the Coalition forces, the EF-111 was a major contributor to the low allied aircraft loss rate and the general breakdown of Iraq's Integrated Air Defense System. An analysis by the Air Force Electronic Warfare Center concluded that when EF-111As were supporting Coalition aircraft, Iraqi abilities to detect, track, and pass target information were seriously impaired and in some cases completely denied.[201]

 **EC-130H Compass Call:** a specially modified version of the C-130 Hercules. It is used to deny the enemy the capability to execute his battlefield strategy. Modifications to the aircraft include an electronic countermeasures system, air refueling capability, and associated navigation and support systems. These modifications give the aircraft an electronic warfare capability that is used to confuse and disrupt the enemy's command and control communications and thus reduce his ability to wage warfare. The system operates in either an automatic response or manual mode. The aircraft's crew includes up to thirteen people; four are responsible for aircraft flight and navigation and nine operate the electronic warfare mission equipment. Aided by an automated system, the nine operators analyze the signal environment and ensure that the equipment is operating properly against designated targets.[202]

Compass Call aircraft flew 450 sorties in Desert Storm.[203] It provided 24-hour surveillance of Iraqi command, control, and communications for 44 consecutive days. Compass Call was also effective in disrupting voice systems. But because of the scarcity of air-to-air engagements during the

---

[200](U) GWAPS *Statistical Compendium*, Table 81, "Total Sorties by U.S. Service/Allied Country by Aircraft Type."

[201](S) AFEWC *Operation Desert Storm EC Effectiveness Analysis*, pp 10-1 - 10-15.

[202]USAF EC-130H Compass Call Fact Sheet.

[203](U) GWAPS *Statistical Compendium*, Table 81, "Total Sorties by U.S. Service/Allied Country by Aircraft Type."

war and Iraqi adherence to emissions control, Compass Call capabilities were frequently underutilized. Nonetheless, postmission reporting during the war indicated that when present, Compass Call effectively jammed-tactical air, antiaircraft artillery, surface-to-air missiles, battlefield, and communications.[204]

Collectors

E-3 Sentry AWACS: a modified Boeing 707 commercial airframe with a rotating radar dome. Its radar system permits surveillance from the Earth's surface up into the stratosphere, over land or water. The radar has a range of more than 200 miles for detecting low-flying targets and even farther for detecting aerospace vehicles flying at medium to high altitudes. It can look down to detect, identify, and track enemy and friendly low-flying aircraft by eliminating ground clutter returns that confused other radar systems. Console operators perform surveillance, identification, weapons control, battle management, and communications functions. The radar and computer systems on the E-3 Sentry gather and present broad and detailed battlefield information. Data are collected as events occur and include position and tracking information on enemy aircraft and ships, along with location and status of friendly aircraft, naval vessels, and ground troops. In its tactical role, the E-3 provides information needed for interdiction, reconnaissance, airlift, and close air support for friendly ground forces. As an air defense system, the E-3 detects, identifies, and tracks airborne enemy forces.[205]

Five E-3s initially were deployed to Riyadh, Saudi Arabia, arriving on 8 August. An E-3 orbit was established the next day about 110 to 125 miles from the Kuwaiti and Iraqi borders. During Operation Desert Shield, the number of E-3s gradually increased in Riyadh until 11 were available by 16 January. On 15 January, three E-3s deployed to Incirlik

---

[204](S) *AFEWC Operation Desert Storm EC Effectiveness Analysis*, pp 9-26, 9-27.

[205]USAF E-3A Fact Sheet.

in Turkey to begin operations in Southeast Turkey, about 120 miles from the Iraqi border.[206]

At the start of Operation Desert Storm, four U.S. E-3s were airborne over Saudi Arabia (three forward, one to the rear) and one U.S. E-3 was over southeast Turkey. In addition, a Saudi E-3 was airborne in southern Saudi Arabia and was used primarily for communications relay. The rearmost U.S. E-3 in Saudi Arabia was primarily used to manage air refueling operations. This configuration of airborne E-3s was maintained twenty-four hours a day throughout most of Operation Desert Storm. E-3s, at times, overflew Iraq to provide additional radar coverage against deep target areas. Combat air patrols by F-15Cs were established near E-3 orbits for protection.

During Desert Storm, AWACS flew 682 sorties[207] and supported all daily air-tasking-order activity, including pre- and poststrike air refueling. They controlled an average of 2,240 sorties a day and a total of more than 90,000 sorties during the war.[208] The AWACS detected enemy aircraft, controlled friendly fighters, and provided a long-range air picture to theater commanders and other command forces. Throughout Operations Desert Shield and Desert Storm, AWACS provided this primary air picture to the appropriate theater command and control centers through voice and electronic datalink hook-ups. The E-3 also operated in conjunction with Marine Corps, Navy, Army, Air Force, and Saudi Arabian units to provide an air picture that spanned from the Persian Gulf to the Red Sea and provided real-time information to most Coalition command centers. This complete theater air picture was passed through a data-sharing network with the RC-135 Rivet Joint, Airborne Battle Command and Control Center, Tactical Air Control Center, and Navy E-2s.

---

[206]NATO-owned E-3s were used in the Mediterranean to monitor the flow of aircraft towards Southwest Asia and for maritime interception surveillance. They also flew over Turkish territory to maintain Turkish sovereignty.

[207]The U.S. E-3s flew 379 and Saudi E-3s 303 sorties, respectively. (U) GWAPS *Statistical Compendium*, Table 81, "Total Sorties by U.S. Service/Allied Country by Aircraft Type."

[208]*Conduct of the Persian Gulf War*, p T-42.

E-2C Hawkeye: an all-weather, carrier-based airborne early warning and command and control Navy aircraft with a crew of five. Its missions include surface surveillance coordination, strike and interceptor control, search and rescue guidance, and communications relay. Normally, four or five E-2Cs are onboard a carrier, and at least one E-2C stays airborne to provide airborne early warning, command and control, and communications relay functions for a carrier task force.[209]

During Operation Desert Storm, 29 E-2C aircraft were in theater. Of the 1,192 sorties scheduled, 1,183 flown were flown for a total of 4,790 flight hours. The E-2C coordinated communications shifts, provided situational awareness to Coalition aircraft, and supplied backup radar coverage and control for flights in hostile territory. Integration of E-2C and AWACS radar pictures provided superior situational awareness to both platforms, but the lack of an over-the-horizon communications suite was a distinct disadvantage. Also, the lack of in-flight refueling capability limited the E-2C's range and endurance.[210]

TR-1/U-2R: a high-altitude tactical reconnaissance aircraft equipped with a variety of sensors to provide continuous day or night, all-weather, standoff surveillance of a battle area in direct support of U.S. and allied ground and air forces. Both aircraft are single-engine jets with a speed of 430 miles per hour and a range of over 3,000 miles. The four TR-1s and five U-2s used in Desert Storm flew 238 reconnaissance sorties from extremely high altitudes, capitalizing on the aircraft's ceiling of over 70,000 feet.[211]

---

[209]*Ibid*, pp T-36 - T-43.

[210]*Ibid*.

[211]U-2s flew 149 and TR-1s 89 sorties, respectively. (U) GWAPS *Statistical Compendium*, Table 81, "Total Sorties by U.S. Service/Allied Country by Aircraft Type."

RC-135V/W Rivet Joint: [DELETED]. Throughout Desert Shield and Desert Storm, Rivet Joint crews collected valuable information about enemy forces [DELETED]. [DELETED].[212]

RF-4C Phantom II: a multisensor aircraft capable of all-weather day and night reconnaissance in a high- or low-threat environment. RF-4C combat missions can be flown at altitudes ranging from 100 feet to 45,000 feet and at speeds exceeding 600 miles per hour. RF-4Cs use optical, infrared, and tactical electronic reconnaissance systems to accomplish their missions. Optical cameras are used generally for daytime, low-altitude photography but also produce high-quality imagery at higher altitudes. These cameras generate forward-looking and side-looking oblique photography, vertical and mapping photography, and horizon-to-horizon panoramic photography. In addition, the RF-4C has special long-range optical photographic systems with focal lengths from 36 to 66 inches, which provide detailed prints from extended standoff ranges. The infrared sensor locates targets under cover or at night by detecting heat sources and heat differentials and is especially suited for night reconnaissance tasks in high-threat areas. The result is a continuous map of the area beneath the flight path of the aircraft. The tactical electronic reconnaissance system records on tape the identity and location of electronic emitters. This system had datalink equipment, which gives it the capability to provide near real-time information to ground sites.[213]

RF-4Cs deployed to Saudi Arabia during Desert Shield and collected intelligence on Iraqi positions near the Saudi Arabian-Iraqi border before Desert Storm. During Desert Storm, 18 RF-4s flew 822 sorties conducting bomb damage assessment flights;[214] and no RF-4s were lost in combat. Air

---

[212](S) AFEWC *Operation Desert Storm EC Effectiveness Analysis*, pp 3-10, 3-11.

[213]USAF RF-4C Fact Sheet.

[214](U) GWAPS *Statistical Compendium*, Table 81, "Total Sorties by U.S. Service/Allied Country by Aircraft Type."

and ground commanders were frustrated at times by the delay between imaging and delivery for interpretation.

E-8 JSTARS (Joint Surveillance Target Attack Radar System): a joint Army-USAF development program designed to provide near-real-time, wide-area surveillance and deep targeting capability to ground and air commanders for indications and warning, situation development, and target development. The two developmental aircraft, C-135 derivatives, possess an airborne radar, a self-protection suite, and air-to-ground communications modules. They provide information on both moving and fixed targets.[215] JSTARS was able to detect, locate, and track high-value targets such as convoys, river crossing sites, logistics sites, assembly areas, and retreat routes. It flew forty-two sorties, and its performance revalidated the need for a system to locate and track moving ground targets across a wide area and to relay this information to ground and air commanders quickly.

S-3B Viking: a carrier-based, fixed-wing, multimission aircraft designed to provide the carrier battle force with quick-reaction antisubmarine warfare, antisurface warfare, surveillance, and attack capability. The S-3 design meets the need for an aircraft that can (1) cruise at patrol speeds for long periods of time, (2) carry a comprehensive set of sensors and weapons, (3) takeoff and land on a carrier deck, and (4) occupy as little deck and hangar space as possible. The Viking can also carry a D-704 refueling package that allows it to act as an air refueling tanker.[216]

Forty-three S-3 aircraft were in theater and operated from five aircraft carriers. They flew 1,674 sorties on a variety of missions in support of Operation Desert Storm.[217] S-3s participated in armed scout missions in the Red Sea and Persian Gulf and augmented armed surface reconnaissance aircraft assigned to strike missions. Viking aircraft also provided in-flight

---

[215]*Conduct of the Persian Gulf War*, pp T-84 - T-87.

[216]*Ibid*, pp T-109 - T-112.

[217](U) GWAPS *Statistical Compendium*, Table 81, "Total Sorties by U.S. Service/Allied Country by Aircraft Type."

refueling to Combat Air Patrol aircraft in the Red Sea and Persian Gulf along with returning strike aircraft. In addition, they established communication connectivity for strike aircraft going to targets in western and central Iraq and the KTO. They provided command and control backup when E-2C aircraft were unavailable and flew SEAD missions in the KTO during the early days of the war.[218]

Electronic/Reconnaissance Weapons

In addition to the previously mentioned aircraft working in the electronic warfare arena, the Coalition used drones to simulate aircraft and perform tactical deception. In turn, this deception caused early activation of Iraqi radars, which were then targeted by electronic warfare "shooters." This section describes the drones used during Operation Desert Storm and the antiradiation missiles used by electronic warfare "shooters" to destroy Iraqi surface-to-air-missile radar sites.

Drones

Drones are produced in the forms of unmanned aerial vehicles (UAVs) and remotely piloted vehicles (RPVs). Their missions are to decoy radars, conduct reconnaissance, and designate targets. Radar decoys provide tactical deception, reconnaissance drones supply battlefield photography, and targeting drones illuminate targets for sea-launched attacks by various weapon systems. Drones provide an inexpensive and valuable capability in terms of reduced losses of aircraft and aircrews and relative acquisition costs. At low risk and cost, these unmanned aircraft effectively prepare the battlefield for air strikes.

BQM-74: a drone used to decoy radars during the strategic air campaign, create confusion, and false targets. The BQM-74 drone flies a programmed mission profile or can be flown manually. Its radar cross section is adjustable to simulate many different types of aircraft, and the drone can be given a new mission profile in 7 to 10 days.[219] BQM-74s cost $230,000 in FY 91 dollars and can be launched from the ground or aircraft. They

---

[218]*Conduct of the Persian Gulf War*, pp T-109 - T-112.

[219]XOOTT, Point Paper on BQM-74 Capabilities and Availability, 29 Aug 90.

have a nominal 1-hour flight endurance at subsonic speeds ranging from 300 to 550 knots and altitudes of 500 to 40,000 feet with a maximum range of 450 nautical miles.[220] These unmanned aerial vehicles were used for tactical deception and to degrade the ability of Iraqi EW/GCI nets and surface-to-air missiles to acquire incoming Coalition aircraft.

[DELETED].[221] [DELETED]. On the first night of Desert Storm, drones were launched from just south of the Iraqi border towards Baghdad to deceive enemy air defenses and to enhance F-4G Wild Weasel targeting.[222] As planned, Iraqi air defense nets, gun and missile batteries, and radars were activated to deal with the perceived threat. This Iraqi reaction served to identify numerous targets for the Weasel HARM shooters. HARM success rates were very high, and no allied aircraft were lost to Iraqi surface-to-air missile shots during these drone missions.[223] [DELETED].[224]

TALD: a tactical air-launched decoy (TALD). The Navy and the Marine Corps launched numerous TALDs during Desert Storm. [DELETED].[225] [DELETED]. The TALD vehicle adds to enemy confusion by flying different mission profiles involving variations in speed, range, and altitude. TALD is compatible with most Navy aircraft. [DELETED].[226]

Drones are also used in a reconnaissance role. The reconnaissance versions have a daylight TV camera with a zoom lens in the nose of the drone. Video is transmitted via datalink, with a video cassette recorder with inflight replay capability for back-up. These reconnaissance drones are parachute recoverable and can potentially be used for panoramic photography and real-time infrared coverage. During Desert Storm, the

---

[220](S) Briefing Slides on Drone Support for CENTCOM, p 7.

[221]XOOTT, Point Paper on BQM-74, 29 Aug 90.

[222](S) Briefing Slides on Drone Support for CENTCOM, p 5.

[223]*Ibid.*

[224](S) *Ibid.*

[225](S) System Description and Mission Summary, GWAPS Files Document 43-020.

[226](S) *Ibid.*

Navy launched these drones to perform naval gunfire direction and gather real-time battle damage assessment information from behind enemy lines without risking the lives of airborne or ground-based forward spotters.[227] In an unusual incident during the ground war, a group of Iraqi soldiers tried to surrender to a drone.[228]

Drones proved to be inexpensive but effective devices during Desert Storm. They drew premature activity from enemy radars, which then became targets for advance aircraft (shooters) before the main attacking force arrived. This tactic helped to open a corridor that allowed penetrating bombers to funnel through and attack targets. Also, reconnaissance drones provided the Army, Navy, and Marine Corps with real-time battlefield information without risking lives. The next section describes antiradiation missiles used to destroy Iraqi radars by Coalition aircraft.

Anti-Radiation Missiles

During the Gulf War, U.S. forces employed two antiradiation missiles–the AGM-45 Shrike and the AGM-88 HARM. These air-to-ground missiles were designed to detect and destroy surface radars.

AGM-45 (Shrike) Missile: a completely passive missile that uses radiation emitted by a target radar for detection, homing, and detonation. Shrike was designed to detect and destroy enemy radar emitters, and was first used in 1965. Its 149-pound warhead is specifically designed to physically impair the operation of the radar antenna. Fragmentation is the primary kill mechanism.[229] Due to range and employment limitations, only seventy-eight Shrikes were employed during Desert Storm; over half by the Air Force and the remainder by the Navy and Marine Corps.[230]

---

[227](S) *The United States Navy in Desert Shield/Storm*, Department of the Navy, 15 May 91, p 48.

[228]"Gulf War Experience Sparks Review of RPV Priorities," *Aviation Week and Space Technology*, April 22, 1991, p 86.

[229](S/NF) *Aircrew Weapons Delivery Manual (non-nuclear) Supplement, T.O. 1-1M-34-1*, 17 Apr 87, pp 1-87 - 1-91.

[230]The USAF fired 53, USN 18, and USMC 7, respectively. (U) GWAPS *Statistical Compendium*, Tables 188, 189, and 190, "Desert Shield/Storm: USAF, USN and USMC Weapons Cost and Utilization (FY 90/91$)."

[DELETED].[231]

AGM-88 (HARM): a High-Speed Anti-Radiation Missile (HARM) designed to detect, guide to, and destroy radar emitters operating throughout a wide range of frequency bands. [DELETED].[232]

[DELETED].[233] U.S. aircraft fired 1,961 HARMs in Operation Desert Storm.[234]

[DELETED].

[DELETED].[235]

Alarm: a short-range British antiradiation missile. It uses a microprocessor-based, software-controlled broadband, microwave passive seeker to guide the missile toward enemy radar emissions. Power is supplied by a single two-staged solid-fuel rocket motor. Flight control is through aft cruciform moveable fins actuated electrically. The seeker can be programmed before and during flight with appropriate target radar characteristics and threat priorities. The seeker switches on shortly after release and homes directly on to the highest priority target. Should Alarm fail to lock on a target because of transmission shut-down, it climbs to an altitude of 40,000 feet and deploys a parachute upon rocket motor burnout. The missile can hang on its parachute for several minutes awaiting a hostile radar transmission, then dive in on the radar after discarding the parachute. It has a high-explosive warhead with a Thorn-Emi fuze. British Tornados fired 113 Alarms during Operation Desert Storm.[236]

---

[231](S/NF) *Flight Manual Supplement, T.O. 1-1M-34-1*, p 1-87.

[232](S/NF) *Ibid*, p 1-94.

[233](S/NF) *Ibid*, p 1-97.

[234]The USAF fired 1,067; the USN 661; and the USMC 233. (U) GWAPS *Statistical Compendium*, Tables 188, 189, and 190, "Desert Shield/Storm: USAF, USN, and USMC Weapons Cost and Utilization (FY 90/91$)."

[235](S/NF) *Flight Manual Supplement, T.O. 1-1M-34-1*, pp 1-94, 1-97.

[236](S) Operational Research Branch Headquarters Strike Command, p 8.

Air-to-Air Weapon Systems

The Air Force F-15C and Navy F-14 aircraft were the primary air superiority fighters used in Desert Storm, although other Coalition aircraft achieved air-to-air kills. In all, Coalition fighters killed thirty-seven Iraqi aircraft without suffering an aerial combat loss; the F-15C was credited with eighty-seven percent of the total kills.

F-15C Eagle: a single-seat, all-weather, extremely maneuverable fighter designed to gain and maintain air superiority in aerial combat. It has electronic systems and weaponry to detect, acquire, track, and attack enemy aircraft while operating in friendly or enemy-controlled airspace. The F-15's main advantage is its versatile multimode, pulse-Doppler radar system. The system can track high-flying as well as low-flying targets without being confused by ground clutter–a true look-down shoot-down capability. The Eagle first flew on 27 July 1972 and its initial operational capability occurred in 1975. Before the Gulf War began, over 1,100 had been delivered to U.S. Air Force squadrons, and more than 280 additional aircraft had been delivered to or ordered by Israel, Japan and Saudi Arabia.

Two squadrons, consisting of 24 F-15Cs from the 1st Tactical Fighter Wing (Langley AFB, Virginia), were among the first U.S.-based aircraft to deploy to Saudi Arabia on 7 August. A total of 125 F-15Cs eventually deployed to Southwest Asia. This force represented about 28 percent of the total Air Force inventory.[237] The U.S. F-15Cs flew 5,667 offensive and defensive counterair missions during Operation Desert Storm, and the 72 Royal Saudi Air Force F-15s flew 2,080.[238] Sortie lengths ranged between 4.0 and 9.0 hours, as opposed to the shorter durations flown during training exercises.

As the Air Force's primary air superiority fighter, the F-15C was responsible for manning the high-value airborne asset (HVAA) combat air patrols (CAPs) over the mainland and generally for keeping the overland

---

[237]*Conduct of the Persian Gulf War*, p T-57.

[238](U) GWAPS *Statistical Compendium*, Table 96, "F-15C: USAF and Saudi Arabia Sorties by Mission Type."

106

area free of Iraqi aircraft. The Eagles were used extensively for sweep and escort missions early in the war when it was assumed the Iraqi Air Force would contest Coalition air strikes. When the Iraqi Air Force declined the fight, the Eagle was used mostly to protect against a "last gasp" attack against the HVAA aircraft. CAPs were also set up over Iraq to try and intercept Iraqi aircraft fleeing to Iran.

F-15Cs successfully accomplished these missions by flying two- and four-ship formations. Formations included trail, offset trail, and line abreast for sweep and force-protection missions. CAPs throughout Iraq were supported by AWACS as F-15Cs sorted and identified targets ending in pursuit to get within missile parameters for valid shots. [DELETED].[239] In all, U.S. F-15Cs shot down thirty-one Iraqi aircraft; twenty-three kills were with AIM-7s, and eight kills were with AIM-9s.[240] F-15Cs did not use their guns for air-to-air kills, but one did accomplish a first by shooting an IL-76 Candid with its gun while the Candid remained on the ground.[241]

A wide variety of armament could be carried on external weapon stations. The number varied depending on whether the aircraft was fitted with a conformal fuel tank. During Desert Storm, F-15Cs carried an internal M-61A1 20-mm cannon, four AIM-9L/M Sidewinders, and four AIM-7 Sparrow missiles.

 **F-14 Tomcat:** a two-seat, twin-engine fighter with variable-geometry wings. The Tomcat, the U.S. Navy's standard carrier-based fighter, is large, fast, heavy and designed around its long-range AIM-54 Phoenix air-to-air missile and its pulse-Doppler, multimode radar. F-14s also fly with a Tactical Air Reconnaissance Pod System (TARPS) that incorporates optical and infrared cameras allowing the aircraft to perform a photo reconnaissance role without degrading its performance in other roles. The first flight was on 21 December 1970, and initial

---

[239](S) USAF Air-to-Air Kill Matrix, Hq TAC/DOT (A-Team), 13 Nov 91.

[240](S) GWAPS File CHST 8-6, U.S. Air Force Air-to-Air Missile Results, Quick Look, USAFTAWC.

[241](S) *Desert Storm Air-to-Air Engagements*, 3 Mar 92, "Air-to-Air Analysis in Desert Storm," p 32.

operational capability occurred in 1973. During Desert Storm, the F-14 was still in production, and the U.S. Navy had 699 in service.

F-14s were deployed aboard five of the six carriers in theater and operated from the Red Sea and the Persian Gulf. They flew fighter sweep, CAP, escort, and fleet defense missions during Desert Storm. Operations were conducted day and night, at all altitudes, depending on the threat and specific mission objectives. On the opening night of the war, F-14s joined with F-15s to perform a fighter sweep of Iraq, where the Phoenix missile could be employed at its maximum range. Barrier CAP missions also were flown to protect Coalition naval forces and Gulf Cooperation Council coastlines throughout the war. Later in the conflict, F-14s were used to establish and maintain CAPs to intercept Iraqi aircraft attempting to flee to Iran. The additional capability of the TARPS system provided daytime imagery for battle damage assessment, prestrike planning, maritime interception operations, and detection of Scud missile launch site locations.

During Operation Desert Storm, 109 F-14s flew 4,005 sorties.[242] One F-14 was lost, only 6 intercepts were flown, and F-14s shot down 1 Iraqi helicopter.[243]

Armament included an internal 20-mm Vulcan Gatling-type gun with 675 rounds of ammunition, Phoenix, AIM-7, and AIM-9 air-to-air missiles. Up to 8 missiles could be carried on the Tomcat in various combinations: 6 AIM-54 Phoenix and 2 AIM-9s; 6 AIM-7s and 2 AIM-9s; 2 Phoenix and 3 AIM-7s and 2 AIM-9s; or 4 Phoenix and 2 AIM-7s and 2 AIM-9s.

---

[242]The majority of missions were as follows: 2,802 DCA, 607 OCA, and 290 reconnaissance. (U) GWAPS *Statistical Compendium*, Table 95, "F-14: USN Sorties by Mission Type."

[243]*Conduct on the Persian Gulf War*, pp T-54 and T-55.

Tornado F3/ADV: a long-range interceptor with infrared AIM-9, Skyflash radar missiles, and an internal 27-mm gun. [DELETED].[244] [DELETED].[245]

Mirage 2000: an air-superiority fighter and interceptor with initial operational capability in 1984. The French deployed twelve Mirage 2000s, which flew mainly air defense CAPs along the Saudi border. They were armed with IR Magic and radar-guided Matra missiles.

Air-to-Air Weapons

This section begins with a general description of missile types, followed by types of guidance, and ends with aerial missiles used in Desert Storm.

Missile Types

A missile can be either guided or unguided. Unguided missiles follow the natural laws of motion to establish a ballistic trajectory. Guided missiles can either home to the target or follow a nonhoming course. Nonhoming guided missiles are either inertially guided or preprogrammed. Homing missiles can be active, semiactive, or passive. An active missile carries the radiation source on board the missile. Radiation from the missile is emitted, strikes the target, and is reflected back to the missile. The missile then self-guides on this reflected

---

[244]Royal Saudi Air Force Systems Analysis, pp 159, 160.

[245](U) GWAPS *Statistical Compendium*, Table 81, "Total Sorties by U.S. Service/Allied Country by Aircraft Type."

radiation. A passive missile uses radiation originated by the target or by some source not a part of the overall weapon system. Typically, this radiation is in the infrared (IR) region (Sidewinder) or the visible region (EO Maverick), but can also occur in the microwave region (Shrike). A semiactive missile has a combination of active and passive characteristics. A source (launch aircraft) of radiation is part of the system but is not carried in the missile. The source radiates energy to the target, and the target reflects the energy back to the missile. The missile senses the reflected radiation and homes on it.[246]

Types Of Guidance

Guidance is the means by which a missile steers to a target. For ballistic missiles, the guidance occurs before launch in the form of pre-launch attempts to reduce aiming errors. For guided missiles, the guidance occurs after launch. By guiding after launch, the effect of prelaunch aiming errors are minimized. Post launch guidance can be done in the following ways:

Lead Pursuit: the launch aircraft directs its velocity vector at an angle from the target so that missiles or projectiles launched from any point on the course impact on the target if within the range of the weapon.

Deviated Pursuit: the missile tracks the target and produces guidance commands to establish a fixed lead angle. When the fixed lead angle is zero, deviated pursuit becomes pure pursuit. No Desert Storm-vintage missile was designed to fly deviated pursuit.

Pure Collision: a straight-line course flown by a launch aircraft or weapon such that it collides with the target.

Lead Collision: a straight-line course flown by a launch aircraft such that it achieves a single given firing position. The time of flight of the weapon is a constant.

---

[246]*Flight Manual T.O. 1-1M-34*, p 4-2.1.

Command Guidance: the launch aircraft tracks the target with one radar and tracks the missile with a second radar. A computer on the launch aircraft determines if the missile is on the proper trajectory to intercept the target. If it is not, steering commands are generated by the computer and transmitted to the missile.

Beam Rider: the launch aircraft tracks the target with a V-shaped beam. The missile flies at the bottom of the V. If the missile moves out of the bottom of the V, sensing circuits in the missile cause the missile to return to the correct position. As long as the launch aircraft continues to track the target, and the missile continues to ride the radar beam, the missile will intercept the target.

Proportional Navigation: a course flown such that the lead angle is changed at a rate proportional to the angular rate of the line of sight to the target.[247]

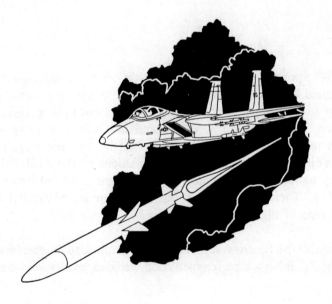

---

[247] *Ibid*, pp 4-2.1 - 4-5.

Figure 9
AIM-7M

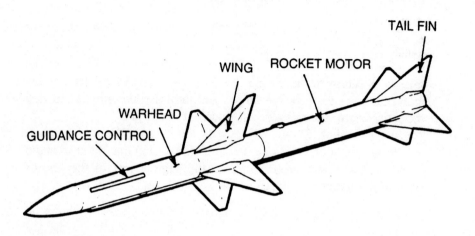

AIM-7 Sparrow Missile: a supersonic, air-to-air radar-guided missile designed for ejection launch. The missile can intercept and destroy targets in adverse weather conditions and does not require visual target acquisition. F-15Cs, F-15Es, F-16s, and F-4Gs can all carry and fire AIM-7M missiles. The AIM-7 is a semiactive homing missile[248] that guides on either continuous wave or pulse Doppler. The AIM-7M homes on energy radiated by the launching aircraft and reflected by the target (Figure 10). Therefore, the target has to be illuminated through-out the missile's time of flight.

The AIM-7M Sparrow represents a quantum leap in capability over older AIM-7s. It has a blast fragmentation warhead, and its solid-propellant

---

[248]A semiactive homing missile had a combination of active and passive characteristics. The source of radiation was part of the system but was not carried in the missile. The source (usually at the launch point) radiated energy to the target, which reflected the energy back to the missile. The missile sensed the reflected radiation and homed on it.

Figure 10
Semi-active Homing

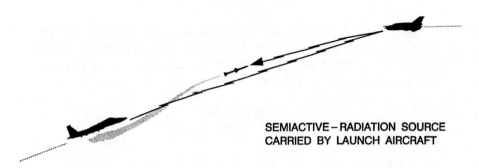

SEMIACTIVE – RADIATION SOURCE
CARRIED BY LAUNCH AIRCRAFT

rocket motor provides boost-sustained thrust.[249] The major improvement is its new digital data processor, which provides the following: (1) programmability to meet future threats, (2) simultaneous track of two targets within the antenna beamwidth, (3) prediction of line of sight rates to make target fades less severe on missile guidance, (4) tracking and avoiding of main beam clutter, (5) improved performance against advanced ECM, (6) improved fuze arming sequence, (7) improved low-altitude performance, and (8) an active fuze.[250]

[DELETED]:[251]

---

[249]The three basic air-to-air missile motor types were all-boost, all-sustain, and boost-sustain. The all-boost motor typically made the missile accelerate rapidly, causing a high peak velocity. The short time of flight (TOF) for a given range caused high missile drag and high aerodynamic heating. This motor type was adequate for rear hemisphere, tail chase encounters. The all-sustain motor produced slow missile acceleration, resulting in less aerodynamic drag and longer flight time, for a given range. Because the motor burned for a long period of time, the motor could be used to overcome gravity in a look-up engagement and provided sufficient velocity for maneuvering at high altitude. This type of motor was suitable for head-on engagements to high altitude. The boost-sustain motor represented an attempt to combine the best features of the all-boost and the all-sustain motors. The boost-sustain motor was designed so that the sustain phase of propulsion maintained the velocity achieved at the end of boost.

[250]*Flight Manual T.O. 1-1M-34*, p 4-12.

[251](S) GWAPS File CHST 8-6, pp 4, 5.

Total AIM-7M Attempts   67
Total AIM-7M Kills   23
[DELETED][252]
[DELETED][253]

The AIM-7M provided look-down/shoot-down capability in Desert Storm, with most of the successful launches hitting targets at low altitude. [DELETED]. Beyond visual range (BVR) was authorized in the majority of the engagements, and no fratricide problems were encountered.[254]

Figure 11
AIM-7M Employment

FIGURE DELETED

---

[252][DELETED].

[253][DELETED].

[254](S) GWAPS File CHST 8-6, p 10.

Figure 12
AIM-9M

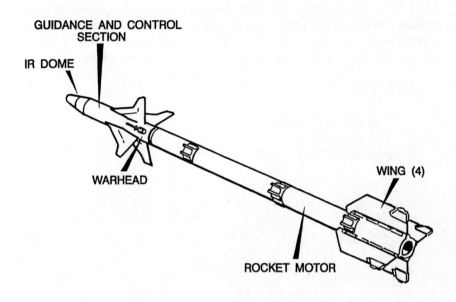

GUIDANCE AND CONTROL
SECTION

IR DOME

WARHEAD

WING (4)

ROCKET MOTOR

AIM-9 Sidewinder Missile: a supersonic air-to-air passive-homing heat-seeking missile. F-15Cs, F-15Es, F-16s, and F-4Gs can all carry and fire AIM-9M missiles. The AIM-9 uses passive homing; that is, it guides on infrared radiation generated by a target. Because no guidance is required from the launching aircraft, the pilot can take evasive action immediately after the missile is launched. Unlike the semiactive radar AIM-7, the Sidewinder is a "fire and forget" missile. It does, however, require visual target acquisition. The AIM-9 seeker converts infrared (heat) energy emitted by the target into electrical signals used to guide the missile. The infrared detector is cooled to improve its sensitivity to infrared energy. The guidance and control unit incorporates inputs from gyroscopic sensors, allowing the missile to "lead" the target and fly what

115

is termed a proportional navigation course.[255] Fragmentation is the primary kill mechanism for all AIM-9 missiles.

Desert Storm AIM-9 variants used active optical target detectors to command detonation. The fuze functioned on either a direct hit or proximity miss. All variants of the AIM-9 used all-boost, solid-propellant rocket motors. The AIM-9M had a more sensitive infrared detector than did older models and an all-aspect capability; that is, it could sense a target's infrared energy from frontal or lateral quadrants and successfully home.

[DELETED].[256]

Total AIM-9M Attempts	11
Total AIM-9M Kills	6
[DELETED].[257]	

---

[255]Proportional navigation was a course flown in such a way that the lead angle changed at a rate proportional to the angular rate of the line of sight to the target. This extended effective range, since a pure tail chase or pursuit curve trajectory consumed more time and energy.

[256](S) GWAPS File CHST 8-6, p 13.

[257][DELETED].

Figure 13
AIM-120A

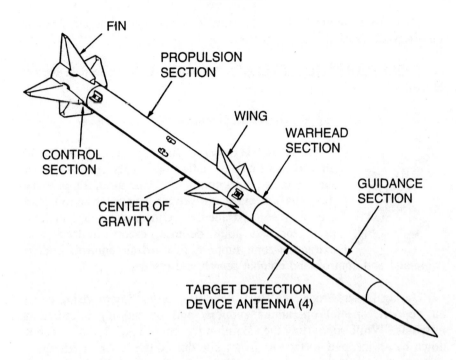

FIN

PROPULSION
SECTION

WING

WARHEAD
SECTION

CONTROL
SECTION

GUIDANCE
SECTION

CENTER OF
GRAVITY

TARGET DETECTION
DEVICE ANTENNA (4)

AIM-120A Advanced Medium Range Air-to-Air Missile (AMRAAM): a new-generation radar-homing air-to-air missile with a blast fragmentation warhead. It has an all-weather, beyond-visual-range capability and serves as a follow-on to the AIM-7 Sparrow missile series. The AIM-120A missile is faster, smaller, and lighter than its predecessors and has improved capabilities against low-altitude targets. It incorporates active radar homing in conjunction with an inertial reference unit. This unit and its microcomputer system make the missile less dependent on the fire control system than were previous radar missiles, enabling the pilot to aim and fire several missiles simultaneously at multiple targets. Like the infrared AIM-9, the AIM-120A is a "fire and forget" missile; the pilot can fire and then perform evasive maneuvers while the missiles guide themselves to targets.

[DELETED]:[258]

---

[258](S) XOOTT, Paper on AMRAAM/F-15 Problems in Desert Storm, 26 Feb 91, p 1.

[DELETED].

AIM-54 Phoenix: the U.S. Navy's long-range fleet air defense missile[DELETED].[259]

[DELETED].[260] [DELETED].[261] No AIM-54s were used in Desert Storm.

Special Aircraft

AC-130A/H Spectre Gunship: a modified C-130 aircraft that first saw action during the final stages of the Southeast Asia conflict.[262] The aircraft's primary missions are close air support, air interdiction, and armed reconnaissance. Other missions include perimeter and point defense, escort, airdrop- and extraction-zone support, forward air control, limited command and control, and combat search and rescue.

During Desert Storm, AC-130s flew 104 sorties[263] comprising close air support, special operations support, and on-call air interdiction missions. While supporting the Coalition forces, one AC-130H was shot down by an infrared surface-to-air missile during the battle of Khafji.

AC-130H armament included two 20-mm Vulcan Gatling Guns with 6,000 rounds capacity and a rate of fire of 2,500 round per minute, a

---

[259]*Desert Score*, p 393.

[260]Gant, p 219.

[261]*Desert Score*, p 393.

[262]These heavily armed aircraft had side-firing weapons integrated with sophisticated sensors, navigation, and fire control systems to provide surgical firepower or area saturation during extended loiter time, at night, and in adverse weather. Its sensor suite consisted of a low-light-level television sensor and an infrared sensor. Radar and electronic sensors also gave the gunship a method of identifying friendly ground forces and of delivering ordnance during adverse weather conditions. Navigational devices included an inertial navigation system (INS) and global positioning system (GPS).

[263](U) GWAPS *Statistical Compendium*, Table 81, "Total Sorties by U.S. Service/Allied Country by Aircraft Type."

40-mm Bofors cannon with 276 rounds capacity and a rate of fire of 100 rounds per minute, and a 105-mm Howitzer with 101 rounds capacity and a rate of fire 3 to 5 rounds per minute.

 **MC-130E Combat Talon:** a C-130E Hercules modified for special operations. It is equipped with aerial refueling equipment, terrain- following radar, an inertial navigation system, a high-speed aerial delivery system, and the surface-to-air Fulton recovery system. During Desert Storm, the aircraft was used primarily for infiltration missions and to resupply special operations units on the ground. The special navigation and aerial delivery systems were used to locate small drop zones and deliver people and equipment. The aircraft also was able to penetrate hostile airspace at low altitude, and the crews were specially trained in night and adverse weather operations.

The MC-130E first entered the Air Force inventory in 1966. Fourteen of these special aircraft were assigned to the Air Force Special Operations Command. Four MC-130 Combat Talons from the 8th Special Operations Squadron participated in Desert Storm and flew eighty-four sorties.[264] They conducted psychological operations by flying multiple leaflet-drop missions. In addition, MC-130s dropped eleven BLU-82/B GP bombs.

 **HC-130 Hercules:** an extended-range, search and recovery version of the C-130 transport aircraft. Modifications to the HC-130 include updated engines and search and rescue equipment for the recovery of aircrews. The HC-130 also has advanced direction-finding equipment and an air-to-air recovery system. The four HC-130P/N aircraft flew 107 refueling and support missions for special operations helicopters in Desert Storm.[265]

---

[264](U) *Ibid.*

[265]The air refueling system consisted of air refueling pods on each wing. Each pod housed an air refueling hose, low speed drogue, and its associated mechanical and hydraulic system. It was used to refuel MH/HH-53, MH-60, and other helicopters.

Helicopters

MH-53J Pave Low III: a redesigned 1950s helicopter with upgraded avionics and sensors. Designed for the Marine Corps as a heavy-lift logistic support helicopter, the Sikorsky H-53 (fore-runner to Pave Low III) was procured in limited numbers by the Air Force starting in 1967, and extensively modified for use as a long-range combat rescueaircraft.[266] The H-53s were progressively modified to MH-53J Pave Low III standards with the addition of FLIR, high-resolution terrain-avoidance radar, improved avionics, and cockpit symbology. By the eve of Desert Shield, all Air Force H-53s had been modified to Pave Low III standards, were equipped with flare and chaff dispensers, GPS for precise navigation, and 50-caliber machine guns.

In Desert Storm, the MH-53J proved capable of penetrating deep into Iraqi airspace. The Pave Low's FLIR and terrain-following radar permitted safe flight at extremely low altitudes at night. GPS permitted precise navigation. Poor visibility and lack of visual cues rendered attempts to fly and navigate with only night vision goggles (NVGs) dangerous except under optimum conditions[267] Of Coalition helicopters, only the MH-53J was able to operate consistently on dark, moonless nights. The 13 Pave Lows flew 282 sorties[268] and participated in combat search and rescue operations, infiltration, exfiltration, and other important missions into threat areas. The MH-53 aircraft opened the war by guiding Apache AH-64s to their targets.

---

[266] The H-53 had its origins in the Sikorsky HR2S, a reciprocating-engine Marine Corps heavy-lift helicopter designed to a 1951 requirement, which entered service in 1956. The initial Marine Corps version, the CH-53A, which first flew in 1964, inherited many of the basic technologies from the HR2S; specifically, the dynamic rotor head components and extruded titanium rotor blade spars. The Air Force combat rescue version, the HH-53B/C, entered service in late 1967. Earl H. Tilford, Jr., *Search and Rescue in Southeast Asia* (Office of Air Force History; Washington, D. C., 1980), p 70.

[267] Lt Col Comer, the MH-53J Squadron Commander, expressed the problem succinctly: "As far as flying operations went, we found . . . that we had a real problem with visibility. The wind blew the sand around all day in about fifteen to twenty knots of wind. It was very light sand and would remain suspended in the air. At night, if there was no moon, the suspended sand created a haze that reduced visibility to one mile and often less. The terrain was so uniform of surface that it was hard to discern any features." Under these conditions, Comer considered NVGs "almost useless." Comer, *History*, p 8.

[268] (U) GWAPS *Statistical Compendium*, Table 81, "Total Sorties by U.S. Service/Allied Country by Aircraft Type."

In addition, the MH-53J was used for the first successful combat recovery of a downed pilot in Desert Storm.

MH-60G Pave Hawk: a modified UH-60A Blackhawk used for night operations and combat search and rescue. The Pave Hawk has several special-mission, night, all-weather upgrades. The upgrades include an additional 117-gallon internal fuel tank, in-flight refueling capability, a doppler/inertial navigation system, electronic map display, Pave Low III FLIR, satellite communications, and a 600-pound capacity external rescue hoist that anchors a "fast-rope" repelling system. It is armed with a 12.7-mm machine gun.

The Pave Hawk entered operational use in September of 1987. In Desert Storm, 8 MH-60s flew 284 sorties,[269] primarily for combat search and rescue and for transporting reconnaissance teams into Kuwait and Iraq.

Aircraft and Weapon Systems Not Employed

B-1B Lancer

The B-1B Lancer is a long-range bomber originally designed for the nuclear strategic role. Lancer joined the Strategic Air Command alert force on 1 October 1987. At the time of Desert Storm, its conventional capability had not been fully developed.

The B-1B role in Desert Shield and Desert Storm was primarily to assume the nuclear alert commitments of B-52 squadrons deployed in the war. SAC chose this role for the B-1B because of its munitions incompatibilities, crew training focus, relationship to arms control treaties, and limitations on its electronic warfare equipment. The significant resources available to the Coalition meant that this non-use was never a critical factor.

---

[269](U) *Ibid.*

During Desert Storm, the only conventional munition the B-1B was certified to carry was the 500-pound MK-82 air inflatable retard bomb. A total of 84 bombs could be carried by each aircraft. Although the B-1B could carry a large number of weapons, its accuracy, especially when combined with medium- or high-altitude deliveries and the long (1,700-foot) narrow shape of its weapon impacts over the ground, limited its usefulness against point and area targets.[270] A more desirable pattern was produced by a cell of B-52 aircraft, which could lay a dense pattern of cluster bombs within a rectangle of considerable size.

The B-1B's extensive and unique preloading requirement compounded the difficulty of using this aircraft. It needed a large facility for bomb-rack buildup. Since the facility was not mobile, flying missions directly from the CONUS would have taken less time than loading the B-1's bomb racks at a forward location.[271] [DELETED].[272] [DELETED].[273]

A possible B-1B role, launching conventionally armed cruise missiles, did not emerge because START guidelines and national policy dictated that the B-1B would not be loaded with operational air-launched cruise missiles until the cruise-missile-modified B-52s were retired.[274]

Another reason for its nonparticipation was that an insufficient number of B-1B crews were trained to accomplish conventional bombing missions. Focus on the strategic nuclear role of the bomber meant that little or no emphasis had been placed on developing crew capability to bomb accurately with conventional ordnance.

In addition to weapon, fuze, and training problems, the B-1B was ECM deficient. In its war time configuration, the B-1B was less capable of evading enemy threats than the B-52. A protracted problem remained in the ECM portion of the AN/ALQ-161 defensive avionics system

---

[270](S) Bob Byzewski, *Point Paper on B-1B Conventional Operations Capability*, 3 Aug 90.

[271](S) *Ibid.*

[272](S/NF/WN/RD) *History of the Strategic Air Command*, p 292.

[273][DELETED].

[274](S/NF/WN/RD) *History of the Strategic Air Command*, p 63.

122

designed to detect, identify, and jam enemy radars. A flawed receiver design, detected during flight testing, prevented the system from meeting SAC's ECM requirements for the 1990s.[275]

Other B-1B problems existed at the time of Desert Shield and Desert Storm. Installation of a fire protection and fuel isolation modifica-tion had not been completed.[276] Yet to be installed was a stability enhancement function to augment the aircraft's stall inhibitor system and expand its flight envelope at low altitude while carrying more weight.[277] B-1Bs also had chronic engine problems. Approximately a year before the start of Desert Storm, B-1B flight missions had been cancelled because of persistent engine problems.[278] These dilemmas, along with CINCSAC's decision to place the bombers on Single Integrated Operations Plan alert, put a stop to plans for deploying B-1Bs to Southwest Asia.

The B-1B long-range strategic bomber was not completely ready to perform as a conventional bomber in a tactical role in Desert Storm. Its problems were too great to overcome before the outbreak of hostilities. Further modifications of the B-1B were required before it could have an effective role in conventional operations.

Have Nap

The AGM-142 Have Nap is a highly effective, precision-guided rocket-propelled air-launched missile.[279] This 3,000-pound missile has a 750-pound blast fragmentation warhead.[280] [DELETED].[281] Rafael Industries, in Haifa, Israel, designed and built the Have Nap weapon system.

---

[275](S/NF/WN/RD) *Ibid*, p 64.

[276]*SAC/LGMMB Point Paper on the B-1B Overwing Faring Modification*, 11 Jun 91.

[277]*SAC/LGMMB Point Paper on the B-1B Stall Inhibitor System 2/Stability Enhancement Function*, 12 Apr 90.

[278](S/NF/WN/RD) *History of the Strategic Air Command*, p 314.

[279](S) Maj Karns, "Bullet Background Paper on AGM-142 (Have Nap)," Hq SAC/DOOQ, 11 Feb 92.

[280]1990 Weapons File, p 5-A-10.

[281](S) Maj Karns, "Bullet Background Paper on AGM-142 (Have Nap)."

Have Nap, although a very capable weapon system, was not used during Desert Storm. It is fair to speculate that it was not used because of the policy implications of launching an Israeli-made weapon against an Arab country. Though not used during the Gulf War, Have Nap's capabilities and characteristics are worth mentioning.

[DELETED].[282] [DELETED].[283]

Representative targets for Have Nap include power plant transformers, generators, and cooling towers; POL refinery cracking/distillation towers; radar or communication site control vans/buildings; and research and development facilities.[284] Upgrades to the Have Nap weapon system, still ongoing after Desert Storm, included an imaging infrared seeker and an I-800 penetrating warhead.

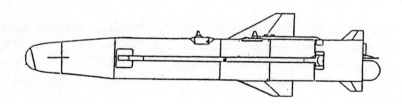

---

[282](S) *Ibid.*

[283](S) *Ibid.*

[284](S) *Ibid.*

(Above) AIM-7E Sparrow Missile. (Below) AIM-9L Sidewinder Missile, a supersonic air-to-air passive-homing heat-seeking missile.

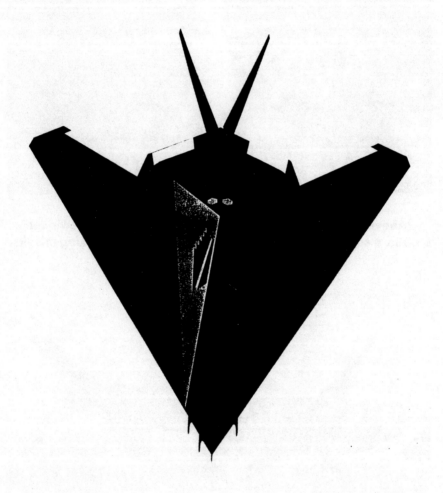

126

3

Coalition Tactics - Fundamentals

Aerial Employment Tactics

As noted in Chapter 1, Coalition air forces enjoyed a decided advantage in the quality of aircraft and weapons they brought to the Gulf War. The outcome in combat, however, was determined by more than the relative capabilities of the equipment of the opposing sides; how that equipment was employed ultimately determined the victor. This section addresses the basic tactics employed by Coalition air forces during Desert Storm. The discussion begins with the point of contact with the enemy and works backward, addressing factors required for successful mission accomplishment. The first topic is ordnance delivery, including target acquisition. Supporting air-to-air missions and electronic warfare considerations, are the second and third topics, followed by en route navigation and defensive formations. Next, all of the general planning considerations for any mission are addressed, followed by the special requirements for large-scale, multimission strikes. The section concludes by addressing the conduct of an actual mission.

Placing Bombs on Target

Many tactical considerations influenced the delivery options selected by Operation Desert Storm aircrews. Enemy defenses, type of target, available ordnance and other factors drove delivery profiles. Basic delivery maneuvers were level, dive, and loft. Level and dive deliveries are flown at both low- and medium-altitudes, whereas loft deliveries are generally considered only low-altitude maneuvers.[1] Each basic delivery method incorporates options tailored to mission effectiveness. Level

---

[1]Since aircraft transitioned early on from low to medium altitude, loft deliveries were used sparingly for only the first few days of Desert Storm and henceforth will not be covered extensively in this section.

attacks can be flown using radar, visual, or infrared (IR) sensors; dive attacks can be flown using visual or IR sensors; and loft attacks can be flown using radar or IR sensors. These next sections describe how aircrews in Desert Storm found and delivered bombs on targets. They first address visually acquiring targets through dive deliveries, then discuss acquiring targets through onboard radar or IR sensors during level deliveries, and finish by examining the unprecedented capability of firing a laser beam at a target to deliver precision-laser-guided bombs (LGBs).

Visual Attacks

Visual attacks are normally conducted by using dive deliveries. During visual deliveries, the pilot has to physically see the target and successfully maneuver the aircraft to position the pipper in the heads-up display (HUD), or optical-sight, on the target at release (see Figure 14).

Figure 14
Pilot's HUD With CCIP Aimpoint

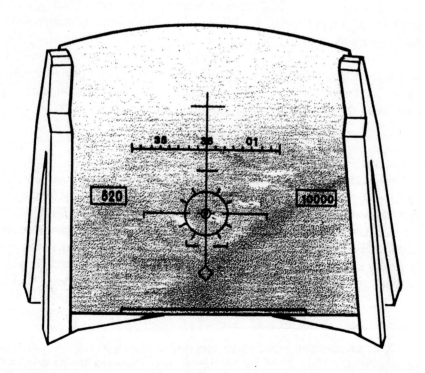

As seen from the above figure, the pipper is over the target. The pilot also has displays of dive angle, airspeed and altitude, along with additional information to cross reference during the attack.

The various factors involved in placing unguided bombs on targets using visual dive deliveries are shown in Figure 15.

Figure 15
Dive Delivery Factors

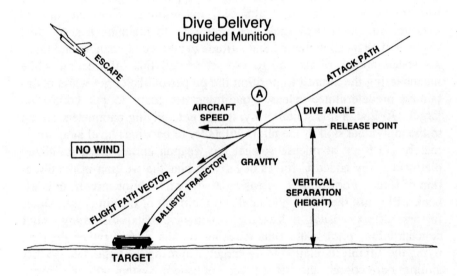

With visual deliveries, the pilot basically has two means available to release bombs; a system delivery utilizing Continuously Computed Impact Point (CCIP) or similar system, and a manual release. CCIP deliveries use aircraft system inputs of velocities, dive angle, heading, winds, altitude, and weapons information to position the drift-stabilized aiming pipper on the HUD. In this delivery, the aircraft is maneuvered in three dimensions so that the pilot can view the target through the HUD, stabilize the aircraft and release the bomb at the correct point in space for weapons ballistics and wind conditions. The aircraft computers continually update the pipper and indicate where the bombs will impact on the ground if released at a particular moment. When the pilot is ready and the pipper is over the target, he pushes the "pickle" button to release the bombs. Manual deliveries require the pilot to insert a milliradian pipper setting (i.e., angular reference setting) into the bombsight for the appropriate release conditions and weapons load, then fly the aircraft to arrive at the point "A" (Figure 15) at the proper dive angle, altitude, and airspeed. Since manual deliveries require the pilot to deal simultaneously with many variables to hit the target, they are normally considered backup options.

In Desert Storm, most visual attacks were accomplished using high-angle dive deliveries. This was done to aid target acquisition, increase impact angles, and give pilots usable pipper settings.[2] Of primary importance were dive angle, airspeed, and altitude. Constant forward pressure on the control stick was necessary to maintain a steep dive angle, and airspeed increased and altitude decreased at phenomenal rates. As stated above, pilots had to crosscheck all this information while maneuvering the aircraft to position the pipper on the target while maintaining predetermined release conditions necessary to put bombs on target. Although this sounds easy, it was not. Flying parameters are up to the individual skill of the pilot. Pilots try to be wings level in approximately 1G flight at release so that the weapon comes off a stabilized platform. Any added G forces negatively bias the weapon in the direction of force. For example, releasing a weapon with the aircraft in a left bank will cause the weapon to land short and left of the aimpoint. Other factors affect visual releases: enemy threats disturbing pilot concentration; pilot's attention focusing on the pipper rather than on flying the aircraft in relation to the target; acquiring the target late, so that aiming corrections can not be accomplished; system altitude errors causing bombs to hit long or short of targets; or the target size when masked by the two-milliradian pipper.[3]

---

[2]Flying lesser dive angles, depending on weapons, could cause the pipper to be depressed beyond the limits of the HUD. Every HUD or optical sight has limitations on how far down the pipper can be depressed before remaining at the bottom of the sight. This is a mechanical limitation that throws off the pilot's tracking capability and puts time in the sight. Due to this fact, visual level releases were not flown in Desert Storm because the resultant depression angles went beyond the capability of all aircraft optical systems.

[3]For a more in-depth analysis on pipper size at altitude versus ground coverage, see the subsection titled "Smart Platform/Dumb Bomb Vice Dumb Platform/Smart Bomb," under the "Air-to-Ground Issues" section in Chapter 2 of this report.

Radar Deliveries

Ordnance could also be delivered by using onboard ground-mapping radars for target acquisition. By using these radars, F-111s, F-15Es, B-52s, A-6s, and to a lesser extent F-16s and F/A-18s, provided the Coalition forces with an all-weather, day and night attack capability. Aircrews could attack by using the radar to acquire the target or by using suitable offset aimpoints when targets did not generate sufficient reflected energy (i.e., no-show targets). Radar deliveries were usually accomplished using level releases.

Figures 16, 17, and 18 are three photos of a radar scope presentation that demonstrate a technique used to deliver ordnance on targets. Figure 16 is a longer range, wide field-of-view display showing prominent geographic features surrounding a radar return from an urban center. This return could be used to update the aircraft position en route to the target area. Initially, the cursers, the white lines crossing in the middle of the screen, were positioned by the aircraft inertial navigation system. The weapons system operator (WSO) or bombardier (B/N) then moved the cursers to the precise predetermined point on the presentation to update his true position.

Figure 17 shows the next step. The scope presentation was downranged[4] and expanded around the cursor intersection to display a smaller area with finer details. In this figure, the urban returns separate into individual buildings. Once again, the aircraft position was updated by moving the cursers to a known point.

---

[4]"Downrange" means to decrease the range of the radar.

Figure 16
Wide Field-of-View Radar Picture

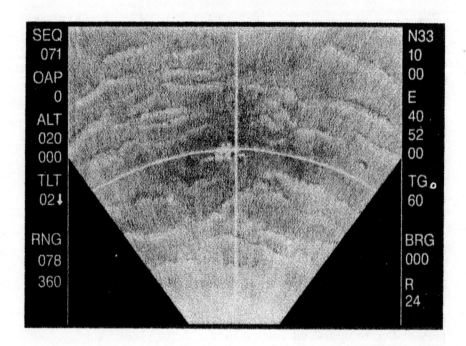

Figure 18 shows a final "bombing" scope presentation. Here the cursers were moved for final aiming on the target, and gain and antenna tilt were adjusted to make the target return as distinct as possible.[5] The adjustment corrected as much as possible for discrepancies caused by the physical features of the radar beam. Using radar to identify the target location, the inertial system's computers then provided steering to the proper position in the sky to deliver the ordnance on the target.

---

[5]Gain was adjusted to provide better resolution and tilt was moved up or down to produce a complete presentation of returns; this concentration of radar energy on the target provided a more accurate bombing "picture."

Figure 17
Moving Radar Crosshairs to Update Steering

Figure 18
Bombing
Scope
Presentation

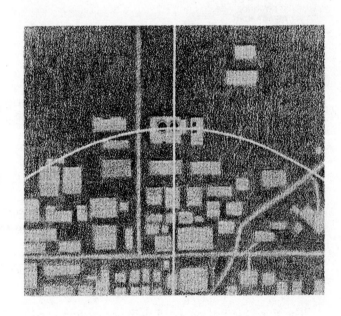

Level-flight radar deliveries could be conducted from any altitude. The factors involved in a level radar delivery are portrayed in Figure 19. The weapons computer considered the effects of the aircraft's altitude and speed, the ballistic fall of the particular bomb due to gravity, and winds present.

Figure 19
Level Radar Delivery

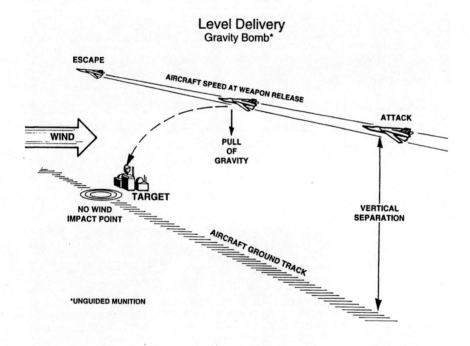

While radar deliveries from the altitudes used in Desert Storm were not as precise as laser-guided bombs, the effects were further enhanced by using strings of bombs or cluster weapons.

Infrared and Laser Deliveries

The third kind of onboard delivery system used in Desert Storm was IR imagery. Infrared system acquisition was normally done in conjunction with laser self-designation, and since IR systems allowed more precise crosshair placement, aircrews sometimes used them with unguided bombs. Note that laser designation had two functions: to designate the desired point of impact for an LGB and to provide more accurate range data for unguided, free-fall munitions. This capability permitted both day and night operations along with a limited adverse-weather capability.

The main physical limitation of IR systems was target acquisition field-of-view (FOV). Looking for a target with an infrared sensor was sometimes described as looking through a soda straw. Without accurate target coordinates and updated systems, finding targets with an IR system was difficult. At medium altitude, the FOV was wider than at lower altitudes, which helped target acquisition. Figure 20 depicts the two FOVs available in the F-111F Pave Tack IR system at various altitudes. Narrow FOV reflects a 33- by 44-milliradian display whereas wide FOV reflects a 132- by 176-milliradian display.[6] The target in view is a football field. At 500 feet, wide FOV covers only an area of about 25 square yards. Ground coverage increases at 10,000 feet, with narrow FOV covering a little more than a football field in size, and wide FOV covering approximately five football fields. This increasing ground coverage at higher altitudes was relatively marginal when an aircraft was searching for small targets without precise coordinates and accurate systems. The best way to find precise aimpoints required photos or accurate sketches of the target area. The next section discusses the combining of IR sensors and laser designation to deliver LGBs.

Laser-Guided Bomb Deliveries

During Desert Storm, infrared sensors were most often used in conjunction with laser designators to deliver laser-guided bombs.[7] Two methods were used: self-designation and "buddy" designation. Self-designation will be discussed first. The placement of the crosshairs of the infrared system depended on other systems: the radar in most aircraft,

---

[6]*F-111F Operations Manual for Pave Tack*, Ford Aerospace, Feb 81, p 5-9.

[7]F-111Fs, F-117s, A-6s and a handful of F-15Es had self-designation capability in Desert Storm.

Figure 20
Comparative FLIR Field of View[8]

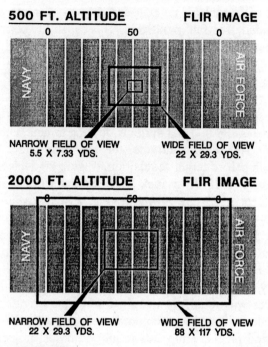

500 FT. ALTITUDE   **FLIR IMAGE**

NARROW FIELD OF VIEW
5.5 X 7.33 YDS.

WIDE FIELD OF VIEW
22 X 29.3 YDS.

2000 FT. ALTITUDE   **FLIR IMAGE**

NARROW FIELD OF VIEW
22 X 29.3 YDS.

WIDE FIELD OF VIEW
88 X 117 YDS.

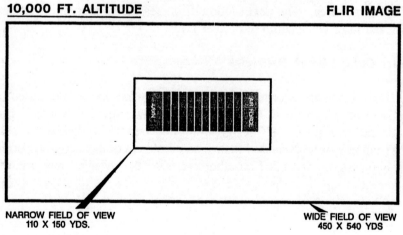

10,000 FT. ALTITUDE   **FLIR IMAGE**

NARROW FIELD OF VIEW
110 X 150 YDS.

WIDE FIELD OF VIEW
450 X 540 YDS

---

[8] *Ibid*, p 5-10.

136

and the inertial navigation system in the F-117. Maximizing the accuracy of these systems was essential before searching by means of IR displays. The F-117's accurate navigation system normally placed the IR crosshairs within the FOV of a target. This allowed the pilot, after sufficient target study, to find the target without using other onboard systems. In other aircraft, the WSO or B/N updated the inertial system by accurately placing his radar crosshairs on the target or an associated aimpoint with good quality coordinates. Then he would transition to his IR display and search for the target.[9] After the target was acquired, the aircrew tracked and fired a continuous beam of laser light at the appropriate time.[10] Light from the laser was reflected off the target and received by the laser-guided bomb's special seeker, which was tuned to the frequency of the laser beam. It was critical that the bomb be released into the area (or cone) of energy reflected from the target. Once the seeker acquired the reflected laser light, it maneuvered small control surfaces to guide the bomb to the target. Figure 21 shows how laser-guided bombs were delivered.

Aircraft without this laser capability could be paired with laser-capable aircraft to double the number of precision weapons available on a given mission. In these "buddy" operations, one aircraft or other source (e.g., handheld laser designator) directed the laser energy at the target while a separate aircraft delivered the weapon. Again, it was critical that the delivery aircraft release the weapon so it could see the reflected laser energy and guide into the target. The "buddy" operations were most often used by the United Kingdom; the British Tornado aircraft dropped 1,000-pound LGBs and the Buccaneer supplied lasing for guidance. Also, Saudi F-5s paired with laser-capable Tornado aircraft, and the U.S. Marine and Navy aircraft fired laser-guided Mavericks and AGM-123 Skipper missiles that received terminal laser guidance from other sources. Additionally, buddy lasing was always available as a backup option for two or more laser-capable aircraft when one developed maintenance problems. Figure 22 depicts the various modes of buddy deliveries.

---

[9]This does not mean that a radar was necessary to find targets by means of IR scopes. However, the radar's much wider FOV helps the WSO or B/N find the general target area before going to the narrow FOV's associated with IR receivers

[10]Laser light is very coherent, which means that it does not disperse as would light from an ordinary flashlight. It is also one very precise color (i.e., frequency).

Figure 21
Laser-Guided Bomb Release

Aircraft Lasing Target & Turn Away

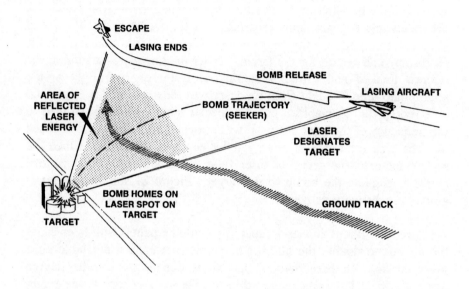

After the transition to medium-altitude operations in Desert Storm, aircrews flew mostly high-angle dive and level-flight deliveries. The following sections summarize the inherent advantages and disadvantages associated with these deliveries.

As stated earlier, aircrews began medium-altitude dive deliveries by proceeding to a predetermined distance from the target and making either a tactical turn to place the target 30 to 45 degrees off the nose of the

Figure 22
Buddy Bombing

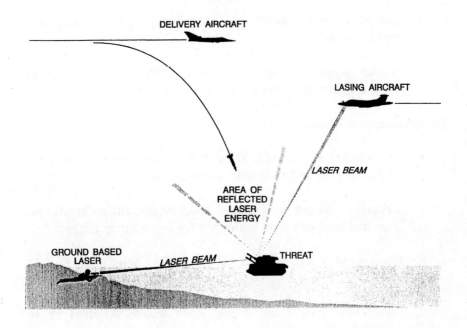

the aircraft or flying directly to a planned roll-in point. Then the pilot accomplished a push-over to the desired dive angle predetermined for release. Most of the day visual deliveries flown in Desert Storm were of this nature. As with any visual delivery, the biggest limitation was target acquisition. The pilot had to see the target to release his ordnance effectively. Another limitation was the propensity for system altitude errors associated with a computer release at medium altitude. These limitations resulted in less than stellar results against small point targets when aircrews released "dumb" bombs during dive deliveries. Accuracy just was not there, and the small sticks of bombs dropped by fighters were not enough to cause permanent damage. On the other hand, precision-guided munitions released during dive deliveries were very accurate. But during Desert Storm, precision-capable aircraft usually flew at night and used the more reliable level deliveries. The following lists advantages and disadvantages associated with dive deliveries.

Advantages at Medium Altitude:

- Aircrews in Desert Storm did not have to worry about safe escape and/or fragmentation deconfliction among aircraft.

- Aircraft faced a reduced threat from small arms fire, most AAA, and IR missiles.

- Impact angles were very high, since pilots released weapons in dives ranging anywhere between 30 to 60 degrees.

Disadvantages at Medium Altitude:

- The attacker was in the heart of the surface-to-air missile (SAM), air interceptor, and radar AAA environment.

- Accuracy was not good against point targets, since aircraft systems and weapons were optimized for low-altitude releases.

- Clear weather was required from the roll-in point to the target.

- The HUD pipper was not precise at medium altitude and could completely cover small targets when release occurred above 15,000 feet.[11]

Medium-altitude level attacks flown in Desert Storm were mostly radar and laser-guided deliveries. Radar deliveries were best used against large area targets to offset associated inaccuracies inherent with "dumb" bombs released from long slant ranges. Precision-guided munitions changed this targeting process by giving aircrews an accurate capability against point targets. The following were advantages and disadvantages associated with level attacks.

---

[11]For some aircraft, the center of the HUD pipper was a 2-milliradian dot. At 15,000 feet, this pipper covered an area 30 feet on the ground, which could be larger than some artillery pieces.

Advantages at Medium Altitude:

- The aircraft were outside AAA real-time zones.

- Standoff weapon range was greater than at low altitude.

- Navigation and target acquisition were easier because of less terrain obscuration and wider field-of-view coverage.

- Penetrating munitions were much more effective, with greater impact angles and faster impact velocities.

Disadvantages at Medium Altitude:

- Tactical surprise was lost due to detection by early warning and ground control intercept (GCI) radars, and the aircraft were more vulnerable to some enemy defenses, notably surface-to-air missiles.

- Accuracy was reduced for all weapons except precision-guided munitions.

- Weather obscuration became more pronounced and took away precision-guided munition and visual attack capabilities, leaving only radar deliveries, which were far less accurate.

Aerial Missions (Air-to-Air)

The most basic air-to-air mission is defensive counter air. Fighters in Desert Shield and Desert Storm flew three primary air-to-air missions. The first was the sweep, which established air superiority over a designated area for a limited time by seeking out and destroying enemy aircraft in the air. The most noteworthy use of this tactic in Desert Storm was the mission into Iraqi airspace by F-15Cs and F-14s, which followed the initial F-117 strikes in the Baghdad area during the opening minutes of the air campaign.[12] Sweep can be conducted autonomously by using onboard fire-control and identification systems. But in an all-aspect threat environment, maximum effectiveness was achieved by using all available resources to increase capabilities beyond visual range and to heighten overall battle situation awareness. These resources included GCI and AWACS. The second method was combat air patrol (CAP). Two types of CAPs were used during Desert Storm, point and screen or barrier CAP. A point CAP protected high-value assets such as airfields, command, control, and communication (C³) facilities, storage facilities, and lines of communications. A barrier CAP prevented the enemy from reaching an asset and was established at some forward point between the enemy and that asset. For example, barrier CAPs protected AWACS, Compass Call, and other vulnerable air assets, or established a screen well forward of airfields or friendly troop concentrations. The third method was escort, which was normally used in a force protection role tied to large attack packages. Escort could be employed in close proximity when fighters were tied to a particular package or asset, or in a detached mode when escort fighters were flying close to the assets being protected.[13]

When a fighter was vectored by AWACS to intercept an inbound enemy aircraft, it first searched on its air-to-air radar. When it acquired the aircraft, it had to confirm that the aircraft was, in fact, Iraqi. The confirmations were made to prevent inadvertent attacks on friendly aircraft, which were much more numerous in the skies over Iraq. After confirming the target as hostile, the aircrew developed a fire-control solution for whatever missile was appropriate. Radar-guided Sparrow missiles were usually used for longer range or BVR shots, while the heat-seeking Sidewinder was used for targets at closer ranges.[14]

---

[12](S) *Master Attack Plan*, "First 24 Hours with Changes 1, 2, and 3," 16 Jan 1991. See Chapter 3 section titled "Attacking The Iraqi Air Defense and Air Force." As the F-15C commenced their sweep, the rest of the first wave of F-117 attacks hit targets in the Baghdad area, F-15Es attacked fixed Scud installations in northwestern Iraq, and TLAMs hit targets in Baghdad. The F-15Es egressed and the other friendly forces ahead of the sweep were either stealthy or unmanned, giving the sweeping F-15s a clear field of fire.

[13](S/NF/WN/NC) *MCM 3-1*, Volume 1, "General Planning and Employment Considerations," 4 Jul 1989, pp 2-3, 2-4.

[14]For a more detailed analysis of the missiles used in Desert Storm see the "Air-to-Air Weapons" section in Chapter 2 of this report.

Threat From the Ground

In the threat area, aircrews had to be concerned about enemy defensive systems as well as delivering their ordnance. Prior training and tactical thought had concentrated on low-level ingress and attack to minimize the SAM threat. By the third day of Desert Storm, however, the SAM threat was effectively suppressed and the Iraqi air-to-air threat was minimal. This left antiaircraft artillery as the primary threat. As a consequence, Coalition aircraft normally operated above 10,000 feet for the balance of the war. The ensuing discussion addresses the tactics used to deal with and suppress the Iraqi electronic threat–primarily the SAM threat–in this tactical environment.

Tactical aircraft flying into target areas had radar warning receivers to help identify threats. These receivers displayed, on small scopes, the types and relative positions of enemy threat radars. Most aircraft also had self-protection radar jamming capability. When a SAM threat appeared on the radar warning scope, the aircrews would evaluate the threat and take appropriate evasive maneuvers. Radar warning receivers provided aircrews with two kinds of warnings: the first indicated that the aircraft was being observed or tracked; the second indicated that a missile had been launched.

When a valid launch indication was present, aircrews maneuvered, dropped bundles of chaff, and tried to acquire the incoming missile visually. [DELETED][15] [DELETED].[16]

---

[15][DELETED]

[16](S) *MCM 3-1*, Volume VI, "Tactical Employment - F-111," 14 Feb 91, p 3-18.

Figure 23

FIGURE DELETED

144

[DELETED].[17]

[DELETED].

Figure 24

FIGURE DELETED

---

[17](S) *Ibid*, p 3-23.

[DELETED].

[DELETED].[18]

([DELETED].

Iraqi Anti-Aircraft Artillery (AAA) was relatively easy to defeat from the medium-altitudes at which most Coalition aircraft flew. When aircrews observed airbursts or tracers in front of a formation, they simply maneuvered to avoid the area. When aircrews observed aimed AAA fire or suspected its presence, they jinked away from the site [DELETED]:[19]

[DELETED]

---

[18](S) *Ibid*, pp 3-24, 3-25.

[19](S) *Ibid*, p 3-25.

Figure 25

FIGURE DELETED

[DELETED]. The key to defeating aimed AAA was to not fly the aircraft in a predictable fashion. Conversely, jinking was not effective against barrage fire. The best tactic against barrage fire was to penetrate and egress as rapidly as possible.

Navigation

Accurate navigation was a crucial planning consideration, since the success of an attack hinged on precise navigation and timing. Dead reckoning, supplemented by positioning determined by onboard systems, was the primary means of navigation. Pilots using dead reckoning start from a positively identified point and flew preplanned headings, flight times, and distances, correcting for winds. The most basic and important concept behind dead reckoning was maintaining general situational awareness of time and space; knowing the location of the aircraft, the target, and the recovery base.

The most important segment of the route was from the initial point (IP) to the target; threats were usually greatest, and navigation and timing most crucial. Just as target vulnerability was a prime consideration in determining a final attack axis, the choice of IP was of equal importance. [DELETED]. Navigational routing also considered safe-passage corridors and procedures, the location of friendly troops, and munition restrictions. [DELETED]. Planning for IR missions was even more extensive. For night missions using IR systems, each navigation turnpoint had to be analyzed for IR significance under predicted weather and absolute humidity conditions. [DELETED]. The flight leader was responsible for navigation, but all flight members had to familiarize themselves with the entire route in order to anticipate turns better, execute tactics better, and provide better mutual support for the formation.

Formations

Flying combat missions with formations of aircraft was based on teamwork. The basic combat unit employed by tactical fighters was a two-ship element. The wingman's main duty was to fly formation on his leader and to support him. A four-ship flight consisted of two mutually supporting elements. Formations were one of the planning factors aircrews could control. The enemy controlled defenses and target vulnerability. Nature was responsible for terrain and meteorology, and higher headquarters established rules of engagement, special instructions, force requirements, and munitions. Flight leaders controlled not only the formation but also release parameters and (to some degree) the navigational problem. The formation selected by the flight leader ideally capitalized on weaknesses in enemy defenses and took advantage of weather and terrain. The purpose of any tactical formation was to provide an offensive capability while maintaining security against enemy defenses. Formations were designed to enter and depart the target and engagement areas in a fighting posture and survive. The typical basic formations flown by fighter aircrews were as follows:

Figure 26
Line Abreast

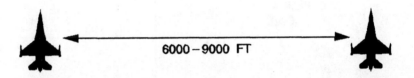

6000 – 9000 FT

Line abreast provided the best lookout and mutual cross coverage for two aircraft. The selected spread distance had to be close enough for mutual support. If the formation was too close, maneuvering became more difficult and a large blind spot existed at the six o'clock position. Conversely, when the spread distance was too great, air threats could sneak in undetected. Generally, 6,000 to 9,000 feet separation provided the best tradeoff between maintaining mutual support and difficulties in maintaining formation.

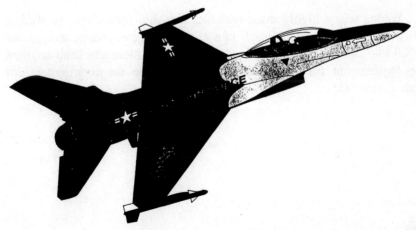

Trail formations were normally used at night and in bad weather. Both aircraft took off as a flight, but were basically on their own after flight split-up. Rejoins could occur at a predetermined rendezvous point at any time during the flight.

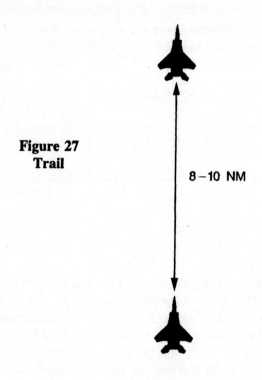

**Figure 27
Trail**

8–10 NM

Wedge

Wedge was a highly maneuverable, two-ship formation. In wedge, the wingman positioned himself in a 45- to 70-degree maneuvering cone 3,000 to 9,000 feet aft of the leader. This formation was used anytime the requirement for hard maneuvering overrode the requirement for mutual support.

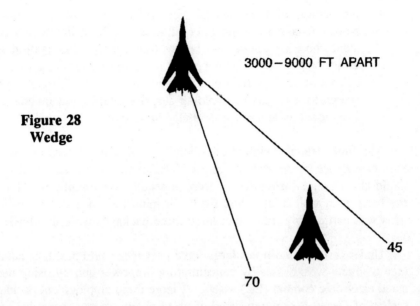

3000 – 9000 FT APART

Figure 28
Wedge

45

70

Offensive potentiᴧl was at times sacrificed for defensive posture as flight members relied upon each other for security and mutual support. Also, in structuring the formation, the flight leader traded off defensive requirements against offensive potential. For example, aircraft size, visibility, clouds, or terrain affected separation distances and altitude stacking; AWACS support could allow the formation to be less defensive, and onboard self-protection weapons (AIM-9, AIM-7, and gun) could permit wider lateral separation. Medium-altitude formations were essentially the same as for low-altitude formations. However, the following items applied specifically to medium-altitude operations.

- Visibility was better at medium altitude, and this allowed increased lateral separation. Increasing spread distances gave better cross coverage, especially of the dangerous six o'clock area.

- Whenever possible, tactical formations were ideally separated vertically by 4,000 feet or greater. This afforded better three-dimensional lookout and made acquisition more difficult for enemy systems. If the sun was a factor, the aircraft closest to the sun stacked low, making visual lookout easier for the wingman

151

and posing greater difficulties for an enemy aircraft attacking out of the sun.[20]

- At medium-altitude, aircraft were vulnerable in all three dimensions. Attack from the same altitude was least likely, and constant checking above and below was critical. Navigation was easier and ground clearance was not a factor, so aircrews could devote more time to providing mutual support. Diligent visual search as a means of avoiding surprise attacks and maintaining situational awareness was vitally important.

The flight leader weighed coordination with other forces and wingman experience before determining which formation to use. Formations could also change during the mission, depending on conditions. Having the basic plan well briefed and firmly in mind helped avoid confusion. This was particularly true when large force packages were involved.

Under certain conditions, large force packages could best take advantage of threat weaknesses by concentrating firepower and by using dedicated electronic combat (EC) assets. A large force employment package, typical of Desert Storm, consisted of up to ninety aircraft, preceded by a dedicated suppression of enemy air defense (SEAD) package of Wild Weasels and EF-111A aircraft. The tactic was to exploit the principles of mass and economy of force.[21] Large packages suppressed and overwhelmed defenses while providing greater destructive energy on targets. Coordination of EC assets in support of a limited number of large forces was easier than employing limited EC assets in support of numerous smaller attack packages. Large force packages also needed dedicated CAP for protection from enemy fighters. Finally, large force employment packages demanded a great deal of coordination, and the time and effort required for coordination increased dramatically with the size of the package.

---

[20]*TACM 3-3*, Volume VI, "Fighter Fundamentals - F-111," 1 Aug 1990, p 3-42.

[21](S/NF/WN/NC) *MCM 3-1*, Vol I, pp 1-1, 1-2. The principles of mass and economy of force guide commanders in tailoring forces to achieve objectives. Tactical resources must be sufficiently massed to achieve the objective rather than dispersed unnecessarily. Conversely, a small force assigned a supporting objective can contribute disproportionately to a large combat effort or tie up large enemy forces in support of the main objective. The main objective is the paramount consideration in prioritizing for mass and economy of force.

Air Crew Planning

Planning a tactical mission was a complex process that had to consider multiple factors to ensure success. When organizing a tactical plan, a flight leader considered the enemy's total complement of threats and balanced his aircraft and crewmember capabilities with desired weapons effects. Sometimes this balance was not perfect, but the main goal was to maximize accuracy and survivability. Hauling iron bombs for long sortie durations, only to miss the desired objective of total target destruction, was a definition of combat futility. There was no single, best solution to any tactical situation, and pilots developing plans for a given situation approached the problem from differing perspectives. The most important concepts in developing a tactical plan were building in unpredictability and denying the enemy any intelligence as to where, when, or how the attackers would appear.

Aircrews considered thirteen tactical factors in planning combat missions:[22]

    (1) Air Targeting Order (ATO) Mission Objectives
    (2) Enemy Defenses
    (3) Terrain
    (4) Weather and Meteorological Factors
    (5) Target Type/Vulnerability
    (6) Rules of Engagement (ROE)/Special Instructions (SPINS)
    (7) Force Requirements
    (8) Navigation
    (9) Formations
    10) Munitions
    (11) Release Parameters
    (12) Fuel Considerations
    (13) Command and Control.

While each factor may appear to be discrete, all interrelated to various degrees. Depending on the mission, some were more significant than others. The following are generic mission planning considerations related to each of the thirteen factors listed above.

---

[22](S/NF/WN/NC) *Ibid*, pp 5-1, 5-2.

The *Air Tasking Order* (ATO) was a message ordering the mission, listing targets and aircraft, and sometimes recommending weapon loads. Once aircrews received the ATO, the tactical planning process began. In the following sample, the actual ATO message is in bold type with the explanation below.

SAMPLE ATO[23]

TASKUNIT/48TFW//   [DELETED]
Tasks the 48 Tactical Fighter Wing

MSNDAT//   [DELETED]
Mission data//

TGTLOC//   [DELETED]
Target location//

REFUEL//   [DELETED]
Refuel//

AMPN/REMARK IDENTIFIER (S): A W H P
Remark A read "see tanker spins for air refueling information." Remark W read "use west comm plan." Remark H read "coordinate with mission numbers - 0401A, 0403A, 0405A, 0407A, 0461W (4F-4G), 0471X (2EF-111A), 0241C (4F-15C)." Remark P read that "mission 0405A was the package commander."

COMMENTS: H2 AFLD//
The target is H2, an airfield in western Iraq.

Enemy defenses drove tactics and represented a key planning factor. This was surely the case during Desert Storm where the enemy threat dictated medium-altitude weapons delivery. There were three basic types of threats: AAA, SAMs, and aircraft. Each had a variety of tracking systems that used radar, infrared, optics, or a combination of the three. Although diversified and capable of autonomous operation, the Iraqis had the KARI system, which was designed to coordinate their defenses. The threat posed by these systems was the reason why destroying Iraq's integrated air defense system was an early priority of the Coalition air campaign. Aviators sought to minimize exposure to high-priority threats,

---

[23](S) This sample ATO was taken from an actual ATO processed on 20 Jan 1991 at 1555 Zulu time. It can be found in section 18 out of 94.

be unpredictable, deal with threats through a see-and-avoid concept, and use the best available resources to suppress enemy air defenses. Minimizing exposure to known threats was done by flying around, over, or under the known threat envelopes. Unpredictability was used to limit the enemy's ability to anticipate tactics. Different penetration formations, navigational routes, attack axis, delivery parameters, and multiship tactics were also used to create confusion. Finally, see-and-avoid procedures and the use of radar warning receivers in combination with a "heads out of the cockpit" navigation technique increased the chance of proper recognition and response to enemy threats. Although radar warning receivers aided in detecting and avoiding threats, visual detection was the real basis of timely and effective reaction.

Terrain was a planning consideration that dominated low-altitude tactics. In training before the Gulf War, aircrews usually planned to use terrain features to counter enemy defenses and as navigational aids to and from the target. However, in Desert Storm, the nature of the enemy threat dictated that few low-altitude missions were flown.

Meteorology was a crucial factor often overlooked during mission planning. During Desert Storm, target acquisition and navigation were both adversely affected by poor weather. Aircrews planned for the worst anticipated weather conditions and had backup options available when real weather differed from forecasted weather. Some weather conditions may not have hindered bombing, yet enhanced the enemy's defenses. For example, flight under an overcast was more predictable, established a known maximum altitude, and made visual acquisition easier. Weather also played a significant role in missions involving use of infrared sensing equipment.

[DELETED].[24] [DELETED].[25] [DELETED].

[DELETED].[26] [DELETED].

---

[24](C) Mission planning for an IR low-level mission added two hours of preparation during the ingress phase and one additional hour for terminal guidance targeting. (S/NF/WN/NC) *MCM 3-1*, Vol I, p 5-19.

[25](S/NF/WN/NC) *Ibid*, p 5-22.

[26](S/NF/WN/NC) *Ibid*, p 5-32.

When attacks were made against closely spaced targets, the wind's velocity became a factor determining attack direction and in minimizing effects of smoke and debris on follow-on strikers. [DELETED]. The tactical decision aid (TDA) (see Table 6) was a major advance for this specialized aspect of mission planning.[27] Specific route, tactics, and target information were input into the TDA computer program, which melded the data with the IR emissivity of the target against its background. Trained weather forecasters used this information to predict the quality and characteristics of the target in the aircrew cockpit display.[28] The TDA also predicted acquisition and lock-on ranges. Aircrews thus knew how hard the target would be to find and when and in what direction to start looking.

Most targets were most vulnerable to attack from a particular direction, determined by the target's structural weakness, vital components, gaps in enemy defenses, terrain, and weather. [DELETED]. Long, narrow targets such as runways, bridges, and roads created special targeting problems. An attack along a major axis would miss if azimuth error were off slightly, and attacking directly perpendicular with a string of bombs could waste bombs because the space between falling bombs might coincide with the target, even if the release was otherwise perfect (see Figure 29).[29]

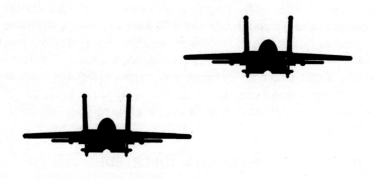

---

[27]TDA uses target/background contrast, atmospheric transmission, and sensor performance computer models to provide this data for all IR and optical systems.

[28](S/NF/WN/NC) *MCM 3-1*, Vol I, p 5-34.

[29]Strings of bombs are released after aircrews input footage or microseconds spacing values into the aircraft's weapon delivery system. Theoretically, these values symmetrically place delivered weapons on the ground with the center of the string over the intended aimpoint.

Table 6
TDA Target Information Worksheet[30]

ALL PURPOSE CHECKLIST	PAGE	OF	PAGES
TITLE/SUBJECT/ACTIVITY/FUNCTIONAL AREA TDA TARGET INFORMATION WORKSHEET	OPR	DATE	

NO.	ITEM (Assign a paragraph number to each item. Draw a horizontal line between each major paragraph.)			
	TARGET/WEAPON INFORMATION FOR TACTICAL DECISION AID COMPUTATIONS The following information is provided by the aircrews of intel people. It should be phoned in. Acquisition Sensor/Device: Weapon: Field of View: Narrow Wide Laser TDA: Receiver Range Designator Range Colocated Range Receiver Height _____ ft Designator Height _____ Aircraft Height (AGL) _____ feet. Target Lat/Long _____ Time over Target _____ zulu Target Elevation _____ feet MSL Target Description: (e.g. T-72) Target Background: (e.g. Snow, trees, sand, etc.) Aspect angle _____ degrees (0° = head-on, 180° = tail-on) Operating Condition OFF IDLE EXERCISED POC _____ Phone _____ Call/Pickup Time _____ Sun Angle Required: YES NO Mission Debrief Time _____ Place (Bldg/Room No.) _____			

---

[30](S/NF/WN/NC) *Ibid*, p 5-35.

Figure 29
Perpendicular Attack

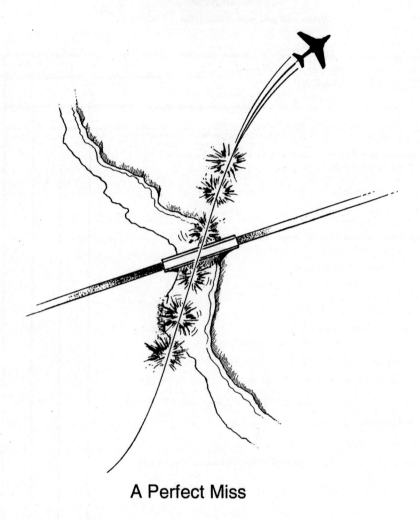

A Perfect Miss

Target vulnerability was a major tactics determinant. The vulnerability of many targets was determined empirically from controlled tests and entered into a Joint Munitions Effectiveness Manual (JMEM) equation to determine the number of sorties required to inflict a specific level of damage on a target.[31] [DELETED].[32] [DELETED].

Rules of engagement (ROE) were derived from policy considerations and tactical restrictions. [DELETED]. ROE were relayed to aircrews in the form of special instructions (SPINS). SPINS were continuously updated and briefed before all missions.

Force Requirements entailed not only parsimony, but prioritization, judgment, and planning. Factors such as ingress altitude and routing, timing, defense suppression, command and control, availability of electronic countermeasure assets, and delivery tactics determined the best attack plan and size of force. Composite attack forces derived synergy from the unique capabilities of various aircraft types. [DELETED]. Therefore, in planning composite attacks, aircrews had to consider flexibility, strength, and mutual support. The mission commander normally did not have control over the composition of his forces, but had to be aware of all contingency factors affecting his planning. Knowing what assistance was available, when it could come, and where other operations would occur spelled the difference between success and failure. Supporting factors included:[33]

- Aerial refueling

---

[31]JMEM is a useful planning document, but it gives statistical averages and probabilities, not guaranteed solutions. JMEM is basically what the "average" pilot delivering "average" ordnance against representative targets may achieve. And, when applying JMEM statistical data to a tactics problem, aircrews must also consider other factors: the status of aircraft systems, the level of aircrew proficiency, and the intensity of enemy defenses. For example, JMEM may dictate the use of four laser-guided GBU-24s against an aircraft shelter. It does not look at the status of the F-111's Pave Tack system scheduled to fly this sortie, nor does it know aircrew proficiency or tactical constraints related to enemy defenses. JMEM is based on past historical evidence and does not conform to the complexities involved with aerial combat.

[32](S/NF/WN/NC) *MCM 3-1*, Vol I, p 5-37.

[33](S/NF/WN/NC) *Ibid*, pp 5-38, 5-39.

- ECM–standoff or escort

- Counter air–CAP, screen, sweep or escort

- Defense suppression–Wild Weasel or other attacks

- Radio relay–frequencies needed to accomplish the mission

- Combat rescue

- Command and control centers–ground, airborne battlefield command and control center (ABCCC), or AWACS

- Target intelligence–pre- and postattack bomb damage assessment.

In summary, mission commanders had to consider the roles of all supporting aircraft. Coordination was often intense and lengthy, and secure telephone and facsimile capability were invaluable in this respect during the Gulf war. Personal interaction was crucial, and having all the players together at one location permitted the mission commander to talk directly to other experts when formulating his gameplan. Full understanding is more likely with personal contact, supporting the teamwork requirement during execution of the plan.

As discussed earlier, accurate *navigation* to the target was an important part of mission planning. Most aircraft in Desert Storm had some sort of onboard inertial navigation computer system, and a few had Global Positioning System (GPS) capability. Selection of the proper route was also important to avoid enemy defenses and provide for visual reference point backups.

Combat *formations* (which were also discussed earlier) varied as the war progressed. In most cases throughout Desert Storm, elements joined larger force packages to take advantage of threat weaknesses, concentrate firepower, and use dedicated EC assets effectively. Operating with a larger formation demanded a great deal of coordination. Large, highly coordinated packages were most common during the first few days of the war. Later, the relatively low Iraqi antiair threat reduced requirements for close coordination between attackers, defensive fighters, and EC aircraft.

The selection of *munitions* and fuzing were important mission planning factors. Although the ATO normally dictated munitions for a given mission, the mission commander could request a change when more effective ordnance was available. [DELETED].[34] [DELETED]. Premission planning had to balance all factors. After munitions selection, aircrews had to determine release parameters.

Factors affecting *release parameters* included target acquisition, fuzing, separation, and minimum exposure to hostile fire. Weapons could be released in level, loft, or dive profiles. Level and dive deliveries forced the aircraft to overfly the target, while loft deliveries offered standoff capability. The flight leader's primary goal was to choose release parameters and delivery modes that would best achieve desired weapons effects on the target set. Assessing threats, targets, and survival priorities helped form his choices. Backup plans were needed to account for system failures or bad weather conditions.

Fuel was a basic mission planning consideration. Fuel requirements affected aircraft range, loiter time, ingress and egress speeds, enemy defense engagement options, and recovery contingencies. Aircrews had to plan for potential delays, threat reactions, and responses in case of premature external fuel tank jettison or tanker nonavailability.

The *command and control* (C^2) environment affected fighter tactics in two ways. First, theater commanders dictated ROE and weapons employment, and their battle staffs exercised control over assigned forces. The additional presence of GCI, AWACS, and ABCCC affected the real-time control commanders retained over fighter forces. Second, the effective-

---

[34]Carriage and release limits are found in each aircraft's operation manual. Carriage limits specify aircraft speed limitations for specific weapons loads, along with bank angles and maneuverability restrictions. Release limits tell the aircrew how fast specific weapons loads can be released, depending on delivery attitude.

ness of C^2 was crucial to carrying out a mission successfully. C^2 includes radar monitoring, flight following, threat warning, tanker rendezvous, intercept control, target assignment, radio relay, and navigation assistance. These traditional C^2 services had to be integrated into tactical fighter operations. Mission planners had to also consider the effects of communications jamming, ECM, and GCI attrition and have backup plans available.[35]

None of the planning considerations discussed previously were rigid requirements; however, they were guidelines that had to be considered in combat mission planning. Tactics changed in response to new threats and the need to accomplish the mission safely and effectively–as was evident when the intense Iraqi AAA at lower altitudes dictated a move from low to medium- and high-altitude tactics.

All crews had to consider these thirteen planning factors to properly plan for a combat mission. Mission Commanders controlling the larger attack packages had further considerations to develop, and these will be covered next.

Large-Scale Mission Planning

Most missions in Desert Storm involved more than one type of aircraft. For the large-scale missions, a designated mission commander was placed in overall command of the entire strike package. To prepare for the mission, he first reviewed the ATO, SPINS/ROE, and weather. In addition, he received an intelligence update for the proposed route of flight. The mission commander extracted the mission information from the ATO. The SPINS/ROE were read to extract the following: general information; electronic combat information; overall communication plan; CAS coordination; command and control; air campaign instructions; air refueling information; and airspace control order information. The

---

[35](S/NF/WN/NC) *MCM 3-1*, Vol I, pp 5-46, 5-47.

general weather briefing helped to determine routing and target area tactics. Intelligence updates were used for route planning.

From this information, the mission commander developed a basic routing plan. He then coordinated with other package members to utilize their capabilities best. Since most were at other bases, much of this information was passed on secure telephones. Often, for larger packages, the mission commander delegated some tasks to subordinate aircraft package leaders, who then developed their own routing and target attacks on the basis of his general guidance. The mission commander was the glue that held the plan together as he gathered information, set priorities, and delegated tasks to other flight members. [DELETED]. The mission commander then ensured that his total package would not cause conflicts in space, time, or altitude, and that adequate force protection was provided. Deconfliction was probably the hardest factor to manage, since airplanes took off from different bases, utilized different tanker tracks, and flew separate routes to the same target.

The safest way to hit a large target was to overwhelm the enemy defense with massive attacks over a short period. In addition to reducing exposure to enemy defenses, this action also maximized the accompanying electronic combat aircraft's ability to suppress these defenses and reduced the strain on force-protection air-superiority fighters. As with all concentrated attacks, the time of most vulnerability is at the merge over the target.

Figure 30
Gorilla Package

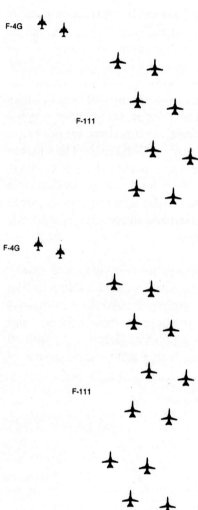

Concentrated attacks are like spokes on a wheel with the center axle as the target. All attacking aircraft fly down the spokes and merge at the center axle. Since the enemy threat is more of a force around a target, the possibility of aircraft collisions and loss of aircraft due to weapon fragmentation over the target increases dramatically with poor mission planning.[36] Air superiority fighters either maintained assigned CAP stations or flew escort missions for force protection, although many attackers carried air-to-air missiles. Ordnance limited aircraft maneuvering and would normally be jettisoned when attacked by enemy fighters so that they could defensively flee, or turn and engage offensively.

---

[36]Weapon fragmentation was only a factor during low-altitude deliveries.

164

In addition to the above duties, the mission commander also had the following responsibilities:

- Determining go/no-go mission-abort criteria by deciding which equipment or support assets were essential to safe mission accomplishment. [DELETED].

- Selecting effective ingress and egress formations for the overall package. For example, the mission commander could place the "swing" fighters (fighters with an air-to-air as well as a bomb-dropping capability) in front of the package or rely entirely on air-superiority fighters for air defense. In planning the spacing of formations, the commander must consider the special needs of large formation attacks such as a "gorilla" package, and projected threat reactions. A gorilla package was one way to place a large number of aircraft over the target in a short period of time, and a typical F-111F gorilla package is depicted in Figure 30. Planning time and effort increased dramatically with the size of the package.

- Planning tanker-fighter air-refueling; the flow of fighters on and off the tankers, and fuel amounts for the mission. The mission commander aimed for efficient, rapid refueling to get the most out of each sortie.

- Planning, integration, and execution of coordinated tactics with electronic combat assets.

- Ensuring that target area tactics safely inflict the desired results and that targeting aircraft deconflict successfully.

- Contingencies affecting the overall force. Anticipating and developing possible reactions to abnormal circumstances and unforeseen developments.

The commander was ready to brief and fly the mission, only after he had considered all of the above requirements.

Mission

During Desert Shield, Coalition forces conducted face-to-face briefings on aircraft capabilities, timing requirements, tactics, and support requirements. These briefings were vital to an understanding of how the various units intended to operate in the Gulf arena. The information exchanges improved everyone's ability to integrate more effectively into the large offensive packages that were common during Desert Storm and helped to ameliorate some planning problems, once the war began.[37]

The following describes how an actual mission might have been planned and flown. This mission was taken from the *Master Attack Plan* and scheduled for 1745Z on 17 January 1991, the first day of the war.[38] It consisted of twenty-two aircraft with the following assignments:

4 F-4Gs	SEAD
2 EF-111s	SEAD
4 F-111Fs	Al FuleJah Radio Relay Station
4 F-111Fs (MSN CDR)	Al Jarrah Airfield Facilities
4 GR-1s	Al Jarrah Airfield Runways
4 F-15s	Fighter Sweep

The fact that these twenty-two aircraft came from different airfields complicated the already difficult task of mission planning and coordination.

The first step was the mission commander briefing.[39] It began with a marshalling plan to bring parked aircraft to the runway. Runway lineup through aircraft rejoin after takeoff was then briefed. Next came the preattack refueling sequence on the tanker followed by the routing and formations to the target. Expected threat reactions were briefed along with contingency plans. Electronic combat support aircraft flight tracks were shown, and the role of the fighter sweep aircraft was discussed. Then, target attack plans were briefed to ensure aircraft deconfliction.

---

[37](S/NF/WN/NC) *Tactical Analysis Bulletin*, Volume 91-2, Jul 1991, p 9-2.

[38](S) *Master Attack Plan*, "First 24 Hours," p 18.

[39]The reader can see the difficulty of organizing, directing, and planning a mission from remote locations via telephone. This was done frequently during Desert Storm, but compliance and understanding was much better when a mass briefing was held at one location. A postmission mass debrief also allowed aircrews to learn what worked or did not, so that the same mistakes would not be repeated.

Postattack return routing was discussed along with poststrike refueling. After the mission commander's briefing, flight leaders conducted individual briefs within their elements.

The flight leader brief detailed the specifics of the upcoming mission. Routine procedures, such as taxiing, takeoff, and rejoin procedures were briefed as "standard."[40] The crux of the briefing focused on target attacks. The flight leader addressed tactics, weapons, release parameters, safe escape, timing, altitudes, deconfliction, weather, aimpoints, threats, and back-up deliveries. Formations selected for the mission were then briefed as were flight reactions to known threats along the route and go/no-go decisions. Secondary targets were briefed in case the target was obscured by weather. These were targets of lesser priority than the primary target, but still of sufficient importance to justify commitment of the force. Most missions in Desert Storm were of long duration and consumed large amounts of aircraft fuel. [DELETED]. Finally, the briefing covered airspace control. When the flight leader briefings were complete, the aircrews walked to their aircraft.

Takeoffs and Refueling

Aircrews took off to rendezvous at the appropriate time with the tanker supporting their mission. Refueling was particularly critical for the F-4G Wild Weasels because of their high fuel consumption rates.

Ingress

Once aircraft refueled, the attack package crossed into Iraqi airspace and began flying their ingress route to targets. Ingress routes were set up to minimize the enemy threat and maximize the chances for a successful attack. Timing along the route of flight was also critical. Aircrews had to fly over the target at the same time the support aircraft were ready on station. [DELETED]. The positioning of the support assets, while

---

[40]"Standard" items were written down and committed to memory by the aircrews. The term "standard" cuts down on briefing time, which gives aircrews more time to do more important things such as study their targets.

flexible, was fairly consistent, especially in the early phases of Desert Storm. [DELETED].[41]

Timing through the target area was critical. Low-level attack, jamming, and other tactics rehearsed during Desert Shield were used on this mission because of the perceived threat. The tactics used by the individual types of aircraft on this mission were typical of other Desert Storm missions and were as follows:

F-15Cs

The F-15C's coordinated with AWACS as well as with the attack mission commander. If Iraqi aircraft rose to meet the attack group, the F-15s were vectored by AWACS to intercept them. If not, F-15s remained in the target area as the attack aircraft conducted their mission. Upon completion of the attack, the F-15s followed the attack group out of the region, alert for any Iraqi reaction. [DELETED].[42]

F-4Gs

The F-4G Wild Weasels had already studied the target area and identified the most dangerous SAM sites. As the attack group approached their targets, the F-4Gs positioned themselves to launch HARM missiles. [DELETED].[43]

EF-111s

Their orbits put EF-111s in a position to jam the enemy radars, which posed the highest threat as determined by premission target area study. [DELETED].

---

[41](S/NF/WN/NC) *Tactical Analysis Bulletin*, Vol 91-2, p 4-23.

[42](S/NF/WN/NC) *Ibid*, p 2-12.

[43](S/NF/WN/NC) *Ibid*, p 9-4.

F-111s

F-111Fs were the primary attack aircraft on this mission. To reduce their exposure to enemy defense, they coordinated among themselves to ensure a minimum time over target for all aircraft. The aircrews attacked the target from multiple headings, deconflicting by using time and altitude differences. [DELETED]. After the first three days, most attacks were flown at medium altitude using level deliveries.[44]

GR-1

The Tornado GR-1 was the Royal Air Force equivalent of the F-111. During the attacks of the first four days of Desert Storm, they attacked airfields, such as Al Jarrah, with JP233. This airfield denial weapon cratered the runway surface and scattered mines to hamper expeditious repair. Each aircraft carried two weapons that required delivery from low altitude.[45] Tornados also made deliveries from medium altitudes on targets other than airfields with 1,000-pound bombs.

Egress and Refueling

After the last attacker was off target, he transmitted a "clear" call; support (SEAD EC) aircraft ceased suppressing the target and also retired from the area. Egress to the poststrike refueling point was as important as the ingress. Aircrews had also to be aware that the postflight drop in adrenalin flow could cause an unjustifiable sense of complacency and relaxation and possibly effect safe operations. The crews had to be alert to the fact that the mission was not over until the aircraft returned to base and the debrief was completed.

---

[44](S/NF/WN/NC) *Ibid*, p 7-9.

[45]After the first few days of operations, the JP233 delivering aircraft were accompanied by other GR-1s releasing 1,000-lb bombs and ALARM antiradiation missiles for air defense suppression.

The importance of a short, thorough debrief can not be overemphasized. It was vital that threat information, lessons learned, and estimated bomb damage assessment be passed to other aircrews and to the planners in Riyadh as expeditiously as possible. Later in the war, the value of the cockpit-recorded video tapes showing the bomb hits was realized and integrated into the bomb damage assessment process.

This section covered the "generic" tactics and employment of the aircraft in the Gulf War. The discussions considered factors that all aircraft fighting in Desert Storm had to address. The following sections will be more specific and will consider the employment of air power against specific target categories.

Attacking The Core Of Iraqi Power

Two technological breakthroughs combined to make the application of air power in Desert Storm much different than in previous wars. First, stealth technology made direct attacks on the most heavily defended enemy areas possible without the need for supporting forces and before traditional air superiority was attained. Secondly, precision-guided munitions were capable of quickly destroying key targets, a task that required many more sorties in previous conflicts. On the basis of these new capabilities, a tactical plan was developed to attack a wide range of targets in the first few hours. These attacks were designed not only to achieve air superiority but also to strike at targets of Iraq's strategic core of power, paralyzing the national leadership and neutralizing major offensive threats such as nuclear, biological and chemical (NBC) and Scud missile capabilities. When this initial, overwhelming blow achieved its objectives, follow-on attacks against the rest of the core targets could be conducted in the face of a greatly reduced threat.

This section concentrates on the efforts employed to reduce the targets of the strategic core. These target sets comprised the real basis of Iraqi power and included Iraqi leadership, command, control and communications (C^3), electrical power sources, oil facilities, NBC capabilities, Scuds, and bridges. The destruction of the target sets was a key element of the goal of reducing the Iraqi military threat. The discussion focuses on the tactics used in the first hours of the air war, examines the close interaction between the efforts to gain air superiority and those directed against the strategic core, and concentrates on the synergistic effects among the various missions. Then, since so many targets of the strategic core were contained in heavily protected buried structures, the discussion addresses the tactics used in what was called "bunker busting." The discussion ends by describing special tactics and efforts employed against each of the strategic core target sets.

The First Hours

Initial attacks on Iraq's strategic core were simultaneous air strikes against elements of the entire target base; the intention was to stun the enemy's command structure and ultimately cause a theaterwide paralysis. The most important objectives of the initial strikes were to establish air superiority and to prevent the Iraqis from using chemical and biological weapons. Each mission was designed to successively degrade Iraqi capabilities, thus reducing both the offensive threat to Coalition operations and the air defense threat to follow-on missions.

The Initial Plan

The overall game plan called for the attack to begin with surprise attacks by F-117s, F-15Es, and cruise missiles, supported by electronic warfare aircraft. The F-117s were to attack key nodes of the Iraqi air defense system, while Tomahawk Land-Attack Missiles (TLAMs) would attack the electrical power grid to force Iraq's air defense system onto backup power. Additionally, the forces would attack major elements of the national command authority and communications networks to counter a possible Iraqi attack on Israel. F-15Es were to attack the fixed Scud sites in the west. These first attacks were to be followed by a wall of F-14s and F-15s that would enter Iraq to shoot down any Iraqi fighters launched in response to the initial attacks. As the Iraqis shifted to backup electrical power and restored their air defense system, they next would be overwhelmed with a massive attack on that system. This attack would involve drones, jammers, and aircraft equipped with high-speed anti-radiation missiles (HARMs). It was thought that the numbers involved in this suppression of enemy air defense (SEAD) attack would overload the Iraq's air defense net. Closely following would be a second attack by the F-117s. The Iraqis would thus experience periods of bombs from apparently invisible aircraft exploding on targets, alternating with periods of seeing waves of aircraft overhead (fighters and drones) that did not appear to drop bombs. All this would happen while their main national command centers and communications nets were being attacked. The strikes were coordinated to cause mass confusion and major disruption in the Iraqi air defense system. This would allow other Coalition aircraft to execute follow-on attacks with greater safety.[46]

Carefully executed deception operations had been conducted to support these initial attacks. During Desert Shield, the Coalition had conditioned the Iraqis to a 'standard' air picture through a series of training exercises. A conscious effort had been made to accustom the Iraqi radar operators and air defense personnel to seeing tankers, AWACS, Rivet Joint, and combat air patrols flying in predictable patterns in the general vicinity of the border.[47] An "Early Warning (EW) line" had been developed connecting points south of which Coalition aircraft flying at that altitude would not be acquired by the Iraqi air defense system.

Desert Storm

On the night of 17 January, before the first attacks, the Iraqis saw the 'standard' air picture on their scopes. All aircraft involved in the initial missions completed their marshalling and refueling south of the EW line. The first group of aircraft to cross the line were the F-117s, which used stealth characteristics to operate in Iraqi airspace without being detected. The first major target an F-117 struck was the intercept operations center (IOC) in southern Iraq at nine minutes before H-hour. The center, a primary air defense node in central Iraq, was responsible for directing enemy fighters in that region. It was attacked to ease the passage of the F-15E/EF-111 flight package soon to pass through that region, on their way for attacks on western Scud sites around H-2 airfield. It was hoped that the attack on the center would prevent information about further incursions from being passed on to higher headquarters.

The second group of aircraft to penetrate Iraqi airspace was Task Force Normandy, which combined the navigational ability of Air Force

---

[46](S) *Master Attack Plan*, "First 24 Hours," pp 1-8, and (S) Briefing, CDR Donald McSwain, USN, Black Hole Air Campaign Graphics with Post War Annotations, Jan 1991, GWAPS Files NA-302.

[47]Briefing, "Electronic Combat in Desert Shield/Desert Storm," Brig Gen Larry Henry, CENTAF/EC. GWAPS Files - NA-358. Also Intvw, Murray Williamson with Brig Gen Henry, GWAPS, Aug 1992.

MH-53s with the firepower of Army AH-64 Apaches. This attack destroyed two border EW sites twenty-one minutes before H-hour to give the F-15E/EF-111 strike package heading for the Western Scud sites a "hole" in the EW coverage. While the attack was successful, the EW sites must have issued some warning because the antiaircraft artillery batteries in Baghdad began firing immediately before H-Hour.

To maximize the shock to the rest of Iraq's air defense system at H-hour, other F-117s attacked eight key air defense centers ranging from the National Air Defense Headquarters in Baghdad to selected important IOCs. Also, striking at core targets in an attempt to prevent a coordinated national defense, they attacked the two main national military command bunkers and the presidential grounds near Abu Ghurayb. In addition, the main telephone exchange and other key communication nodes were struck. These attacks were level, medium-altitude deliveries with infrared acquisition and GBU-27 penetrating laser-guided bombs.

Shortly after the F-117 strikes, fifty-two TLAMs struck their designated targets. Approximately one-third were targeted against the electrical power grid, since it was believed that the air defense system depended on the national electrical grid for most of its power. Disabling it would force the air defense system off line for a period.[48] The remaining TLAMs were targeted against core targets: Ba'ath Party Headquarters, the Baghdad Presidential Palace, and the Taji surface-to-surface missile (SSM) support facility.[49] These attacks were designed to stimulate confusion in the national decision-making structure and to remove a portion of its offensive capability.

Following Task Force Normandy's preparation, a strike package consisting of 22 F-15Es and 3 EF-111s struck Western Scud launch areas in the vicinity of H-2 airfield. Supported by KC-135s, this strike package formed south of the EW warning line, then headed north. After

---

[48](S) Interviews with electrical engineers had given the planners a good knowledge of specific, critical targets and possible Iraqi workarounds to keep the system going. Interview, GWAPS Task Force VI personnel with Lt Col Dave Deptula confirmed that the Black Hole's major intention in striking the power plants was to disable the air defense system.

[49](S) *Master Attack Plan*, "First 24 Hours," p 2.

final refueling the attack package penetrated Iraqi territory. The F-15Es attacked fixed Scud sites with a combination of free-fall bombs and cluster weapons. The EF-111s provided jamming support for the F-15Es during the attack and then exited to provide jamming support for the F-117s returning from the Baghdad area.

As the F-117s and F-15Es exited south, a fighter sweep of twenty-four F-15Cs and F-14s crossed the border into Iraq to reach the areas from which the Iraqis were expected to launch fighters in reaction to the first Coalition attacks. While the Iraqi reaction was much less than expected, these fighters did succeed in downing four enemy aircraft and watching one other Iraqi aircraft shoot his wingman down before crashing into the ground himself.

At H+40 minutes, the air campaign moved into its next phase–attacks by several massive SEAD packages aimed at the H-3, Kuwait, and Baghdad areas. The attacks were timed to occur just as the Iraqis were expected to bring their air defense nets back on line after shifting to backup electrical power. As the Iraqis reactivated their radars, they were expected to detect literally hundreds of contacts, which, it was hoped, would overload the KARI system. The tactics for these attacks involved drones, jamming aircraft, and Wild Weasel and other HARM-firing aircraft, and are discussed in detail in the section titled "Attacking The Iraqi Integrated Air Defense System" in this chapter. At about the same time, B-52s and Tornado GR-1s attacked the Iraqi Air Force dispersal fields utilizing low-level tactics. The Tornados dropped the JP233 munition designed especially for runway denial; the munition required a low-level delivery to be effective.

A third wave of F-117 attacks followed the SEAD strikes and attacks on the airfields. This time, more of the targets were in the strategic core–mostly leadership and communications related. By this time, also, other nonstealthy packages had begun striking at Scud shelters, NBC capabilities, and the communications network. Most of these attacks were flown by combined packages of bombers and SEAD aircraft. In a sense, the bombers acted as the 'stimulators' for the SEAD aircraft, the role drones had performed in the earlier large-scale SEAD missions.

The interaction between the tactics chosen for successive strikes was critical to the success of the first few hours of the air war. Aircraft missions were usually conducted to enable the success of follow-on missions. Key also was the employment of overwhelming Coalition assets against the whole range of targets, both strategic core and air defense. While the Iraqi command and control structure may not have been totally paralyzed, the tactics employed by the Coalition certainly degraded the Iraqi defensive capabilities to a degree where they could not defend themselves against the successively more aggressive Coalition attacks.

Bunker Busting

A particular problem faced by the Coalition was the need to penetrate the hardened bunkers protecting many of the strategic core targets. Command and control centers, NBC weapons storage facilities, and communications relay equipment were examples of the targets protected in this manner.

The Coalition encountered four classes of bunkers during Desert Storm. The first class was basement bunkers, usually located directly beneath an existing building. The difficulty with these targets was that weapons had to penetrate the buildings in addition to the underground bunkers. The buildings themselves created "voids" above the bunkers, negating the effects of most penetrating weapons by deflecting the weapons, causing detonations before penetration, or attenuating the effects of the blasts. The second class was the earth-covered bunker. These Iraqi bunkers typically had approximately twenty feet of earth above reinforced concrete.[50] The bunker walls were usually five to ten feet of reinforced concrete.[51] Some Iraqi bunkers were classified as superhardened (i.e., nuclear resistant). These superhardened bunkers had sixteen feet of earth covering 6.5 feet of reinforced concrete above a five-foot prefabricated steel mat.[52] The third class was mountain bunkers. Mountain bunkers were extended natural caves or tunnels located primarily in northern Iraq. They were very difficult to locate, target, and destroy because of their depth and camouflage. The fourth bunker class was revetted hardened

---

[50](S/NF) GWAPS File, AF/IN Briefing on THREAT (BUNKERS), CHST Folder 16.

[51](S/NF) *Ibid.*

[52](S/NF) *Ibid.*

aircraft shelters, which will be discussed as a subset of air superiority activity in the section titled "Defeating The Iraqi Air Force."

The primary tactics of penetrating hardened bunkers evolved around the I-2000 weapon, which was basically an improved 2,000-pound bomb. It had a slimmer, harder case than the standard MK-84 general-purpose bomb and contained 550 pounds of tritonal high explosive in its blast warhead, as opposed to 945 pounds in the MK-84.[53] The case was a single-piece forging of one-inch high-grade steel. The weapon usually was mated with a laser-guided kit to form the GBU-10I, GBU-24 A/B, or GBU-27. It was delivered by F-117s and F-111Fs in Operation Desert Storm.

Aircraft delivering a penetrating weapon strived to achieve angle and impact velocity to result in the deepest penetration. [DELETED]. [DELETED]. Smaller impact angles decreased penetration capability. Shallow impact angles also contributed to the phenomenon called J-hooking. J-hooking results when a weapon's movement after impact was more lateral than down, diminishing penetration (see Figure 32).

Table 7[54]
GBU-24 A/B (F-111F)
Level Release

[DELETED]

GBU-27 (F-117)
Level Release Horizontal Target

[DELETED]

F-117s and F-111Fs used I-2000 laser-guided weapons against numerous hardened bunkers throughout Desert Storm. F-117s dropped individ-

---

[53]*T.O. 1-1M-34*, Aircrew Weapons Delivery Manual, 15 Feb 1986, pp 1-14, 1-20.

[54]GWAPS Microfilm, Reel #23996, Frame #1025 (C) and 1026 (S).

ual weapons, whereas the F-111Fs dropped bombs in pairs and sometimes released their full load of four weapons. Targets had to be selected and planned by knowledgeable weapons officers, since it was imperative that aircrews received specific aimpoint guidance and coordinates along with a correct weapon mix to successfully destroy targets.[55] These I-2000 weapons devastated most Iraqi hardened targets.

Figure 31[56]
I-2000 Perforation Limits (Thickness of Bunker Roof)
Earth Overburden, 3° Angle of Attack

FIGURE DELETED

Figure 32
"J" Hooking Effect

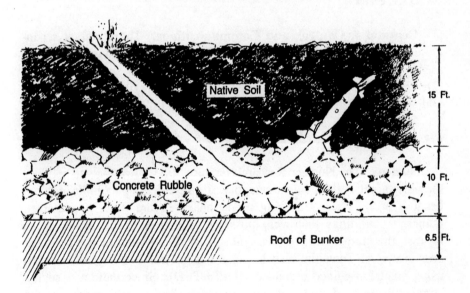

---

[55](S/NF/WN/NC) *Tactical Analysis Bulletin*, Vol 91-2, p 5-8.

[56](S) GWAPS Microfilm, Reel #23996, Frame #1030, Memorandum for TAC/DRA, Dense Penetrating Weapon, 28 Jan 91.

The Strategic Target Sets

Most of the targets in the strategic core target sets were attacked by using the tactics as discussed previously in this Chapter. Some targets were more difficult to attack and required special tactics and weaponeering to destroy them. This section discusses some of the tactics developed for use against the more challenging target sets.

Leadership. The Leadership target set included targets associated with the highest levels of the Iraqi government. Target sets included the Baghdad and Abu Ghurayb presidential palaces, the Ba'ath Party Headquarters, and the North Taji command bunker. This target set was almost exclusively the domain of the F-117, F-111Fs, and TLAM. F-117s and F-111Fs conducted infrared sensor acquisition and laser guided bomb delivery against these targets, using penetrating warheads against the harder targets and GBU-10s against the softer ones.

[DELETED].[57]

Command, Control, and Communications. The C^3 target set included the Iraqi nationwide communications system's most important elements such as radio relay facilities and satellite ground stations. [DELETED]. Penetrating weapons with delayed fuzing were employed and successfully fractured the communications links.

NBC (Nuclear, Biological, and Chemical)

Nuclear. The Nuclear Research Facility at Al Tuwaitha was initially the only target in the nuclear category. It presented a particular problem because of its size. Covering more than a square mile, it contained numerous buildings that were possible subtargets. The initial strike against this target was a mass attack of F-16s delivering free fall ordnance. Al Tuwaitha also became a target for F-117s and F-111Fs using precision-guided ordnance. [DELETED]. Since there was such a large collection of point targets, planners checked off targets in the complex as they were attacked.

---

[57](S) GWAPS Files, CHP Folder #14, "Additional Leadership Targets," 31 Jan 91.

[DELETED].[58] [DELETED].[59]

Biological. Probably the most challenging targets faced by the Coalition planners were the suspected biological storage sites. The Iraqis had been suspected of pursuing a biological weapons program and had amassed quantities of toxins in refrigerated bunkers. Initial considerations of the danger of releasing these agents into the atmosphere while trying to destroy them required conducting experiments on how best to attack them. [DELETED].[60] [DELETED].[61]

The method used in Desert Storm was a combination of timing of attacks and choosing proper munitions. [DELETED].

Chemical. The Iraqi threat to use chemical weapons against the Coalition or against Israel caused the Al Samarra Labs to be struck by TLAMs on the first night. The attacks hit chemical production buildings; however, the chemical materials were stored in S-shaped or cruciform bunkers at several sites. The Iraqis also sought to confuse the issue by constructing numerous dummy bunkers. After identification, subsequent attacks on these bunkers were carried out with penetrating GBU-24/27 weapons.

Bridges. The initial bridge attacks were flown by "smart" aircraft using "dumb" bombs. While these tactics achieved some success, the results were judged insufficient and, as in Vietnam, laser-guided bombs (LGBs) were employed. F-117s, F-111Fs, F-15Es, and A-6s attacked and cut designated bridges with LGBs. In addition to these attacks, river reconnaissance missions were flown to patrol the waterways and ensure that the crossings remained closed. These missions were flown by F-16s during the day and F-111Fs at night, and were tasked to attack any bridging and crossing activities such as pontoon-building or ferries.

---

[58](S) GWAPS Files, CHP Folder #14, "Emergency War Termination Plan," 29 Jan 91.

[59](S) Damage to Iraqi Nuclear Facilities, Hq Air Force Intelligence Agency, 25 Jan 91.

[60](S/NF) Intvw, Perry Jamison, Rich Davis, and Barry Barlow, Center for Air Force History, with Lt Gen Charles A. Horner, 4 Mar 92, p 32, GWAPS NA-303.

[61](S) Intvw, Kurt Guthe, GWAPS, with Capt. John R. Glock, 2 July 92.

Not all bombing problems could be solved with readily available weapons. Various methods to destroy deeply buried and hardened facilities were proposed but were either not fully developed or not shipped to theater before the war ended. For example, the GBU-11 was a 3,000-pound laser-guided bomb from the Vietnam era; planners remembered and attempted to ship it to the theater. The GBU-11 provided greater explosive blast than a 2,000-pound bomb, creating more destruction over a greater range of targets. But, the war ended before the weapon could be used.

[DELETED].

Unlike prior examples, the GBU-28 went from idea to operational use before the war ended. This weapon was designed to meet the requirement to penetrate very deep hard targets and is discussed extensively in the Logistics Report. Two GBU-28s were used on the last day of the war against the North Taji Weapons Manufacturing Facility No. 2.

The attacks on the strategic target sets during Desert Storm added a new dimension to aerial warfare. Using new technologies and weapons, the Coalition was able to seize the initiative and define the battle beyond any Iraqi hope of resistance. As the campaign unfolded, continued tactical innovations neutralized most of the difficult targets and contributed significantly to the Coalition's success.

Figure 33
Conventional Weapons Enhanced Penetration (CWEP)
"Nail Driver"

FIGURE DELETED

Attacking The Iraqi Air Defense And Air Force

The highest priority of Coalition air operations was gaining and maintaining air superiority by neutralizing the Iraqi Integrated Air Defense System (IADS) and rendering the Iraqi air force ineffective. Iraqi forces had to be neutralized before follow-on attacks could be conducted with acceptable losses by nonstealthy aircraft.

This section discusses tactics associated with operations used to gain and maintain air superiority. Central to the effort were denying Iraqi commanders both the ability to understand what was happening and the capability to command and control their forces. To accomplish these goals, electronic combat missions would blind early warning sensors, disrupt communications, deny ground controlled intercepts, and destroy surfaced-based air defenses. Fighter sweep aircraft would engage the Iraqi fighters in the air, destroying their airborne defense capability and ensuring the success of Coalition fighter bombers. Fighter bombers would deny the Iraqi air force the use of their runways and their ability to retaliate and defend, ultimately forcing them into hardened shelters. Finally, F-111Fs and F-117s would destroy those impervious shelters, and in the process, destroy the offensive capability of the Iraqi Air Force. As the shelter busting campaign heightened, Iraqi aircraft attempted to flee to Iran, and Coalition forces countered with combat air patrols over Iraq.

Attacking the Iraqi Integrated Air Defense System (IADS)

Six elements of offensive strategy were used to negate the Iraqi IADS. *Electronic Surveillance* aircraft such as the RC-135 and EP-3 were used during Desert Shield to determine the nature and extent of the enemy threat. *Tactical deception* masked the intentions of Coalition forces

181

during their buildup and training phases. The air campaign began with attacks on Iraqi sector operations centers, early warning sites, and command and control nodes using stealth and a variety of SEAD aircraft along with decoys to provide a false tactical air picture to ground radars. *Bombing attacks* were coordinated with and complemented dedicated SEAD mission assets. Later, attack packages were *accompanied by dedicated SEAD aircraft*–Wild Weasels, jammers, and HARM-carrying aircraft –which responded to mobile and target area threats. In addition, the air war in the KTO involved *roving bands of dedicated SAM killers and carefully located jammers* to destroy Iraqi SAM capabilities in the area. In this way, air superiority over ground-based air defense was gained and maintained throughout the war.

Reconnaissance and Surveillance Measures

The air defense threat faced by the Coalition was formidable, both in density and sophistication. A combination of old and new weapons coordinated by the computerized KARI control system presented a credible threat to Coalition aircraft. The Coalition's task was to determine the extent and nature of this threat. Aircraft such as RC-135s, TR-1/U-2s, and P-3s, flew near the Iraqi-Saudi border, and gathered data. [DELETED].[64] Another phase of this collection effort involved obtaining technical data from the French, who had developed and installed the KARI system.[65] These efforts enabled Coalition planners to assess the strengths and vulnerabilities of the system more accurately.

Electronic intelligence (ELINT) systems maintained a constant presence. [DELETED].[66] Collection aircraft developed an extensive picture of the Iraqi IADS. Figure 35 depicts the command and control structure of the Iraqi air defense system.

---

[64](S) Intvw by Dr. Williamson Murray, GWAPS, with Brig Gen Larry Henry, the CENTAF Electronic Combat coordinator, Aug 1992.

[65](S) Naval Operational Intelligence Command SPEAR Group Briefing, GWAPS, 15 May 1992.

[66][DELETED]

Figure 34
EC Combat Preparations[67]

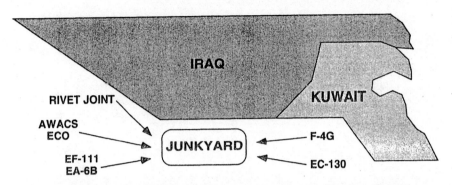

Numerous EC Preparation Missions Throughout Desert Shield

- Joint use of EC Assets
- Border Runs for Real Time ELINT Recce
- Built Aircrew Confidence / Timing / Calibrated Systems
- Coordination with AWACS / RIVET JOINT / TACC

Tactical Deception

Careful review of Coalition operations during Desert Shield gives a sense of the way in which the gradually increasing scale of operations was orchestrated to desensitize the Iraqi defenders. Beginning in September 1990, the tactical deception operation began. A consistent mix

---

[67](S) From Briefing Slide "Electronic Combat in Desert Shield/Desert Storm," by Brig Gen Larry Henry describing pre-war EC efforts.

Figure 35
Iraqi Air Defense Command and Control

FIGURE DELETED

Figure 36
Iraqi SAM Coverage (16 Nov 90)

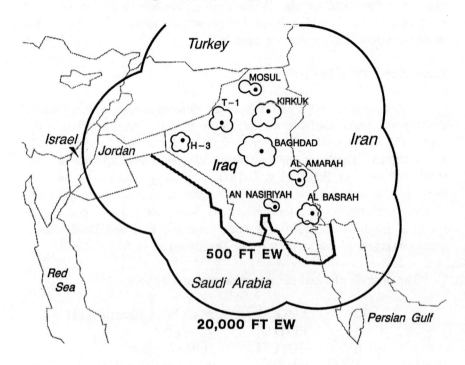

of Coalition aircraft flew the same flight tracks on a regular basis. By the night of 17 January, Iraqi radar operators, observing Coalition activities, saw a similar pattern. AWACS, Rivet Joint, Combat Air Patrols (CAPs), high-value airborne assets (HVAA), and tankers were all in their familiar tracks. Most of the attack aircraft remained south out of the range of Iraqi radars until it was time to go north and attack targets.[68]

The initial attacks by F-117s and TLAM cruise missiles were aimed at air defense operations centers and electrical power plants supporting the air defense net. The intent was to force activation of emergency electrical

---

[68]Most Coalition aircraft penetrated Iraqi airspace at low altitude to avoid radar detection.

power, create confusion, and isolate commanders while emergency power was being brought on line. Meanwhile, attacking aircraft would proceed toward their targets. When the Iraqi air defense system resumed operations, it would suddenly have to process hundreds of aircraft. This would overload the air defense system.[69]

Large Scale SEAD Strikes

The prewar analysis of the Iraqi air defense structure was used to develop the portion of the master attack plan designed to disable the IADS. The first two days of the plan provided for twenty-five large-scale SEAD attacks. The large SEAD aircraft package directed against the area south and west of Baghdad at H-Hour plus forty minutes on the first night of the war provides examples of the tactics used during these efforts. The attack was a joint effort; Air Force aircraft attacked targets south of Baghdad, and Navy aircraft from the Red Sea Battle Force attacked targets in the vicinity of Al Taqaddum.

The aircraft planned for this mission were as follows:[70]

12	F-4G	SEAD Wild Weasel/HARM
3	EF-111	SEAD ECM
6	BQM-74	Drone Support
3	EA-6B	SEAD ECM (Jammer)/HARM
3	F-14	Escort for EA-6B
10	F/A-18	SEAD/HARM
8	A-7	SEAD/HARM
4	A-6	SEAD/TALD

The plan was to approach the target area from numerous directions, force a reaction, then destroy the radars. The Air Force and the Navy used different tactics based on the types of equipment employed. The mission was flown as pictured in Figure 37.

---

[69](S/NF/WN/NC) *Iraqi Threat to U.S. Forces*, Navy SPEAR, Naval Intelligence Command, NIC-26605-018-90, Dec 1990, p 3-20.

[70]Numbers of aircraft derived from both (S) *Master Attack Plan*, "First 24 Hours," p 4; and (S/NF/WN/NC) CNA Rpt, "Desert Storm Reconstruction Report, Volume VIII: C³/Space and Electronic Warfare," Jun 1992, p 3-8.

**Figure 37
H-40 Large Scale
SEAD Strike**

FIGURE DELETED

187

In the south, Air Force EF-111s proceeded to their jamming positions and established orbits. BQM-74 drones were launched to stimulate the IADS.[71] As Iraqi target acquisition radars activated, EF-111s jammed, forcing the Iraqi radars to increase their vulnerability to HARM missiles.[72] Wild Weasels, loaded with HARMs, approached the Iraqi radars. Each aircraft was tasked to destroy high-threat mobile SAMs within their assigned area of responsibility. [DELETED].[73] [DELETED]. Sixty HARMs were fired during the mission.[74]

In the west, EA-6Bs established orbits. A-6s launched tactical air launch decoys (TALDs) to cause individual SAM operators to react to the air threat.[75] EA-6Bs jammed, causing increased radar activity, and developed a radar environment more conducive to HARMs launched by A-7s and F/A-18s. [DELETED].[76] [DELETED]. Navy aircraft fired fifty-one HARMS on this strike.[77]

Bomb damage assessment could not be obtained on all radars, but ELINT operators noted a significant reduction in electronic activity.[78] Numerous SEAD missions of the type just described were conducted on the first day of the war.[79] Although causal relationships cannot be definitively established at this time, the Iraqi electronic defenses were

---

[71](S) "Operation Desert Storm Electronic Combat (EC) Effectiveness Analysis," Air Force Electronic Warfare Center, Jan 1992, p 11-3.

[72][DELETED]

[73][DELETED]

[74](S) 52d Fighter Wing Desert Storm - A Success Story, Briefing slides 10 and 12 and p 2.

[75](S/NF/WN/NC) CNA Rpt, Vol VIII, p 3-9.

[76](S) *Ibid*, p B1.

[77](S) *Ibid*, p 3-9.

[78](S) "Operation Desert Storm Electronic Combat (EC) Effectiveness Analysis," p 11-9.

[79](S) *Master Attack Plan*, "First 24 Hours."

never fully reconstituted. While individual air defense radars continued to pose a localized threat, the SEAD missions fractured the backbone of centralized control.

Attacks Against Air Defense Nodes–Command, Control, Communications Countermeasures (C³CM)

The primary objective of C³CM is to deny or degrade the ability of hostile military commanders to command and control their forces effectively.[80] A large portion of the F-117 missions on 17 January had this objective. Twenty air defense nodes were targeted in the first two waves of F-117s.

The air defense and communications nodes, in hardened bunkers, presented challenges in weapons selection and delivery. As described previously, Coalition forces encountered four classes of bunkers in Desert Storm. The F-117 and F-111F delivered I-2000 penetrating laser-guided bombs, which proved particularly effective against these bunkers.

Large-scale SEAD attacks and attacks on particular elements of Iraq's air defense structure combined to eliminate their ability to operate in a coordinated fashion. The remaining air defense challenge became the individual SAM and AAA systems.

Direct and Area Support of Attack Missions

Individual SAM and AAA threats were dealt with primarily by assigning SEAD and ECM aircraft to attack groups. Jammers and HARMcapable aircraft would support attack packages based on analysis of the expected threats. Aircrews would communicate with mission commanders before

---

[80](S/NF) *Tactical Air Forces Guide for Integrated Electronic Combat*, USAF Tactical Air Warfare Center, Oct 1987, p 3-2.

189

flight to establish tactics for each particular situation. The positioning of jammers and HARM aircraft was critical to protect the flights.

[DELETED].[81]

In the early phases of the war, both the EF-111 and EA-6B were tasked primarily in the direct support role. The EF-111s, provided target area suppression while flying between the threat and the attack force.[82] The EA-6Bs, in general, flew behind their strike groups.

Navy HARM aircraft flew to preplanned positions, salvoed their missiles at known radar locations, and worked in unison with EA-6Bs to ascertain the presence of active systems. The EA-6B, although used primarily as a jammer, had the ability to fire a maximum of two HARMs. NAVCENT policy dictated that Navy attacks not proceed into Iraq or the Kuwait Theater of Operations (KTO) without an accompanying EA-6B.[83]

---

[81](S/NF) *USCENTAF Electronic Combat in Desert Shield and Desert Storm After Action Report*, Oct 1991, p 1-2.

[82](S/NF/WN/NC) *MCM 3-1*, Vol 1, p 7-10.

[83]CDR William J. Luti, U.S. Navy, "Battle of the Airwaves," U.S. Naval Institute Proceedings, Jan 1992, p 53.

Figure 38
Jamming Tactics

FIGURE DELETED

Dedicated ECM Stations–The "Weasel Police"

As the ground offensive approached, the SAM threat to attack aircraft in the KTO, while greatly reduced, was still present in the form of mobile SAM batteries. The make-up of Coalition attack missions had also changed from large packages to flights of two or four aircraft. To provide ECM protection for these flights, SEAD aircraft were assigned to orbit positions surrounding the KTO. These "Weasel Police" missions are depicted in Figure 39.[84]

Overall, the Coalition campaign against the Iraqi air defense system reduced the threat to Coalition aircraft.

The combination of JSEAD, packaging, and the aggressive destruction campaign against critical C^3 nodes contributed greatly to the overall low attrition rate and success of the offensive air campaign.[85]

Defeating The Iraqi Air Force

As discussed in Chapter One, the Iraqi Air Force presented a potential threat to Coalition forces. While the quality of its pilots could be questioned, its potential could not be overlooked. Fighter sweeps, various types of combat air patrols, and attacks on airfields and aircraft on the ground were all used to defeat or neutralize this threat.

The Fighter Sweep

In a "fighter sweep," large numbers of fighter aircraft, operating independently, proceed through an area with the intent of overpowering any enemy fighters encountered. The most prominent use of this tactic occurred just after H-Hour on the first night of the war. Twelve elements (twenty-four aircraft) of F-15Cs and F-14s were positioned to cover the entire Iraqi border. Their goal was to engage any enemy aircraft launched in reaction to the initial attacks. Additionally, the intent was to intimidate the Iraqis and cause them to think twice about engaging future

---

[84](S) 52d Fighter Wing, Desert Storm Brief, GWAPS Files, slides 15 left and 17 right.

[85](S/NF) *USCENTAF Electronic Combat in Desert Shield and Desert Storm After Action Report*, p 5-2.

Figure 39
Typical Weasel
Police Station

FIGURE DELETED

193

Coalition missions. Five Iraqi aircraft were downed in this initial sweep, all by F-15s.

Smaller sweeps flew throughout the initial phases of the war. On these smaller missions, the F-15Cs preceded the attack aircraft. The objective was to clear the target area before the attack aircraft arrived. These sweep tactics were developed to counter an aggressive opponent. But, as the war progressed, the Iraqis changed their tactics by engaging outbound attackers from the rear. F-15Cs countered by remaining in the target area long enough to protect Coalition attackers from Iraqi fighters.

Typical of these fighter sweeps were the operations of Citgo and Penzoil Flights in the early morning hours of the 17th of January 1991.[86] These two flights of four F-15Cs each embarked on an offensive counter-air sweep[87] missions in support of numerous strike packages.[88] The sweep became an engagement when AWACS spotted "bandits"[89] as the flights were air-refueling. AWACS directed Penzoil Flight to leave the tanker and respond to the bandits. Citgo Flight remained south of the Iraqi border to minimize the chances of early-warning-radar detection. Meanwhile, the F-15Es were approaching H2 and H3 airfields, and the SEAD aircraft were already north of the border.

The initial formation used by Penzoil Flight was tactical spread, and the individual elements divided (see Figure 40). Navigation responsibilities fell to the element lead (number three aircraft), who also left his

---

[86](S) These aerial combat missions were liberally extracted from "Desert Storm Air to Air Engagements, 3 Mar 92, 33d Fighter Wing Air to Air Engagements Desert Storm," pp 1-11.

[87]Offensive Counter Air (OCA) sweep aircraft seek out and destroy or neutralize enemy air power in a designated area for a specific time period.

[88](S) The overall air-to-air gameplan called for surprise attacks by F-117s, F-15Es, with support by EF-111s. The F-117 targets included higher headquarters communication nodes, and the F-15Es were tasked into the H2/H3 area. The main attack package followed behind with numerous strategic targets. It was projected that the Iraqis would flush their aircraft from alert in response to the loss of communication links with Baghdad, leaving the air superiority F-15Cs poised for attack.

[89]Bandits are known enemy aircraft. The term originated from RAF World War II usage.

194

formation lights on for visual identification. All other flight members flew with their lights off as the aircraft left the tanker northbound.

Figure 40
Tactical Spread

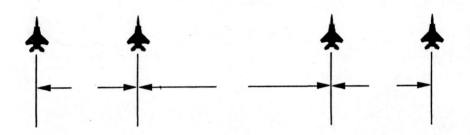

As Penzoil Flight neared Mudaysis airfield, three separate groups of aircraft were "painted" on radar. AWACS labeled two of the groups as friendlies, the last group was identified as bandits. Penzoil Flight was continuing to monitor the groups when a pop-up group appeared at two o'clock and forty nautical miles. AWACS replied with a "bogey"[90] radio call. The flight lead handed this contact off to the element lead and went back to monitoring the initial bandit group ten to fifteen miles north of Mudaysis (see Figure 41).

The bandits north of Mudaysis turned west to land while still thirty to thirty-five miles away from Penzoil Flight. Meanwhile, the element lead received a pop-up contact at thirty-five nautical miles.[91] AWACS was unable to determine hostile, friendly, or unknown status. In fact, due to prev-

---

[90]A bogey is a radar/visual contact with an aircraft whose identity is unknown.

[91][DELETED]

Figure 41
Mudaysis Airfield Attack

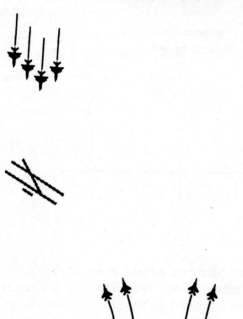
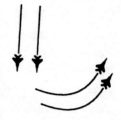

ious friendly tracks in the area, AWACS never declared the bandit hostile before the shot. Penzoil's element lead continued northbound and locked on to the unknown aircraft at thirty nautical miles away. [DELETED].[92]

One Penzoil Flight member called possible multiples in the group, [DELETED]. The element lead asked AWACS if any friendlies were at this altitude and received a negative reply. At this time, the number four aircraft turned to the west as the element lead determined the oncoming aircraft to be a bandit. [DELETED]. The element lead fired a radar AIM-7M missile towards the head-on bandit. The shot parameters were as follows:

---

[92][DELETED]

Figure 42
MIG-29 Kill

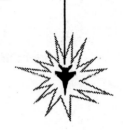

Bandit

Alt:
Speed: [DELETED]
Heading:
Aspect:[93]

Shooter

Alt:
Speed: [DELETED]
Heading:

After firing his missile, the element lead executed a hard turn to the east while number four continued his turn to the west northwest. [DELETED]. No visual launch was observed from the bandit, and the element checked back towards the bandit to observe missile detonation on a single aircraft. The element lead rejoined his flight to regain mutual support, as the friendly train of F-15Es safely egressed their target below.

When Penzoil Flight departed the tanker early to commit on targets near Mudaysis airfield, Citgo Flight trailed by about 60-65 miles. Citgo Flight initially followed at an altitude in the middle to upper 20,000s. Element lead was 20-25 nautical miles in trail offset to the west (see Figure 43). Citgo Flight viewed Penzoil's engagement as they flew north towards Mudaysis.

---

[93](S) Aspect angle is the angle between the defender's longitudinal axis and the line of sight to the attacker. The angle is measured from the defender's 6 o'clock position, and the attacker's heading is irrelevant.

As Citgo Flight approached to within 40 nautical miles from Mudaysis, two groups of suspected enemy aircraft were spotted tracking the F-15Es coming off target (see Figure 44).[94]

Figure 43
Citgo Flight Sequence No. 1

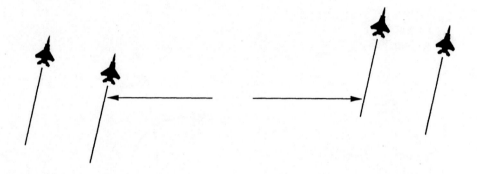

[DELETED].[95] Meanwhile, AWACS called bandits launching from Mudaysis, twenty-five to thirty nautical miles off Citgo's nose.[96] The F-15Es were still forty to forty-five nautical miles away, proceeding eastbound. The far northern group of bandits had turned back north, and then west, away from the F-15Es, taking them out of this engagement (see Figure 45).

---

[94](S) The F-15Es reported to have taken a single AIM-9M shot on a Fulcrum, but the tone was bad and the missile did not guide.

[95][DELETED]

[96]It appeared that the Iraqis were flushing their fighters off at 5-nm intervals. The runway lights were still on as Citgo Flight flew through, even though Penzoil Flight had already shot down a MIG-29.

Figure 44
Citgo Flight
Sequence No. 2

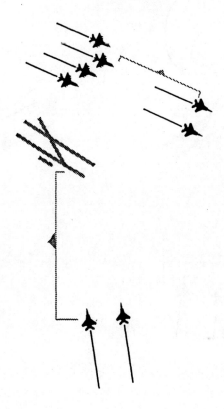

At this point, the Citgo leader locked on to a group 25 nautical miles away from Mudaysis. This bandit group was in a left-hand climbing turn out of 4,500 feet, vectoring in the direction of Citgo Flight. [DELETED]. [DELETED].

Figure 45
Citgo Flight Sequence No. 3

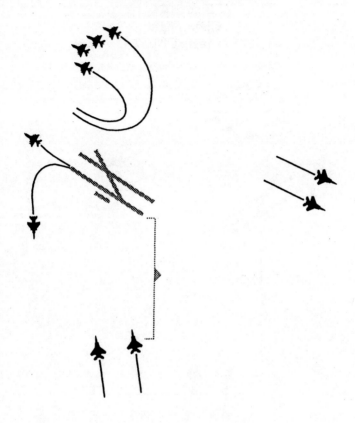

The flight leader shot a single radar-guided AIM-7M at the Iraqi aircraft (see Figure 46).[97] The following launch parameters applied:

---

[97](S) The F-1 did not fly any offensive or defensive maneuvers. This reaction was common for Iraqi aircraft during the rest of the Gulf War.

Figure 46
Citgo Flight Sequence No. 4

Bandit

Alt:
Speed:
Heading: [DELETED]
Aspect:

Shooter

Alt:
Speed: [DELETED]
Heading:

As the missile impacted the target, Citgo Flight observed a large fireball followed by an even larger fireball as the F-1 hit the ground. At this time, Citgo 2 locked on to another bandit group taking off from Mudaysis. The bandits flew to the west as Citgo 2 pursued in a tail chase. Pursuit stopped as the bandits flew over the SAM ring around H2 and H3 airfields. AWACS confirmed them as bandits, but the SAM presence forced Citgo Flight to return to its preplanned combat air patrol between Mudaysis and H2 airfield. No other engagements occurred during this mission, and Citgo Flight egressed behind Penzoil Flight on the way back to home station.

Combat Air Patrol

Various types of combat air patrols were employed. Defensive patrol stations were established along the northern border of Saudi Arabia to protect the kingdom and the Coalition forces, as depicted in Figure 47. [DELETED]. The Saudi F-15C that shot down two Mirage F-1s on 24 January was on such a mission. Combat air patrol stations were also maintained over the northern Persian Gulf to protect Coalition ships and the

Arab Gulf states. [DELETED].[98] Fighter protection was also provided to attack missions, called escort or target combat air patrol. High-value airborne asset combat air patrols or high-value unit combat air patrols were launched to protect important aircraft that had limited or no means of self-protection. [DELETED].[99]

Figure 47
Desert Storm CAP and AWACS Stations

FIGURE DELETED

---

[98](S) "Desert Storm Reconstruction Report," Volume 1, Summary, Center for Naval Analyses, CRM-91-219, Dec 1991, pp 83, 84.

[99](S) *Master Attack Plan,* "First 24 Hours," pp 1, 4, 6, 10, and 14.

Airfield Attacks

The Coalition conducted a campaign to destroy the Iraqi Air Force on the ground and to neutralize its capability by attacking its airfields. During the first three days of the air war, almost all airfields in Iraq were struck. The primary targets were the runways, taxiways, ramp space, hangars, and munitions areas.

The Iraqis built airfields with multiple runways and stressed taxiways capable of being used as runways. This situation posed significant tactical problems (see Tallil Airfield, Iraq Photo). As long as one unbroken length of 3,000 feet of concrete remained, the field was, at least in principle, capable of supporting air operations. Shutting down an Iraqi airfield completely was clearly a daunting problem. Even if a runway was damaged, the Iraqis had first-rate runway repair equipment.

The following strike package planned for a mission in the Tallil area is typical of this type of mission.[100] All aircraft were Marine except for the British GR-1s.

4	EA-6	SEAD/ECM
6	F/A-18	SEAD/HARM
4	F/A-18	Fighter Sweep
1	F/A-18	SEAD/TALD
[DELETED]	GR-1(UK)	Tallil Airfield
4	F/A-18	Nasiriyah Power Plant
4	A-6	Tallil Airfield Scud Shelter
2	F/A-18	Tallil Airfield Scud Shelter
4	A-6	Qurna Airfield FAC Scud Shelter
2	F/A-18	Qurna Airfield FAC Scud Shelter

All of the elements of a total strike package were present: the tactical air-launched decoy to stimulate enemy radars, SEAD aircraft to jam radars and fire HARM missiles, fighter sweep F/A-18s to engage enemy fighter aircraft, and strike aircraft loaded with weapons to hit their particular targets.

---

[100](S) *Ibid*, p 7.

The tactical core of this attack was the United Kingdom GR-1 Tornados armed with JP233 munitions. [DELETED].[101]

(Left) JP233 damage at Tallil Airfield, Iraq.
(Right) Indicates runway repair work at Tallil Airfield.

"Shelter Busting"

After the first few days of the war, Iraqi aircraft rarely launched to challenge Coalition attacks. When not flying, the Iraqis placed all aircraft in shelters to protect them from Coalition bombing. There were three

---

[101](S) Debrief, British Ministry of Defence to GWAPS, May 1992.

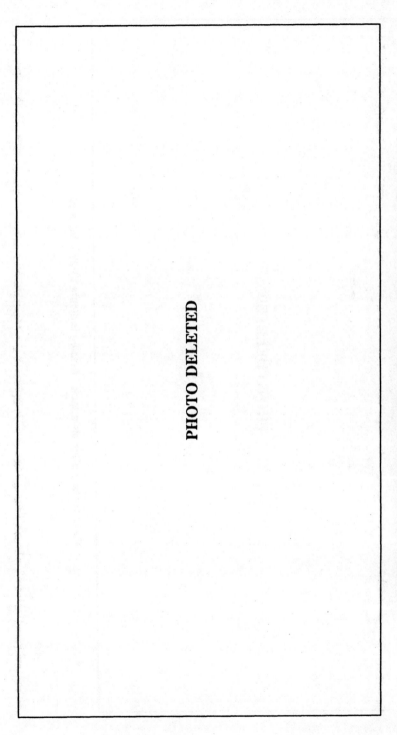

PHOTO DELETED

Tallil Airfield, built with multiple runways (A1,A2) and taxiways capable of being used as runways (B1,B2). Photo includes additional targeting annotations.

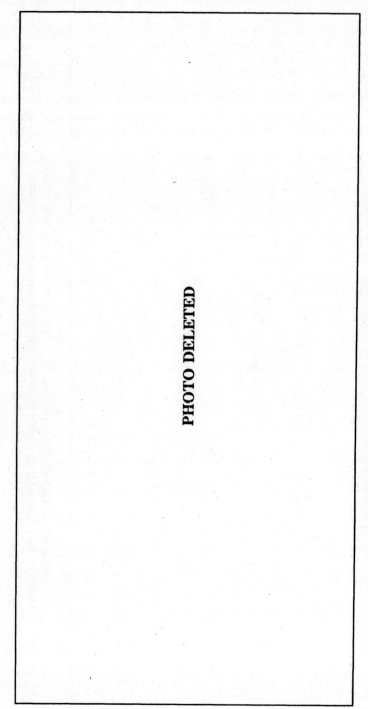

PHOTO DELETED

Tallil Airfield after air attack. Arrows indicate JP233 damage.

types of aircraft bunkers.   The Tab-Vee, the most common bunker, [DELETED].[102]
The Trapezoid shelters [DELETED].[103]

PHOTO DELETED

---

[102](S) AFIA/INKT, Paper on Bunker Descriptions, GWAPS Files, CHST Folder 16.

[103](S) *Ibid.*

PHOTO DELETED

Trapezoid Shelters – Talill Airfield, Iraq. Top photo depicts trapezoid shelter under construction. Bottom photo indicates finished shelter.

PHOTO DELETED

The third type of bunker was Yugoslavian. [DELETED]. The Iraqis placed their highest priority aircraft in them.[104]

These hardened shelters were distributed as indicated in Table 8.

Sheltered aircraft remained a potential threat. As a force in being, presumably being saved for the commencement of ground operations, these aircraft still gave Iraq a capability to launch a massive offensive raid. So, on the seventh day of Desert Storm, plans were developed to destroy the hardened shelters.[105]

These operations became known as "shelter busting," and were flown mainly by F-111Fs, F-117s and F-15Es. Locating the shelters on the airfields was relatively simple. The runways and taxiways acted as pointers to the targets [DELETED]. Attacking a large array of shelters was a complex process requiring a detailed plan. For a single target, the most critical factor was the specific aimpoint or desired mean point of impact. [DELETED]. The shelter effectively became a blast containment vessel, enhancing the effects of explosion. The fuel in the target aircraft added to the force of the blast. On occasion, 2,000-pound doors were blown off and thrown 430 feet by the force of these penetrating weapons.

---

[104](S) AFIA/INKT Paper on Bunker Descriptions.

[105](S) Briefing Slide, "Shelter Busting Forces: Iraqi Exodus to Iran," GWAPS Files, CHP folder #14.

PHOTO DELETED

Yugoslav Shelters, Shayka Mazhar Airfield – Top photo depicts double-bay drive through shelter under construction. Bottom photo indicates single bay drive through shelter.

PHOTO DELETED

Table 8
Iraqi Shelter Types by Airfield[106]

Airfield Name	Tab-Vee	Trapezoid	Yugoslav
QAYARRAH	X		
KIRKUK	X		
BALAD			X
AL TAQADDUM	X	X	
SHAYKA MAZHAR			X
UBAYDAH		X	
TALLIL	X	X	
JALIBAH	X		
SAHIBAH		X	
H-2	X		
H-3	X	X	
AL ASAD	X		X
AL SAHRA	X		
SADDAM INT'L		X	
HABBANIYAH		X	
TALL AFAR	X		
TUZ KHURMATU	X		
KUT AL HAYY	X		
QALAT SALIH	X		
AS SALMAN	X		
WADI AL KHIRR	X		
MUDAYSIS	X		
SAMARRA	X		

2,000-pound case hardened penetrating laser-guided bombs, were used against all aircraft shelters. The I-2000 was an improved 2,000-pound bomb

---

[106](S/NF) GWAPS Files, CHP folder #14.

with a slimmer harder case than the standard MK-84 general-purpose bomb. The weapons were usually mated with a laser-guided kit to form the GBU-10, GBU–24 A/B, or GBU-27, and were dropped by F-111Fs and F-117s.[107]

This Tab-Vee Shelter door was blown over 430 feet from the shelter in the background. To the left, note the destroyed personnel bunker.[108]

Combat Air Patrols East of Baghdad

As the Coalition "bunker busting" campaign began to take effect, the Iraqis moved some aircraft out of the shelters into open fields or populated areas in an attempt to protect them. They also tried to preserve their top-line fighters by flying them to Iran. The Coalition responded by establishing combat air patrol stations Cindy, Elaine, and Wendy deep in Iraq, effectively surrounding Baghdad with the objective of intercepting the fleeing aircraft (refer to Figure 47 earlier). These operations included tanker support flown over Iraqi territory. [DELETED].

---

[107]All I-2000s dropped in Desert Storm were laser-guided.

[108]Oral interview and photograph provided by DIA.

During one such mission, Zerex Flight, an element of two F-15Cs, shot down four Iraqi aircraft.[109] Zerex Flight was flying barrier patrol east of Baghdad when AWACS reported an initial contact 60 nautical miles northwest of Zerex's position. Zerex Flight armed its ordnance and located the bandits at ten o'clock 60 nautical miles away. [DELETED].[110] [DELETED]. The Zerex Flight leader turned his formation into the engagement to cutoff the bandits, who were heading for the border. At 40 nautical miles, Zerex Flight picked up multiple contacts in close formation. The bandits turned 10-15 degrees to the left and headed eastbound for the border. Zerex Flight turned further to the right to cutoff the bandits, and at 35 nautical miles, radar painted multiple returns (see Figure 48).

[DELETED].

[DELETED].

The flight lead picked up a visual tally on two MIG-21s heading eastbound. At the same time, Zerex Four spotted two Frogfoot aircraft further north, also heading eastbound. The bandits had apparently split into two elements to escape the oncoming F-15Cs (see Figure 49). The wingman fired an infrared AIM-9M missile on the northernmost Frogfoot. He then pulled 60 degrees to the right and fired another infrared AIM-9M at the second Frogfoot. Both missiles tracked and destroyed their targets. At the same time, the flight lead converted on both MIG-21s and fired two AIM-9Ms, which destroyed both targets. No defensive reactions or countermeasures were observed.[111] Zerex Flight exited the engagement zone to the south.

The Coalition effort against the Iraqi Air Defense System and air force was an unqualified success. The combination of weapons and delivery tactics, particularly laser-guided weapons and SEAD, allowed the

---

[109]These aerial combat missions were liberally extracted from "Desert Storm Air to Air Engagements, 3 Mar 1992, 53d Fighter Squadron Air to Air Engagements Desert Storm," pp 12-17.

[110][DELETED]

[111]The Iraqis never reacted to missile smoke or attacks from behind their aircraft. The only defense they exhibited was flying at very low altitude.

Figure 48
Zerex Flight Sequence No. 1

FIGURE DELETED

Figure 49
Zerex Flight Sequence No. 2

FIGURE DELETED

Coalition to gain air superiority and eventually air supremacy. This control of the air provided the basis for the successful efforts against other targets, and can be seen as a major contributor to the Coalition victory in Desert Storm.

Attacking The Iraqi Ground and Naval Forces

This section examines the tactics used by Coalition aircrews in attacking Iraqi ground and naval forces. It places particular emphasis on Close Air Support/Battlefield Air Interdiction (CAS/BAI) missions; that is, missions flown at the request of the ground commander. Where possible it discusses how tactics were adapted to particular situations and how and why they may have differed from tactics practiced during prewar training. The section pays special attention to the contributions of Air Force and Marine Corps fixed-winged aircraft, describes Navy and allied aircraft where appropriate, and includes a section on Army and Marine Corps attack helicopters.

To understand air support of ground operations, the reader must understand the objectives of the ground offensive and the maneuvers employed. Aviation had to be responsive to the priorities of the ground commanders. It had to make a direct contribution to the overall ground plan of attack (scheme of maneuver). Simply killing people and destroying things was not enough. The Army and Marine Corps ground forces were assigned strikingly different missions. The Army, supported by British, French, and other Coalition forces, conducted a wide, sweeping, high-speed, flanking maneuver. The Marines executed an extensive counter-barrier operation against Iraqi fortifications. Interestingly, these different missions produced similar priorities for air support. Both Army and Marine Corps commanders were far more interested in Iraqi indirect fire systems–artillery, free rocket over ground (FROGs) systems, and multiple-launch rocket (MLRs) systems–than in direct fire systems such as tanks and armor.[112]

Air missions in support of the ground forces began on the first day of the war and continued until the cease fire. Early air support to the

---

[112]During GWAPS interviews with both Gen Franks, USA, commander VII Corps, and Gen Boomer, USMC, commander I MEF, they made it clear that they placed a higher priority on Iraqi artillery than on tanks.

ground scheme of maneuver concentrated on isolating the battlefield by cutting communications and disrupting or halting resupply. As the time for the ground assault approached, priorities shifted to enemy forces closer to the front.

Background

The Air Tasking Order (ATO)[113] was employed to control and coordinate the flow of air missions. While the ATO process was necessary to deconflict and coordinate aircraft during the strategic phase of the campaign, ground commanders did not perceive the ATO process, with its seventy-two-hour development time, as being responsive to their needs during the battlefield preparation and ground assault phases of the war.[114] To increase the volume of air support available to the ground commander, a "push flow" system was implemented. A description of the system and how it worked is presented later in this section.

The "push flow" system produced the desired number of CAS sorties, but for a variety of reasons, including the relative lack of enemy resistance, little opportunity or need arose for classical, troops-in-contact CAS missions.[115] Other reasons included the speed of the ground advance, the extensive night operations, the poor weather, and the presence of obscurants (notably, smoke from burning oil wells). All of these reasons combined made distinguishing friendly from enemy forces difficult, and had the important tactical consequence of rendering CAS missions more dangerous to execute. In simple terms, the potential for casualties from "friendly fire" was high.

---

[113]Additional information on the ATO process can be found in the *Command and Control* Report.

[114]Numerous sources allude to the perceived difficulty the ATO process had in being responsive to the tactical ground situation; for examples, see the interview with Lt Gen Royal N. Moore, Jr. USMC, "Marine Air: There When Needed," *Naval Institute Proceedings,* Nov. 1991, pp 63-64, and (S) Institute for Defense Analysis, "Desert Storm: Fixed Wing BAI/CAS Operations and Lessons Learned," *IDA Document D-1080,* Alexandria, VA, p 62.

[115]JCS Pub 1 Definition: Air action against hostile targets in close proximity to friendly forces and which require detailed integration of each air mission with the fire and movement of those forces. In a "classic" case, CAS is air used as a supporting arm against targets that are directly effecting ground operations; CAS is support to "troops in contact." Integration is normally through a specially trained Forward Air Controller (FAC).

216

Often, CAS missions were defined as those conducted inside the fire support coordination line (FSCL),[116] while those beyond the FSCL were considered air interdiction[117] or battlefield air interdiction.[118]

Even a cursory look at the number of different criteria used to document CAS missions during Desert Storm highlights the problem of definitions. The Central Command Air Force commander called missions inside the fire support coordination line CAS missions and all others outside the line, AI missions, which deleted BAI as a type of mission.[119] The Center for Naval Analyses in its reconstruction of Marine air operations also used the FSCL as a rough divider between CAS and deep air support missions.[120] The Institute for Defense Analysis took the position

---

[116]JCS Pub 1 Definition: A line established by the appropriate ground commander to ensure coordination of fire that is not under his control but may affect current tactical operations. The fire support coordination line is used to coordinate fires of air, ground, or sea weapon systems using any type of ammunition against surface targets. The fire support coordination line should follow well defined terrain features. The establishment of the fire support coordination line must be coordinated with the appropriate tactical air commander and other supporting elements. Supporting elements may attack targets forward of the fire support coordination line without prior coordination with the ground force commander, provided the attack will not produce adverse surface effects on, or to the rear of, the line. Attacks against surface targets behind this line must be coordinated with the appropriate ground force commander.

[117]JCS Pub 1 Definition: Air operations conducted to destroy, neutralize, or delay the enemy's military potential before it can be brought to bear effectively against friendly forces, at such distance from friendly forces that detailed integration of each air mission with the fire and movement of friendly forces is not required.

[118]HQ AAFCE Manual 80-3, "Conventional Offensive Operations Planing Guide," Definition: Air action against hostile surface targets that are in a position to directly affect friendly forces and which require joint planning and coordination. While BAI missions require coordination in joint planning, they may not require continuous coordination during the execution stage. And TAC/TRADOC Pamphlet, "General Operating Procedures for Joint Attack of the Second Echelon (J-SAK)" Definition: Air Interdiction (AI) attacks against land force targets that have a near-term effect on the operations or scheme of maneuver of friendly forces, but are not in close proximity to friendly forces, are referred to as Battlefield Air Interdiction (BAI). The primary difference between BAI and the remainder of the air interdiction effort is the near-term effect and influence produced against the enemy in support of the land component commander's scheme of maneuver.

[119](S) "Concept of Operations for Command and Control of TACAIR in Support of Land Forces," CENTAF/DO, 22 Feb 1991.

[120](S) Center for Naval Analyses, "Marine Corps Desert Storm Reconstruction Report Vol IV: Third Marine Aircraft Wing Operations," Alexandria, VA, p 67.

that a tactical air strike in the KTO under forward air controller (FAC) control was CAS, while one not under FAC control was BAI.[121] Arguments over definitions were not simply a sterile exercise in terminology. Definitions were important to the commanders involved because they determined who set the priorities for aviation, who picked the targets, which weapon systems were employed, and which tactics were therefore used.

Battle of Khafji

Although the battle of Khafji absorbed only a small portion of Coalition air assets, it provided the first real challenge to the responsiveness of the CAS/BAI capabilities. The battle was important not because of the size of the force or the actual battle, but because of what it told Coalition forces about the Iraqis. On the evening of 29 January 1991, Iraqi forces crossed the border in three places: Ras Al Khafji, Wafrah, and Umm Hujul (Observation Post-4). Coalition forces, particularly Saudi ground forces in conjunction with the 3d Marine Air Wing and the Joint Force Air Component Command, successfully repelled the attacks. A wide variety of aviation assets were used at the battle of Khafji; unmanned aerial vehicles and the Joint Surveillance Target Attack Radar system to provide near real-time target information, a wide variety of platforms for signals intelligence, and AC-130 Spectre Gunships, AH-1 Cobras, A-10s, AV-8Bs, F/A-18s, B-52s, and F-16s for interdiction, CAS, and close-in fire-support missions.[122]

At the request of the Marine Commander, Lieutenant General Boomer, and with the approval of Lieutenant General Horner, CENTAF, a B-52 strike and two tactical air packages were diverted from Republican Guard targets to southern Kuwait where Iraqi armor was moving to reinforce the initial Iraqi penetration. The tactics employed, while not standard, resulted in a successful attack on approximately one-hundred Iraqi armored vehicles. As described in a field report, the effect of the B-52 strike was "like turning on a light in a cockroach infested apartment." The B-52 strike sent the vehicles scurrying for survival only to find that their movement was awaited by tactical air, eager to "squish

---

[121](S) *IDA Document D-1080*, p 16.

[122](S) MARCENT SitReps, 29 Jan - 2 Feb 1991.

them like bugs."[123] For additional information about the battle of Khafji, see the *Operations and Effects* report.

The purpose of the Coalition ground offensive was to cut lines of communications, destroy Republican Guard forces, and liberate Kuwait.[124] Preparations for the ground offensive moved into the final phase on 22 February, two days before G-Day, as Coalition forces moved into attack positions and the already significant air support being devoted to battlefield preparation moved into high gear. Table 9 shows the number of CAS/AI and direct support missions flown by Air Force and Marine Corps aircraft from 22 February to the cease fire. Figures do not include all Coalition missions flown on these days, i.e., CAP, Scud hunting, etc. After one-hundred hours of ground war, Iraq capitulated at 0800 on 28 February 1991.

<hr/>

[123](S) USCINCCENT, Sitrep, 012115Z Feb 91 and TACC notes, dated 30-31 Jan 91, 1900-2100 hours, by TSgt Hosterman.

[124]USCINCCENT OPLAN, Desert Storm, dated 16 Dec 90.

Table 9[125]
Close Air Support/Interdiction Sorties by Day

Air Force Aircraft	22	23	24	25	26	27	28
OA-10	21	20	22	22	19	21	4
A-10	175	208	216	212	220	207	26
F-15E	52	51	60	56	80	56	4
F-16A/C	305	310	275	312	342	274	8
F-111F	71	62	69	64	59	55	
B-52	51	43	47	47	37	29	

Marine Corps Aircraft	22	23	24	25	26	27	28
A6-E	32	35	38	35	26	2	1
OV-10	16	21	23	24	24	9	1
EA-6B	16	16	16	16	15	5	2
AV-8B	136	211	174	152	186	63	0
F/A-18	192	204	175	135	166	102	4

Tactical Aircraft (TACAIR)[126]

Since most CAS/BAI missions were flown by Air Force and
Marine Corps TACAIR, this discussion will begin with those aircraft. The

---

[125]Sortie data extracted from the (S/NF/WN/NC) GWAPS Composite Sorties Data
Base. Sortie numbers, while generally close, do not always agree with those generated
for other studies. Variations in numbers appear to result from the use of different source
documents and the application of different definitions to CAS/BAI/AI. The numbers, while
open to possible debate, are relevant because they reflect order of magnitude efforts
devoted to particular missions. OV-10 sorties were listed as C³ and EA-6B sorties were
listed as EW.

[126]Except where specifically attributed to another source, the basic information in
this section, particularly the data on Air Force and Marine Corps aircraft, was extracted
liberally from (S) *IDA Document D-1080* and (S/NF/WN/NC) *Tactical Analysis Bulletin*,
Vol 91-2.

220

effective suppression of the Iraqi radar-guided SAM threat made antiaircraft artillery (AAA) and infrared SAMs the primary threats. As a result, operations at medium altitudes were most survivable, and after Day 3 of the war, medium-altitude tactics were used almost exclusively. These tactics were a departure from the much exercised low-level weapons delivery that had been in vogue throughout the U.S. armed forces for many years. Fortunately, in many cases, Desert Shield allowed aircrews time to refine their medium-altitude tactics.

U.S. Air Force - OA-10 Forward Air Control (Airborne)[127]

The OA-10s were used primarily to acquire targets from medium altitude (above 10,000 feet). Two-ship employment was preferred for mutual support. But, because of the limited number (twelve) of OA-10s in theater, usually only one was on station at a time. Single aircraft formations increased vulnerability and made low-altitude target identification passes dangerous. OA-10 crews were left with two undesirable options: descend unprotected into the AAA and IR SAM threat envelope, or wait for the fighters to arrive to provide cover. When the first option was adopted, two OA-10s were lost and a third was seriously damaged. Waiting for fighters, the second option, wasted the time of attacking aircraft, but was considered the best option in more highly defended areas. The OA-10 used the 30-mm gun with high explosive incendiary (HEI) ammunition to mark targets.

U.S. Air Force A-10

A-10s usually flew in two-ship formations for combat missions. In high-threat areas, A-10s were sometimes packaged in groups of from four to eight aircraft, accompanied by EF-111 and F-4G aircraft. The A-10s were used to attack armor, artillery, trucks, and other targets.

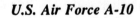

[127]The information on OA-10 and A-10 tactics was drawn from (S) *IDA Document D-1080*, pp 25-32 and (S/NF/WN/NC) *Tactical Analysis Bulletin*, Vol 91-2, Chapter 6-1.

The preferred munition against armor was the AGM-65 Maverick missile. The typical attack profile of an aircraft carrying the electro-optical Maverick (AGM-65B) started with a 30-degree dive from an altitude of between from 10,000 and 15,000 feet; the aircraft then fired a single missile at two- to three-nautical miles slant range from the target. Approximately 30 percent of the Mavericks shot were the electro-optical version. The typical attack profile with the imaging infrared (IIR) Maverick (AGM-65D) started at 15,000 to 20,000 feet with a 20- to 30-degree dive; a single missile was fired at four- to five-nautical miles slant range. The A-10s fired approximately 90 percent of the over 5,000 Mavericks used during the Gulf War; about half of the Mavericks fired were the IIR version.

The GAU-8, a 30-mm Gatling Gun, was also effective against armor when fired from an aircraft in a 45- to 60-degree dive from below 10,000 feet.[128]   Aircraft usually fired 150-200 uranium-core armor piercing rounds, using one long or two short bursts. The gun fired at a rate of 2,100 shots per minute; shell velocity was 3,747 feet per second.

A-10 pilots, using medium-altitude release tactics, had difficulty hitting armor with MK-20 Rockeyes. To compensate, they selected a ripple release mode that released all weapons on one pass against a single target. Steeper dive angles generally produced more accurate deliveries, but bad weather frequently caused pilots to use shallower dive angles.

The preferred munition for attacking artillery was a MK-82 fuzed for an air burst. The standard tactic was to ripple release all bombs against a single target. The normal dive angle was 45- to 60-degrees at 400 knots. The MK-82 was also used against trucks and other soft-skinned vehicles.

Cluster Bomb Units (CBUs) were also ripple released against a single target. The attack run was normally a 45- to 60-degree dive, with bomb release starting at 10,000 to 12,000 feet. CBUs were used against soft targets, vehicles, personnel in the open, and artillery.

Night CAS was restricted to using freefall munitions delivered parallel to the front lines to minimize the possibility of friendly fire casualties.

---

[128](S/NF/WN/NC) *Tactical Analysis Bulletin*, Vol 91-2, p 6-6.

Maverick attacks were permitted if over two kilometers from friendlies; guns when over one kilometer from friendlies. The A-10s were all equipped with the PAVE PENNY[129] system, but very few pilots had an opportunity to use the system on a CAS mission. The A-10s were also limited during night attacks by not having OA-10s available to find targets, since they did not operate at night. Most night targets were fixed artillery, fixed armor, and moving convoys. The A-10s used the IIR Mavericks and/or flares to aid in acquiring targets at night. The aircraft delivering weapons normally released them while in a shallower dive and from lower altitudes than in day attacks because of the reduced effectiveness of Iraqi AAA and IR missiles at night.

U.S. Marine Corps OV-10 FAC(A)[130]

Usually, the twenty Marine Corps OV-10s flew FAC missions inside the FSCL and conducted radio relay and visual reconnaissance missions. Because of an early combat loss, the OV-10 was restricted to flying over friendly territory. With the start of the ground war, OV-10s maintained twenty-four-hour coverage of the battlefield. The OV-10 also laser-designated targets for Marine AV-8s. The OV-10's night capability was due primarily to its FLIR sensor.[131]

---

[129]The AN/ASS-35(V) PAVE PENNY laser receiver/tracker was operational on all the A-10 aircraft used in Desert Storm. PAVE PENNY was a day and night target detection set used to detect the reflected energy from a laser designator. Used in conjunction with a laser designation system (either ground-based or in cooperation aircraft), it can rapidly designate specific targets for attack. The system provides accurate steering data on the HUD to assist the pilot in delivering unguided or laser-guided weapons.

[130]The information on OV-10 tactics was drawn primarily from (S) IDA Document D-1080, pp 32-33, unless otherwise noted.

[131]Of the 20 Marine OV-10s deployed to Desert Storm, 11 had the AN/AAS-37 FLIR nose-mounted in the aircraft. The rotating ball turret mount provided almost full lower hemisphere coverage (elevation coverage was from minus 82° to plus 16°). The total system weight was about 420 pounds. The FLIR had two fields-of-view: 15 x 20° and (for higher-magnification) 5 x 6.7°. The real-time IR picture was displayed on a TV monitor in the cockpit. The system also included a laser ranger and illuminator for designating targets.

U.S. Marine Corps AV-8B[132]

 A total of 86 AV-8B Harriers were deployed to Southwest Asia. Land-based AV-8Bs were equipped with a 25-mm Gatling gun and carried a typical combat bomb load of six MK-82s or four MK-83s or six MK-20 Rockeyes. In addition to the gun, ship-based Harriers normally carried four MK-82s, or two MK-83s, or four MK-20s. To maintain a high sortie rate during the ground assault, the aircraft refueled and rearmed at Tanajib, only five minutes from the Kuwait border.

AV-8B pilots delivered primarily MK-82s and Rockeyes using medium- to high-altitude dive bombing tactics. They used MK-82s against artillery, trucks, and other soft targets and Rockeyes against armored and light armored vehicles. Early problems with delivering MK-20s were corrected and accuracy improved as the war progressed. MK-83s with nose plugs and delayed fuzes were used against bunkers and similar hardened targets. Guns were employed mainly to suppress low-level point defenses during delivery of other weapons. The AV-8Bs also used their guns to strafe targets at the Battle of Khafji. The pilots used an inertial navigation system combined with a shallow dive to find the assigned target and the heads-up display video to assess battle damage. AV-8B tactics are also discussed in the push flow and artillery raids portions of this section.

Target location and control of sorties beyond the FSCL were accomplished by a variety of means, chief among them AWACS, ABCCC, Fast FAC, Killer Scouts, and Joint STARS. Targets beyond the FSCL included assembly areas, road convoys, command posts, artillery, mobile rocket launchers, and surface-to-surface missiles (FROGs and Scuds); and maneuver forces such as tanks, APCs, and other mechanized equipment.

---

[132]The information on AV-8B tactics was drawn primarily from (S) *IDA Document D-1080*, pp 33-34.

U.S. Air Force F-16 "Killer Scouts"[133]

During Desert Storm F-16 missions included day air interdiction, Low-Altitude Navigation and Targeting Infrared (system) for Night (LANTIRN) operations, armed reconnaissance, and "Killer Scouts." For a variety of reasons an airborne platform was stationed in the interdiction area to validate ATO targets and, when required, to find new targets. From sunrise to sunset, GPS-equipped F-16 "Killer Scouts" flew this mission. The Scouts patrolled kill boxes and essentially flew armed reconnaissance missions. They carried a mix of ordnance to mark targets, conduct SEAD, and kill fleeting targets. The Scouts normally updated the target location, provided an overall ground situation brief, and marked the target before passing it over to incoming attack aircraft.

U.S. Air Force F-16 Tactics

The F-16s dropped primarily general-purpose, unguided ordnance by using a 30- to 60-degree, high-altitude dive bomb release procedures. These medium-altitude deliveries effectively negated the Iraqi AAA and IR SAM threats. If SAMs were seen, they could be defeated by a combination of flares and evasive maneuvers. But, medium-altitude weapon accuracy was less than desired, resulting, at least initially, in weapons falling short of the target and unpredictable scatter patterns.

The two LANTIRN-equipped F-16 squadrons achieved almost as good results at night at they did during the day.[134] GPS combined with the lower delivery altitudes achievable with LANTIRN were responsible for the increased bombing accuracy at night. The normal F-16 night package was two aircraft, with the wingman flying 1,000 to 2,000 feet above and 1 to 4 miles behind the lead aircraft. Aircraft flew with lights off and used the forward-looking infrared/heads-up display (FLIR/HUD) to maintain

---

[133]The information on F-16 tactics was drawn primarily from (S) *IDA Document D-1080*, pp 43-47 and (S/NF/WN/NC) *Tactical Analysis Bulletin*, Vol 91-2, Chapter 4-1.

[134]The F-16C carried the LANTIRN navigational pod externally either under a wing or fuselage. The pod contained a wide field of view FLIR and terrain-following radar, together with the associated power supply, pod control computer, and environmental system. The FLIR imagery from the pod was displayed on a wide field-of-view holographic heads-up display. The purpose was to allow the pilot to acquire the target and deliver unguided munitions at night with accuracy similar to daytime attack.

position. They usually carried free-fall munitions along with an occasional IIR Maverick. Typical targets for the LANTIRN-equipped F-16s were bridges, bunkers, armor, and artillery.

A typical F-16 weapon load was six MK-82s or two MK-84s, or four CBUs. In daytime, ordnance was released by using the continuously computed impact point system. At night, the F-16s used the FLIR to find targets and released weapons at a nominal altitude of 10,000 to 12,000 feet while in a 30-degree dive. They used higher altitudes and steeper dive angles against the same targets in the daytime. Night attacks were considered safer because of Iraqi difficulty in acquiring the aircraft and the aircrews' improved ability to see and therefore avoid AAA and IR SAMs.

U.S. Marine Corps F/A-18D Fast FACs[135]

The F/A-18D aircraft flew primarily Fast FAC missions in Desert Storm; a significant number of these missions were flown at night. They conducted visual or tactical reconnaissance of the battlefield and reported back to the ground commanders almost immediately on sighting major hostile force movements or hot spots. Generally, F/A-18Ds performed FAC missions for deeper strikes, while OV-10s acted as FACs for CAS missions. All F/A-18D aircraft had a FLIR targeting system. The system was designed to provide the aircraft with a day, night, and limited adverse weather attack capability. It presented the pilot with real-time thermal imagery for locating, identifying, and attacking tactical targets.

Pilots sometimes located daytime targets by using binoculars, marked the targets with 5-inch Zuni white phosphorous rockets and passed the target locations to a flight of attack aircraft. Battlefield familiarity helped F/A-18Ds perform their FAC missions. At night, pilots used night vision goggles, navigation FLIR, digital color moving maps, and some targeting FLIRs. Procedures were similar to those employed during the day.

---

[135]The information on F/A-18 tactics was drawn primarily from (S) *IDA Document D-1080*, pp 47-49.

226

U.S. Marine Corps F/A-18A/C

F/A-18A/C employed tactics similar to those of the AV-8B. Aircraft flew at ingress altitudes as high as 30,000 feet and dive angles of 10- to 20-degrees until target acquisition. Upon target acquisition, the dive angle steepened to about 45-degrees with a recovery altitude of 14,000 feet, later reduced to 12,000 and finally to 10,000 feet. Reduced enemy capabilities and poor visibility were reasons why aircrews flew at lower altitudes as the war progressed. The F/A-18A/Cs favored a mix of MK-80 series bombs and MK-20 Rockeyes. Marine aircraft dropped a total of 15,828 Rockeyes against armor, artillery, and antipersonnel targets.[136] As the war progressed and the threat diminished, aircraft flew at lower altitudes, thereby correcting Rockeye delivery problems and high dud rates. By the later phases of the war, the Marines considered MK-20 a flexible, effective weapon. F/A-18A/Cs also fired a few antiarmor Maverick missiles. The typical F/A-18 combat bomb load was a gun plus either six MK-82s, four MK-83s, or four MK-20s. Additionally, F/A-18A/Cs performed SEAD with HARM missiles.

U.S. Marine Corps A-6[137]

The night, all-weather capabilities of the Marine Corps' A-6Es allowed them to fly 98.8 percent of their 850 Gulf War sorties at night. A typical weapon load for the A-6E was 11 MK-82s or MK-20s and one laser-guided bomb, usually a GBU-16. A-6Es were tasked to attack specific targets or targets within a designated Kill box. Normally operating as single aircraft, the A-6E used its radar to navigate and locate and attack fixed targets while using its moving target indicator mode to locate and attack

---

[136]GWAPS *Statistical Compendium*, Table 190, "Desert Shield/Storm: USMC Weapons Cost and Utilization (FY 91$)."

[137]The information on A-6E tactics was drawn primarily from (S) *IDA Document D-1080*, pp 49-51.

moving targets. The A-6E also used its target recognition and attack multisensor[138] as an integrated day and night weapon delivery system.

Normal A-6E ingress and target acquisition was at altitudes between 25,000 and 30,000 feet. The bombardier/navigator (B/N) used the aircraft radar to acquire the target and the boresighted FLIR sensor to bring the target into close-up view. Once the target was satisfactorily acquired, the B/N lased the target for LGBs.

U.S. Air Force F-15E[139]

Both of the F-15E squadrons deployed to Southwest Asia were equipped with LANTIRN navigational pods, whereas only a handful of LANTIRN targeting pods were used during Desert Storm.[140] Aircraft with targeting pods normally carried eight GBU-12s when flying armor missions. When only one aircraft had a targeting pod, "buddy lasing" was used, or the aircraft without the pod carried free-fall ordnance, such as twelve MK-82s or six CBU-87/89s or four MK-84s, or four GBU-10s. Targets included bridges, Scuds, C3I nodes, bunkers, and fixed armor.

Almost all F-15E sorties were flown at night. The LANTIRN system allowed aircrews to locate targets at night, hit them with LGBs, and obtain real-time bomb damage assessment. Although the F-15Es flew an assortment of missions, about one-third were tank-busting or "tank-plinking" sorties. The preferred ordnance for these missions was the GBU-12. Most attacks were from medium altitude with weapons release at between 12,000 and 14,000 feet. Altitudes changed depending on weather and threat conditions.

---

[138]This system included a forward-looking infrared sensor, a laser designator/ranger and a laser receiver. The equipment was contained in a precision stabilized turret mounted under the nose of the aircraft. The system was designed to provide target acquisition and guidance capabilities for a wide range of laser-guided weapons.

[139]The information on F-15E tactics was drawn primarily from (S) *IDA Document D-1080*, pp 51-53 and (S/NF/WN/NC) *Tactical Analysis Bulletin*, Vol 91-2, Chapter 3-1.

[140]The AN/AAQ-14 targeting pod contained a stabilization system, wide and narrow field-of-view FLIR, laser designator/ranger, automatic multimode tracker, automatic infrared Maverick missile hand-off system, environmental control unit, pod control computer, and power supply.

U.S. Air Force F-111F[141]

 As with F-15Es, F-111Fs were used to conduct a variety of missions, mostly at night. The missions, after the first few days of the war, were conducted primarily from medium altitude. The principal targets were bridges, bunkers, armor, and artillery. The weapons of choice were LGBs, and the F-111F was the only aircraft to employ the GBU-15 glide bomb. This munition destroyed the oil storage tank manifolds, halting the flow of oil into the Gulf. Typical combat munitions loads for the F-111F were eight CBUs or twelve MK-82s or four MK-84s, or four GBUs. For tank-plinking missions, the weapon of choice was again the GBU-12. In addition to the GBU-15, F-111Fs were the only aircraft to drop GBU-24s and GBU-28s.

All F-111F squadrons were equipped with the infrared Pave Tack system,[142] which employed FLIR target acquisition sensors and laser designation/ranging.[143] The Pave Tack sensor had full lower hemisphere coverage, giving the aircrew nearly total freedom in choosing flight paths. Once tracking was initiated, the target was lased for laser-guided munitions. The Pave Tack computer also aided in delivery computations for unguided munitions. The F-111F used its onboard virtual image display (VID) to show radar, FLIR, and weapons data, which was normally recorded for postmission bomb damage assessment.[144]

---

[141]The information on F-111F tactics was drawn primarily from (S) *IDA Document D-1080*, pp 53-56 and (S/NF/WN/NC) *Tactical Analysis Bulletin*, Vol 91-2, Chapter 7-1.

[142]The F-111F carried a large, 1,300-pound Pave Tack pod under the fuselage aft of the nose gear. The pod was in two major sections. The fixed-base section contained the aircraft interface unit, computer, power supplies, cooling system, the CRT interface, and the video-tape recorder, which recorded the crew's video display and provided bomb damage assessment. The rotating head section contained the FLIR, laser, and range receiver, and allowed full lower hemisphere coverage.

[143]The FLIR and the laser were boresighted. The stabilized FLIR imagery provided a wide field-of-view (176 x 132 mrad) display for target acquisition and had a narrow field-of-view (44 x 33 mrad) with 3-power magnification for target identification and tracking.

[144]The aircraft capable of recording bomb impact points (F-111F, F-15E, and F-117 units) kept and distributed their own bomb damage assessment within and between the units.

In addition to the platforms discussed above, Navy and Coalition TACAIR and other aviation platforms directly and indirectly supported the ground effort. Navy and Coalition TACAIR flew only approximately fifty CAS/BAI missions in support of the ground offensive. There is no indication that the weapons or the tactics used by these aircrews differed in any significant respect from those just described. The tactics used by the Navy against maritime targets will be discussed later in this section. Air Force B-52s flew tactical missions in support of the Battlefield Preparation Phase of the war. Electronic warfare, tanker, command and control, reconnaissance, and other specialized aircraft also supported the ground offensive. Additionally, unmanned aerial vehicles and both Army and Marine Corps attack helicopters played significant roles.

B-52s

B-52s flew 1,741 missions and dropped 27,000 tons of munitions, which amounted to 30 percent of the overall Gulf War tonnage. The bomber's long-range capability was demonstrated on the third day of the war when 7 B-52s launched from Wurtsmith AFB in Michigan, bombed Republican Guard targets in the KTO, and landed in the theater.[145]

B-52s attacked mostly large area targets, dropping unguided general-purpose and cluster bombs from above 30,000 feet. Targets included "dug in" armored units, suspected Scud storage and production facilities, and troop concentrations. However, their main effort (37 percent of all B-52 sorties flown) was against the Republican Guard.[146]

B-52 support must be measured not just in terms of direct hits or physical damage but also in terms of the psychological effects it produced. Recognizing the impact of these bombing missions, General Schwarzkopf directed the B-52s to focus on the Republican Guard. The

---

[145](S/NF/WN/RD) *History of the Strategic Air Command*, p 252.

[146](S/NF/WN/RD) *Ibid*, p 253.

result was a three-ship formation of bombers striking troops in the KTO every three hours, twenty-four-hours a day.[147]

[DELETED] [148]

B-52s conducted four distinct missions during the Gulf War: attacking strategic fixed targets, Scud hunting, attacking Iraqi Army and Republican Guard targets, and supporting breaching operations.[149] [DELETED].[150] [DELETED].

To prepare the battlefield for the ground assault, B-52s dropped dual-fuzed MK-82s designed to break up barriers, berms, and obstacles such as multistrand concertina wire. Near the end of the war, B-52s dropped CBU-87s on Iraqi tank and vehicle columns along the highways leading north out of Kuwait.[151]

Unmanned Aerial Vehicles (UAVs)

The employment of UAVs during Desert Storm was the first time U.S. forces used them in combat. There were three UAV systems: the Pioneer, the Pointer, and the Exdrone. UAVs were operated by the Army, Navy and Marine Corps. The real-time battlefield surveillance and detection capabilities of the UAVs directly enhanced the targeting of both fixed and mobile targets and affected the employment of CAS/BAI and close-in-fire support (CIFS) assets.

---

[147]Intvw with Capt Rich Cleary and Capt Jim Wright, B-52 Planners for USCENTAF Strategic Forces, conducted on 1-2 Sep 92.

[148](S/NF/WN/RD) *Ibid*, pp 265-268.

[149](S/NF) Maj John Masotti, "Operation Desert Shield and Desert Storm Bomber Story," Hq SAC/DOBX, 18 Sep 1991, pp 32, 33.

[150][DELETED]

[151](S) *IDA Document D-1080*, p 57.

The Marine Corps deployed seventy-nine AH-1s to Southwest Asia. Typical AH-1 missions included antiarmor, close-in fire support, armed reconnaissance, and helicopter escort. Poor weather, blowing smoke, and the rapid advance of the ground forces all combined to make classic "troops in contact" CAS difficult and unnecessary in most cases. But, on those occasions when troops in contact did need support, the Cobra gunships used extraordinary tactics and techniques to provide it. Marine AH-1s, in coordination with other Coalition aircraft, also played a significant role in repulsing the numerous Iraqi incursions into Saudi Arabia (Khafji) during the period 29 January to 2 February 1992.

The First Marine Division used the AH-1s en masse; they used them in conjunction with light armored vehicles and occasionally AV-8Bs as an additional maneuver element, called Task Force Cunningham.[152]

On G+2, AH-1s and a UH-1 supported Task Force Ripper in the battle with the Iraqi 3d Armored Division. The UH-1N with FLIR and a laser designator capability led two divisions of Cobras through smoke and under power lines to attack Iraqi forces facing the Marines. The Huey designated targets for the Cobras' Hellfire missiles. On another occasion, Cobras worked with light armored vehicles to thwart an Iraqi mechanized infantry brigade counterattack against the 1st Marine Division's command post.[153] During Desert Shield, Marine AH-1Ws fired Hellfire missiles with targeting and laser spotting assistance from Army OH-58Ds. Although successfully exercised before the war, there is no evidence the tactic was actually employed during Desert Storm. This nonuse was probably due to a scarcity of OH-58Ds.[154]

---

[152]Intvw with Maj Gen J. M. Myatt, USMC, "The 1st Marine Division in the Attack," *Naval Institute Proceedings*, Nov. 1991, pp 71-75. Gen Myatt organized his assets into Task Forces.

[153]*Ibid.*

[154]U.S. Army Aviation Center, Coordinating Draft, *Operation Desert Shield/Storm After Action Report*, 22 Nov 1991, p 9.

Army Attack Helicopters

The Army deployed approximately 145 AH-1 Cobras, 130 OH-58D Kiowa Warriors, and 277 AH-64 Apache attack helicopters to Southwest Asia.[155] They carried out armed reconnaissance, antiarmor, and helicopter escort missions. Additionally, the Army made extensive use of massed attack helicopters as integrated maneuver elements,[156] and conducted large armed reconnaissance missions jointly with U.S. Air Force CAS and support aircraft. Army attack helicopters worked with USAF A-10s, F-16s, EF-111s, Compass Call, Wild Weasels, and J-STARS.[157] Army attack helicopters conducted numerous long-range missions into Iraq, some out to approximately 100 miles.[158] Most of these missions were joint Army-Air Force undertakings involving tactics never previously practiced. When Army helicopters needed TACAIR, they would typically request it through the AWACS onguard frequency.[159] Army attack helicopters, especially Apaches, regularly scouted and screened for ground forces. Major General Griffith, CG 1st Armored Division, reflected the attitude of the Army commanders when he said, "I don't want another minute to go by without Apaches out in front of this division."[160] The Army was able to employ the Apaches in this role because of the unique capabilities of the aircraft, the scheme of maneuver of the Coalition ground forces, and the disposition of the Iraqis.

"Push flow"

In support of the land components, CENTAF initiated a push flow system of TACAIR to generate large numbers of sorties in a target-rich environment. The system called for aircraft to launch in accordance with a time schedule to achieve an advertized CAS sortie flow rate per hour.

---

[155]U.S. Army Aviation Center, Draft Report, *Army Aviation in Desert Shield/Storm*, Ft Rucker, AL, 8 Jun 1992. Figures on number of attack helicopters in theater from pp 42, 210, 39, respectively. It should be noted that figures do not appear to agree with summary chart on p 26.

[156]*Ibid*, p 34.

[157]*Ibid*, p 35.

[158]*Ibid*, pp 34, 72.

[159]*Ibid*, p 35.

[160]*Ibid*, p 206.

Sorties without an appropriate CAS target were normally directed to the ABCCC for an AI mission. In all cases, the objective was to keep aircraft moving through the system to provide land component commanders with a ready supply of air support. A tactical air control center (TACC) log entry sums up the thinking behind establishment of the push flow system. "When asked, What air is where? Answer, There is a continuous flow of anything you want anywhere you want it."[161]

U.S. Marine Corps Push CAS[162]

The Marine Corps adapted the push CAS system to ensure adequate air support to Marine ground forces. The 3d Marine Aircraft Wing began surge operations using the system on 22 February, two days before the start of the ground assault. The push CAS system called for aircraft to launch according to a specific schedule, but without a specific mission or target. Aircraft checked in with the Marine tactical air command center and the tactical air operations center and were then passed to the direct air support center. After checking in with the direct air support center, they preceded to the "main stack" to fill requests for CAS missions. Figure 50 illustrates the locations of the various holding points, orbits, and aircraft operating areas referred to in the description of the push CAS system. If the aircraft were not used for a CAS mission within a specified period of time (seven and one-half minutes during the day and fifteen minutes at night), they were handed off to the direct airborne support center for further handoff to a Fast FAC for deep air support (DAS). The goals of the procedures were to maintain control and continue to "push" aircraft to missions.

Joint Force Air Component Commander (JFACC) air was used primarily beyond the FSCL. JFACC air would contact the Marine tactical air operations center for deconfliction and would then be sent to one of two JFACC stacks. Navy aircraft were sent to the East stack and Air Force aircraft were sent to the West stack. JFACC aircraft contacted the

---

[161](S) "Concept of Operations for Command and Control of TACAIR in support of Land Forces," CENTAF/DO, 22 Feb 1991.

[162]"Push CAS" procedures were promulgated in 3d MAW msg 201630 Feb 1991, "Coordinating Instructions for Third MAW Air Control Procedures for Operation Desert Storm." The description of how the Marine Corps implemented the "Push CAS" system is from the (S) CNA Rpt, Vol IV, Third Marine Aircraft Wing Operations."

Figure 50
Push CAS System

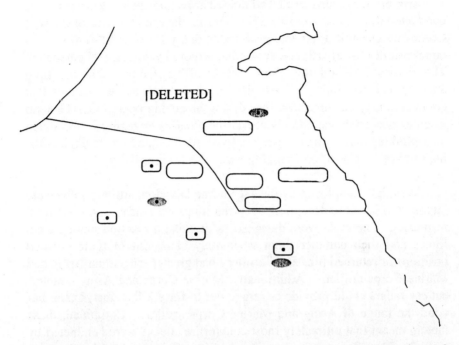

[DELETED]

airborne direct air support center en route to their assigned stacks and were handed off to a Fast FAC. To ensure that the system was understood by all concerned, messages were sent, liaison visits were held, briefings were conducted, and the plan was first flown on 12 February. The plan called for surge operations to begin approximately two days before G-Day.

East and West CAP stations were manned continuously by electronic warfare assets. These aircraft were available to conduct electronic support measures, jam surveillance and counterbattery radars, jam early warning and SAM radars, and fire HARMS. OV-10s provided twenty-four-hour coverage of three positions. They were used for TAC(A)/FAC(A) missions. F/A-18Ds were used exclusively in a Fast FAC role. During daylight, these aircraft flew two Fast FAC orbits continuously. At night, the intent was to provide one Fast FAC for thirty minutes out of each hour. Plans called for A-6Es to be used exclusively at night in the CAS/DAS/armed reconnaissance role. F/A-18A/Cs and AV-8Bs also flowed through this push CAS system, beginning when the ground forces moved into their attack positions.

Artillery Raids[163]

Artillery raids, also termed combined arms raids by the Marines, were conducted throughout Desert Storm. During the initial phases of the war, Command General, First Marine Expeditionary Force (I MEF) directed a target priority list of artillery, armor and armored vehicles, and personnel. The rationale behind this prioritization of targets was that the Iraqi artillery had the ability to mass fire and deliver chemical weapons that could seriously endanger Marines during breaching operations. General Boomer was so concerned about Marine aviators engaging in too much tank-plinking that he made a personal visit to the squadrons to explain the importance he placed on stripping away the Iraqi artillery.

As initially employed by the 1st Marine Division, artillery raids were intended to promote deception, keep the Iraqis off balance, and test Iraqi responses. The raids were designed to provoke a reaction among Iraqi forces and then hammer them when they came out of their fortified positions or returned fire. Iraqi artillery had greater range than Army and Marine Corps artillery. Additionally, Marine Corps and Army counterbattery radars could provide coverage out to forty kilometers; again, beyond the range of Army and Marine Corps artillery. Combined, these factors meant that ultimately most counterfire attacks were conducted by aircraft. The almost immediate availability of air provided by the push CAS or push flow system made aerial attack of targets easy to arrange.

Marine EA-6Bs supported counterfire operations by jamming Iraqi counterbattery radars. Marines learned that the enemy quickly returned fire if fired upon; they also learned that Iraqi artillery fire was woefully inaccurate. Buoyed by this knowledge, Marine artillery moved forward and fired. Counterbattery radars, Fast FACs, and attack aircraft all waited until the Iraqis returned fire, then located the Iraqi artillery and attacked. Enemy prisoner of war reports indicated that the certainty of counterfire was so pervasive that Iraqi cannoneers frequently pulled their lanyard once and then "ran like hell" to get to protected positions before the "iron

---

[163]Most of the information on Combined Arms or Artillery Raids was gathered from Marine Corps Research Center, Research Paper #92-0007, "Fire Support/Coordination During Desert Storm."

236

rain" began. When the ground assault began, I MEF target priorities began to shift, and the nature of the artillery raids changed; but the tactics used to conduct counterfire operations remained basically the same.

Maritime Operations: Attacking the Iraqi Navy

At the beginning of the war, the Iraqi Navy had approximately 178 vessels, 13 of which could fire surface-to-surface STYX or Exocet missiles. They also had 5 sets of equipment to fire the Silkworm missile, a coastal defense weapon. The Silkworms were of particular concern to the amphibious forces as preparations continued for a possible amphibious assault. Neutralizing the Silkworm threat came under the purview of two commanders; CENTAF, in his capacity as the Joint Forces Air Component Commander, and NAVCENT, who considered defeating the Iraqi's Silkworm threat an element of Battle Force defense.

The JFACC, through his Strategic Planning Cell, set up a Naval target category. Targets included naval bases, port facilities, and Silkworm sites; it grew to include twenty-one targets. These targets were scheduled in the ATO, and the tactics used to attack them were similar to those used on other ground targets.

On the maritime side, the Anti-Surface Unit Warfare Commander (ASUWC) of the Composite Warfare Commander structure was the officer charged with defending the Battle Group against surface threats. Normally, his role was defensive in nature—conducting search programs to identify possible threats, then requesting the Strike Warfare Commander to conduct an attack to destroy or neutralize the threat. Beginning 21 January 1991, the ASUWC in the Gulf developed a new, more aggressive tactic. Instead of using patrol aircraft, he used armed attack aircraft to conduct armed surface reconnaissance (ASR) missions, and their task was to immediately attack any surface vessel identified as Iraqi. A surface ship in the Northern Gulf was in charge of the effort and was assisted by either a P-3 Orion or a British Nimrod patrol aircraft.

The A-6 Intruders were the aircraft most often used in this armed surface reconnaissance role, although F/A-18s were also used. The normal weapons load for an A-6E mission was one GBU-12 laser-guided bomb and two MK-20 Rockeyes. This load could be brought back to the carriers if not delivered, and weapon deliveries were normally from level flight. Since there was a reduced AAA threat at sea, the aircraft worked at lower altitudes. Silkworm missile sites were also attacked by armed surface reconnaissance aircraft. If a Silkworm site became active, the ASUWC would divert the aircraft to strike. In this way, the Silkworm sites, targets of a fleeting nature, could be struck in a timely manner.

Helicopters armed with rockets and missiles were also employed in the antisurface unit effort. Some U.S. Army aviation units operated from Navy frigates. They patrolled, watched for Iraqi vessels, provided bomb damage assessment, and raided offshore oil platforms. The British Lynx helicopter, firing the Sea Skua missile, was also successful in attacking Iraqi shipping. The joint-combined efforts of U.S. Army, Navy, and Marine Corps helicopters, Navy TACAIR, and British ships and helicopters accounted for 143 Iraqi vessels either sunk or damaged.[164]

Observations

It is worth noting that even during the Gulf War when the Coalition enjoyed air superiority, the enemy threat had an appreciable effect on air-to-ground tactics. On one hand, attack aircraft were able to use a medium- to high-level weapons delivery because there was literally no air-to-air threat, and the SEAD campaign had been so successful it had virtually neutralized all of Iraq's radar-controlled SAMs. On the other hand, barrage AAA and IR SAMs caused major problems when aircraft descended below approximately 10,000 feet during daylight hours. The selection of medium-altitude tactics to minimize the Iraqi threat caused Coalition aircraft to sacrifice some target recognition and identification capabilities and adversely impacted conventional weapons delivery accuracies.[165]

---

[164]*Army Aviation in Desert Shield/Storm*, pp 83-85.

[165]Multiple sources including, USN *Interviews of USAF Desert Storm Vets*, "A Study of Night Attack Experiences During Desert Storm," Naval Air Systems Command, Washington, DC, p 11.

The unrehearsed B-52/U.S. Air Force TACAIR strikes in support of Coalition forces at Khafji, and the joint impromptu U.S. Army attack helicopter and Air Force TACAIR armed, long-range, reconnaissance missions are just two examples of a phenomenon that was quite common during Desert Storm. Many of the successful tactics employed were improvised; they happened spontaneously, almost by accident. The success of these kinds of tactics are a direct result of a mutual confidence often evident among, and within, the different U.S. Services during Desert Storm. In many cases the success of Coalition forces can be compared with that of a championship-caliber athletic team. The participants demonstrated great anticipation; a knowledge of, and confidence in, the skills of others; and a feel for how their particular capability fit into the larger whole.

4

Special Issues

Low Observables and Stealth

A Stealth aircraft has to be stealthy in six disciplines: radar, infrared, visual, acoustic, smoke and contrail. If you don't do that, you flunk the course.[1]

Ben Rich
Director, Advanced Development Products Division
Lockheed Aircraft Company

This section deals with two related concepts, low observability and stealth. Both terms are technical descriptions of specified tactical capabilities. Both terms are also used to describe engineering disciplines aimed at suppressing detection signatures;[2] that is, reducing emissions from a given platform or vehicle that might be used to detect and attack it. Low observability as an engineering discipline involves the systematic suppression of the detection signatures in various emission spectra, including, but not limited to, radar. Stealth technology focuses specifically on radar emissions. Suppression of the radar signature is the essential technical characteristic of a stealth platform or delivery system. It is also the tactical essence of low observability. Tactically, low observability is the ability to penetrate enemy territory and strike directly at the heart of enemy power without having to suppress enemy air defenses in advance. A stealth platform is one whose radar signature has been sufficiently suppressed to render enemy radars ineffective against it. Three platforms used by U.S. forces in the Gulf War satisfied the tactical definition of low observability: the F-117 piloted stealth attack aircraft

---

[1]Bill Sweetman, *Stealth Bomber: Invisible Warplane, Black Budget* (Osceola, Wisconsin: 1989), p 101.

[2]We will use the term signature in the technical sense to mean the distinctive observable return of a given platform in a given spectrum, e.g., visual, aural, infrared, or radar. For an informed, reasonably nontechnical discussion, see Bill Sweetman, *Stealth Bomber*, Chapter 4, "Under the Skin," pp 84-119.

and two autonomously guided long-range precision-guided munitions, the Tomahawk Land Attack Missile (TLAM) and the Conventional Air Launched Cruise Missile (CALCM).

Three points must be made: First, there is no such thing as an invisible airplane, in the radar spectrum or in any other. Signatures can be suppressed; they cannot be eliminated. Second, and even more basic, technology cannot be divorced from tactics. Stupid tactics can negate seemingly overwhelming technological advantages, while intelligent tactics applied in a timely and decisive manner can overcome seemingly crippling technological deficiencies. Third, low observability can be achieved either tactically or technologically.

Detection Spectra Characteristics

Of all active means of detecting aircraft in flight, radar has the longest range and is least affected by weather and atmospheric conditions. For this reason, passive suppression of radar signature is the essence of stealth technology: if the radar signature cannot be suppressed, there is little point in trying to suppress the other means, with the partial exception of the visual. Camouflage paint offers important, if limited, advantages in suppressing visual and infrared signatures. Infrared systems rank after radar in effective range and vulnerability to atmospheric interference. Infrared systems derive considerable tactical importance from the fact that anything that moves, shoots, or emits radiation–in short, any military system–produces heat. This makes passive detection feasible, and the overwhelming majority of military infrared detectors, sensors, and terminal homing systems are passive.[3] Detection by light in the visual spectrum is, generally speaking, shorter ranged than infrared detection and more affected by atmospheric interference.[4] The principal advantage of detection by visual light is the accuracy, resolution, and flexibility of the human eye and the speed with which visual inputs can be incorporated

_____

[3]That is they emit no energy, in contrast to active systems, such as radar, which do. Some of the earliest operational infrared systems were active, combining a viewing device with an infrared illuminator, as with the World War II sniper scope and similar devices attached to tanks. Improvements in the sensitivity of viewing devices have largely eliminated the need for illumination.

[4]This generalization summarizes a complex set of relationships, and there are exceptions to it. Fog, for example, is more easily penetrated by visual light than by infrared radiation.

into the individual tactical decision-making process. Exhaust smoke and contrails are special visual signatures that permit detection at exceptionally long distances. Aural energy is the shortest ranged and least precise detection spectrum. Sound alone does not provide information sufficiently accurate to aim antiaircraft missiles or guns, but it can alert defenders that something is overhead and give an idea of direction of flight, speed, and perhaps identity. Finally, intercepted radio and radar transmissions can be used to locate aerial platforms with considerable accuracy at ranges limited only by the strength of the signal.

F-117 Strengths

The "Black Jet," as it is called by its pilots, represented the single greatest technological advance fielded in Desert Storm. The tactical effectiveness of the F-117 rested on four pillars: the extremely low radar signature of the aircraft; the capabilities of the mission planning computer, nicknamed Elvira;[5] the effectiveness of the GBU-27 and the infrared target acquisition and laser designator system; and the skill and training level of the pilots. The first and most critical of these was the low radar signature, and it is fair to say that the F-117 was safe from detection by all tactically relevant Iraqi threat radars. It is possible that the odd Iraqi radar operator detected a brief perturbation on his scope as an F-117 passed through his radar coverage. Such perturbations, however would have been brief in duration, difficult to detect, and next to impossible to exploit tactically. The relevant datum is that the F-117's radar signature has been selectively tailored to provide the greatest protection against systems representing the greatest threat; that is to say, "shooter" systems–surface-to-air and air-to-air missile acquisition, guidance, and control radars and antiaircraft artillery fire control radars. [DELETED].[6] In fact, the evidence suggests that the F-117 was detected rarely, if at all, and certainly not by "shooter" systems within their engagement envelopes. The aircraft's record of 1,299 sorties without damage argues persuasively that the F-117 was not detected by Iraqi radars in any tactically useful manner.

---

[5]The nickname was inspired by a vampire-like female comic book character, Elvira, Mistress of the Night.

[6]Bill Sweetman and James Goodall, *Lockheed F-117: Operation and Development of the Stealth Fighter* (Osceola, Wisconsin: 1990), pp 58-60.

The primary supporting element and the second pillar of the F-117's tactical effectiveness is Elvira, the mission planning computer. [DELETED]. As an F-117 pilot on the GWAPS staff put it, "We walk in the shadows and Elvira finds the dark corners for us."

In addition to the F-117's low radar signature and Elvira's flight path optimization, Gulf War planners and tacticians used the presence of additional aircraft providing radar targets in the same general airspace to further reduce the possibility of detection. This enhancement to low observability was partly technological, partly physiological, and partly psychological. Quoting a former commander of the F-117's parent unit, the 37th Tactical Fighter Wing, "The F-117 is not an invisible airplane, but it gets a lot closer to being invisible when people on radar scopes are occupied with seeing lots of other, more observable, aircraft on the scopes."[7] This phenomenon reflects the limits of radar technology at the interface between scope display and human operator. Most current-generation radars, particularly airborne radars, have computer-generated displays that "clean up" the scope by removing clutter and false returns from the visual scope display through various analytical algorithms. The algorithms are highly effective in increasing display clarity, but they tend to eliminate precisely the kinds of weak and ambiguous returns a stealthy platform produces. Bypassing the computer-generated display and reverting to raw return would increase the chances of painting a low observable target such as the F-117 on the scope, but would also reintroduce clutter and increase the number of false returns.

Those connected with the F-117 program were well aware of the above phenomena because of their extensive experience on the Tonopah ranges well before Desert Shield. Nevertheless, pre-deployment tactical concepts envisioned Black Jets operating autonomously.[8] The idea of using the F-117s as part of an integrated attack plan emerged early in Desert Shield, primarily as a means of enhancing total force effectiveness. Black Jets were assigned the most heavily defended targets because they were least vulnerable to detection. The F-117 did not depend on

---

[7]Brig Gen Anthony Tolin, oral intvw with John F. Guilmartin, Nellis AFB, NV, 30 Jan 1992. Then Col Tolin handed over command of the 37th to his replacement, Col Al Whitley, on 15 Aug 1990. He then served briefly as F-117 liaison with Headquarters TAC before proceeding to Riyadh, where he served in the "Black Hole" planning cell under Brig Gen Buster Glosson.

[8]Tolin intvw, p 10.

electronic warfare support to penetrate Iraqi defenses–to the contrary, on several occasions, friendly jamming posed a threat to F-117s by stimulating Iraqi barrage fire–but planners were aware that the presence of multiple targets in hostile airspace would give the Black Jets an extra margin of safety. [DELETED].[9] [DELETED].

An important component of the F-117's stealthiness is its low visual signature. Low observable technology was in its infancy when the F-117 design concept gelled in 1975.[10] The result was an aircraft which was, and is, essentially a bomb dropper. The F-117 has the normal maneuverability one would expect from a fighter aircraft of its size, weight, and planform,[11] but cockpit visibility is poor and the F-117 would be extremely vulnerable to a visually aimed gun attack in air-to-air combat. The obvious solution is to attack under cover of darkness, a logical choice, since the F-117 is just as vulnerable to optical-tracking antiaircraft artillery or surface-to-air missiles as any other aircraft . . . if the gunners can see it. The F-117's black RAM (radar absorptive material) and faceted design serve to reduce visual signature as well as radar signature, and the Black Jet is extremely hard to acquire visually in the dark.[12]

The third pillar of the F-117's tactical effectiveness in the Gulf War was its offensive ordnance suite. The suite had two main components.

---

[9](S) Information from Maj Robert Eskridge. Maj Eskridge, an F-117 pilot, was a Black Hole mission planner and flew seven F-117 missions during Desert Storm.

[10]Before 1975, Lockheed Aircraft Company engineers had used state-of-the-art computer analysis to design a small piloted aircraft that could, quoting F-117 Program Manager Paul Martin, "traverse the same threat field as an SR-71, but at a speed and altitude that would permit accurate weapons delivery." On the basis of these tests, Ben Rich, Director of Lockheed's Advanced Development Projects Division—the so-called Skunk Works—received company approval to submit an unsolicited bid to the Air Force to build two flight test vehicles to demonstrate the feasibility of a stealth fighter. The proposal was funded in mid-1976 under the code name Have Blue. Have Blue produced two sub-scale prototypes of what was to become the F-117; Sweetman, "Lifting the Curtain," p 159.

[11]Planform is defined as the shape of an aircraft's lifting surfaces when viewed from above. Deep delta planforms similar to that of the F-117 exhibit a sharp rise in induced drag, that is, drag produced attendant to lift, in high-g maneuvering flight. In lay terms, they slow down rapidly when they turn hard.

[12]Obviously, all aircraft are more difficult to see under low light conditions, but normal aircraft have a multitude of curved and angled reflective surfaces that pick up and reflect even small amounts of light, facilitating visual detection.

First was the GBU-27, a Paveway III laser guidance kit mated to a BLU-109/I-2000 bomb body with the tail fins shortened slightly to fit the F-117's bomb bay.[13] The second component was the combined FLIR/DLIR (forward looking infrared/downward looking infrared) imaging system with an integral laser designator.[14] The FLIR/DLIR system, peculiar to the F-117, provides 360 degree coverage beneath the aircraft and has an excellent cockpit display and high-quality video. In combination with the F-117's ability to safely attack from medium-altitudes, this suite consistently yielded high accuracy. The ability to achieve this accuracy in a high-threat environment was unprecedented.

The fourth pillar comprised the high standards of morale, motivation, and training of 37th Tactical Fighter Wing pilots, a matter of relevance here, since it was expressed operationally in terms of bombing accuracy. It is revealing as well that the 37th produced a particularly complete and historically useful cockpit video record of its attacks.[15]

Ironically, the faith of senior commanders and staff members in the Black Jet's accuracy had been compromised by press coverage of its first and only previous combat employment, in Operation Just Cause. In that operation, two F-117s had been tasked to drop bombs about fifty meters from a Panamanian Defense Force Barracks as a diversion. The pilots dropped as ordered and achieved hits close to the barracks. In the aftermath of the operation, an enterprising reporter obtained a quote from a DOD official implying that the bombs were to have been dropped precisely fifty meters from the barracks. He then visited Panama, measured the distance from the craters to the barracks, obtained a value greater than fifty meters, and filed a widely published story implying that

---

[13]Sweetman and Goodall, pp 58-60.

[14]*Ibid.*

[15]Comment by Capt Edward Wolfe, USAF, 11 Aug 1992, supported by authors' observation. An ordnance effects engineer formerly assigned to the USAF Weapons Test Laboratory, Eglin AFB, FL, and assigned to the Defense Intelligence Agency at time of writing, Wolfe compiled as comprehensive a record of cockpit attack video footage as possible so he could undertake a systematic comparison of bombing results observed and claimed against specific categories of targets, notably hardened shelters and bunkers. The 37th videos were significantly more complete and better processed than those from other units.

the F-117 was inaccurate.[16] This helped to produce an interesting divergence in confidence in the Black Jet's essential systems in the prelude to Desert Storm. F-117 pilots were utterly confident of their ability to place their bombs precisely on their designated mean points of impact, but the fighter's stealthiness remained an unproven quality to them.[17] Conversely, as one ascended the chain of command–bear in mind that the F-117 had only recently come out of the "black" world–there was increasing faith in the aircraft's stealthiness and increasing skepticism of its bombing accuracy.[18]

F-117 Limitations

If acquired visually, like all aircraft the F-117 would have been subject to visual air-to-air interception. Simply put, its best defense against aerial interception was its ability to defeat both radar and visual acquisition. This meant, in practical terms, that it is best employed at night. [DELETED].

F-117 in Desert Storm

Operating exclusively at night, the F-117 penetrated the densest and most sophisticated Iraqi air defenses with impunity. Its success was primarily a product of its inherent stealthiness, but smart tactics increased the tactical advantage. Most Black Jet strikes were flown after the Iraqi air defense net had been seriously degraded, but it is well to remember that F-117s initiated attacks on those defenses when they were still operating at something at least theoretically approaching full capability. Stealth comprised half of the F-117's tactical effectiveness; the second half of the effectiveness equation was offensive capability. Simply put, a platform that could drop 2,000-pound bombs precisely on selected targets, an inherent product of being able to drop from medium altitudes in straight and level flight, was an enormous asset to Coalition planners. More than any single platform, the Black Jet made Desert Storm fundamentally different tactically from previous air campaigns.

---

[16]Michael R. Gordon, "Stealth's Panama Mission Reported Marred by Error," *New York Times*, National edition, Wednesday, April 4, 1989, p B5.

[17]Gen Tolin reports F-117 pilots suiting up for the first night's attacks over Baghdad saying "I sure hope this stealth s___ works!" under their breath; Tolin intvw, p 12.

[18]*Ibid*, pp 13-14.

The Navy Tomahawk Land Attack Missile (TLAM) and the Air Force Conventional Air Launched Cruise Missile (CALCM) had their genesis in the early 1970s as an early military exploitation of miniaturized microchip-based guidance and navigation systems. TLAM uses terrain contour mapping (Tercom) radar to update the inertial guidance and navigation systems supplemented by terminal updates from digitized scene matching area correlation (DSMAC).[19] CALCM uses global positioning system (GPS) for both en route navigation and terminal accuracy. TLAM and CALCM differ from earlier air-breathing cruise missiles in three important respects: accuracy, reliability, and size. Both missiles are extremely accurate, although CALCM's accuracy depends on the accuracy of the GPS coordinates. Given terrain suitable for DSMAC updates within a reasonable distance of the target, TLAM can be expected to strike within tens of feet of the selected point of impact.[20] CALCM is not terrain dependent and has an accuracy of a similar order.[21] Note, however, that accuracy depends on the precise accuracy of the target coordinates, whereas DSMAC updates do not. Both TLAM and CALCM displayed remarkable reliability in light of their con-siderable complexity; this was almost entirely attributable to the inherent reliability of microchip circuitry. The diminutive sizes of the missiles are in part a product of the extreme compactness of microchip avionics and in part a product of the efficiency of the small, high-performance turbojet engines that power them. The engines are designed for an extremely short service life and can hence be made considerably lighter than would be possible otherwise.

The abilities of both missiles to penetrate enemy defenses are functions of their extremely small radar and visual signatures and low cruising altitudes. They fly almost entirely below ground-based radar coverage,

---

[19]Tercom develops terrain profiles using a radar altimeter; DSMAC views an area of land beneath the missile, digitizes the picture, and compares it with a similarly digitized picture of the same terrain stored in memory to determine the missile's precise position.

[20]This accuracy is primarily due to the precision of the inertial navigation systems, but even the best inertial systems have a certain amount of "drift"; that is, the indicated position departs from the actual position as a function of time. Tercom and terminal DSMAC updates ensure accuracy by re-zeroing the inertial system.

[21](S) Maj Karns, "Bullet Background Paper on Conventional ALCM in Desert Storm," Hq SAC/DOOQ, 3 Mar 92, p 1.

and while they are potentially vulnerable to detection from above by airborne doppler radars, their radar signatures are sufficiently small to counter known active and semiactive radar homing air-to-air missiles. They are extremely difficult to acquire visually, which protects them from a gun attack by an intercepting fighter, and their small infrared signatures render them essentially immune to infrared homing missiles. Finally, their engines are relatively quiet. With low aural and visual signatures, particularly from the front, TLAM and CALCM strike with little warning.

The basic TLAM C warhead is a 1,000-pound high-explosive "Bullpup" warhead, effective against light structures and general-purpose buildings of mixed concrete and steel construction.[22] It is not adequate for attacks on hardened targets. In addition to the normal horizontal attack profile, TLAM has a pop-up attack mode in which the missile dives into the target. One TLAM variant is fitted with a cluster munition dispenser for attacks on "soft" targets such as aircraft and vehicles in the open.

The CALCM's terminal effects reflect the missile's role as a conventional suppressive munition designed to support penetration of enemy defenses by piloted bombers. The CALCM's high explosive fragmentation warhead is designed to attack soft targets.[23] Nevertheless, CALCM was apparently effective in Desert Storm against electrical generator switching facilities and exposed communications relay facilities.[24] In contrast to TLAM, generalizations concerning CALCM effectiveness in Desert Storm must be treated with caution in light of the small number fired.

During Desert Storm, 282 TLAMs were launched, attained cruise flight, and proceeded toward their targets. Of these, 226 were timed for

---

[22]David A. Fulghum, "Secret Carbon-Fiber Warheads Blinded Iraqi Defenses," *Aviation Week and Space Technology*, 27 Apr 1992, pp 18-19.

[23](S) CENTCOM/J3 Msg 281950 Jun 91.

[24](S) Maj Karns, p 2.

daylight impact and 56 were timed to hit at night.[25] [DELETED].[26] 35 CALCMs were successfully launched.[27] [DELETED].

Tables 10 and 11 summarize CALCM and TLAM targeting in the critical first 48 hours of Desert Storm. The 137 TLAMs and CALCMs fired in the first 24 hours were more or less evenly distributed among "strategic" targets with indirect or limited tactical value: twenty-four missiles attacked leadership targets and 54 missiles attacked strategic targets with no tactical value (that is, chemical and oil facilities). Forty-two missiles attacked targets associated with electrical power generation; while not tactical in the normal sense, these targets were selected in part to interfere with enemy tactical communications. Seventeen missiles attacked command and control targets with direct tactical relevance. These strikes encompassed no less than 79 percent of night TLAM firings.

TLAM and CALCM Limitations

[DELETED].[28] [DELETED].

TLAM and CALCM in Desert Storm

TLAM and CALCM were capable of precision daylight strikes in areas denied to piloted platforms by the density of Iraqi defenses, particularly radar-guided surface-to-air missiles, and were the only Coalition weapons with this capability. TLAM effectively complemented the F-117 by keeping pressure on the most heavily defended areas by

---

[25]There were 298 attempts to fire; (S/NF/WN/NC) GWAPS *Statistical Compendium*, Table 202, "Desert Shield/Storm: USN Weapons Cost and Utilization (FY 91$)." (S/NF) Of the firing attempts, 9 missiles failed to launch and 6 failed in boost phase; (S/NF) May 1991 briefing on *Tomahawk Employment and Effectiveness During Desert Storm*, by Cmdr Roy Balaconis from JCS/J-3.

[26](S/NF) Cmdr Balaconis Briefing.

[27]GWAPS *Statistical Compendium*, Table 188, "Desert Shield/Desert Storm: USAF Weapons Cost and Utilization (FY 90)."

[28]CDR Steve Froggett, USN (Ret), "Tomahawk in the Desert," U.S. Naval Institute Proceedings, Jan 1992, p 72.

Table 10
TLAM and CALCM Targets: First 24 Hours[29]

Day or Night	Nature of Targets	Type of Missiles Fired
Night	electrical	TLAM
	leadership	TLAM
	chemical	TLAM
Daylight	electrical	CALCM
	C2	CALCM
	electrical	TLAM
	chemical	TLAM
	leadership	TLAM
	oil	TLAM

Table 11
TLAM Targets: Second 24 Hours[30]

Day or Night	Nature of Targets	Type of Missiles Fired
Daylight	leadership	TLAM
	oil	TLAM
	electric	TLAM
	air defense	TLAM
	electrical	restrikes (may not have gone)

---

[29](S) *Master Attack Plan*, "First 24 Hours," 16 Jan 1991, for numbers of CALCMs assigned against specific target sets.

[30](S) *Ibid.*

day. In terms of terminal effects, the TLAM C was highly effective against soft structures, mixed-construction buildings, and nonhardened command and control facilities. Air defense-associated communications facilities were particularly suitable targets. The reader is urged to consult the appropriate sections of the *Effects and Effectiveness* report for a comprehensive overview, but it is fair to say that daylight TLAM strikes in the Baghdad area helped maintain the tempo of offensive air operations, particularly during the first 48 hours of the air campaign. Only speculative conclusions can be drawn concerning the psychological impact of TLAM strikes as the campaign wore on; however, the unheralded detonation of warheads at night and the eerie spectacle of small vehicles homing on targets with seemingly human intelligence must have had an impact.[31]

Precision Attack Versus Mass Bombing

Desert Storm witnessed a fundamental change in the tactical and technological means of causing a given amount of destruction to a specific target. Previously, the requisite level of destruction could be increased by increasing the mass of bombs dropped, by improving the inherent accuracy of the bombing platform, or both. In Desert Storm, the availability of precision-guided air-to-surface munitions, particularly laser-guided bombs (LGBs), caused a fundamental rethinking of the means of achieving the destruction goal. The following pages address how and why that change took place. The discussion concentrates on bombs in the narrow sense. While there is an overlap in tactical function between precision-guided bombs and certain air-to-ground missiles, notably the AGM-65 Maverick, bombs were–and are–far less costly, both in cost per round and in cost per unit of destructive energy expended.[32] The air-to-

---

[31]The only available direct evidence of this conclusion is in press reports based on eyewitness observations by reporters in Baghdad in the initial stages of the air campaign. A British correspondent, from his room in the Al Rasheed Hotel, observed a Tomahawk fly down the street below him, turn the corner, and strike the Communications Ministry building at the end of the next block. His story reflected a positive and surprised reaction to the missile's technological sophistication; National Public Radio broadcast.

[32]A rough comparison of numbers and cost of munitions dropped or fired in the Gulf War by U.S. forces by category (HQ USAF/LGS, Combat Support Division and 1990 Weapons File; pp 585-89) yields the results tabulated below. The AGM-62B Walleye free fall EOGB is included in the guided-bomb totals and the powered AGM-123A Skipper and AGM-84B SLAM are in the air-to-surface missile totals. The AGM-114 Hellfire and

ground missiles fall into a category distinct from aerial bombs in terms of complexity, cost, and delivery tactics, and are therefore excluded from the following analysis. In light of the Gulf War's nature, the analysis deals almost entirely with attacks on ground targets and focuses on the relative merits of mass (or pattern bombing) and precision—meaning precision-guided—bombing. The section addresses many of the same tactical issues as found in the next section, "Twenty-Four-Hour Air War," but from a different perspective, and should be read in conjunction with it.

In the early days of aerial warfare, bomb-aiming systems were limited by the visual acuity of the human eye, the ballistic and aerodynamic characteristics of the bombs,[33] and the ability—or inability—to predict accurately the density and movement of the air through which the bombs fell. As long as these conditions applied, the primary substitute for accuracy in achieving target destruction was to increase the number of weapons dropped, to increase their individual size, or to increase the explosive yield of the bomb filler. Efforts were made to increase accuracy by maximizing the effectiveness of eyeball-controlled release, but these invariably ran up against the fundamental limits of visual acuity mentioned above. The classic attempt was the Norden bombsight of World War II, a tactical linchpin of the U.S. Army Air Forces precision strategic bombardment campaign. This sight effectively integrated the bombardier's eye and the aircraft as the two travelled together in a three-dimensional medium, seeking the precise point in time and space from which bombs released at a given forward velocity would hit the target under the prevailing atmospheric conditions. Although highly accurate for its day, it was not capable of precision bombing as we now

---

the BGM-71 TOW helicopter-fired missiles are included in the air to surface missile totals:

Unguided Bombs	Number Dropped	Total Cost
MK-82/83/84, M-117, UK-1000, CBU-52/72/78/87/89, MK-20	209,940	$431,960,550.00
Guided Bombs		
GBU-10/12/15/16/24/27/28, AGM-62B	9,473	$307,592,641.00
Air-to-Surface Missiles		
AGM-123A, AGM-84B, AGM-65, AGM-114, BGM-71	5,647	$550,797,084.00

[33]The ballistic and aerodynamic characteristics of free-fall bombs affect accuracy in two ways: First, some shapes and combinations of shape and mass are inherently more accurate than others. Second, variations between bombs in shape and mass produce variations in trajectory.

understand the term. In addition, as with all optical bombsights, the Norden was of limited value at night.

The enormous tactical advantages of being able to bomb in darkness and through meteorological obscuration—the fundamental impediments to visual aiming—were apparent from the beginning of aerial warfare.[34] Celestial navigation could be used to determine aircraft position above an undercast and was effective at night, but never approached the levels of accuracy necessary for blind bombing. This spurred attempts to develop methods of locating targets by electronic means. The Germans used directional radio beams to mark attack axes and bomb release points during the Battle of Britain; their methods, while sufficiently accurate for attacks on city-sized targets, proved vulnerable to electronic countermeasures.[35] The Royal Air Force, followed by the U.S. Army Air Forces, applied aerial radar to blind bombing after 1942.[36] Success was initially limited, but by the end of the war, blind bombing from medium-altitude under ideal conditions could approach visual bombing in accuracy.[37]

Bombing from low altitude was recognized as an effective solution to the accuracy problem from the beginning, but as long as visual aiming was necessary, the tactical disadvantages generally out-weighed the gain in accuracy. Low-altitude visual attacks against defended targets were and are inherently dangerous. If visibility is good enough for the pilot

---

[34]This impetus was felt most strongly in Europe, where the weather is cloudy and the nights long for most of the year. Limiting bombing to daylight gives the enemy automatic sanctuary about half the time, and adverse weather adds to the effect. Similarly, clouds and rain are less of a detriment to repair and restoration of bomb damage than a heavy overcast is to bombing.

[35]The British "bent" the beams by transmitting on the same frequency with the appropriate direction and power.

[36]*The Army Air Forces in World War II, Vol II, Europe: Torch to Pointblank, Aug 1942 to Dec 1943*, 7 Vols (Chicago, IL: The University of Chicago Press, 1950), pp 660-90, 720. Edited by Wesley Frank Craven and James Lea Cate.

[37]*The Army Air Forces in World War II, Vol III, Europe: Argument to VE Day, Jan 1944 to May 1945* (Washington D.C., Office of Air Force History, 1983), pp 19-20, 667. See also USSBS, Oil Division Final Report, p 4 of Figure 7. In attacks on three selected oil plants, 8th AF bombers dropping visually put 26.8 percent of their bombs within the plant area. RAF Bomber Command attacks dropping on parts designated by radar-equipped path finders achieved 15.8 percent.

or bombardier to see the target, it is good enough for defending gunners to see and engage the attacking aircraft. Under some circumstances, the gain was felt to justify the risk—the Ploesti raid of August 1943 is a classic example—but losses were almost always high.[38] Low-altitude night attack provided a solution in principle, but not in practice. While darkness provided concealment from visually aimed defensive systems, flying into obstacles or the ground was a major problem, and target acquisition was difficult to impossible. Only the advent of capable terrain-avoidance/terrain-following radar in the mid-1960s made possible the exploitation of the inherent accuracy of low-altitude bombing by night. The developments and relationships in question are discussed further in the next section, "Twenty-Four-Hour Air War." Here, it is sufficient to say that low-altitude bombing achieves accuracy by reducing the time and distance from release point to target.

The problem of achieving precision accuracy from all altitudes was solved, in principle, by the transistor revolution, which made possible the development of electro-optically guided bombs (EOGBs) and laser- guided bombs in the late 1960s. Previously, two basic methods existed for increasing the likelihood of target destruction. The first was to build larger aircraft capable of carrying heavier loads. The second was to send out greater numbers of aircraft. Within the radius of destruction produced by a large aircraft carrying a large bomb load, planners could determine statistical expectations of destroying various kinds of targets. The method was particularly appropriate for large fixed targets. It was virtually useless against moving targets such as ships or tanks, since the density of bomb strikes within the circular error probable (CEP) of the bombing platform was insufficient to ensure effective destruction.[39] Moreover, if military targets were located in urban areas, collateral damage to surrounding facilities and civilian life could be considerable. In WW II, both sides considered the responsibility for such collateral damage to lie with the national owner of the target, since the collocation of target and urban area were his responsibility. The attacking air force was required to ensure only that bombing was not indiscriminate, wantonly without

---

[38]*The Army Air Forces in World War II,* Vol II, pp 477-83. An analogous example in naval warfare is the use of dive and torpedo bombers against warships in World War II; again, losses were almost always high.

[39]*The Army Air Forces in World War II,* Vol III, p 192.

aim or military purpose.[40] During the Vietnam War, however, this willingness to accept and inflict collateral damage came increasingly under challenge and has remained so since, on political if not on legal grounds. This factor should be borne in mind, in considering the relative merits of precision and mass bombardment.

Once technologies capable of precisely guiding bombs to a point analogous to the designated mean point of impact (DMPI) became available, moving point targets could be destroyed with a single weapon. That, however, did not eliminate the tactical value of platforms carrying large numbers of unguided weapons. Notable among these in Desert Storm was the B-52, although the F-111, A-6, and F-15E performed the same role on occasion, and the F/A-18 and F-16 dropped dumb bombs almost exclusively. The analysis presented here will focus on the B-52, since it is, by virtue of its large bomb load and lack of a LGB designator capability, the limiting case. As did its ancestors, the B-17, B-24, and Lancaster, the B-52 in a conventional bombing role in Desert Storm depended on releasing a large number of bombs into a defined circle to produce statistically predictable levels of destruction. The B-52's vulnerability and resultant exposure of a large crew to enemy defensive systems were the principal drawbacks; the large tonnage of bombs it carried was the primary benefit. That benefit came into play in situations in which precision was not the most efficient, most effective, cheapest, lowest risk, or most humane method of achieving the desired tactical objective. In short, some targets in some situations were more effectively and efficiently attacked in the old fashioned way: through mass and statistical inevitability.

One such target in the Gulf War was the Taji weapons manufacturing complex north of Baghdad. Described in the Strategic Air Command History of the Gulf War as a "classic strategic target," the Taji complex sprawled over several square miles and contained multiple complexes and facilities. In assessing the nature of this target and the appropriate tactics to use in attacking it, the USCENTAF Commander stated:

---

[40]W. Hays Parks, "Air War and the Law of War," *The Air Force Law Review*, Vol 32, No. 1, p 55.

We wanted to attack Taji [with fighters] but its size and defenses just didn't justify the exposure of airplanes carrying one or two bombs, because they'd take out only one or two buildings, so we had to send the B-52s against it.

In fact, B-52 pattern bombing proved effective (see Taji weapons manufacturing complex photos).[41]   From 10 to 27 February, B-52Gs attacked the complex with sixty-eight sorties, carrying nearly three thousand bombs, and inflicted widespread and severe damage on the complex.[42]

By contrast, numerous targets in Iraq demanded precision weapons, although they were statistically vulnerable to destruction by mass bombing. This was due to the limited resources available for operational reasons and/or to the desire to limit collateral damage to civilians or nonmilitary infrastructure. In principle, individual Iraqi Defense Ministry buildings scattered throughout Baghdad could have been attacked with mass drops of gravity bombs from a variety of platforms, including the B-52. That option was rejected for straight-forward reasons: the large number of sorties required to accomplish the desired levels of destruction to individual buildings; the increased risk to the weapons delivery system; the high collateral damage caused by bombs that, while statistically on target (that is within the CEP), would miss the precise aimpoint; and the inability to achieve the strategic paralysis inflicted on the Iraqi command and control infrastructure by the near simultaneous detonation of high-explosive ordnance on critical nodes in the Iraqi system.   These considerations drove planners toward choosing almost exclusively precision weapons to attack the targets in question.

The systematic attack on the bridges in Iraq is another example of how the choice of weapon systems impacted operational decisions. The challenge was to deliver a weapon to a point where its detonation would collapse enough of the bridge to render it impassable. Again, this could be determined by statistically analyzing the predicted effects of the bomb blast and factoring in the probability that the aircraft would deliver the munition or munitions to the desired point on the bridge.

---

[41](S) Checkmate INTEL Target Files, CIT Folder #101, Taji Suspect BW Facility.

[42](S) Bomb damage assessment indicated that nearly complete reconstruction would be required to reach to prewar levels of production; (S/NF/WN/RD) History of the Strategic Air Command, Vol I, 1 Jan - 31 Dec 1990, pp 260, 275.

PHOTO DELETED

(Top) Taji weapons manufacturing complex, 8 September 1990.
(Bottom) Taji complex after B-52Gs attacked the complex with 68 sorties,
and carrying nearly 3,000 bombs.

PHOTO DELETED

The Air Force has long recognized a multiplicity of solutions in choosing among available weapons for specific targets. Based on many years of quantified weapons testing data, the Joint Munitions Effectiveness Manual is the foundation upon which predicted weapons effects are compared with desired damage levels to guide operations planners in selecting from available weapons, delivery platforms, delivery tactics, and other relevant parameters. The result is an empirical, statistical methodology that allows the planner to match specific aircraft and weapons to designated targets to produce the desired level of damage with the fewest resources and the least risk to aircraft and aircrew. The JMEM provides a range of answers to the question, what bomb on what airplane is best suited for a particular target?

Examination of a representative target illustrates this point. The target-to-weapon match is not intuitively obvious, yet produces clear results. The illustration involves the requirement to severely damage a bridge by dropping any span, with the goal of rendering it impassable for an extended time. The bridge in question was assumed to be a reinforced-concrete deck bridge with five spans, each 75 feet long and 22 feet wide. JMEM data and standard U.S. Air Force weaponeering procedures used in Desert Storm yield an array of choices. The performances of the following weapon-aircraft combinations are compared: an F-111F delivering precision electro-optical GBU-15 2,000-pound bombs; an F-16 carrying MK-84 2,000-pound bombs; and a B-52 loaded with MK-82 500-pound bombs. While each alternative had a theoretical capability of severely damaging the bridge in question, the F-111F/GBU-15 combination was clearly the best for the mission (see Table 12).

Analysis of attacks on bridges during the war indicates that not all precision weapons were effective against these targets. [DELETED]. The same hard penetrating munitions with fuzing delays caused the bomb to explode well beneath the surface of the bridges with little damage to

Table 12
Weapons and Sorties Required
to Destroy a Reinforced Concrete Bridge[43]

Target Description: Steel plate girder, reinforced concrete deck, deck-type highway bridge with five spans.

Criterion: Drop any span

Weapon System Alternatives:

1. F-111F W/ GBU-15
   Fuze: Set for impact
   Delivery Tactic: [DELETED]
   Single-Sortie Probability of Damage:[44] High
   Sorties Required for Probability of Damage of 0.7: one

2. F-16A W/ MK-84
   Fuze: Set for impact
   Delivery Tactic: 2,000 feet, [DELETED], High Stress Conditions[45]
   Single-Sortie Probability of Damage -Low
   Sorties Required for Probability of Damage of 0.7:Greater than one

3. B-52G W/ MK-82
   Fuze: Set for impact
   Delivery Tactic: [DELETED]
   Single-Sortie Probability of Damage: Very low
   Sorties Required: Much greater than one

---

[43](C) Results derived from paper provided by Air Force Intelligence Support Agency, Directorate of Targets, Subject: Bridge Weaponeering Problem, 18 Sep 1992.

[44](C) Single-Sortie Probability of Damage is the mathematical probability that the platform in question, dropping the weapon or weapons indicated, will achieve the level of damage desired on a single pass.

[45]That is, the single-sortie probability of damage is adjusted to account for the high aircrew stress anticipated when using the delivery tactics indicated in a hostile environment.

the structure.[46] Conversely, when the appropriate bomb-fuzing combinations were used, laser-guided bombs proved highly effective. The same comment applies to electro-optically guided bombs dropped by French Jaguars and laser-guided bombs dropped by Royal Air Force GR-1s using buddy laser designation from Buccaneers.[47]

The advantages and limitations of the Smart Plane/Dumb Bomb concept are embodied in the F-16 weapons delivery system. The heart of the visual bombing system in the F-16 (and several other fighter aircraft) is the continuously computed impact point (CCIP). The fire control computer receives spatial data from onboard systems and instruments, including radar, INS, and air data computer, combines the data with the known ballistic characteristics of the weapon selected for delivery, and calculates the predicted impact of the weapon, should it be released at that instant. A pipper, displaying the predicted impact point, appears on the heads-up-display (HUD). The pilot maneuvers the aircraft to superimpose target and pipper and releases his weapons. From this point the "smart" airplane can do nothing more to influence the impact point of the "dumb" bombs. The impact point is determined by the ballistics of the weapon, wind, altitude, and other uncontrollable variables. Pilots of smart airplanes, such as the F-16, F/A-18 and F-15E, increase accuracy by placing their aircraft in the best possible positions to release the weapons. The CCIP and fire control computer systems are designed to eliminate as much error as possible before weapons release. Chapter 3 of this report contains a description of the process, and Figure 15 graphically illustrates the impact of the uncontrollable variables affecting dumb bombs released from smart airplanes.

The value of mass bombing from large, high-capacity bombing platforms is the confluence of physical destruction and psychological effects that these weapons produce. These effects contrast sharply with those of precision weapons bombing. Within the radius of the circular error probable, no target is certain to be hit, but all targets are liable to be hit by precision weapons. An individual soldier observing the destruction of high-value targets by precision-guided munitions could survive, and even keep himself combat capable, by staying away from

---

[46](S/NF/WN/NC) *Tactical Analysis Bulletin*, Vol 91-2, Jul 1991, pp 7-11, 7-12.

[47]Carole A. Shifron, "Britain's Gulf Role Highlights Value of Flexible Tactics, New Technology," *Aviation Weekly* and *Space Technology*, 22 Apr 1991, pp 104-107.

valuable equipment likely to be targeted. In Desert Storm, Coalition psychological operations reinforced this obvious conclusion by dropping leaflets specifically warning Iraqi soldiers to stay away from heavy equipment.

Large maneuvering units in the field were excellent targets for mass bombing. Maneuvering units remained effective until the individual members decided that cohesion was no longer desirable, worthwhile, or possible. A huge number of precision sorties, at overall greater risk and expense, would have been needed to break the cohesion of the soldiers if the technique had been to strike only high-value targets within the defined area. In fact, logistics and risk factors were actually greater for precision weapons, since repeated attacks would have been necessary until a large number of armored weapons, artillery, and combat vehicles were destroyed, and also until the effective means of feeding and otherwise supplying the remaining troops were eliminated. How many precision sorties this would have taken is problematical, but certainly a large number. The expense of the precision weapons, the fuel for the multitudes of small aircraft, the feeding of the pilots, maintenance personnel, and replacement spares for the aircraft would have been considerable. Once the Iraqi soldiers realized the nature of the attack, they could have made themselves fundamentally immune from personal harm by distancing themselves from observable military targets. This would have, at least potentially, maintained unit cohesion, requiring ground assault to eliminate the unit as a threat. There is some evidence that Iraqi soldiers and units responded in this way.[48]

The evidence suggests that the Iraqis were used to defending their positions without using mobile armor and that they expected ground assaults by light infantry, as they had faced in the Iran-Iraq War.[49] The evidence further suggests that ground assault, Iranian-style, would not in itself have been sufficient to produce the sudden collapse that characterized the ground phase of Desert Storm. Precisely why front line Iraqi troops surrendered quickly and in large numbers remains a matter for speculation. The fact remains, however, that these units were repeatedly hit by B-52s, and the statistical randomness of the bombing, combined with its inherent massiveness, is very likely the answer. As

---

[48](S) 513th Military Intelligence Brigade, JDC Report #0052, 11 Mar 1991.

[49][DELETED]

indicated earlier, uncertainty is an inherent characteristic of statistical attack. The evidence suggests that in the Gulf War, the physiological results of surviving near misses by 500-pound bombs went beyond the merely unpleasant and affected an Iraqi's basic will to fight and his expectation of survival.[50]

The use of precision-guided munitions can be inappropriate or impossible against some types of targets. The classic example is a large mobile military unit, in which precise location and identification of individual targets is impossible or impractical. It would be possible to cripple an armored unit by destroying each of its vehicles individually with precision-guided munitions. This tactic of attrition by precision munitions would, however, take many sorties, much time, and considerable quantities of relatively expensive precision weapons. In the Gulf War, this technique could not be effectively undertaken by smart planes-dumb bombs combinations, such as the F-16, from medium- or high-altitudes; the bombing systems were not sufficiently accurate and the bomb loads were too small to make up the difference. In short, some targets are appropriate for the statistically oriented JMEM approach. The following paragraphs explain why in some detail.

The destruction of some units by precision weapons would have required an enormous and costly effort, especially when the same units could be functionally destroyed by relatively dumb airplanes dropping dumb bombs. Destruction of a unit's tanks one by one would be unnecessary if the unit as a whole, and particularly its moral cohesion, could be broken by massive bombardment. Experience dating back to WW II has demonstrated that high-level bombing of armored units is unlikely to destroy tanks; chance alone produces a few hits close enough to destroy individual tanks. However, an armored unit is functional only as a cohesive unit, not as a collection of individual tanks, and incessant aerial pounding can break a unit without destroying all, or even a majority, of its parts. The real limit is the ability of the troops to absorb the pounding, since individual decisions to cease fire will eventually render the unit useless tactically. Soldiers may desert (leave their unit and go home), defect (present themselves as prisoners), or, if unable to leave the killing ground, desert in place, that is, consciously or unconsciously cease to be a functioning member of the unit. Backing up

---

[50](S) Intelligence Information Report #2 340 2494 91.

the aerial bombardment by specific suggestions through psychological operations radio, leaflets, and loudspeakers can speed up the process if the bombardment is perceived as personally threatening by the members of the unit. The minimum accuracy is therefore defined as a perceivable credible strike distance that maintains individual fear at a high pitch. This distance does not necessarily coincide with the location of the unit. Should an attacker be known for having an inexhaustible supply of aircraft and bombs, the effect and the effective psychological distance will be increased. Should the personal motivations of those in the targeted unit be low, the perceived credible distance can grow to the point that the circular error probable desired becomes the range of human hearing of the detonating bombs. Even bombs that miss all units will be assumed by members of each unit to be hitting someone else, and if severed communications ensure they can not compare notes, total misses will add to the overall effect. Iraqi prisoners were very specific about the effect the bombing of other units within earshot had on their combat capability and morale. Although the Iraqis were rarely able to differentiate between the systems bombing them, they were always impressed by the results. They also confirmed the importance of random bombing in inducing helplessness and surrender among enemy troops before launching a ground assault.

Although the A-10 was able to create the same anxiety as more random systems, it generally functioned as a precision weapon by firing its GAU-8 gun and Maverick missiles at tanks. According to Iraqi prisoner reports, the principle source of anxiety produced by A-10s was the aircraft's sustained loitering capability. As long as the A-10 was in the target area, everything within eyesight was subject to attack. Given their great accuracy, the psychological effects of the A-10s were: the enemy did not know which target would be attacked, and the aircraft seemed omnipresent.[51] Any soldier could suddenly become the target; if he were unfortunate enough to attract the attention of the omnipresent weapon, death seemed certain. The only alternative was defection, and many took it. The lack of any effective air defense gave rise to complete hopelessness, which magnified the effect.[52]

---

[51][DELETED]

[52][DELETED]

Randomness and helplessness combined to achieve the same effect. The B-52s used both 500-pound iron bombs and cluster bomb units. One prisoner, apparently a veteran of the Iran-Iraq War, stated that Coalition bombing had been "the worst thing he had ever experienced in a combat" and went on to assert that the B-52s were particularly bad. [DELETED].[53] [DELETED]. Effects were uneven; the Republican Guard apparently remained cohesive to the bitter end, but there can be little doubt as to the overall adverse effect of B-52 area bombing on the Iraqi ground forces.

[DELETED].[54] [DELETED]. These reported effects were anticipated and are validated by the reported experience of communist recipients of B-52 Arc Light strikes in the Vietnam War. A particularly eloquent account by a senior National Liberation Front (Viet Cong) cadre described the effects of a B-52 attack in the following terms:

> . . . it seemed, as I strained to press myself into the bunker floor, that I had been caught in the Apocalypse. The terror was complete. One lost control of bodily functions as the mind screamed incomprehensible orders to get out.[55]

The same source stated that,

> for all the privations and hardships, nothing the guerrillas had to endure compared with the stark terrorization of the B-52 bombardments . . . translated into an experience of undiluted psychological terror, into which we were plunged, day in, day out for years on end.[56]

Warned by foreign radio stations that bombing would occur, Iraqi troops did not anticipate the ferocity of the attack. The prisoner cited above described the attacks as so continuous that the troops were rarely

---

[53](S) JDC Rpt #0052.

[54][DELETED]

[55]Truong Nhu Tang with David Chanoff and Doan Van Toai, *A Vietcong Memoir* (Vantage Books: New York, 1986), p 168.

[56]*Ibid*, pp 167-70. Truong describes the effect of a B-52 strike on a visiting Soviet delegation: "When it was over, no one had been hurt, but the entire delegation had sustained considerable damage to its dignity, uncontrollable trembling and wet pants from the all-too-obvious signs of inner convulsions."

able to sleep for more than two hours at a time. The bombers eventually did not have to hit within his area to produce an effect because vibrations and sound travel great distances in the desert. The "horrified" men would quiver in fear as units far away were hit. He specifically stated that the sound effects spawned suspense and the fear that their unit would be next.[57] Again, the randomness appears to have contributed to the effect. This same deserter clearly remembered and obeyed the Coalition leaflets' exhortation to move away from heavy equipment, as did his compatriots.

In conclusion, the experience of Coalition and U.S. air forces in Desert Shield and Desert Storm indicates that bombs delivered by precision guidance to a specific point and bombs delivered en masse to inflict statistically predicted damage had complementary roles. On one hand, precision-guided bombs were particularly suited for bombing high-value, dense targets, particularly where dispersion and consequent collateral damage had to be tightly controlled. The least expensive and most commonly used precision-guided bombs were LGBs. On the other hand, dumb bombs were particularly suited for mass bombing of targets when goals included widespread damage and demoralized enemy troops. A number of platforms executed mass bombing effectively, but the B-52, with its 38,250-pound maximum bomb load and the ability to deliver it from high altitude, was considered the optimum performer.[58] Also, the B-52 used cheap, nonprecision bombs and was able to deliver them effectively with the help of accurate navigation and near-real-time electronic surveillance.

Twenty-Four-Hour Air War

From the dawn of aerial warfare, military airmen appreciated the tactical advantages that would accrue from being able to penetrate enemy defenses under cover of clouds and darkness. They also sought to exploit the advantages of increasing pressure on an enemy by bringing air power to bear around the clock. The practical obstacles to achieving those goals, however, were formidable, and until recently, the notion of applying airpower unconstrained by weather and time of day was an unattainable ideal. Cursory analysis of the Gulf War suggests that the old limita-

---

[57][DELETED]

[58](S) USCENTAF Combat Plans Handout, B-52 Standard Conventional Loads (SCLs).

tions no longer apply. A higher proportion of Coalition aerial platforms could deliver ordnance accurately at night than in any previous conflict, and the tempo of air operations varied little between daylight and darkness. Under certain circumstances, Coalition air power was able to strike more powerful blows at night than by day; the obvious example is the use of F-117s in the Baghdad area, where heavy defenses prevented overflights by manned platforms in daylight. Closer examination, however, suggests that the ability of Coalition air forces to strike Iraqi targets around the clock was simply a function of improved technical capabilities. This 24-hour coverage depended on an array of complex and connected variables including human factors, the capabilities of Iraqi defensive systems, and the bombing accuracy of specific systems.

The ability to mount all weather air operations around the clock depends on several discrete but tactically related capabilities: First, and most basic, is the ability to fly in clouds and at night, a reality since the development of effective flight instruments and piloting techniques in the 1920s and 1930s. Second is the ability to navigate accurately and locate targets at night and through clouds, smoke, and haze with sufficient precision to deliver ordnance. Airborne radar was used for this purpose with limited success in the latter stages of World War II (see the Chapter 4 section titled "Precision Attack Versus Mass Bombing"). Offset radar bombing, the ability to bomb a designated point by reference to the radar return of a presurveyed natural feature or cultural object some distance from the target, came of age in the 1950s, but bombers were unable to penetrate enemy defenses safely in darkness or adverse weather at altitudes low enough to defeat ground-based radar-controlled antiaircraft defenses. High-altitude bombing was sufficiently accurate only for area targets.

The ability to bomb accurately at night and in adverse weather demonstrated in Desert Storm emerged from two developments of the mid-1960s: The first was the emergence of ground mapping and terrain-avoidance radars that made low-altitude penetration of radar-controlled, ground-based enemy defenses tactically feasible. That capability was first fielded operationally in the A-6A in the autumn of 1965,[59] and the F-111A demonstrated the same capability in the Linebacker II offensive in late 1972. These aircraft could penetrate below enemy radar and put

---

[59]Frank Uhlig, Jr., ed., *Vietnam: The Naval Story*, (Annapolis, MD; 1987), p 27.

bombs on target.[60] The tactical nub of the matter was that the A-6 and F-111 were able to penetrate at night, at altitudes which were low enough, generally below 1,000 feet above ground level, to keep them masked by terrain enough of the time to defeat enemy radars. The second development, night viewing devices capable of discerning point targets–individual buildings, vehicles, and installations–appeared at about the same time.[61] These devices were first used operationally on side-firing gunships, notably the AC-130, first tested in combat in early 1968.[62] The AC-130 could place rounds within feet of its target and proved highly effective in missions where accuracy counted and loiter time was at a premium. However, the AC-130 carried only a limited ordnance load and required a relatively permissive operating environment (see the Chapter 4 section titled "Special Operations Forces and Air Power"). The pivotal development was the coupling of night viewing devices, notably forward-looking infrared (FLIR), with designators for laser-guided bombs. Previously, accuracy in night bombing could only be achieved in low-altitude attacks. Now, genuine precision–the ability to hit point targets–can be achieved at night from any altitude so long as the target can be observed on FLIR and the laser designator brought to bear.

The FLIR and laser designator were combined earlier to provide precision-guided bombing capability in the Pave Spike system; a strap-on pod mounted on the F-4E during the final stages of the Vietnam War.[63] Pave Spike was the ancestor of the Pave Tack system used in the Gulf War on the F-111F. Pave Nail was a parallel development used on OV-10 forward air control aircraft to designate targets for tactical

---

[60](C) CINCPACFLT Analysis Staff Study 2-71, "Analysis of A-6A Radar Bombing Accuracy," 15 July 1971: [DELETED]

[61]The first of these was the starlight scope used as a gunsight on the side-firing AC-47 gunship, used in combat in February of 1965. The AC-47, armed with 7.62-mm machine guns, was followed by the cannon-armed AC-130, first tested in combat in February of 1968, which used FLIR (forward-looking infrared) and LLLTV (low light level television) for the same purpose. The definitive version, the AC-130H, was armed with 20-mm cannon, 40-mm cannon, and a 105-mm howitzer. Jack S. Ballard, *Development and Employment of Fixed-Wing Gunships, 1962-1972* (Washington, D.C.: Office of Air Force History, 1982), p 28.

[62]*Ibid*, pp 77-93.

[63]Marcelle Knack, *Encyclopedia of U.S. Air force Aircraft and Missiles*, Vol I, Post World War II Fighters - 1945-1973 (Office of Air Force History, 1978), pp 281-282.

fighters. OV-10s were used successfully in this manner in the final stages of the Vietnam War, but in insufficient numbers to realize the full tactical potential of the system. By contrast, a relatively high percentage of the tactical aircraft deployed in Desert Shield possessed an autonomous FLIR-laser designator capability, notably the F-117, F-111F, and A-6E. In addition, some F-16s and all F-15Es deployed in Desert Shield were fitted with AN/AAQ-13 low-altitude navigation and targeting infrared (system) for night (LANTIRN) pods, though only a handful of F-15Es were fitted with the AN/AAQ-14 designator pod.[64] The AGM-65D Maverick imaging infrared homing missile was used at night to find targets and could be fired by most U.S. tactical fighter and attack aircraft. Table 13 summarizes the day and night, all-weather capabilities and limitations of the more important Coalition systems.

Coalition Capabilities

Beyond a doubt, the most significant weapons at the disposal of Coalition air forces for extending the reach of airpower around the clock were the precision-guided missiles (PGMs), which could be used at night. By far the most important of these in terms of tons delivered were laser-guided bombs (LGBs) dropped from manned platforms; Air Force aircraft dropped the lion's share. The aircraft included, but were not limited to, the F-111F, F-15E, F-117, and A-6E. Although these platforms could attack in daylight as well as at night, Coalition planners chose to exploit their night capability. The imaging-infrared (IIR) homing AGM-65 Maverick missile, fired mainly by A-10s plus a few from F-16s, was also useful in extending the reach of airpower into the hours of darkness, although much less so than LGBs in combination with FLIR. A few GBU-15 infrared-guided bombs were also dropped at night; however, the potential of this weapon was limited by the facts that only the F-111F was equipped with the requisite datalink for guidance and few crews had trained with it.

Through its ability to attack heavily defended areas at night, the F-117 made a major contribution to overcoming the iron rule of the clock. B-52s made a major contribution through their ability to drop

---

[64]Only two F-16 squadrons were LANTIRN-equipped. Only the half dozen target designator pods available were rotated among F-15Es.

Table 13
Bombing Capabilities by Platform

	Visual Bombing: Day	Night	Radar	LGB Self-Designation	Air-to-Air Swing Role	Comments
F-117		FLIR/DLIR		X		Night, limited bomb load (2 x 2,000 lb); extremely accurate bombing platform.
F-111F	X	Pave Tack	X	X		Large bomb load for tactical aircraft; air-to-air missiles for defense only.
F-111E	X		X			Large bomb load for tactical aircraft; air-to-air missiles for defense only; analog avionics.
A-6E	X	TRAM	X	X		Large bomb load for tactical aircraft; multi-role capability (e.g., SEAD with HARMs); logistically constrained (few LGBs aboard ship).
F-15E	X	LANTIRN-equipped	X	X	X	Large bomb load for a tactical aircraft; aircraft FLIR designator pods in theater; new aircraft–crews accomplished familiarization in theater.
F-16C	X	LANTIRN-equipped aircraft	X		X	LANTIRN pods available for only two squadrons.
GR-1	X		X			Qualified for JP233 runway denial munition; effective only with low-altitude delivery.
B-52			X			Exceptionally large bomb load; unsuitable for point targets.
A-10	X	X				Precision accuracy with 30-mm GAU-8 cannon; limited night capability with IIR AGM-65.
F/A-18	X		X		X	Highly capable air-to-air aircraft.
TLAM						Day and night precision capability; unmanned; limited numbers avail-able; TLAM C suitable only for point targets.

large tonnages of bombs in all weather, day or night, but only after air superiority was achieved. Although the B-52s had no LGB guidance capability, they dropped bombs on large area targets and Iraqi forces in the field and added significantly to the total weight of ordnance delivered. B-52s, and to a lesser extent F-111s, A-6s, and F-16s, dropping "dumb" bombs by day and night, effectively complemented precision bombing (see the Chapter 4 section titled "Precision Attack Versus Mass Bombing"). The F-16 is an extremely accurate low-altitude bombing platform by day and, with LANTIRN navigation pods installed, by night. It did not, however, have a designation capability for LGBs and was markedly less accurate when visual bombing from medium altitudes. The relative weights of day and night attacks delivered by these platforms are reflected in Figure 51.

Autonomously-guided cruise missiles also made an important and distinctive contribution to twenty-four hour operations: these were almost entirely Navy TLAMs, although a few CALCMs were fired in the first twenty-four hours of the air campaign. Both TLAM and CALCM are insensitive to time of day, and TLAMs were used extensively in night attacks on strategic targets during the first forty-eight hours of the air campaign. TLAM's biggest contribution to twenty-four-hour air operations, however, was in striking targets in the heavily defended Baghdad area during daylight. Extremely accurate, and with no pilot at risk, TLAM was the ideal weapon for maintaining pressure on heavily defended areas by day.

Although many Coalition platforms were more or less equally suited for day and night operations, manning limitations forced individual units into either day or night operations (see Figure 51). The greater weight of F-16 strikes in daylight hours primarily reflects the number of units committed to daylight operations rather than equipment limitations. In simple terms, a unit must have a very high crew ratio and must be overmanned in both operations support and maintenance to conduct twenty-four-hour operations; this was a luxury which few if any Coalition units enjoyed.

Inspection of Figure 51 reveals a number of significant tactical considerations. The perceptible drop in sorties on targets during twilight hours reflects two phenomena: The first is poor visibility for visual ordnance delivery at twilight, that is, within about thirty minutes of sunrise and sunset. The difficulty of acquiring and attacking targets under

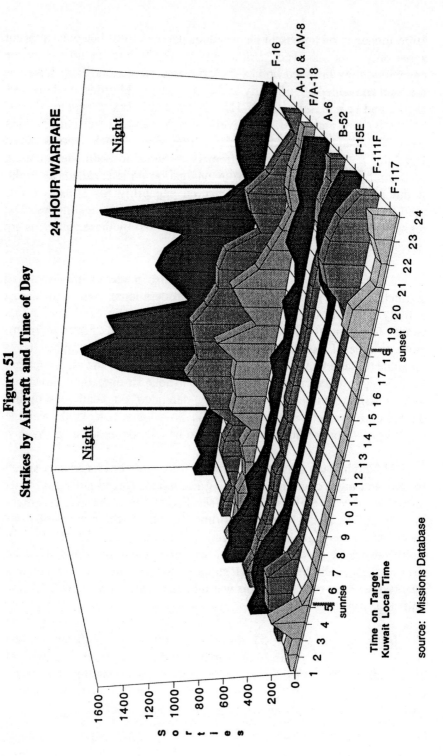

Figure 51
Strikes by Aircraft and Time of Day

24 HOUR WARFARE

Night

Night

F-16
A-10 & AV-8
F/A-18
A-6
B-52
F-15E
F-111F
F-117

1 2 3 4 5 6 7 8 9 10 11 12 13 14 15 16 17 18 19 20 21 22 23 24

sunrise

sunset

strikes

1600
1400
1200
1000
800
600
400
200
0

Time on Target
Kuwait Local Time

source: Missions Database

272

low-sun-angle and dim-light conditions is one of the most enduring realities of aerial combat. The second is the shift in the infrared contrast gradient after sunrise and sunset, a factor that was particularly significant in the KTO where vehicles and equipment were major target sets. Sand warms and cools more quickly than metal; hence, the contrast between the two was greatest shortly after evening twilight when the sand had cooled and the heat-soaked metal of vehicles and equipment was still hot. The difference gradually diminishes throughout the night and reverses shortly after sunrise, reaching a transient condition of equality when the sun has warmed the sand to the same temperature as the metal.[65]

Tactical Results

While there were distinct limitations in the ability of Coalition airpower to bring pressure to bear on Iraqi forces regardless of time of day or meteorological conditions, those limitations were much less restrictive than in previous conflicts. In all previous conflicts, there was a marked tradeoff between accuracy and time of day, and the vast majority of accurate bombing attacks took place in daylight. That generalization held true through the end of the Vietnam War, although with somewhat less force than for Korea and World War II. In the Gulf War, LGBs delivered with FLIR designators evened the balance, and reversed it to a degree, since the infrared sensors with their ability to penetrate haze, enjoyed an appreciable advantage over optical systems.[66]

In summation, Coalition forces could attack the vast majority of targets under prevailing conditions most of the time. There were, however, significant limitations on twenty-four-hour, all-weather operations. The most important of these was the need for relatively clear visibility to deliver LGBs, day or night. Weather was thus a constraining factor and had an adverse effect on F-117 operations in particular. TLAM helped to pick up the slack with daylight attacks in the most heavily defended areas but was not effective against hardened targets. F-111Fs, A-6s, and F-15Es, though unable to penetrate the heaviest Iraqi defenses with the same impunity as the F-117, were able to bomb by radar; these

---

[65]See, for example, *Maverick Operations Supplement: IR Maverick* (Hughes Aircraft Company: 1 Jul 1988), "IR Predictions," pp 1.5-1.6.

[66]Note, however, that optical systems can penetrate mist and fog better than infrared systems.

aircraft thus had a genuine all-weather capability and were capable of considerable accuracy at low altitudes. This advantage was somewhat degraded by the decision to reduce the effectiveness of Iraqi antiaircraft artillery, optically aimed by day and barrage fired by night, by attacking from medium altitudes. The F-111E was also able to radar bomb but had analog avionics and was thus less accurate at medium altitudes than the other aircraft mentioned. Intelligent tactics and scheduling compensated, in part, for the limitations of individual systems. Black Hole schedulers, for example, learned to schedule F-117 sorties around the poor ceilings and visibility associated with frontal weather passages and to attack targets suitable for radar deliveries with F-111s, F-15Es, A-6s, and, on occasion, B-52s when weather in the target area was poor.[67]

Although impossible to quantify, the next most serious constraint on twenty-four-hour operations was aircrew fatigue. Although not a natural routine, entire squadrons could be put on a night schedule operationally. Because essential administrative functions had to be accomplished in daytime, aircrews flying outside the normal duty hours almost inevitably faced a heavier fatigue toll than their daylight-tasked equivalents. To this must be added the psychological toll of routinely penetrating enemy defenses, a toll that sooner or later found expression in physiological form. To cite a relevant example, a competent observer characterized F-117 pilots–a group explicitly trained for night operations–as "tired" by the end of Desert Storm.[68] To make matters worse, the key mission planners and analysts in tactical wings and squadrons in Desert Storm were almost all operational aircrew members who had to fly to maintain currency.[69]

The Scud Hunt

The anti-Scud campaign was conducted in two overlapping but tactically distinct phases. The first phase was part of the Master Attack Plan and was directed against fixed launchers, support facilities, and storage areas. Since this phase was an integral part of the strategic air

---

[67]See the *Effects and Effectiveness* Report.

[68]Tolin intvw, p 14.

[69]37th TFW tactical mission planning was largely accomplished by weapons and tactics officers who stayed up to do the work after flying their nocturnal missions, information supplied by Maj Robert Eskridge.

campaign, it is not discussed in detail here. The second phase, termed the Scud Hunt, was triggered by Scuds being fired at Israel and Saudi Arabia from mobile launchers. The second phase was thus aimed at locating and destroying Iraq's mobile launch assets.

The first Scud hunt sorties were launched during the night of 18 January with the diversion of three AC-130H gunships.[70] During the following two nights, three more AC-130 sorties were committed to anti-Scud armed reconnaissance.[71] Then, on the night of the 21st, an AC-130 engaging a possible a Scud site drew an SA-7 launch and was taken under fire by 23-mm and 37-mm antiaircraft artillery. After evading the Iraqi fire, the AC-130 was diverted to another possible Scud site. En route, it was engaged by early-warning radar followed by an SA-8 launch. The crew narrowly evaded the missile but over stressed the aircraft.[72] The following night, the launch of an AC-130 against mobile Scud targets in western Iraq, marked the last use of AC-130s in the Scud Hunt.

The Scud Hunt proper got under way as the AC-130 commitment ended and continued until the cessation of hostilities.[73] The effort absorbed a significant proportion of strike assets in theater: about twenty-five percent of F-15Es, seven percent of A-10s, twenty-five percent of LANTIRN-equipped F-16s, and eight percent of F-111Fs were dedicated to the Scud hunt; F-117s, B-52s, Navy A-6Es and F/A-18s, and Royal Air

---

[70]The crews encountered low clouds in the search area and termed their efforts "zero percent effective." (S) "AC-130 Gunship Desert Storm Mission Summary," atch. to 16SOS/CC ltr to the Office of the Secretary of the Air Force, 14 May 1992, subj: "AC-130 Desert Storm Information."

[71](S) *Ibid.* One sortie was diverted on the 19th. Two were launched with the assigned mission of anti-Scud armed reconnaissance on the 20th; these claimed two Squat Eye/Flat Face radars and several associated vans destroyed.

[72] The aircraft was returned to duty only after extensive maintenance in Germany.

[73](S) The 20 January start date correlates with the first entry in the so-called Scud Chasing Log maintained by The Tactical Air Control Center (TACC) under CENTAF Headquarters; (S/NF/WN) Christie and Barlow, *Desert Storm Scud Campaign*, Apr 1992, Appendix C, "Scud Chasing Log." (S) This Table lists 255 separate Scud-related events, defined as a reported activity involving an aircraft involved in anti-Scud operations, between 20 January and 27 February.

Force GR-1 Tornados were used on occasion as well.[74] The tactical essence of the Scud Hunt was to place strike aircraft in orbit over known launch areas poised to attack mobile Scud sites as soon as they could be detected and located. Detection, location, and the direction of strike aircraft toward their targets were undertaken by a variety of reconnaissance, intelligence, and command and control platforms.

The objectives of the Scud Hunt were to locate, attack, and destroy mobile Scud launchers and associated support equipment and, secondarily, to suppress launch activity. The Scud Hunt is of historical interest as the first air campaign against a mobile ballistic missile force.[75] It is of tactical and operational interest, since it is unlikely to be the last such campaign.[76] The Scud Hunt pressed to the limit Coalition strike, intelligence, and command and control systems, as well as aircrew skills and the powers of innovation and adaptation of Coalition staffs, planners, and commanders.

Background

The technical characteristics and tactical capabilities of Iraqi mobile ballistic missile systems were well known to U.S. and Coalition intelligence analysts before the Gulf War (see Figure 52). It was apparent to Coalition commanders that the possession by Iraq of

---

[74]In a postwar press briefing, Chief of Staff of the Air Force Gen Merrill McPeak stated that anti-Scud operations absorbed three times the resources anticipated; "Scud Chase" press briefing, 15 Mar 1991, quoted in (S/NF/WN) Christie and Barlow, *Scud Campaign*, p D–4.

[75]Operation CROSSBOW, the air campaign against German V weapons mounted by the U.S. Army Air Forces and Royal Air force in WWII, offers strong parallels to the Scud Hunt in terms of training, intelligence organization, and the role of political factors in the allocation of resources. The parallel breaks down tactically, since no attempt was made to target mobile V-2 launchers; observation by Capt Edward O'Connell, USAF, DIA Targeting Officer. See *The Army Air Forces in World War II*, Vol III, Ch 4, "CROSSBOW," pp 84-106 and 525-46.

[76](S/NF/WN) Christie and Barlow, *Scud Campaign*, p 1. Secretary of Defense Richard Cheney made the comment, "Mobile missile hunting was difficult and costly; we will need to do better."

Figure 52
Scud Functional Flow to Launch Positions (Soviet Model)

FIGURE DELETED

significant numbers of Al Husayn (also called Al Hussein), and perhaps Al Abbas ballistic missiles, posed major problems for the Coalition.[77] These problems were compounded by the possible use of chemical or biological warheads. The primary concern was that Scud attacks against Israel might prompt Israeli intervention and split the Coalition. This overriding concern gave the Scud Hunt its tactical priority.[78]

During the war, neither chemical nor biological warheads were used, and the Scud did not pose a militarily significant threat to Coalition forces.[79] The relatively small high-explosive warhead and 1,500 to 2,000-meter circular error probable (CEP)[80] of the Al Husayn reduced the missile to a psychological and harassment weapon.[81]

Scope and Concept of Operations

The Scud Hunt campaign had three main components: First, U.S. Army Patriot missiles defended selected point targets in Saudi Arabia and later, Israel. Second, Coalition air forces located, identified, and neutralized or destroyed Scud missiles, mobile launchers, support

---

[77](S/NF/WN) Ibid, pp I–10, I–11. Al Husayn and Al Abbas were Iraqi modifications of the Soviet Scud B, which in crude terms doubled the range of the original by extending the fuel tankage and halving the weight of the warhead.

[78](C) In August 1990 contingency planning for an Iraqi invasion of Saudi Arabia CINCCENT expressed concern over the prospect of "chemical and perhaps biological warheads threatening cities, airfields, ports, and troops" and emphasized the importance of suppressing Scud attacks quickly once hostilities began; he was also concerned about the use of Scud attacks on Israel as a means of splitting the Coalition. During the war, 42 Scuds were fired at Israel and 45 at Saudi Arabia; 1 landed in Qatar; (S/NF/WN) Christie and Barlow, *Scud Campaign*, pp I–14 - I–17.

[79](S) *Cf.* Desert Storm Scud Missile Working Group Conference, Working Group III (Tactics) Summary (Washington, D.C., 28-30 May, 1991), p 2, henceforth Scud Conference Group III Summary.

[80]W. Seth Caras and Joseph S. Bermudez, Jr., "Iraq's *Al-Husayn* Missile Programme," *Jane's Soviet Intelligence Review* (May 1990), pp 204-248, 206.

[81]For the psychological effects of the Scud threat on Coalition military personnel, see J. R. Galle-Tess, *Usage Et Limite de la Notion de Stress de Combat a L'Experience de la Guerre du Golfe*, a paper presented at the Gulf War International Symposium and World Psychiatric Association Meeting, Paris, 27 Jan 1992. Galle-Tess reports several instances of French aircrew members whose psychological reaction to the Scud threat led to their being relieved of flying duty.

278

vehicles, and support facilities. Finally, Special Operations Forces (SOF), including British Special Air Service (SAS) and Special Boat Service (SBS) and U.S. Army Special Forces, were deployed into Iraq.

Destroying Scud research and development centers, command and control installations, production and storage facilities, and fixed launch sites amounted to only a small part of the total effort after the first few days of the campaign. Since the fixed Scud launchers were not used,[82] and since attacks on these sites were tactically no different from attacks on any fixed installation, they are of no concern here.

The ability–or inability–of Coalition air forces to find and destroy mobile launchers and support systems was the key to attaining the objectives of the Scud hunt. The terminal effects of available ordnance were not a limiting factor, since bombs in the MK-80 series and cluster munitions of various kinds were more than adequate to destroy the soft-skinned targets associated with mobile Scud operations.[83] Accuracy was not a problem either, because if the target could be seen, LGBs (laser-guided bombs) had more than the requisite accuracy. When the target could not be seen visually or on infrared cockpit imagery, platforms with a radar bombing capability, notably the B-52, F-15E, A-6E, and F-111E/F, could in principle attack with sufficient accuracy to destroy mobile Scud targets.

There were three critical tactical challenges in the anti-Scud campaign. The first was the ability to detect Scud launches in timely fashion. The second was the ability of aircrews, using onboard visual, radar, and infrared aircraft systems, to spot mobile Scud launchers, vehicles, and support systems associated with mobile launch operations. The third was the ability to place ordnance on the targets once detected. Of these challenges, detection had to be met first, since there could be no strikes without detection. The ability of Coalition systems to detect the signatures of the various components of the mobile Scud system was thus a key to a successful Scud hunt.

---

[82](S) 27 Jan INKS Briefing. As of 27 January, there was no conclusive evidence that the estimated 30 fixed launchers had been used.

[83](S) Scud Conference Group III Summary, p 8.

[DELETED][84]. [DELETED][85]

[DELETED]. The Iraqis, made little or no use of radio communications for controlling Scud operations. [DELETED].[86] [DELETED]. Iraq apparently exercised command and control via encrypted communications over secure land lines and, possibly, couriers.[87] Consequently, underground communications cables believed to be associated with mobile missile operations–specifically, fiber optic cables–were identified as potential targets of the Scud hunt. [DELETED].[88] [DELETED].

Vehicles associated with mobile Scud operations were readily identifiable on imagery . . . if they could be seen. The qualification is critical because the Iraqis were adept at hiding mobile launchers and associated vehicles. [DELETED].

[DELETED][89]

The signature of the Scud missile itself was the principal means of launch detection. [DELETED].[90] Defense Support Program (DSP) satellites, successfully detected all eighty-eight Scud launches.[91] DSP

---

[84](S/NF/WN) Christie and barlow, *Scud Campaign*, p 1-7, para. 2 b.

[85][DELETED]

[86](S) 193d Special Operations Group, JULLS Long Report No. 41843-33473 (00004); 193d Special Operations Group (Air National Guard) GWAPS interviews, 20-21 Jan 1992.

[87](S) INKS briefing.

[88](S/NF) *USASOC History, Army Special Operations in Operations Desert Shield/Desert Storm*, atch. to ltr., Richard W. Stewart, Command Historian, to HQ, USSOCOM, attn. Dr. Partin, MacDill AFB, FL, subj: "Review of Historical Monograph on Desert Shield/Desert Storm," 22 April 1991 (henceforth *USASOC History*), p 45. [DELETED]

[89](S/NF/WN) Christie and Barlow, *Scud Campaign*, Summary p 12.

[90](S/NF/WN) *Ibid*, p I–11.

[91](S) *Defense Science Board Final Report on "Lessons Learned During Operations Desert Shield and Desert Storm,"* (8 Jan 1992), p 65; two of the 88 missiles launched failed in flight and did not reach their target areas.

coordinates delineated Scud launch areas.[92]   Strike crews did visually observe some Scud launches, but could not attack because they had no way to determine the precise location of the launches, particularly at night.[93] [DELETED].[94]

For tactical purposes, the most important visual, radar, and infrared signatures of the mobile Scud system were those of its component vehicles.   The most characteristic and important of these was the eight-wheeled Soviet-built MAZ-543 transporter-erector-launcher (TEL). [DELETED].[95] [DELETED].[96] [DELETED]. The Iraqis also fielded a number of locally constructed mobile-erector-launchers (MELs), launch rails on a flatbed truck in essence, to supplement the MAZ-543s. While these vehicles lacked the MAZ-543's superior mobility, they were probably capable of off-road operations. Post-war analysis indicated that Scud launches took place near paved highways. This would have been consistent with movement from hide locations[97] and with the use of MELs. [DELETED].[98]

All of the Scud vehicles were easily camouflaged and difficult to detect visually from the air.   All had large radar signatures plus prominent infrared signatures when their primary propulsion systems, auxiliary power units, generators, and heaters or air-conditioning units were operating. The signatures, however, could be readily imitated by decoys with varying degrees of fidelity, depending on the expense and attention to detail put into the decoy. [DELETED].

---

[92][DELETED]

[93](S) This would not have been true in the unlikely event that the launch took place within the field of vision of the strike aircraft's targeting radar or infrared systems, which did not happen.

[94](S) [DELETED]

[95](S/NF/WN) *Ibid*, pp I–2, 6, 11.

[96](S/NF/WN) *Ibid*, pp I–5, I–6.

[97](S) *Defense Science Board Final Report*, p 65.

[98](S) [DELETED]

The evidence suggests that tactical deception played a major role in Iraqi mobile Scud operations. [DELETED].[99] [DELETED].[100] [DELETED].

[DELETED][101] Postwar intelligence suggests that the estimated number of missiles was somewhat high, the estimated number of TELs and MELs was somewhat low, and predictions of tactics and organizational structure were inaccurate.[102] [DELETED].

[DELETED].[103] [DELETED].[104] [DELETED].[105]

[DELETED].[106] [DELETED].[107] [DELETED].[108]

In assessing the effectiveness of Iraqi tactical deception and the formidable problems facing Coalition airmen in attempting to locate mobile Scud systems, an important caveat must be made. Whether they

---

[99](S) [DELETED]

[100](S/NF) [DELETED]

[101]As quoted in OPLAN Desert Storm dated 16 Dec 1990, cited in (S/NF/WN) Christie and Barlow, *Scud Campaign*, I–10. The improvised MELs used Scania tractor transports as the prime mover. There was a wide band of uncertainty in estimates of numbers of missiles on hand, re (S) INKS briefing, which estimates that the Iraqis possessed 30 mobile launchers and 350-950 missiles on the date indicated. The DIA estimate was a total of 36.

[102](S/NF/WN) Christie and Barlow, *Scud Campaign*, p I–13.

[103](S) Comments provided by DIA analysts.

[104](S) [DELETED]

[105]Forward air controllers used this technique successfully in the Vietnam War, but flew specialized observation aircraft with more spacious cockpits, many of them two-seaters such as the OV-2 and OV-10. The side windows could be opened on many of these aircraft to avoid optical distortion from looking though the canopy, and the operating altitudes were generally considerably lower.

[106](S/NF/WN) Christie and Barlow, *Scud Campaign*, p I–15.

[107](S/NF) The tests were conducted at the Fort Campbell, KY, reservation and from Nellis AFB, NV, on the Yuma Proving Grounds, Arizona; information from [DELETED], who was involved in TOUTED GLEEM as a DIA targeting officer. See also (S/NF) TOUTED GLEEM: F-15; F-16 LANTIRN Adaptive Video.

[108](S) Information from Capt Jeff Hodgdon. Captain Hodgdon participated in TOUTED GLEEM as an F-111F weapons system operator.

were effective or not, the Iraqis obviously feared detection, particularly in daylight. Eighty-one percent or seventy-one of all Scud launches were in darkness,[109] and the few daylight launches occurred shortly after dawn. Specifically, launches took place between twenty minutes after dusk and one hour after dawn, and the great majority were launched between 2130 and 0345 Baghdad time.[110] The most likely explanation for the concentration of launch activity at night is that the Iraqi's were attempting to prevent Coalition Scud combat air patrol pilots from obtaining a visual fix on the launch location and attacking before the mobile launcher could move.

Tactical Execution

When the Scud offensive began, Coalition air forces were faced with the daunting prospect of searching virtually the entire western and southeastern quadrants of Iraq for mobile launchers and associated equipment.[111] This situation changed for the better with the discovery, made during the first days of the air war,[112] that Scuds were being fired to their maximum range of just over 600 kilometers, a pattern followed throughout the campaign. On the basis of this observation plus historical knowledge of previous launch sites and the known target areas–Haifa, Tel Aviv, Riyadh, and Dhahran–it was possible to define the launch areas with considerable accuracy.[113] (See Figure 53.) The intelligence community had plotted the locations of presurveyed Scud launch points in southeastern Iraq on the basis of a search of historical imagery

---

[109](S) *Defense Science Board Final Report*, p 65. The source does not specify, but "darkness" in this context probably means between evening nautical twilight (by definition, when the horizon can no longer be seen) and morning nautical twilight.

[110](S) As of 27 January, 68 percent of all launches had occurred in the 2130 to 0345 window, (S) INKS briefing.

[111](S/NF) DIA analysts had isolated likely mobile Scud launch areas on the basis of LANDSAT imagery and terrain analysis in advance of the air campaign, re (S/NF/WN) DIA Desert Storm Adaptive Planning Target Material, OPAREA India (ADTM 1-91), information cutoff date 7 Feb 1991, but air campaign planners were not aware of this.

[112](S) Precisely when the connection was made is unclear, but Checkmate team members are in agreement that it was during the first few days of the air war. The 27 Jan INKS briefing treats this as an established fact.

[113](S) *Defense Science Board Final Report*, p 66; and (S/NF/WN) Christie and Barlow, *Scud Campaign*, p I-18.

augmented by new imagery and HUMINT during Desert Shield, and these locations generally coincided with the Scud baskets.[114]

The Iraqi practice of launching only at maximum range can be accounted for by two complementary hypotheses, one technical and one tactical. The technical hypothesis is that launching at maximum range burns propellants to depletion and thus avoids aerodynamic instability resulting from center-of-gravity shifts on reentry that lead to tumbling and breakup of the missile body. The tactical hypothesis is that the Iraqis were preregistering and calibrating their launchers and missiles to the same (maximum range) settings on each launch. This procedure would save time by minimizing prelaunch adjustments after the missile was rolled into firing position, and also improve speed and efficiency

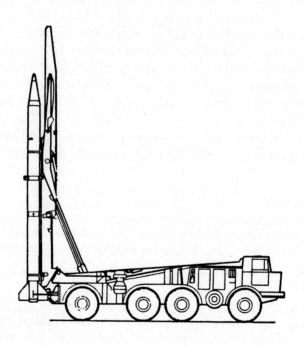

[114](S/NF/WN) Christie and Barlow, *Scud Campaign*, p I–12; a similar correlation was made for launch baskets in western Iraq after the initiation of hostilities.

Figure 53
Scud Targets and Launch Sectors

FIGURE DELETED

through standardized procedures.[115] The second hypothesis agrees with the notion that the Iraqis were concerned about risking detection by staying at a firing site too long. If that were the case, the adoption of "shoot and scoot" tactics to preserve mobile launch assets would logically follow. While neither hypothesis is provable in any rigorous sense, both fit what was known about Iraqi objectives and patterns of operations.

While many anti-scud tactics were considered, maintaining standing Scud combat air patrols (CAPs) over the launch baskets on a twenty-four-hour basis was favored. Night CAPs were maintained by F-15Es equipped with synthetic aperture radar and LANTIRN targeting pods in the western

---

[115](S) This hypothesis emerged within the CHECKMATE cell charged with monitoring Scud issues, (S) INKS briefing.

launch area and by F-16s equipped with LANTIRN and Global Position System (GPS) in the eastern area (or "box").[116] The F-16s, and occasionally the F-15Es in the western area, worked in conjunction with JSTARS. A-10s were used for daylight armed reconnaissance in both areas. Scud CAPs were supplemented by preplanned strikes against fixed targets.

During the Scud Hunt Campaign, formations of F-15Es patrolled the western box and F-16 formations patrolled the eastern box at night, using LANTIRN for reconnaissance of their assigned areas. If they did not locate targets during patrol, they attacked targets provided by intelligence. If no targets were available from intelligence, the patrols expended ordnance on preplanned Scud-related targets before returning to base.[117] Daylight Scud CAPs were flown by ten A-10s assigned to Al Jouf. These aircraft conducted daylight road reconnaissance in pairs, and the pilots used binoculars to assist their visual search. Both day and night Scud CAP aircraft normally flew at 12,000-15,000 feet to remain above effective antiaircraft artillery fire.[118] A-10 pilots used infrared imagery from Maverick seeker heads to augment their visual searches. [DELETED]. Those directing the Scud Hunt were well aware of the importance of suppressive efforts and issued their orders accordingly.[119] An idea of the range of weapons and tactics used and the ebb and flow of daily Scud hunting activity can be gained from Table 14.

[DELETED]

---

[116]Only one squadron of F-16s had GPS; they were the only Coalition tactical fighters so equipped.

[117](S/NF/WN) Christie and Barlow, *Scud Campaign*, p III–6.

[118](S/NF/WN) *Ibid*, p III–7.

[119](S) E.g., USCENTAF/DO to 4 TFW/CC message 040900Z Feb 91, directing F-15E crews on Scud CAP to maintain their patrol until relieved, even if they had expended all their ordnance.

Figure 54
Scud CAP Notification Net

FIGURE DELETED

[DELETED].[120]   Linking these disparate scud-hunt detection, communications, and tactical assets into a near-real-time command and control network was a remarkable achievement. The significance of that achievement, however, must be qualified when put in tactical context. The mobility of the Scud system and the brief warning time its various signatures afforded provided minimal engagement time, even when everything worked perfectly. It should be noted, however, that warning times   improved   significantly   as   the   campaign   progressed.

---

[120](S/NF/WN) Christie and Barlow, *Scud Campaign*, p II–25.

Table 14
Resources Committed to Scud Hunt Operations
27 January 1991[121]

Western Area

Mission Category	Resources	Ordnance	Targets
Scud CAP Night Only	F-15E • on ground alert • on Scud CAP,	CBU- GBU-	As provided by intelligence or targets of opportunity.
Armed Reconnaissance Daytime Only	A-10 • sorties, 2 on station at a time	AGM- CBU- 30-mm cannon	Intelligence provided launch locations and targets of opportunity.
Preplanned Missions	F-111F	GBU-	Large culverts and other potential hide sites.
	B-52G	CBU-	Storage and support facilities; H-1 and H-2 airfields.
	A-6E	not stated	
			Selected launch locations, storage and support facilities;
Supplemental missions	F-117	GBU-	Hardened sites at H-1, H-2, and H-3 airfields.

Eastern Area

Mission Category	Resources	Ordnance	Targets
Scud CAP Night Only	F-16C • on ground alert • on Scud CAP,	CBU-	As provided by intelligence and JSTARS or targets of opportunity.
Supplemental missions	B-52G as available	not stated	As provided by Intelligence or JSTARS.
	F/A-18 as available	not stated	Via ATO/FRAG order.

[121]Developed from (S/NF/WN) Christie and Barlow, *Scud Campaign*, Table III–1, p III–3.

**Figure 55
MobileScud
Exposure
Time**

FIGURE DELETED

[DELETED].[122]

[DELETED].[123] [DELETED].[124] [DELETED]

[DELETED].[125]

The difficulties of locating and attacking individual mobile Scud targets eventually drove tactical planners to an increased emphasis on suppressive tactics, which included dedicated B-52s armed with CBU-58s, (cluster munitions), making preemptive strikes in the Scud boxes from 19 February through the end of hostilities.[126] The B-52s arrived on station with CBU-58s and dropped them at intervals during their time on station. Dropped from high altitude, the high-explosive and fragmentation effects of the bomblets scattered over a wide area, putting thin-skinned mobile Scud vehicles and fueled missiles at risk. The B-52s freed five Scud CAP F-15Es for other targets and were deemed to have done the same suppressive job equally well.

Tactical Effectiveness

[DELETED][127] [DELETED].[128]

[DELETED]. The ability, or inability, of Scud-associated vehicles to move freely from staging areas to hide sites and back was a key determinant of tactical effectiveness. Those responsible for developing the ATO

---

[122](S/NF/WN) *Ibid*, Fig. 11-6, p II–32.

[123](S/NF) USASOC History, pp 46-48.

[124](S/NF/WN) Christie and Barlow, *Scud Campaign*, pp II–27, 28.

[125](S/NF/WN) *Ibid*, pp III–12, III–13. An F-15E entry cited that the anecdotal evidence alluded to above involves an unplanned radio contact between a Scud CAP aircrew and an individual on the ground with a British accent who directed a successful strike.

[126](S) 26 Feb 91 memo, subj: "B-52 Scud Hunter Mission," identified as probably written by Black Hole operative Cpt James Hawkins, Checkmate File 19-7. The CBU-58 submunition is a baseball-sized high explosive/fragmentation bomblet fuzed for instantaneous detonation.

[127](S/NF/WN) Christie and Barlow, *Scud Campaign*, p III–6.

[128](S) *Defense Science Board Final Report*, Fig. 2.6-4, p 72.

were well aware of this. They approached the problem by targeting potential hide sites such as culverts, overpasses, and bridges, whether Scud movement was observed around them or not–an idea developed within the Checkmate staff in coordination with DIA.[129] These targets were attacked by a variety of aircraft, including F-111Fs and F-117s, and involved the use of denial ordnance to inhibit free movement in and around suspected staging and launch areas. CBU-89/B GATOR, a cluster munition combining magnetically-fuzed antitank submunitions and trip-wire-fuzed antipersonnel submunitions, was used extensively for this purpose. GATOR would seem to have been ideal for limiting and delaying Scud movement in and around hide sites and staging areas, although conclusions concerning effectiveness remain an area of speculation, barring access to Iraqi records.[130] Similarly, the targeting of culverts, overpasses, and bridges capable of sheltering Scud-associated vehicles may have had some suppressive effect. The simple presence of Scud CAP aircraft overhead may have had suppressive effect as well, a supposition discussed later in the chapter.

[DELETED].[131] [DELETED].[132] [DELETED].

Scud hunting tactics were ineffective if measured in terms of numbers of Scud-associated vehicles confirmed destroyed. Cockpit imagery and reports by SOF ground forces hold open the possibility that some mobile launchers were destroyed, but this cannot be confirmed. Assertions by denigrators of the air campaign that no mobile launchers at all were destroyed are equally unprovable.[133] [DELETED].[134] On

---

[129](S) This took place on or about 23 January; information from, DIA.

[130](S/NF/WN) Christie and Barlow, *Scud Campaign*, p III–10, cite several "informal documents" to that effect, albeit without naming them. The CBU-89 is a free-fall cluster weapon consisting of the SUU-64/B dispenser containing 72 BLU-91/B antitank and 22 BLU-92/B antipersonnel submunitions. The BLU-91/B is a 4.31 pound antitank mine with a mass focused warhead fuzed with a magnetic sensor; the BLU-92B is a 3.75-pound antipersonnel mine with a fragmentation warhead triggered by tripwires.

[131](S/NF/WN) *Ibid*, Appendix C.

[132](S/NF/WN) Ibid, pp III–15-17.

[133]See, for example, Mark Crispin Miller, "Operation Desert Sham," *The New York Times*, 24 Jun 1992. See also "Claims of Scud Destruction Unverified," *Washington Post*, 25 Jun 1992, p 5.

balance, the evidence suggests that few mobile launchers were destroyed by Allied air power.

It seems unlikely that Iraqi mobile Scud operations remained unaffected. [DELETED]. The scud-hunt no doubt discouraged road movement by Scud units. It is worth noting in this regard that both the total number of Scuds launched and the weekly launch rates were significantly lower than one would expect on the basis of equivalent data from the "War of the Cities" phase of the Iran-Iraq War. [DELETED].[135]

Crossing the physically clear but analytically fuzzy line between destruction and suppression, analysis of Iraqi tactical behavior suggests considerable respect for Coalition Scud hunting capability. The most revealing datum in this respect is the Iraqi unwillingness to launch in daylight, and if the Iraqis were unwilling to launch at all in daylight, it seems unlikely that they felt able to do so with impunity at night.

Although the two cannot be cleanly separated, it seems clear that the destructive and suppressive effects of anti-Scud tactics combined to significantly reduce the launch rate. This conclusion is supported by the fact that the weekly launch rate was some thirty-four percent lower than in the War of the Cities phase of the Iran-Iraq War, during which the Iranians made no attempt to strike or suppress Scud launch activity. This was true despite the probability that the Iraqis had some thirty percent more missiles to expend than in the earlier conflict.[136] Figure 56 depicts a comparison of Scud launch rates in the War of the Cities with those in Desert Storm. These data suggest that anti-Scud operations reduced the

---

[134](S) The classic example involves the release of cockpit video footage in the course of a Riyadh press briefing, which was billed as showing a mobile Scud launcher being destroyed. In fact, the vehicle in question was probably a fuel truck.

[135](S) Point Paper, "BDA–Desert Storm, Operator's Look," briefed to Checkmate as of 29 Jan 0900 Baghdad time, CBDA Folder 13-1. In addition a "monumental" secondary explosion was noted following a B-52 strike on the Rumaylaw ammunition storage site on the morning of 28 Jan, re. Pentagon Operations Directorate 282330Z Jan 91 msg, p 2. This may or may not have been Scud related.

[136](S/NF/WN) Christie and Barlow, *Scud Campaign*, esp. Fig IV–2, pp IV–10-11.

number of Iraqi launches by something on the order of fifty percent.[137] The counter argument can be made that the slope of the two curves is remarkably similar, suggesting that the initial drop in firings and subsequent recovery was attributable mainly to internal logistic or operational factors. This argument bears closer examination. The most likely reason for the sharp drop in launches after the first two weeks in either case was the depletion of forward stockpiles of missiles, warheads, and fuel. According to this hypothesis, the "trough" in the launch curves represents a period of replenishment and the up turn at the end represents the expenditure of stocks moved forward during the period of reduced activity. In principle, the forward displacement of missiles, warheads and fuel would have been vulnerable to air interdiction. The difference in gross launch rates between the two cases is therefore, in principle at least, partly attributable to the difficulty of moving under the watchful eye of air power.

Two other considerations support the notion that anti-Scud operations significantly affected mobile Scud operations. First, the Iraqi ability to coordinate Scud launches appears to have declined as the campaign wore on. While forty of the first forty-two Scuds fired were launched in salvos, no less than twenty-seven of the last thirty-

---

[137](S) This estimate is based on several assumptions concerning the capabilities of the Iraqi mobile missile force in the absence of a suppressive effort: first, that it could have equalled the average weekly launch rates achieved during the War of the Cities with the same number of missiles on hand. Second, that thirty percent more launches could have been achieved had thirty percent more missiles been available. The above analysis is based on weekly averages. Close examination of launch patterns on an hour by hour basis correlated with air activity might well produce a somewhat different picture.

Figure 56
Comparison of Scud Launch Rates

FIGURE DELETED

nine were launched separately.[138] This may be attributable to a change in Iraqi tactics, but on balance this seems unlikely. Second, launches against King Khalid Military City (KKMC) did not begin until 14 February, some four weeks after the start of the Scud Hunt. These firings came from a new launch area immediately north of Baghdad,

---

[138](S) *Defense Science Board Final Report*, p 70; there were 13 multiple launches with salvo launch times totalling 15 seconds or less; 4 of these included launches from more than one Scud box.

much closer to presumed missile stockpiles than the others, and better served by road. Since the Iraqis surely accorded Israeli targets higher priority than Saudi targets, and since Riyadh was presumably a more lucrative target politically and psychologically than KKMC, this shift in effort is suggestive. The notion that the change in targeting was forced on the Iraqis by tactical considerations rather than voluntarily adopted for policy reasons is supported by a comparison of targets struck in the first and last twelve days of the Scud campaign. Of the fifty Scuds fired during the initial twelve day "spike," no less than twenty-seven, or fifty-four percent, fell on Israel. It is all but certain that the bulk of these missiles were in forward staging areas when the air war started. Note, too, that twenty of the fifty were fired before the Scud Hunt proper began. Of the twenty-eight fired in the final twelve days, nine, or thirty-two percent fell on both Israeli and KKMC targets.[139]

Conclusions

The salient conclusion is that U.S. and Coalition air forces found it extremely difficult to locate, find, and destroy mobile Scud targets. The absence of unequivocal evidence concerning the number and nature of targets destroyed strengthens this conclusion: a timely, accurate, and reiterative bomb damage assessment process is an essential part of any successful air campaign, and the assessment did not exist. Conversely, several considerations suggest that the campaign placed significant tactical and operational constraints on Iraqi mobile Scud operations. First, the reluctance of the Iraqis to fire during daylight provides clear, if indirect, evidence that mobile Scud forces were unable to operate with impunity in daylight. Second, the markedly lower numbers and rates of Scud launches in the Gulf War in comparison with those in the War of the Cities strongly implies that an inhibiting factor constrained mobile Scud operations. The only such factor evident is air power. The same point applies to the shift in firings from Israeli to Saudi targets toward the end of the Scud campaign. While the estimates of numbers of missiles and launchers available on which this point is based are soft, the point holds across the spectrum of estimates.[140] The implication is that the effects of air power multiplied the impact of whatever logistical constraints were at work.

---

[139](S/NF/WN) Christie and Barlow, *Scud Campaign*, Fig. 1, p 8.

[140](S) For numbers of Scuds available and fired, see *Report of the United Nations Special Commission Special Mission to Iraq*, Annex C, 27-30 Jan 1992. [DELETED]

Special Operations Forces And Air Power

This section discusses the weapons and tactics used by Special Operations Forces (SOF) in support of the Desert Shield and Desert Storm air campaign. Special Operations Forces began arriving in Saudi Arabia 10-12 August. SOF employed by the Commander-in-Chief, US Central Command (CINCCENT), included Army, Navy, and Air Force units. Missions performed included Coalition Warfare Support, Psychological Operations (PSYOP), Combat Search and Rescue (CSAR), Direct Action, Combined Special Reconnaissance, Civil Affairs, and Military Reconstruction in Kuwait.[141] These missions are addressed in turn.

Command Relationships

Command relationships were fragmented and complicated and, in some cases, had a negative impact on tactical effectiveness. With certain exceptions, SOF, including the Joint Special Operations Task Force (JSOTF), were under the command of CINCCENT and under the operational control of Special Operations Command, Central Command (SOCCENT). Civil Affairs units remained under the operational control of the Army Component (ARCENT), while AC-130 Spectre gunships and EC-130 Volant Solo PSYOP aircraft were under the operational control of the Air Force Component (CENTAF). Additionally, sea-air-land (SEAL) platoons and Special Boat Detachments were under the operational control of the Naval Component (NAVCENT) (see Figure 57).

Relationships established between Central Command (CENTCOM), SOCCENT, CENTAF, and Special Operations Command Europe (SOCEUR), serve to illustrate the problems associated with command and control of SOF air assets. Shortly after arrival in theater, Commander SOCCENT set about consolidating his air assets at King Fahd International Airport.

---

[141](S) USSOCOM Command Brief, prepared by USSOCOM/SOJ3, 1992. It is important to note that each SOF mission had an air component.

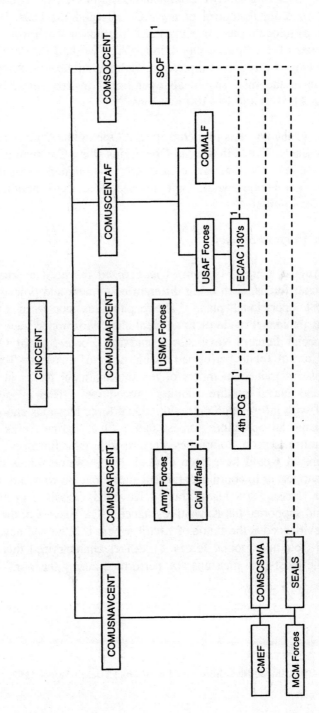

**Figure 57
Operational Control of SOF Forces
Split Among Different Components**

1 (U) Shows how OPCON of SOF forces was split among different components.

However, the acting CENTAF Commander, Major General Thomas Olson, retained operational control of the AC-130s and EC-130s. He agreed, however, to relocate them to King Fahd International Airport. Thus, the Commander of 1st Special Operations Wing worked for both SOCCENT and CENTAF. He reported directly to Colonel Johnson at SOCCENT, but did not have the final say in all operational matters, especially those involving AC-130 and EC-130 missions.[142]

Also in theater was the 39th Special Operations Wing from Rhein-Main Air Base. The 39th Special Operations Wing Commander reported to Commander SOCEUR, while SOCCENT maintained tactical control. European Command would not release forces to another theater commander-in-chief.[143]

Coalition Warfare Support

In August, Central Command recognized the need to integrate the multinational forces, each using different equipment and procedures, into a coherent operational plan. The capabilities possessed by special operations personnel made them an ideal choice to support such an effort. Army Special Forces, Navy SEALs, and Air Force Special Operations Combat Control Teams performed a wide range of missions. Teams from these missions trained members of the multinational forces in close air support and Naval gunfire spotting procedures. They also provided CINCCENT with information on multinational force locations and activities. Other nonspecial operations forces, such as the Marine Corps' Air and Naval Gunfire Liaison Companies, performed similar functions. Without these teams, it would have been difficult for Coalition forces to receive U.S. fire support or to coordinate tactical air operations with U.S. and other Allied air forces. SOF teams trained Kuwaitis, Saudis, Egyptians, and Syrians and supported the Kuwaiti resistance. The success of the program was first evidenced at the Battle of Khafji, where U.S. air and naval gunfire supported Coalition ground forces. CINCCENT characterized this effort as "one of the most vital missions SOF performed during the war."

---

[142](S) AFSOC unpublished history of Desert Shield/Desert Storm, 1992, p 3.

[143](S) *Ibid.*

298

Psychological Operations

As the crisis in the Gulf unfolded, the need for a psychological operations campaign became apparent.[144] Language qualified and regionally and culturally oriented, PSYOP personnel were specifically organized, trained, and equipped for such operations. By the end of October, a combined cell had been formed with representatives from the United States, Saudi Arabia, Egypt, and the United Kingdom.[145] By 12 January 1991, everything was in place to begin the psychological operations campaign. Actually, the PSYOP machinery had been in place since 30 August 1990, but permission to implement the plan was granted only after a 5 December personal message from General Schwarzkopf to the Joint Chiefs of Staff.

EC-130 Volant Solo is the only airborne PSYOP platform in the U.S. inventory. As an Air National Guard asset, the Volant Solo operation presented unique unit and personnel rotation policies. Active duty participation was based on prefiled volunteer statements and not on mobilization.[146] The National Guard Bureau specified thirty day rotations of personnel, since thirty days is the maximum volunteer period. Many guardsmen returned for three or four rotations.

During Desert Shield, the flight orbits of broadcasting aircraft were moved progressively closer to the Iraq/Kuwait border. The first Volant Solo broadcast was on Thanksgiving Day, 22 November 1990, when they began rebroadcasting Voice Of America service. [DELETED].

---

[144](S) JCS issued deployment orders to CINCSOC directing movement of the 193d SOG (a one-of-a-kind PSYOP asset).

[145]Before October, Saudi representatives were very concerned about using PSYOP for fear they would provoke an Iraqi invasion.

[146]193d Special Operations Group. After Action Rpt and Intvws. Harrisburg, PA, Jan 1992.

The recovery of downed U.S. aircrews has traditionally enjoyed a high priority in wartime.[147] Doctrinally, combat rescue was the responsibility of the Joint Force Commander. Each component commander was responsible for planning and conducting CSAR in support of his own operations. CSAR was a Service responsibility.[148] The Special Operations CSAR responsibilities were no greater than that of any other Service or functional component.

The crisis in the Gulf confronted the Air Force with a dilemma. The Air Force had recently reestablished the Air Rescue Service (ARS), but without helicopters capable of penetrating a high-threat environment.[149] In the aftermath of the failed April 1980 Iranian rescue operation, most CSAR aircraft, the HC-130s and HH/CH-53s, had assumed special operations roles. The most capable ARS helicopter, the MH-60 Pave Hawk, was available only in small numbers and was considered capable only for a medium-threat environment. None of the Services possessed forces trained and equipped solely to conduct classic combat rescue missions. In Desert Storm, SOF aviation assets were the only forces with the requisite capabilities to penetrate enemy territory, recover a downed pilot, and egress safely.[150] Special Operations Forces, however, are equipped and trained for night missions. A 24-hour on-call search and rescue mission could put Special Operations Forces in enemy territory during daylight hours–a circumstance they are taught to avoid.

The above problems notwithstanding, and with a campaign plan that called for the use of hundreds of aircraft flying thousands of sorties around the clock, a strategy had to be created and forces positioned for

---

[147]Aerospace Rescue and Recovery Service, the principal CSAR force in Vietnam, was disbanded in 1983, and its components and equipment were absorbed by Special Operations Forces (SOF). Air Rescue Service was (re)constituted in 1989, but was not combat ready and was not equipped with helicopters capable of penetrating a high-threat environment.

[148]JCS Pub 3-50.2, Doctrine for Joint Combat Search and Rescue.

[149]In 1989, the 41st Rescue Weather Reconnaissance Wing was realigned under the Military Airlift Command and renamed the Air Rescue Service.

[150]The only SOF aviation assets configured to penetrate enemy airspace were the U.S. Air Force MH-53 and MH-60, and the U.S. Army CH-47 and UH-60.

accomplishing CSAR. CINCCENT tasked the mission to SOCCENT, who in turn designated Air Force Special Operations Command, Central Command, to be the single manager for all CSAR aviation.[151] CENTCOM Army,[152] Navy, and Air Force aircraft were responsible for on-call CSAR for Kuwait and Iraq, south of 33 degrees, 30 minutes north latitude. The area north of 30 degrees, 30 minutes north latitude was covered by EUCOM forces in Turkey. By the time Desert Storm began, aircraft supporting CSAR missions were located at five bases in Saudi Arabia and at two in Turkey.

A CSAR plan was developed and a joint rescue coordination center (JRCC) was established within the Tactical Air Coordination Center (TACC). Once established, Special Operations personnel and aircraft were on 24-hour CSAR alert for over eight months. The mission continued into the postwar period.

Air Force Special Tactics personnel conducted CSAR exercises and provided communications, escape, and evasion training to aircrews. They also helped develop and implement weapons, survival, first aid, and medical training for Air Force Special Operations Command (AFSOC) personnel.[153]

CSAR Procedures

Central Command's CSAR guidelines required reasonable confirmation of a downed aircrewman's survival and location before a CSAR

---

[151]AFSOCCENT provided mission guidance to AFSOF assets at Rafha, Ar'Ar, and Al Jouf and to the Army's 3/160 assets at King Khalid Military City. All assets responded to the Joint Recovery Coordination Cell (JRCC) at Riyadh, and final mission approval rested with SOCCENT. U.S. Army Special Ops CMD, Historical Monograph on Desert Shield/Storm, 1992, p 4-5.

[152]The Army 3d Battalion, 160th Special Operations Aviation Regiment, working with Air Force Special Operations, developed procedures and techniques for conducting CSAR. Using these techniques, Army SOF aviators rescued one F-16 pilot. The Army flew MH-47 (Chinook) and MH-60 Blackhawk helicopters.

[153](S/NF) Air Force Special Tactics personnel were augmented by Air Force Survival instructors (SOCCENT E&E After Action Rpt, 5 Mar 1991).

mission launch.[154] First Special Operations Wing personnel visited each flying wing and briefed aircrews on CSAR procedures, and detailed information on SOF capabilities and requirements.[155] The CSAR system was set-up so that once a crewman ejected and reached the ground, fighters, would be diverted to the designated area. The JRCC, then alerted AFSOCCENT to execute the mission (see Figure 58). Due to dense enemy concentrations on the battlefield and Iraqi use of radio direction-finding equipment, downed pilots were frequently captured immediately after parachuting to the ground. As a result, only seven CSAR missions were launched, resulting in three saves.

The first save, January 21, was a daylight recovery[156] of a Navy F-14 pilot (Lieutenant Devon Jones) downed deep in Iraq by antiaircraft fire. The E-3 AWACS directed two A-10s to the area of the downed pilot, over 160 miles inside Iraq. Meanwhile, a MH-53 Pave Low helicopter

---

[154]Some aircrews found fault with Central Command's CSAR procedure requiring confirmation of a survivor before a mission launch. The following are comments by Lt Col Trumbull, 550 TFTS, interviewed 17 Jun 91. "The other thing I think was missing was SAR (search and rescue). Our DO and his backseater were on the ground for three and one-half days in western Iraq. Nobody'd go in and pick them up, and they eventually became prisoners of war. The advertised special operations guys that came down to talk to us before the war said, 'no sweat, we'll come get you anywhere you are.' That from my perspective, was a big lie. When I've got guys on the ground for three and one-half days and they don't go pick them up, we basically decided at that point that if anybody went down, you were on your own. Nobody was going to come get you." Lt Col Trumbull refers to the Eberly and Griffith shoot down. Poor communication prevented contact, location authentication, and recovery efforts. The officers were captured when they walked into a border guard post. Three recovery attempts were made before their capture.

[155](S) Air Force Special Operations Command (AFSOC) Desert Storm After Action Rpt, 1991, p 9-10.

[156]SOF CSAR preferred to operate in darkness, the time when they were most likely to survive.

Figure 58
CENTCOM CSAR Procedure

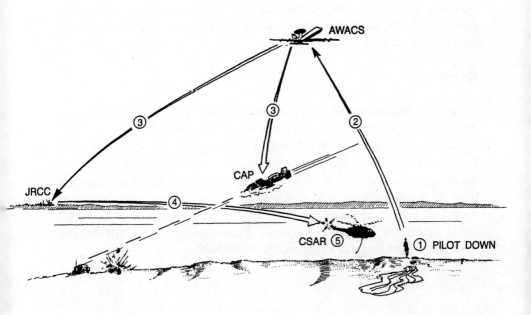

was launched. As the helicopter arrived in the rescue area, the A-10s destroyed an Iraqi radio-intercept truck closing in on the downed pilot. Two Special Tactic Paramedics, part of the MH-53 helicopter crew, assisted the downed pilot to the helicopter and conducted a preliminary physical examination.

Other rescue missions did not go as smoothly. On 27 February 1991, AWACS received a call of a downed F-16 pilot in hostile territory (Iraq) and reported the data to the JRCC. [DELETED].[157] [DELETED]. The Army directed a UH-60 Blackhawk to refuel, pick up a flight surgeon, rendezvous with two armed AH-64 Apache[158] attack helicopters, and attempt a rescue. The pilot's exact location was unknown. The plan was

---

[157](S) Intvw, Capt Greg Eanes, USAF, Chief, Escape and Evasion, SOCCENT during Desert Storm, Sep 1992.

[158]The UH-60 Blackhawk and the two AH-64 Apache helicopters were from the 101st Airborne Division.

to get the rescue helicopter to the general area of the downed pilot and attempt to establish radio contact. As the three helicopters entered the area of the downed pilot,[159] they came under heavy Iraqi fire. All three helicopters began evasive maneuvers, but the rescue helicopter was shot down.[160] Both escort helicopters sustained damage, but were able to return to home base.[161]

Escape and Evasion

As the Executive Agent for Aircrew Escape and Evasion, SOCCENT was tasked with developing and executing an escape and evasion plan.[162] In response, SOCCENT developed a contingency Blood Chit (see Figure 59) that could be photocopied and passed out to aircrews and special operators as needed. It was also recommended that a contingency fund be established to pay indigenous persons for assisting downed American pilots and crews. One Coalition member used a Blood Chit in his successful evasion to freedom. Fortunately, Blood Chits did not have to be used in great numbers. [DELETED].

---

[159]The pilot was captured by Iraqi soldiers. He was repatriated on 6 Mar 1991.

[160]Five crew members died in the crash; the three survivors were captured by Iraqi soldiers. They were repatriated on 6 Mar 1991.

[161]Intvw, Lt Col Joseph Hampton, USAF, Commander, Joint Rescue Control Center during Desert Storm, Sep 1992.

[162](S) Capt Greg Eanes, USAF, SOCCENT J2/E&E officer Evasion and Escape Rpt 1991.

Figure 59
Blood Chit

117516   117516

ARABIC

انا امريكي ولا اتكلم لغتك. انا احتاج
الى مساعدتك للحصول على الطعام
والمأوى والوقاية. ارجوك ان تأخذني
الى من يستطيع ان يحميني وان يرجعني
الى اهلي. سأعمل بكل طاقتي لحمايتك
من اي ضرر. وان حكومتي ستكافيك
مكافأة على مساعدتكم لي عندما
تقدمون لها هذا الرقم مع ذكر
اسمي.

PERSIAN (FARSI)

امريكايی هستم - زبان شما حرف نميزنم -
بمناسبت دچار بدبختی مجبورم از شما
مساعدت خوراک و بناه، و بست بخواهم -
خواهشمندم مرا بکسی که وسایل سلام
مرا فراهم کند ببرید و مراقبت کنید که من
تحت نظارهی دولت خود واگذار شوم -
نهایت کوشش خواهم کرد که هیچ اسیبی
بشما نیاید - دولتم بشما پاداش تلافی
خواهد داد -

KURDISH

من له مریکیم و به زمانی نیوه قسه ناکه م
من به هیچ جوربك هه زیه تو ناره حنیو
ناخوشیتان بی ناك به ته
برادهره کان تکاتان لی ته که م که یارمه تیم
بدهن به ئابه به بی بر خواردنؤ خوارزه
به نی وجلو به رك و ته که ر بیوبستی
دکتور (حکیم) بم
هه ر وه ها برادهره کانم سیاستان ته که م
ته که ره بوخه نه ده ستی له شکری برادهران
و هه رجی ولاتیك که وا یارمه تی و
تلسوزی له مریکا ته دا
و مئیش ئه م جانه بی نیوهم له بیر ناهیت
و نه مه ى قازانجیکی زورتان بی بکه یه تم
هه ر ناوی من له که ل نم نمرهیه بدهن
ده ستی بیاوانی حکومه تی له مریکا
بیتر هه ر بترین.

TURKISH

Ben Amerikalıyım ve Türkçe bilmiyorum. Benim size hiç bir
zararım dokunmaz! Sizin halkınıza benden hiç bir kötülük gelmez.
Arkadaşım lütfen bana yiyecek, su, barınak, giyim eşyası, ilaç
ve doktor sağlar mısın? Aynı zamanda benim Amerikalıların ve
onların dostu olan diğer memleketlerin en yakındaki kuvvetlerine
emniyetle gitmemi sağlayın. Benim ismimi ve bu numarayı
Amerikan makamlarına verdiğiniz zaman bana yardım ettiğiniz için
size bir ödül verilecektir.

ENGLISH

I am an American and do not speak your language. I will not harm you! I bear no malice towards your people. My friend, please provide me
food, water, shelter, clothing, and necessary medical attention. Also, please provide safe passage to the nearest friendly forces of any country
supporting the Americans and their allies. You will be rewarded for assisting me when you present this number and my name to American
authorities.

PREPARED AND PUBLISHED BY THE
DEFENSE MAPPING AGENCY AEROSPACE CENTER
ST LOUIS, MISSOURI

BLOOD CHIT
(front/back)

117516

Direct Action

On the evening of 16 January 1991, a MH-53J Pave Low III helicopter crossed into Iraqi airspace leading a flight of Army AH-64 Apache attack helicopters. The Apaches attacked Iraqi radar sites with Hellfire missiles to suppress radar defenses in advance of the initial Coalition strikes. At the same time, special operations teams placed radar beacons along the northern Saudi Arabian border to aid Coalition aircraft in confirming their position when entering and leaving Iraq.[163]

Special operations fixed-wing aircraft also performed direct action missions. The MC-130E Combat Talon dropped 15,000-pound BLU-82 bombs. Five complex missions involving AWACS, electronic jamming, air defense suppression, and support aircraft were executed. Eleven BLU-82s were dropped on nine different Iraqi positions, including Faylaka Island. The weapon's enormous blast effect was exploited to demoralize Iraqi forces. The Commander of the 8th Special Operations Squadron proposed the use of BLU-82s as a mine-clearing and psychological weapon. The proposal was forwarded to CINCCENT, who was interested in using the bomb to clear mine fields. The depot at Hill AFB quickly shipped 18 BLU-82s to King Fahd Airport. The Iraqi air defense threat dictated drop altitudes between 16,000 and 21,000 feet.[164] In addition, more than one was dropped at a time to increase the psychological impact and to take advantage of tactical surprise. As a final precaution, each of the drop aircraft formations included EF-111 Ravens, F-4G Wild Weasels, and EC-130 Compass Call aircraft.[165]

Eleven BLU-82s were dropped, mostly against minefields and troop concentrations.

> While the effectiveness of the munitions in clearing mines and other obstacles has not been determined, the BLU-82s were very effective against enemy troops. Even bunkered troops were severely affected by the blast from these massive bombs. Debriefings from captured troops

---

[163](S) AFSOC Desert Storm After Action Rpt.

[164](S) Air Force Special Ops CMD Paper: BLU-82 Operations in Desert Storm, May 92, p 2.

[165](S) *Ibid*, p 3.

from the vicinity of the BLU-82 missions provided testaments to the effectiveness of this weapon.[166]

No bombs were dropped after G-day. Upon cessation of hostilities, the seven unexploded BLU-82s in country were destroyed by Explosive Ordnance Disposel personnel.[167]

Special operations AC-130 Spectre gunships were also involved in direct action missions. These aircraft, first used in combat missions in Vietnam, were equipped to operate in a low-threat environment. Between 18 and 21 January, AC-130s were diverted from their usual missions to look for mobile Scud targets.[168] On 21 January, an AC-130 crew detected launch indications on their Radar Warning Receiver. The crew evaded the missile attacks but overstressed the aircraft. A second AC-130 on the Scud hunt was also threatened by a number of SAM sites. Both crews were confronted with well-organized and coordinated Iraqi attacks, demonstrating a high degree of command and control. [DELETED].[169] AC-130s were effective in supporting ground forces in Kuwait and in suppressing the Iraqi incursion into Khafji, Saudi Arabia, where a gunship was lost.

Special Reconnaissance

SOCCENT used teams for combined special reconnaissance during Desert Shield and Desert Storm. These missions satisfied a wide range of requirements, from reconnaissance along the Kuwaiti coast to support of conventional tactical operations deep inside Iraq. SEAL units operated in shallow water close to shore. SEAL operations, which took place over several weeks, resulted in intelligence gathering and contributed to tacti-

---

[166](S) SOCCENT, 1991 Command History Desert Shield/Desert Storm.

[167]Before Desert Shield/Storm, no testing had been conducted with the BLU-82 for mine clearing or desert warfare, a shortcoming that impacted desert use. Unfortunately, after the war, no tests were conducted with the unexploded bombs, which were eventually destroyed.

[168](S) 16th SOS Desert Storm Mission Summary Report, 1991.

[169](S) *Ibid*, p 3-4.

cal deception operations. A PSYOP sea- and air-delivered leaflet operation also supported this deception effort (see Figure 60).[170]

Figure 60
Leaflet

Army special forces performed reconnaissance missions in support of XVIII Airborne Corps and VII Corps. Rotary wing aircraft, specifically MH-53J and UH-60 special operations penetrator helicopters, conducted long-range infiltrations and exfiltrations into central and western Iraq. These missions provided commanders with essential information such as trafficability analysis (the ability of the ground to withstand traffic) and other details that could not be acquired by any other means.[171]

---

[170]Leaflets were placed in bottles that were allowed to drift onto Kuwaiti beaches. Iraqi military personnel gathered the leaflets and made inferences. Intvw, Commander 4th Psychological Operations Group, Feb 1992.

[171]Army 5th, 3d and 10th Special Forces Groups were inserted behind Iraqi lines to provide eye-on-target intelligence. Assistance was provided by Air Force, Navy, and 4/17th Cavalry. U.S. Army Special Operations CMD, Historical Monograph.

Civil Affairs[172]

Civil Affairs (CA) units played an important role throughout Operations Desert Shield and Desert Storm. Their missions included emergency support to the civilian sector, assessing the availability of host nation support, and assisting in the control, care, and movement of dislocated civilians and EPWs. The units made use of SOF and Military Airlift Command air assets in carrying out their missions. Special tactics personnel spent a great deal of time setting up contracts for water, fuel, and other airfield critical items. They had little training in this area, and it took them away from their primary duties. Civil Affairs units, however, were specifically trained in developing host nation interface and support agreements. Earlier deployment of CA units would have freed-up special tactics personnel and would have helped major airfields reach an operational status sooner.

Kuwaiti Military Reconstruction

In October of 1990, the State Department directed Civil Affairs planners to assist the Kuwaiti government in planning and executing a reconstruction effort.[173] One of the first tasks involved restoration of the International Airport.[174] Initial work was begun by Air Force Special Tactics units, which were later supplemented by regular Military Airlift Command combat control units.

Special Tactics Groups

The Air Force Special Tactics Group was activated on 1 October 1987 in response to the need for integrated positive control and management of aviation and for on-scene casualty treatment and staging.[175] Previously, these functions had been performed either by different units or, in some cases, not at all. Under certain circumstances, such an informal arrangement was adequate. This was not true during special

---

[172]Intvw, Sgt Maj Eric Patterson, USSOCOM, Crisis Action Team, 1992.

[173]The Kuwait Task Force (KTF), in cooperation with others, accomplished a significant reconstruction effort. Civil Affairs In The Persian Gulf War, A Symposium, USA JFKSWCS, Ft Bragg, NC, Oct 1991, pp 270-271.

[174](S) U.S. Army Special Ops CMD, Historical Monograph.

[175](S) Special Order GA 170, Hq MAC, 28 Sep 1987.

operations, however, where close coordination was a necessity and fragmented and inefficient operations had to be avoided.[176]

Wartime Tasking

During Desert Storm, Special Tactics combat air traffic controllers operated the three forward operating locations (FOLs) while the Pararescue Jumpers were flying as medical crewmen aboard Air Force MH-53s and MH-60s, and Army CH-47s and UH-60s.

At Al Jouf and Ar'Ar airfields, along the Saudi Arabia-Iraq border, Special Tactics combat air traffic controllers recovered and refueled hundreds of aircraft and operated the primary emergency divert airfields for battle-damaged or minimum-fuel aircraft returning from combat sorties in Iraq. Al Jouf also became the main operating base for A-10s in the northern region.

On 22 January 1991, a Special Tactics combat air traffic controller was a member of a special team infiltrated to within fifteen kilometers of Baghdad on a classified mission. His knowledge of close air support and communications procedures provided the team with a reasonable assurance that they would receive support if needed. The team was successful in cutting many lines of communications from Baghdad to outlying areas. As a result of the team's success and the contributions of the Special Tactics combat air traffic controller, the special operations unit requested four more Special Tactics personnel to conduct other clandestine missions.

During Desert Storm, Special Tactics personnel functioned as frontline combat medics, flew aeromedical evacuation missions in support of the Coalition forces, and provided other medical support. They assisted in planning and executing Joint Task Force Charlie; a medical contingency plan designed to provide initial medical support at Kuwait City International Airport.[177]

---

[176]Briefing, Bernie Oder, Special Tactics (USAFSOC), 4 Jun 1992.

[177]Kuwait City International Airport was to act as a casualty collection point, triage, and air evacuation station.

Summary

During Desert Storm, SOF played a unique and important role. SOF operated in all environments–on land, on and under the sea, and in the air–as part of the combined arms team. SOF teams remained behind enemy lines and conducted special reconnaissance. They also supported theater deception plans, performed combat search and rescue, and conducted direct action missions. SOF contributed significantly to Coalition warfare and the reconstruction of the Kuwaiti Military and public infrastructure.[178]

In support of Desert Storm, U.S. Special Operations units were part of the largest special operations force in history. Many of the missions performed during Desert Shield and Desert Storm were identified in prewar plans; others, including the CSAR mission, were worked out during the crisis.

SOF was able to provide the CINC with capabilities and options that effectively multiplied the military force available. Previous training and funding provided SOF with the flexibility to perform CSAR, Direct Action, Reconnaissance, and other missions with the same assets on very short notice.

Air Refueling

Air refueling was critical to the success of Desert Storm–not only the air refueling needed to deploy Coalition forces, but also air refueling for complex tactical operations. For example, during the opening hours of Desert Storm, seven B-52s launched from Barksdale AFB, Louisiana, and flew the world's longest combat mission. The mission lasted over thirty-five hours and culminated with the launch of thirty-five conventional air-launched cruise missiles (CALCMs). The B-52s had to be air refueled five times, requiring support from a mix of thirty-eight KC-135 and nineteen KC-10 tanker sorties.[179]

Since World War II, the United States has invested heavily in air refueling aircraft. These include the Air Force KC-135s and KC-10s, the Navy KA-6s, and the Marine KC-130s. If considered a separate air force,

---

[178]USSOCOM, Posture Statement, Jun 1992, p 2.

[179](S) Hq Strategic Air Command, "Black" Weapon, Covert Mission: The Conventional ALCM, Desert Shield and Desert Storm 1986-1991, 29 May 1992.

all of these refueling aircraft combined, a total of 813,[180] would rank as the world's seventeenth largest force.[181]

All the Services procured air refueling systems to support their unique tactics and requirements. However, only Air Force tankers routinely planned and operated refueling missions supporting all Services in Desert Shield and Desert Storm.[182] These tankers refueled 4,820 Navy/ Marine sorties, offloading 167,705,600 pounds of fuel, or about 13.5 percent of all fuel offloaded.[183]

The scope of air refueling in the Gulf War was enormous and could only have been accomplished by the United States with the U.S. Air Force in the lead role, for no other air force in the world has so totally integrated air refueling into its operational concepts.[184] The operational tactics employed by the U.S. tanker force during the Gulf War evolved from those of the Vietnam war and matured, through exercise and planning, into a layered spread of airborne aircraft that stretched the entire length of the front. As the air war successes became apparent, KC-135s and KC-10s even orbited in Iraqi airspace.

Tracks And Anchors

Desert Shield deployment air refuelings built what can be described as a bridge across the Atlantic and Mediterranean. The tanker tactics required to support the Air Campaign Plan were of a different nature, but responded to the same basic questions: How much gas do you want? Where do you want to start? Where should you be when finished? The driving force behind the tactics employed was the diversity of the fighter

---

[180]At the time of Desert Storm, the USAF had 635 KC-135A, QE, R, and 59 KC-10 in active, reserve, and National Guard; the U.S. Navy had 59 KA-6D, and the Marine Corps had 60 KC-130. Data were compiled through the assistance of Hq USAF, Hq US Marine Corps, and Chief of Naval Operations staff.

[181](S) Based upon data from 480th Air Intelligence Group comparing the world's air forces fixed wing aircraft.

[182]Helicopter refuelings are accomplished by Marine Corps KC-130s and some versions of USAF HC-130s and MC-130s

[183](S) Desert Shield/Desert Storm Tanker Assessment, pp 2-6 - 2-13.

[184](S) The USAF possesses the world's largest tanker fleet, 694 aircraft. Source: 480th Air Intelligence Group.

packages used in the air campaign. Aircraft came from different locations and had different fuel burn rates and different offload requirements. What they had in common was the need to air refuel in the same area and end very nearly at the same time over approximately the same geographic area. This requirement drove the development of tanker anchor orbit areas, which involved several tankers stacked vertically at 500-foot intervals so that they could refuel many aircraft simultaneously. The orbits were designed to meet the fuel demands of the fighter force and, equally important, to provide enough booms to refuel an entire package at the end of its mission within a short time.

Not all aircraft could benefit from the orbit concept. Some aircraft such as the B-52, E-3A, and RC-135 required many thousands of pounds of fuel. They needed long, straight tracks, usually along the most direct flight path required to get the aircraft to its target. These tracks did not have tankers stacked as did the anchor orbits. Rather, they often had two or three tankers in formation available to refuel a multiship bomber cell requiring over 200,000 pounds of fuel. The maze of requirements spread tankers across the battle area right to the forward edge of U.S.-controlled airspace. Figure 61 depicts the planned tanker anchors and tracks available on Day 1 of the air campaign.

Boom Versus Drogue

Differences between the U.S. Services complicated refueling operations. The KA-6D and KC-130 were equipped with drogues designed to mate with the probes on Navy and Marine aircraft.[185] For long duration missions such as trans-Atlantic deployments, offload requirements dictated the use of U.S. Air Force tankers, which have the capability to refuel with either a boom or a drogue. With the KC-135, however, the decision as to which aircraft were going to be air refueled

---

[185]The Air Force standardized on flying boom systems in the 1950s and 1960s, largely because of the enormous offloads required by strategic bombers, frequently exceeding 100,000 pounds per bomber. The Navy, constrained by the need for systems capable of carrier operations, standardized on the lighter probe and drogue systems.

Figure 61
The Tanker Tracks/Anchors Used on Day 1 Desert Storm[186]

FIGURE DELETED

had to be made on the ground, since the KC-135's boom can only be converted to a drogue on the ground. Essentially, the KC-135 can refuel probe- or boom-equipped aircraft, but not both on the same mission. The KC-10 possesses both a boom and a drogue and can use them sequentially on the same mission. While this is more efficient, it also commits the aircraft with the largest capacity to a specific area and mission that might be better filled by the more numerous KC-135s. The tanker planner had to match fuel and boom and drogue requirements with available tankers. [187]

The KC-10 refueling basket was considered superior to that on the KC-135. Navy and Marine pilots found refueling more difficult with the

---

[186](S/NF/WN/RD) *History of the Strategic Air Command*, Vol I, p 366.

[187]*Conduct of the Persian Gulf War*, Final Report to Congress, DOD, Apr 1992, pp T-90 - T-91.

harder basket and shorter hose on the KC-135. They preferred the softer basket and longer hose on the KC-10. The unforgiving characteristics of the KC-135 basket has produced a noticeably higher number of damaged probes on Navy and Marine aircraft.

ATO Process

Air refueling is unique among air operations in that tanker tactics depend on the requirements of receiver aircraft. The ATO process that mated tankers and receivers in the Gulf War is discussed in the *Command and Control* Report of this study. Difficulties with the ATO process arose after the first-phase (48-hours) of the war. Planners had several months to plan the first-phase operations but only 24-hours to plan each succeeding operation. After the War, Brigadier General Caruana commented, "One of the problems that we had here is that the tankers are always assumed in any operation."[188] The important point was that tanker tactics were developed and exercised to be rapidly responsive and flexible. These tactics addressed two elements most critical to the tanker mission, the amount of fuel and number of booms and drogues available.

The limit most frequently addressed concerning fighter refueling was the number of booms. The requirement to have all members of a flight ready at about the same time required groups of tankers flying orbits stacked at 500-foot intervals. This tactic responded to a limitation on the number of fighters that can be refueled in a given period. If insufficient tankers are available for the operation, it is boom limited. [DELETED]. This desire to push fighter flights through the air refueling anchors quickly demanded large numbers of airborne refueling booms during peak operations.

The need to expedite the flow of fighter aircraft through the air refueling anchors led to the development of a new tactic. The procedure was called Quick Flow (see Figure 62). As one fighter was being refueled, the fighter next in a refueling sequence maintained an "on deck" position, flying right wing formation with the fighter on the boom rather than the normal more distant tanker observation position. When the first fighter on the refueling boom was finished, it moved to the tanker's left

---

[188](S) Intvw, Strategic Air Command Oral History with Brig Gen Patrick P. Caruana, USCENTAF STRATFOR, conducted 13 Mar 1991, page 12 of transcript.

wing and the "on-deck" receiver slid left into position with the boom. Because no fore and aft movements were necessary for the "on-deck" fighter to move into position, it was a much faster procedure. This procedure enabled fighters with similar refueling airspeeds (A-10s could not refuel with F-15s for example) to expedite their passage through the air refueling anchors.[189]

Figure 62
Quick Flow Air Refueling Procedures

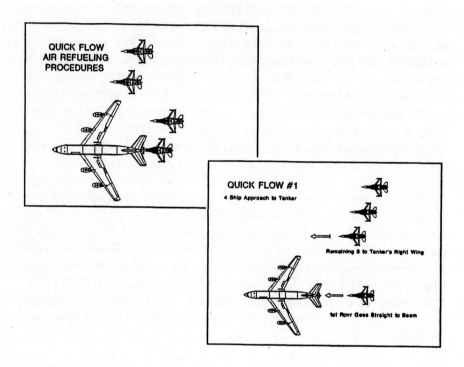

[189]Tanker Tactics in Southwest Asia, 17 Air Division (P) Pamphlet 3-1, 10 Nov 1990, pp 3-6 - 3-7.

Crowded Skies

The sheer number of aircraft involved in air refueling operations created a serious problem, prompting the remark that " . . . the biggest danger was that we would have a mid-air collision somewhere up there in that very congested, confusing arrangement of tracks."[190] This sentiment was echoed by a working group at the Desert Storm Tactics Conference: "Tanker operations were the most dangerous part of the mission (excluding the IP-to-target runs)."[191]

A major challenge was the last minute changes to tanker requirements. This problem was solved, in part, by the addition of a tanker liaison (usually a KC-135 navigator) on the AWACS as part of the Airborne Command Element. The tanker liaison helped coordinate and deconflict tanker sorties, had the authority to move tankers as mission requirements dictated, and became an indispensable problem solver.[192] He was able to identify which tanker was most readily available and capable of making last minute flight changes or of meeting new requests without disrupting scheduled flows of receivers to other tanker aircraft.[193]

Cross Border Operations

A major problem regarding tanker tactics revolved around tanker operations over the Iraqi and Kuwaiti land mass. Regulations that prescribed basic tanker tactics failed to adequately address the special considerations involved in planning and conducting air refueling operations over enemy territory. During the Gulf War, tankers orbited for up to four hours over enemy territory. The major difficulty for the tanker force was the dearth of published tactics on threat avoidance and how to respond to them if encountered.[194]

---

[190]Intvw, Strategic Air Command Oral History, Lt Col Ken Mills, 1703 AREFW, King Khalid, Saudi Arabia, conducted 19 Mar 1991.

[191](S/NF/WN/NC) *Tactical Analysis Bulletin*, Vol 91-2, p 7-6.

[192] Capt Robert Littrell, USAF, "E-3 Desert Storm Air Refueling Operations," Fighter Weapons Review, Vol 40, Summer 1992, pp 21-22.

[193]Intvw, Strategic Air Command Oral History with Maj Scott Hente, Maj John Heinz, Lt Col Jim Philips, and Lt Col Jim Schroder, STRATFOR Tanker Planners, conducted 11 Mar 91.

[194]*Ibid.*

The air refueling tanker was a major contributor to the Coalition's air effort; air refueling was a critical element in U.S. force projection. Twelve different varieties of tanker aircraft from the Air Force, Navy, and Marine Corps and from the United Kingdom, France, Canada, and Saudi Arabia supported the Coalition air effort. USAF tank-ers alone flew over 34,000 sorties, performed over 85,000 refuelings, and offloaded over 1.2 billion pounds of fuel.[195] Tactics were developed and utilized to put the gas where the fighters, bombers, and other receivers needed it. As requirements changed, tankers were diverted to where they were needed. The use of Quick Flow procedures shortened the time that fighters spent in the refueling anchors. These tactics were a critical component in the success of the air campaign. It is clear that the Air Campaign of Desert Storm could not have been accomplished without the contribution of the Coalition's air refueling force.

Tactical Deception

Both sides used tactical deception during Desert Shield and Desert Storm. Coalition forces employed deception to mask the timing of initial air attacks and to confuse the Iraqis as to the final axis of the ground attacks. Each of the Services embarked on deception plans contributing to the overall Central Command deception plan.[196] Air power contributed greatly to the overall success of these Coalition efforts. The Iraqis used tactical deception in the form of decoys, movement, and obscurants to make Coalition targeting and bomb damage assessment difficult.

---

[195](S) Desert Shield/Desert Storm Tanker Assessment, pp 1-1 - 1-3.

[196]Deception is a psychological action that may or may not be part of a greater psychological operation.

Coalition Deception

Central Command's deception plan was built around four goals: mislead the Iraqi military staff as to Central Command's force composition, intentions, capabilities, and timing; encourage Iraq to misallocate resources moving into Kuwait; achieve and maintain a tactical advantage during the battle; and minimize attrition of friendly forces.[200]

To accomplish the Gulf War deception plan, CENTAF was charged with supporting operations that would: condition Iraqi commanders to conclude that Coalition forces believed Kuwait to be the center of gravity; condition Allied air forces to fly a tempo of operations similar to what Iraq would see on the night of the real attack; develop a plan for masking the launch and movement of mission aircraft (air refuelers, etc.); exploit situations where repeated tactics created conditioned responses; and shut down Iraqi reconnaissance assets, thereby allowing Coalition ground forces to move unobserved.[201] These supporting operations efforts can be summed as follows:

> The Iraqi command structure was being conditioned not to react to a set of stimuli that were orchestrated to get just the sort of non-reaction required to keep allied aircraft losses to a minimum during the first critical hours of the war.[202]

Air Force Mission

CENTAF contributed to Central Command's tactical deception objectives by allowing the Iraqis to see the type of training that portrayed Kuwait as the center of gravity. CENTAF placed air refueling tracks so that Iraqi electronic intelligence saw tracks in northeastern Saudi Arabia. The tracks flown in the west were placed far enough south so that they fell outside Iraq's radar coverage (see Figure 63). [DELETED] (see Figure 64). Over time, the picture painted was of a ground frontal assault into Kuwait supported by close air support aircraft. Since Iraq's preconception was a Coalition frontal assault into Kuwait, as evidenced by the placement of troops in the KTO, the deception plan sought to maintain

---

[200](S) AF/XOOU Briefing, *USAF Tactical Deception Program.*

[201](S) *Ibid.*

[202](S) Maj William Holway, *Tactical Deception in the Gulf War,* 1 Jun 1992.

that Iraqi perception,[203] while continuing to mask the time and axis of the Army attack.

CAP and AWACS Coverage. Combat Air Patrols and AWACS radar surveillance were conducted from the onset of Desert Shield (see Figure 65). Central Command planners, recognizing that Iraqi early-warning (EW) technicians would pick up any sudden increase in flight activity, surged the number of CAP and AWACS flights periodically to deemphasize actual increases in air activity as Desert Storm approached.

Nighthawk Scheduling. [DELETED] CENTAF developed a refueling track called "Nighthawk" (see Figure 66). This track positioned F-117s nearer the border and gave pilots time to familiarize themselves with the area and it provided refueling practice; CENTAF also tasked other, aircraft to refuel on the Nighthawk track.[204] In fact, the Nighthawk track was used on the first night while other Coalition forces marshalled just outside the range of Iraqi EW (see Figure 67).

ATO Planning. One of the most detailed and intensive parts of the overall deception plan was the increase in flying patterns established by the ATO. The plan slowly built up the number of aircraft in the air with surges occurring one night a week. [DELETED]. Additionally, major

---

[203](S) *Ibid.*

[204][DELETED]

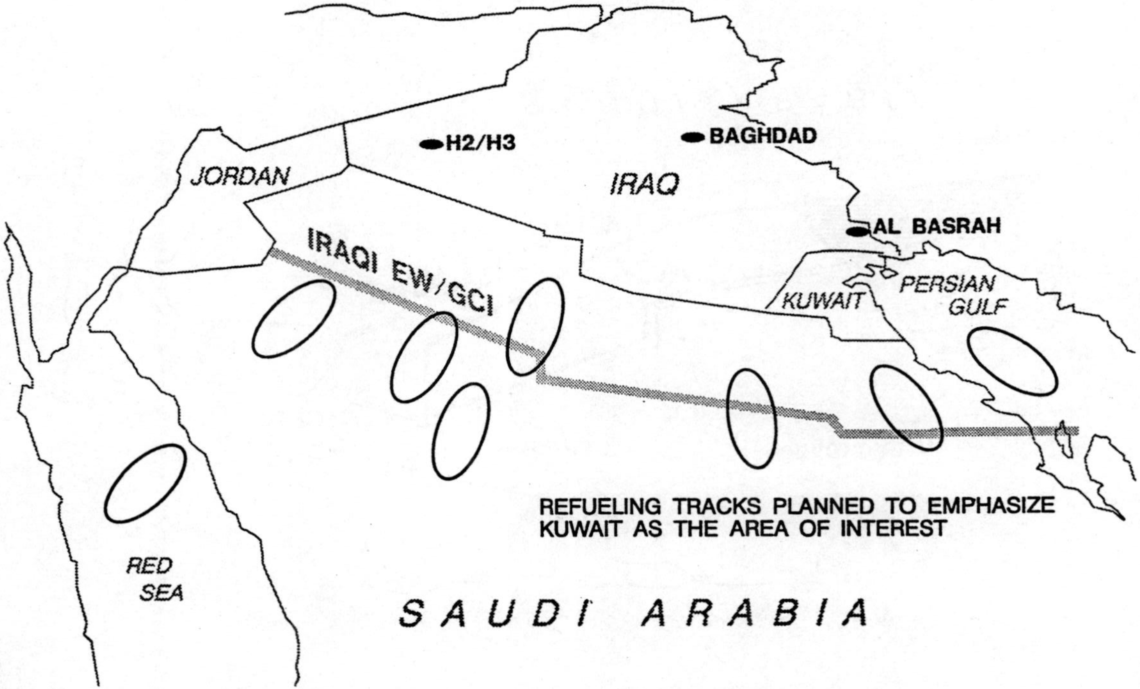

Figure 63
Supporting
the CINC

REFUELING TRACKS PLANNED TO EMPHASIZE
KUWAIT AS THE AREA OF INTEREST

IRAQI EW/GCI

SAUDI ARABIA

JORDAN

IRAQ

BAGHDAD

AL BASRAH

PERSIAN
GULF

KUWAIT

H2/H3

RED
SEA

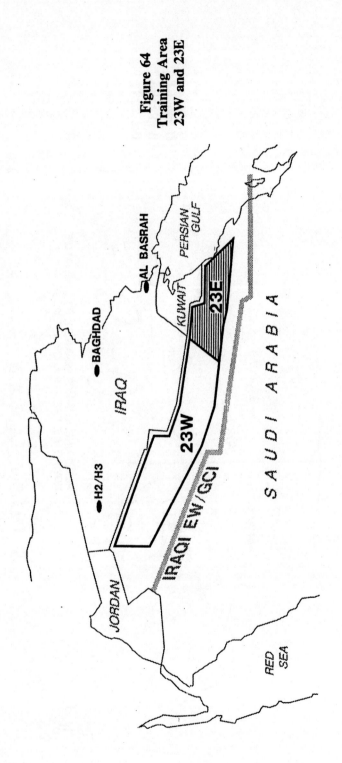

Figure 64
Training Area
23W and 23E

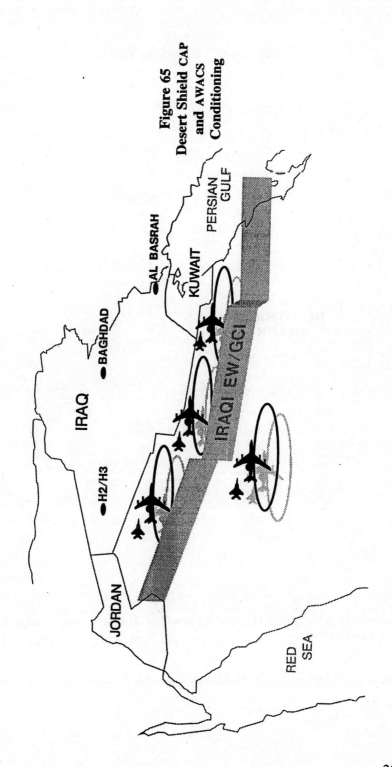

Figure 65
Desert Shield CAP
and AWACS
Conditioning

Figure 66
"Nighthawk" Refueling Track

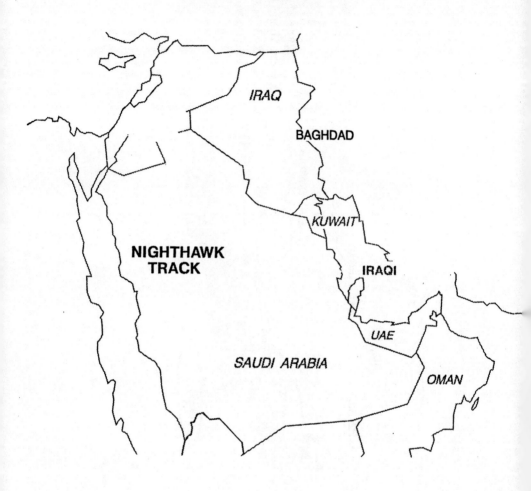

exercises such as Initial Hack and Imminent Thunder were designed to test Central Commands's ability to wage war, and began during this

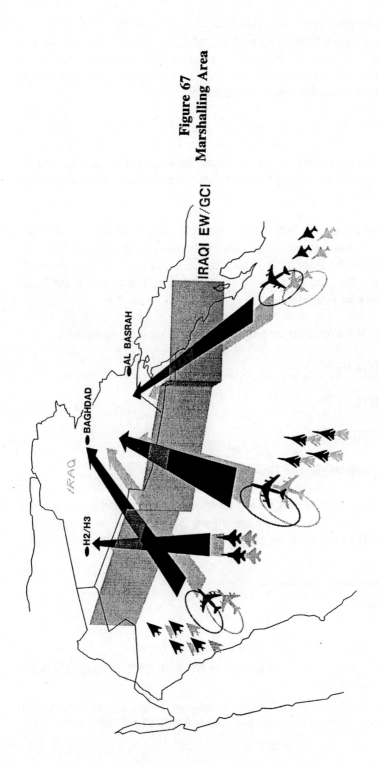

Figure 67
Marshalling Area

designated surge period. By mid-December, surge activity began to align itself with Central Command's plans, and for months before the first Coalition attack, CENTAF showed the Iraqis a high-activity flight profile. The objective was to condition the Iraqis not to be overly alarmed by high activity on the first night of Desert Storm.[205]

Decoy drones compounded Iraqi confusion on the first night. The objectives were to bewilder the Iraqi Air Defense System, lure threat radars to emit earlier and longer for easier SEAD targeting, and induce the Iraqis to waste some missiles. All drones were shot on the first two days of the war.[206]

The integrated deception plan wove a pattern of activity that the Iraqis were inclined to believe. This conditioning enabled the Allied air forces to strike the Iraqi air defense system unexpectedly and eventually to commence the ground war on a scale and direction to which the Iraqis had no ability to respond.

Coalition forces also employed unit-level tactical deception. .

[DELETED].[207]

[DELETED].[208]

[DELETED].[209]

Air Force Support for the Ground Offensive

Coalition aircraft flew a variety of missions in support of the ground offensive. Many missions were flown specifically to support the deception plans of ground units. Central Command required that major

---

[205](S) Maj Holway.

[206](S) *Ibid.*

[207](S) AF/XOOU Briefing, *USAF Tactical Deception Program.*

[208](S) Early jamming times and ingress route of attack axis were continually varied to further deceive the Iraqis.

[209](S) Intvw, MSgt Mike Caflin, crew member of the Volant Solo, 193d Special Operations Group, Harrisburg International Airport, PA, 21-22 Jan 1992.

ground units not "show their hand" by shifting forces west of King Khalid Military City before Iraq was blinded. After the start of the air war, the 18th Airborne Corps began its shift west. With Iraq's reconnaissance capability destroyed or incapacitated, Coalition forces moved unseen.

In its wake, the XVIII Airborne Corps left a large deception cell in Saudi Arabia. Unit positions were left intact, and the deception cell was equipped with electronic deception gear and inflatable decoy equipment.[210]

The Marines utilized Task Force Troy to aid in their deception plans. Task Force Troy built mock artillery pieces, utilized dummy tanks, faked helicopter missions into and out of areas, and continued false radio transmissions to deceive Iraqi intelligence units. In addition, the Marines ran diversionary combined-arms raids into Kuwait supported by air units. The Navy contributed to deception by conducting exercises to pin Iraqi troops into defensive positions on the beaches. Navy SEALs conducted raids, minesweepers prepared waterways, amphibious ships practiced landings, 16-inch guns conducted shore bombardment, and aircraft were tasked onto targets near the likely beaches. Although the Marine Corps did not conduct an amphibious landing in the Gulf War, amphibious forces greatly aided in the deception program. Reports indicate anywhere from two to ten divisions of Iraqi troops were kept in the "fire sack" of Kuwait due to Naval activities in the KTO. None of these operations would have been as easy had the air not been controlled by Coalition forces. Air power played a leading role in strategic and tactical deception efforts.

Iraqi Deception

Iraqi forces also used tactical deception as part of their campaign against Coalition forces. Their support for such activities was limited by several factors. They did not have the reconnaissance assets nor did they have the extensive variety of early-warning equipment as the Coalition forces. The Iraqis did however have one important advantage; they had been on the receiving end of Western intelligence products during the Iran-Iraq war and knew approximately how good our equipment was.

---

[210]*Army Aviation in Desert Shield/Desert Storm*, US Army Aviation Center, Ft Rucker, AL, 36362, 8 Jun 1992, p 14.

They also knew many of the Coalition weaknesses, and they planned accordingly.[211]

[DELETED].

[DELETED].[212]

[DELETED].[213] [DELETED].

After the start of the air campaign, it was apparent that communications between many Iraqi units had been interrupted. Therefore, much of the tactical deception at the unit level was probably accomplished independently by the local commander.

The Iraqis attempted to use smoke to achieve both strategic and tactical success. They applied these measures throughout the KTO and at installations within Iraq to conceal battlefield operations and targets. Besides smoke generators and smoke pots, the Iraqis set a number of different objects ablaze to create clouds of smoke; the objects included oil filled pits, spills along pipelines, oil drums, and tires. Some Iraqi efforts may have been prompted by media coverage reporting that Coalition pilots were reluctant to bomb "cloud covered" targets.[214] The effects of smoke were twofold: as a denial measure, it obscured targets and prevented complete bomb damage assessment; as a deception measure, it created the appearance of previous damage, possibly where no attacks had occurred.

The Iraqis used smoke as a denial and deception tactic at a number of sites. The use of smoke generally followed the Coalition's targeting

---

[211] Iraq had been able to buy a constant flow of Western weapons, parts, and supplies since 1970. The West willingly shared National Asset products with some of the Gulf States. Near the end of the Iran-Iraq War, Iraq was buying French Satellite data. Additionally, Iraq was a prime user of Soviet Bloc sources, training, technology, and intelligence. Efraim Karsh, *The Iran-Iraq War: A Military Analysis,* 1987. Also found in Cordesman, Anthony, and Wagner, Abraham, *The Lessons of Modern War,* Vol II, *The Iran-Iraq War.*

[212] (S) Msg from UTAIS Ramstein AB GE//INOA//P 190450Z Dec 1990.

[213] (S) *Ibid.*

[214] (S) This tactic was indeed effective, since cloud cover did impede Coalition bombing with precision-guided weapons.

priorities. In response to increased Coalition targeting of bridges, smoke from fires set near bridges was used to obscure the structure or give the false impression of bomb damage. At one target site at least ten smoke generators produced clouds of white smoke, concealing portions of the facility. One Iraqi deception tactic used was black smoke seen emanating from an oil/tire fire at an ammunition plant that in reality was undamaged.[215]

[DELETED].

On a more strategic level, the Iraqis utilized deception tactics in employing their Scud missiles.

[DELETED].[216]

In conclusion, both sides used tactical deception tactics to their advantage. Iraq's crude methods of smoke, concealment, decoys, and camouflage aimed at hindering Coalition targeting and bomb damage assessment efforts. On the other hand, Coalition deception practices were completely integrated into overall operations that paralyzed Iraq's ability to conduct warfare.

Psychological Operations and Air Power

Both Iraqi and Coalition forces conducted psychological operations (PSYOP) during Desert Shield/Desert Storm. PSYOP covers a wide spectrum of tactical and strategic political and military operations. This section focuses on psychological operations that directly involved air power.

It was generally acknowledged that the effectiveness of psychological operations was notoriously difficult to judge. By most measures, Iraq's tactical PSYOP against Coalition forces was ineffective. Its strategic campaign, however, met with some limited success. There was also evidence that U.S. PSYOP had a positive effect on the outcome of the war. The United States used a wide variety of air assets in its tactical PSYOP efforts, including MC-130, HC-130, and EC-130 Volant Solo aircraft plus

---

[215](S) *Iraqi Smoke Denial and Deception Measures*, D&D [decoy and deception] Digest 91-03, 21 Feb 1991 AFIA/INID.

[216](S/NF/WN) Christie and Barlow, *Scud Campaign*, p I-18.

B-52s, F-16s, Marine F/A-18s, and Navy A-6s. U.S. PSYOP efforts included dropping 29 million leaflets, coordinating PSYOP missions with tactical air operations, and countering Iraqi PSYOP efforts.

The aims of U.S. PSYOPs were to reduce the morale and combat efficiency of enemy troops and create disaffection within their ranks and to convince enemy, friendly, and neutral nations and forces to take actions favorable to the Unites States and its allies.

Recent conflicts have seen increasingly close integration of PSYOP with combat operations. For example, the 1982 Falklands War, conflicts in Afghanistan, Africa, South and Central America, and U.S. interventions in Grenada and Panama all had important PSYOP dimensions. PSYOP was also a critical part of terrorist operations during the 70s and was part of the Iraqi plan when Saddam implicitly threatened terrorist activities before to the Gulf War.[217]

Iraqi PSYOP

Any analysis of PSYOP must be within the context of the conflict it was intended to support. In this case, PSYOP was triggered by the 2 August 1990 Iraqi invasion of Kuwait. The overall Iraqi PSYOP strategy appears to have been to prevent western intervention, deter Coalition air activity, and once air action started, to limit its effectiveness.[218]

Iraqi PSYOP flowed from the Ministry of Culture and Information under the strict supervision of the Ba'ath Party, the Revolutionary Command Council, and Saddam Hussein. The Iraqi propaganda system was modeled on the Soviet system and was similar in its essentials to that of most other totalitarian countries. The Iraqi PSYOP campaign emphasized religious symbolism, Arab nationalism, and praise of Saddam Hussein. The themes reflected Iraqi culture and politics.[219] A basic

---

[217]Saddam's gathering of terrorists in Baghdad, in early Sep 1990, was a clear message to the Coalition not to start any military action against Iraq. The threat was convincing on the basis of past Middle East terrorist activity. Its effect was felt mostly by the air travel community, both domestic and international.

[218]USSOCOM Post Operational Analysis of Iraq PSYOP, unpublished, 1992, p 15.

[219]*Ibid*, p 16.

fallacy of Iraqi PSYOP planning was its focus on the characteristics of the sender, rather than on the nature of the receiver.

The apparent initial objectives of the Iraqi PSYOP campaign were to rationalize the invasion of Kuwait, gain the support of the Arab masses, discourage nations from participating in the U.N. embargo, and discourage or hinder military attacks on Iraq. To these, an additional objective, rationalizing incorporation of Kuwait as a permanent province of Iraq, was added later.

Iraq placed few restrictions on the means available to achieve a PSYOP desired goal. In many cases, documentation was simply manufactured. Furthermore, the Iraqi campaigns did not follow western logic. For example, Iraqi PSYOP criticized the Coalition bombing as being inaccurate one day and stressed the destruction wrought by highly accurate Coalition bombing the next. The reported accuracy of Coalition bombing varied, depending on how it could best enhance the Iraqi propaganda campaign.[220]

Strategically, Saddam met with some early successes. He used Scud missiles to attack Israel and Saudi Arabia. As political and psychological weapons, Scuds were useful in diverting Coalition attention and military effort away from the main battlefield. The threat of chemical warheads added to the seriousness of the threat.[221] While the impact of the Scuds was militarily negligible, they did produce emotional and psychological effects (see Table 15).[222]

---

[220]Iraq placed military resources around civilian schools, mosques etc., to protect the resources, create civilian casualties, and neutralize Coalition air attacks. Much of the civilian damage shown by Iraq was probably attributable to spent antiaircraft projectiles.

[221]Lt Gen Charles A Horner, Oral History Intvw, by Jamison, Davis, and Barlow. "I don't think any of us, first of all, estimated the political impact of the Scud, the terror induced," 4 Mar 1992.

[222]Lt Col Z Solomon, "Psychological Effects of the Gulf War on High Risk Sectors of the Israeli Population." Presented at the Gulf War International Symposium and World Psychiatric Association meeting, 27 Jan 1992. "The Scud attacks put an incredible amount of pressure on the Israeli population." Tactically, Israelis are prepared to respond to military attack. "Our people and our flight crews were very frustrated just sitting and waiting. However, when the Patriots arrived, even though most knew that their effects might be marginal at best, it was an uplifting experience for the people."

Table 15
Israeli Scud Casualties

Direct Casualties To Missile Impact		Indirect Casualties		
Death	2	Death:	Heart Attack	4
Injured	232	(Gas Mask Use)	Suffocation	7
		Injured: (Running or		
		Driving for cover)	Accidents	40
		(Atropine Injuries)	Atropine	230
		(Hospitalized)	Acute Anxiety	544
Total	**234**		**Total**	**825**

A total of 1,059 Israeli casualties were attributed to Scud attacks. The disparity between the small number killed by Scuds and the enormous Coalition effort devoted to anti-Scud operations highlights the importance of the psychological effects. The number of self-inflicted atropine casualties speak for itself. The Scud attacks induced fear among the Israeli and Saudi populations and threatened the integrity of the Coalition. They combined a limited military technology with a politically effective targeting policy. In addition to their psychological effects, the Scud attacks diverted significant military resources to the difficult and militarily unrewarding task of Scud hunting. Coalition Scud hunting efforts, together with Patriots, helped the Israelis maintain their policy of restraint. Patriots had a calming affect on both the Israeli and Saudi public.[223] A tactical military response thus blunted a psychological weapon aimed at the heart of the Coalition. (See "the Scud Hunt" section in this chapter for additional information.)

Although Iraqi efforts to use western television for propaganda generally failed, they may have had some effect in the Arab world. Saddam's attempt to generate international goodwill through personal

---

[223]*Ibid.*

appearances with hostages was an example of badly misreading a target audience. Another example of Iraq's poor use of western television was its attempt to portray an industrial target struck by Coalition air power as a "Baby Milk Factory" (with signs and workers' jacket logos conveniently printed in English). These efforts were quickly dismissed as crude propaganda by all except the most gullible or antiwestern, but they appear to have had some internal success.[224]

The staged televised appearance of downed Coalition pilots also proved counterproductive. Instead of inducing the Coalition partners to acquiesce to Iraqi policy goals, they alienated a worldwide audience appalled by the battered, physical condition of the captives and their orchestrated, mechanical admissions of guilt. It was obvious that the pilots had been tortured. The resultant backlash produced more, not less, support for the Coalition. This Iraqi propaganda initiative was aimed at U.S. public opinion. The evidence suggests that the campaign was designed to mimic tactics used, with some effect, by North Vietnam during the Southeast Asia conflict.[225] Iraqi propagandists apparently thought that presenting live interviews with captured Coalition pilots would stimulate the U.S. public to call for the withdrawal of U.S. forces. The response to the broadcast came swiftly. All western governments, the public, and the media severely condemned the broadcast, and the use of the downed pilots in this manner.[226] The worldwide condemnation was so overwhelming that the broadcasts, which began on 20 January, ended on 24 January.

Saddam's PSYOP efforts included radio broadcasts to U.S. troops in the field by "Baghdad Betty," reminiscent of those by "Tokyo Rose" during World War II. Intended to lower U.S. troop morale, Betty's messages frequently proved comical as she warned American servicemen that their wives back home were sleeping with "famous movie stars" like

---

[224]In the Diary of an Iraqi Soldier, written during the air and land attacks in Kuwait from Jan 17-Feb 26, 1991, the anonymous author reacted with renewed resolve and anger to news of the Coalition bombing of the "Dairy Factory," indicating that the Baby Milk Factory propaganda was used to motivate Iraqi troops.

[225]USSOCOM Post Op Analysis of Iraqi PSYOP, pp 35-36.

[226]Such use of prisoners is forbidden by the laws of warfare. The failure of the Iraqi plan was partially engineered by the prisoners. LT Zaun, for example, augmented the battering of his face and exaggerated his behavior to inform the world the Iraqis were maltreating him.

Tom Cruise, Arnold Schwarzenegger, and the cartoon character Bart Simpson.[227]

Iraq also used PSYOP leaflets. Their effects on the military forces of the Coalition were minimal. However, the same leaflets were received in a more positive way by some segments of the civilian populations in Coalition and Arab Nations. Some key themes of the Iraqi leaflet campaign were:[228]

- The war was really about access to oil.

- The U.S. was using the air war as an excuse for imperialism.

- The U.S. was propping up a corrupt government in Kuwait. (See Appendix B for examples of Iraqi PSYOP leaflets and hand bills.)

The Iraqi leaflet campaign targeted the populations of Great Britain, Germany, France, Australia, Canada, the United States, and the Arab Nations of the Coalition with varying degrees of success. It was hoped, that like Vietnam, the home population would turn on their own military forces, viewing Coalition aviators as baby killers, milk factory destroyers, etc.

While Iraqi strategic propaganda found a receptive audience in some quarters, neither public opinion nor the world media were moved as the Iraqi president had hoped. Although antiwar demonstrations took place in the United States and certain European Coalition countries, they failed to draw significant popular support. To the contrary, public support for Coalition troops deployed to the Persian Gulf remained strong throughout Desert Shield and Desert Storm.

The main failure of Iraqi propaganda was its lack of credibility. The propaganda was generally far below the level of sophistication of the targeted audiences. Politically aware segments of the population, even

---

[227]Iraqi Baghdad Betty was monitored by both USIS and the ANG 193d "Volant Solo." Troops were able to listen to Baghdad Betty broadcasts from Kuwait.

[228]Iraq's PSYOP War: Targeting the Arab world, United States Army Intelligence Agency and United States Army Intelligence and Threat Analysis Center, October 1990.

those who might be inclined to be antiwar, were in general turned off by the crude Iraqi attempts to manipulate their beliefs.

United States and Coalition PSYOP Planning Phase

The Air Force had no PSYOP doctrine despite its role in planned Joint PSYOP Operations. As a consequence, the planning process was guided by Army doctrine, which called for the conduct of "Psywar" in support of U.S. forces *in combat*. The *in combat* distinction had later repercussions. Early in Desert Shield, at the request of Central Command's Commander-in-Chief, the Commander-in-Chief of Special Operations Command provided a PSYOP planning cell. The cell produced a list of sixty-four strategic PSYOP/International Information proposals for interagency review. The theater PSYOP plan, Burning Hawk, was approved by the Commander-in-Chief of the Special Operations Command on 20 September 1990. From this point on, the PSYOP *approval* system began to display significant weaknesses.[229]

Personnel were not familiar with operational charters and lacked an understanding of the differences between clandestine and covert activities.[230] [DELETED].[231]

Operational Phase

In contrast to Saddam's ineffective PSYOP efforts, Coalition PSYOP did have some effect on Iraqi soldiers. The Coalition employed four primary PSYOP methods: radio transmission, loudspeaker broadcasts, leaflet dissemination, and enemy prisoner of war (EPW) operations.[232] According to information produced by U.S. Special Operations Command (see Figure 68), different types of operations produced different levels of effectiveness.[233]

---

[229]Intvw, USSOCOM PSYOP Planning Cell, CINCCENT, 1992.

[230]*Ibid.*

[231](S) Msg, USCINCCENT/CCCC to CJCS Washington, DC, DTG051300Z Dec 1990.

[232]USSOCOM Post Operational Analysis of PSYOP, p 4-4.

[233]*Ibid*, p 4-5.

Figure 68[234]
PSYOP Effort and Relative Effectiveness in the Persian Gulf

- 29 Million leaflets dropped in theater
- 17+ hours per day of radio transmitting
- 19.5 hours per day aerial broadcasting
- Over 73,000 Iraqi's reached through PSYOP
- Impact on surrenders based on exposure and type of effort

EXPOSURE & EFFECTIVENESS PERCENTAGES

	LEAFLETS	RADIO	LOUDSPEAKERS
% Exposed to PSYOP	98	58	34
% Believed PSYOP Msg	88	46	18
% Influenced to act	70	34	16

---

[234](S) Based on interrogations of Iraqi EPWs accomplished by members of the 13th PSYOP Battalion (Reserve) (EPW), Ft. Snelling, MN. The 13th PSYOP BN is a one-of-a kind unit designed for quality assurance. It does not produce PSYOP; rather, it analyzes and evaluates the PSYOP produced by other units to determine effectiveness and credibility.

It is extremely difficult to measure the overall effectiveness of PSYOP and even more difficult to measure the effectiveness of separate tactical PSYOP efforts. For example, many Iraqi EPWs appear to have been influenced by leaflets but made the final decision to surrender only when exposed to a loudspeaker team.[235] Others reported being influenced by a Volant Solo radio broadcast but made the final decision only after being exposed to a leaflet, hearing reports of effective bombing, being within earshot of a BLU-82, or hearing a favorable report on how EPWs were being treated. In contrast to Iraqi PSYOP, Coalition PSYOP focused on the intended audience and was conducted in concert with overwhelming air and ground campaigns. Of the large number of EPWs, the proportion attributable to PSYOP, as opposed to direct military action, is unknown in the final analysis.

The four sets of operations—radio transmission, loudspeaker broadcasts, leaflet drops, and the actions taken by EPW teams—began at two different times.[236] The Coalition's tactical leaflet and radio activities were initiated in January 1991 to coincide with the start of the air campaign. The loudspeaker and EPW actions began in February with the start of the ground campaign. The following sections explain the major operations.

Radio Transmissions

In the Persian Gulf Theater of Operations, six broadcast platforms were established and used: aerial platforms (EC-130 Volant Solo aircraft) and ground radio stations. The Volant Solo aircraft were available in August; however, their use was put on hold until late November. Volant Solo was first used on Thanksgiving Day, 22 November, when the aircraft broadcasted the Voice of America (VOA) service in Arabic to areas VOA could not reach. Volant Solo operations had the positive effect of establishing an airborne platform as a credible broadcaster.

Loudspeaker Broadcasts

PSYOP loudspeaker operations were accomplished by two- or three-person teams directly supporting forward combat units. Teams normally consisted of one or two noncommissioned officers and an interpreter or

---

[235](S) *Ibid.*

[236]USSOCOM Post Operational Analysis of PSYOP.

communications specialist. Loudspeaker teams broadcasted prepared messages. Occasionally a team would ad lib a broadcast if the pressures of the moment demanded and if the language skill and initiative of the team permitted. Feedback from some EPWs indicated that, while "leaflets and radio showed us how to surrender, loudspeaker teams told us where."[237]

The U.S. Marines of Task Force Shepard employed Army PSYOP loudspeaker and air power in a unique counterbattery tactic. Task Force Shepard was tasked to screen the front of the 1st Marine Division. A PSYOP loudspeaker team was assigned to each company.[238] The loudspeaker teams would drive along the border playing audio tapes simulating the sounds of tanks and light armored vehicles. These tactics elicited responses from Iraqi radar and artillery. Marine F/A-18 Fast FACS would spot the fire and call in Coalition TACAIR to conduct counterbattery fire. The ploy worked ten times. The Marines were also able to draw fire with "Rap" and "Country Western" music. Surrender tapes and rock and roll music did not draw fire.[239]

Leaflet Drops

Leaflets and other forms of printed PSYOP proved especially effective in terms of audience penetration. Of the targeted audience–300,000-plus Iraqi troops–calculations based on EPW interviews suggest that approximately 98 percent read or were otherwise exposed to the 29 million leaflets dropped in the theater.[240] Most EPWs were found clutching leaflets in their hands or hiding them somewhere in their uniforms.[241] The leaflets' language was simple and straightforward. They incorporated

---

[237]*Ibid*, p 4-5.

[238]The Marines used PSYOP loudspeakers at company level and the Army used loudspeakers at Brigade level.

[239]Intvw, Lt Col Clifford Myers, USMC, Commander, Task Force Shepard, 1992. Lt Col Myers acknowledged that the PSYOP/air counterbattery fire was different, but effective. He further states that EPWs coming into his area reported that their officers and NCOs walked the line, shooting anyone attempting to surrender after a bombing/broadcast episode.

[240]Based on interrogations of Iraqi EPWs accomplished by members of the 13th PSYOP Battalion (Reserve) (EPW), Ft. Snelling, MN.

[241]513th Military Intelligence Brigade (Forward), 4th CAG CA Group 2d MARDIV.

visual appeals for an audience that seemed to respond psychologically and emotionally to a visual medium. Weather conditions characterized by low humidity and generally moderate winds translated into good air drops and low loss through scattering and deterioration. These attributes combined with generally effective theme choice, audience vulnerabilities, and effective Coalition military action resulted in large numbers of surrenders.

Examples of leaflets distributed during operations in the Gulf are included in Appendix B. The first set in this appendix shows Iraqi PSYOP leaflets, and the second set shows copies of Coalition PSYOP leaflets.

B-52 Leaflet Operations

An important precept at work in the radio and leaflet operations was *operant conditioning*, using fixed, positive reinforcement. Tactical PSYOPers announced to certain Iraqi ground units that they were to be bombed.[242] That specific unit was then attacked. The repeated cycles of announcement-and-execution helped persuade the audience that the message and delivery means were credible and that surrender was a viable alternative to a useless death.

In late January 1991, the 4th PSYOP Group asked if the Air Force would support a campaign to tell the Iraqis when they were going to be bombed and by what aircraft. A plan was presented and approved to incorporate PSYOP with B-52 strikes along the front lines. The Concept of Operation for such missions outlined a plan to print and disseminate leaflets to specific Iraqi units. The leaflets, together with radio broadcasts, would specify which Iraqi unit or units would be hit the next day (see Figure 69). The following day, CENTAF would bomb the specified unit with three B-52s. This would be followed with another day of leaflets indicating that the same unit would be bombed again and that surviving Iraqi soldiers should defect or desert. The next day, CENTAF would bomb the same unit. CENTAF continued to support this effort. By the start of the ground war, as many as eight B-52s were dedicated to these missions, and the U.S. Army PSYOP commander was effectively influencing the employment of strategic PSYOP forces.[243]

---

[242](S) Intvw, CENTAF PSYOP Liaison Officer, After Action Rpt, 1992.

[243]Maj Jack Summe, CENTAF PSYOP Liaison Officer, memo, 1992.

Figure 69
B-52 Leaflet Operations

إن عاصفة الصحراء واصلة...
اهربوا هرباً حالياً!!

Above:
Translation:

'Desert Storm is coming to your area. Flee Immediately!'

Below
Translation:

"'Saddam's Army intends using your city as a protective barrier to hide behind. Saddam doesn't care about you or your family. But the Joint Forces do not wish to hurt innocent civilians, so take your belongings and head North to a safe place.'

سوف جيش صدام يستخدم مدينتكم كحاجز حماية سوف
يتوارى خلفها ! فصدام لا يهمه مصيركم ولا مصير عائلاتكم
ولكن القوات المشتركة لا تريد إصابة المدنيين الابرياء ، لذلك
خذوا امتعتكم الضرورية واتجهوا الى الشمال والاماكن الامنة

EPW *Operations*

EPW team operations proceeded sequentially and logically from the other operations and provided pretesting and post-testing of PSYOP materials for future missions.[244] During surrenders, loudspeaker and EPW teams helped to counteract the degraded command and control among thousands of Iraqi forces, while at the same time, providing a locus for humanitarian assistance.[245]

Intelligence sources interviewed EPWs from six different Iraqi Army and Republican Guard Divisions who provided similar stories on the combined impact of the air campaign and psychological operations.[246] Two EPW stated that,

> Their own tanks had become the enemy of their soldiers because high flying aircraft could destroy them without warning, even at night.

Others in the same units stated that

> Their desertion rates skyrocketed and the air campaign left their troops weak and demoralized, the A-10 was the aircraft that destroyed most of the equipment, the B-52s induced the greatest fear and the leaflets that announced the impending B-52 strikes prompted desertions. Additionally, the non-stop air strikes made it impossible for Iraqi commanders to stop the flow of soldiers away from their units.[247]

---

[244]USSOCOM Post Operational Analysis of PSYOP, p 4-9.

[245]*Ibid*, p 4-10.

[246]The 513th Military Intelligence Brigade (FWD) is trained for EPW interrogations and uses a variety of methods to validate EPW responses. The findings of the 513th have been independently verified by the 13th PSYOP EPW Company and released by the Joint Staff Information Service Center. Marines of the 4th CAG, CA Group, 2d MARDIV also report similar findings.

[247](S) U.S. Army Special Ops Cmd, Historical Monograph, p 81.

An Iraqi unit, which surrendered to the Marines weeks before the start of the ground war, indicated that leaflets told them how to surrender. Most of the surrendering troops had leaflets on their person.[248]

During Desert Shield and Desert Storm, Coalition forces conducted combined psychological operations. These psychological operations in concert with overwhelming military force proved to be a successful partnership.

---

[248]Intvw, Lt Col James Zumualt, 4th CAG CA Grp 2d MARDN. Sep 1992.

5

Training

An air force's aircraft and weapons may enjoy technical superiority, and it may have developed superior tactics, but if the personnel flying those aircraft are not proficient in executing the tactics, the air force will still be the loser. This chapter addresses training, the means by which tactical proficiency is developed. It asks three basic questions: first, did the U.S. air forces and those of our Coalition Allies train the way they fought? Secondly, were any particular kinds of training more or less useful? Finally, were combat skills honed or degraded during Desert Shield preparations for the war?

These questions will be addressed in the three sections. The first addresses training conducted before the war, considered in light of its significance to Desert Storm. Both the training of the individual and the training of units are considered. The second section addresses training accomplished during Desert Shield. This section pays particular attention to data reflecting on the competing demands of training and combat readiness. It also studies training development and the exercises set up to prepare for the war. The third section looks at training lessons learned during Desert Storm. The focus is on tactics developed and trained for, but proved unsuitable in the war. The topics presented in these three sections are expanded where necessary in the appropriate appendices to the Report.

Maintaining the Combat Edge in Peacetime

In terms of training, the U.S. air forces that deployed during Desert Shield were considered combat ready and able to engage the Iraqis had they crossed the border into Saudi Arabia. This state of readiness reflected a DOD commitment of resources to a peacetime training regimen for a variety of global contingencies. Training efforts in theater further refined this training regimen. Preparing aviators for combat was at the heart of this commitment, and it is a complex evolution. Developing combat readiness in the aviator proceeds in stages, beginning with undergraduate flight training (pilot or navigator), moving through initial weapon system qualification, and concluding with continuation training of the aviator as a member of a mission-qualified, combat-ready aircrew.

The most demanding training environment experienced during the typical aviator's career is undergraduate pilot or navigator training. During this period, basic flying skills are taught at a rapid pace, challenging the individual both mentally and physically. Officer students are evaluated on their ability to master complex tasks in a demanding environment under time constraints and psychological pressure. Those able to complete the undergraduate flight training programs demonstrate the essential personal traits necessary to continue to the next building block in the training experience. All U.S. services conduct separate pilot training (and navigator/flight officer training) to meet their specific requirements. Appendix C provides a summary of the training accomplished.

Before assignment to an operational squadron, the aircrew pilot undergoes specialized training and completes an initial qualification course in an aircraft type relevant to the squadron's overall mission. Acquiring flying skills, systems knowledge, and general tactics in the assigned aircraft are the main objectives of this phase of training. Instructors with considerable operational experience in the specific aircraft type supervise and, in many cases, conduct the training. Tactics training is guided by appropriate regulations: *Multi-Command Manual 3-1* series for the Air Force, and appropriate Naval Aviation Training and Operations Procedures Standardization publications and tactical manuals for the Navy and Marines. The initial qualification training provides pilots with the basic knowledge and skills required to become qualified within the operational unit. Representative costs and course length for the Air Force F-16 replacement training program is given below in Table 16. The figure makes two points, one explicitly and one implicitly. First, training in combat aircraft is intense and expensive. Second, it covers a wide range of mission capabilities.

Following assignment to an operational squadron, but before achieving fully qualified status within the unit, the newly assigned aircrew undergoes local-area orientation, theater indoctrination, and unit-specific tactics. Combat-ready status is achieved upon completion of the mission qualification training. In all U.S. Air Force operational units, the pilots must maintain currencies as dictated by the Air Force regulation 51-50. Table 17 lists the number of days that can elapse before an aircrew's currency status for a specific flight event becomes invalid. These currencies required continuation training during Desert Shield.

Table 16[1]
Flying Training Syllabus For F-16 Replacement Training Unit

Flight Training	Sorties	Hours[2]
Transition	6	8.3
Instruments	*4	6.0
Advanced Handling	1	1.3
Intercepts	5	7.7
Basic Fighter Maneuvers	13	13.3
Air Combat Maneuvers	3	3.0
Surface Attack	13	18.4
Surface Attack Tactical	5	6.5
Night Transition	*1	2.0
Night Surface Attack	*1	2.0
Tankers (included in "*" phases)	(4)	
	52	**68.2**

Training Days	113
Academics	239.5 hours
Simulators	38.5 hours
Cost (FY 91 dollars)	$1,012,310

---

[1]Course data provided by WCR David Millsmith from Hq Air Combat Command, 29 Jun 1992.

[2]Tactical Air Command syllabus F-16 C0B00 PL/M, Oct 1990.

Table 17
Currencies[3]

Event	Experienced	Inexperienced
Demanding Sortie	30	21
Landing	45	30
Night Landing	30	15
ACBT (air combat training)	60	45
Low Altitude Operations	60	45
Weapons Delivery	90	60
Night Weapons Delivery	6	30
Air Refueling	180	180
Formation Takeoff	90	60
Formation Landing	90	60
Precision Approach	45	30

Particular squadron training requirements, beyond those common to all Air Force units, are driven by the tasking of the individual unit. All units are required to maintain proficiency in operations characteristic of those they could expect in their assigned operating region. Table 18 details pre-Gulf War theater tasking for all Air Force flying units that participated in Desert Shield and Desert Storm. It also identifies those units that participated in Green Flag 90-4, the last major joint, Air Force-sponsored, electronic warfare exercise before Desert Shield.[4] A salient fact to emerge from the data is that all units fighting during Desert Storm also had to train for commitment in Europe (USAFE), with the sole exception of the three F-16 squadrons of the 363d Tactical Fighter Wing stationed at Shaw AFB, South Carolina.

---

[3]Maj Stan Hill, CENTAF/XOOTT briefing, "Fighter Training in Desert Shield." The numbers represent the maximum number of days allowed between completion of the required events. In other words, an experienced pilot must complete a demanding sortie at least every thirty days.

[4]Green Flag exercises were conducted by the 57th Fighter Weapons Wing at Nellis AFB, NV, and differ from Red Flag exercises only in that their primary emphasis is electronic warfare. Green Flag 90-4 was in progress when Iraq invaded Kuwait on 2 Aug 1991, and is thus of direct relevance.

Table 18
Unit Taskings Pre-Desert Shield[5]

[DELETED]

[DELETED]

Individual units develop their training programs from theater requirements and relevant directives of their parent Major Command. Routine training to maintain combat proficiency encompasses a wide range of missions and weapons delivery options. Using the F-16 as an example, Table 19 gives the numbers of sorties and desired tactical capabilities for an F-16 pilot in the 363d Tactical Fighter Wing. The key concept here was that of graduated levels of combat capability, a management tool establishing standards of performance in various maneuvers and weapon delivery tactics. The tool provides higher headquarters with a measure of a unit's level of readiness and suitability for a given tactical scenario. Table 19 provides a representative Air Force example of how this concept is applied. The other services use equivalent methods to maintain the desired level of combat readiness. The underlying point is that these methods work.

---

[5](S) The numbers of units deployed and the command relationships came from: USCINCCENT OPLAN 1002, USCINCEUR OPLAN 4102, USCINCPAC OPLAN 5027, and Green Flag 90-4 After Action Report.

Command regulations further quantify and define the required proficiencies. With regard to Table 19, an aircrew "qualified" for an event maintains a higher level of proficiency than one who is "familiar." In many cases, "familiar" means that a requirement has been met without regard to accuracy or proficiency. The goal is to spread the practice of these events throughout the training cycle so aircrews do not lose overall proficiency. The qualification criterion for dropping or firing ordnance is either an actual weapon release or a simulated weapon release within realistic launch parameters. This simulated release is then validated by film recorders in either the training munition or the cockpit.[6] Using these requirements, squadrons can plan training programs to keep all aircrews proficient in the areas required for combat readiness.

Although they share a core of basic requisites and common procedures, flight skills required in each area of the world vary. In Europe, with its peculiar weather conditions, low-altitude flying is stressed. Areas without prominent terrain features for threat evasion and navigation necessitate unique tactics. Individual aircrew readiness is skewed towards the theater for which the unit is tasked for deployment. In addition to individual aircrew readiness, squadrons train regularly with other units and participate in exercises designed to maintain the readiness of the squadron's capability to deploy and fight (see Appendix F, "Flag Exercises").

---

[6]*Ibid*, pp 19-21.

Table 19
F-16 Graduated Combat Capability Requirements, 363d TFW
Minimum Training Required Per Pilot Every Six Months[7]

Sorties	
Air-to-Surface	30
Air-to-Air	17
Air-to-Air Night	–
Advance Handling	1
Other	11

Events	
Radar Laydown	Familiar
VSD (visual system delivery)	Familiar
VLB (visual level bomb)	Familiar
Loft	Familiar
High Angle Dive Bomb	Qualified
LLLD (low level low drag)	Familiar
LRDT (long range dive toss)	Familiar
Dive Bomb	Familiar
Low-Angle Dive Bomb	Qualified
Low-Angle Strafe	Familiar
Maverick	Qualified
Surface Attack w/FAC	2
Low-Altitude Tactical Navigation	8
Combined Force Training	–
Medium-Altitude Tactics	–
Intercepts Day/Night	12/–
Air-to-Air Refueling	3
Joint Maritime Operations	–

The Red Flag series of tactical training exercises conducted at Nellis AFB, Nevada, was the most noteworthy exercise for U.S. and Coalition aircrews and one of the predominant factors in the success of Desert Storm. Red Flag

---

[7]363d Fighter Wing MSG 111040Z Dec 91, F-16 Graduated Combat Capability Program.

affected more tactical aircrew members who flew in Desert Shield and Desert Storm than any other single tactics training program.[8] Moreover, tactical, realistic composite force training lessons learned during Red Flag exercises were generally considered by Air Force commanders to have had a strong positive effect on Air Force performance, a view mirrored by the Coalition partners.[9] Red Flag exercises challenged units, aircrews, and support personnel to implement and evaluate their readiness planning. A more detailed examination of both the history of Red Flag and the typical training provided there are found in Appendix F, "Flag Exercises."

In summary, training to maintain combat readiness in peacetime is a complex problem. Stringent requirements often prepare the squadrons for combat in a particular area of the world. However, well trained personnel can be flexible: routine, ongoing training provided a solid basis for Desert Shield; training during Desert Shield prepared the Coalition air forces for war. This training is the subject of the next section.

Training In Desert Shield

The units initially deployed to Saudi Arabia soon found conflicts between normal proficiency training requirements and preparation for the immediate war at hand. The training programs established during peacetime to quantify the minimum levels of training appropriate for mission readiness (i.e., AFR 51-50 requirements) remained in effect during Desert Shield. As discussed in the previous section, the regulations institutionalized unit training requirements and formed mission objectives for scheduled sorties. However, in the initial days, the Coalition feared that Iraq might continue its push south. It was thus necessary that training strike a balance between preparing for immediate invasion of Saudi Arabia and maintaining proficiency. Crews required to stay on alert, however, would shortly become noncurrent in essential skills and maneuvers, necessitating additional training programs to retrain them.

In the early stages of Desert Shield, units prepared for an Iraqi attack into Saudi Arabia with an expected thrust towards the eastern oil fields, the "D-Day"

---

[8]Intvw, Gen Robert D. Russ, TAC Attack Department of the Air Force, TAC SP 127-1 Volume 31, issue 3, Mar 1991.

[9]Extracted from discussions with personnel from Hq AAFCE on 30 Apr 1992. Content of discussions was the substance of the AAFCE TLP Gulf War Conference Report, AFOOAT/S-078/92.

plan. Training for this attack anticipated the use of air power in close air support and air interdiction roles, which would include limited strategic attacks towards Baghdad. On one hand, to be prepared for combat, aircraft had to be fueled with weapons loaded and readied for launch. On the other hand, the aircraft were needed for combat training, which would subject the aircraft to risk and require additional maintenance. Flight training thus inevitably degraded readiness over the short term.

The 35th Tactical Fighter Wing, an F-4G "Wild Weasel" unit, provides a representative example of this problem. The primary mission of the unit was destroying and suppressing surface-to-air missile systems. After arrival in the Gulf, the unit maintained alert with the appropriate external tanks and ordnance to accomplish the SEAD mission. Aircrews, however, expressed the need for air-to-air training in light of the anticipated Iraqi threat. To prepare aircraft for this training, safety considerations dictated that live ordnance had to be down-loaded and the external tank configuration changed, an obvious compromise to mission preparedness. The solution was to keep the majority of unit aircraft on alert and configured for the primary SEAD mission and reconfigure six aircraft for air-to-air combat training.[10]

Soon after arrival in theater, it became apparent that crews would lose proficiency if training programs were not reinstated. In response, CENTAF initiated a Coalition staff to define and set training priorities and arrange host nation training facilities. Responsibilities for the development and execution of unit training remained with the commanders of service components, but CENTAF maintained the responsibility for developing the operational concept and plans for overall training. CENTAF's priorities were (1) maintain deterrent and defensive posture, (2) practice mission profiles that would be expected during combat operations, and (3) be ready to respond to an Iraqi invasion of Saudi Arabia.[11] Units accomplished as much ground training as possible and requested waivers of other training requirements (such as emergency procedure simulator training), when necessary.

Flight training depended upon air space and weapon ranges and required host nation support. Gradually, Saudi Arabia made national bombing ranges available for military use, which was to include low-altitude training routes

---

[10](S/NF) Charles L Starr, "Special Study History of the 35th Tactical Fighter Wing (Provisional) Operations Desert Shield and Desert Storm," 14 Apr 1992, p 113.

[11] Maj Hill.

351

despite intense competition for existing training airspace. Training was additionally affected by unfamiliar meteorological conditions, notably, blowing sand and dust;[12] austere living and working conditions; extreme heat from August through October; and a lack of practice training. It is important to realize that preparedness is a complex problem, especially in a forward deployed location. Commanders developed programs to maintain proficiency and emphasize the tactics anticipated for the Saudi/Iraq theater. Minimum sortie rates were established to ensure minimum combat capability (see Table 20).

Table 20
Aircrew Sortie Rates[13]

Aircraft	Weekly	Monthly
A-10	7	
EF-111	2	8
F-4G		
F-15	3	11-13+
F-15E	3	11
F-16	2-3+	11-13+
F-111	2	7
F-117	2+	9
RF-4	3	12
AVERAGE	2.5	10

Training accomplished during Desert Shield fell into three broad categories: desert acclimatization, local-area orientation, and mission preparation. Initial training of U.S. and Coalition air forces deployed to Saudi Arabia, and later to Turkey, began with local-area orientation and training designed to familiarize the aircrews with flying conditions peculiar to Southwest Asia. Problems such as haze and sand posed particular difficulties for helicopter crews, for whom low-altitude night operations posed severe hazards.[14]

---

[12]Lt Col Richard Comer, USAF, Commander, MH-53J Squadron *History of Desert Shield/Desert Storm-20 SOS*, undated.

[13]Maj Hill.

[14]Lt Col Comer.

352

Aircrews arriving in Saudi Arabia needed to adjust to local flying conditions and be integrated into the theater planning. Who managed air space control? What navigation aids were available? Landscape in urban areas is surrounded by diffused light at night, but what about the desert? Only CENTAF forces did not regularly train within the theater. Previously, the problem had been compounded by the limited number of in-theater exercises such as Bright Star, and these were limited in scope and involvement.

Desert Acclimatization

Table 18 illustrates the lack of dedicated training for Southwest Asia. The Wild Weasels stationed in the desert at George AFB commented,

> Probably one of the biggest things we learned was how to fly in this desert—which is different than the desert at George. There are different weather considerations, visibility considerations. The effects of heat have modified the way we fly the airplane. Something as mundane as not being able to turn some of our sensors on [radar, etc.] while on the ground has caused us to train in a new way.[15]

Lastly, civilian aviation requirements competed with military aviation requirements by restricting low-altitude training, and the Saudi range restrictions (maximum altitude 15,000 feet MSL) compromised training realism.[16] But, since aircrews were on the verge of war, they needed to know how well everything was going to work and develop tactics to compensate for shortfalls.

As the size and diversity of deployed Coalition air forces continued to grow, airspace and military training areas became saturated. Additional military operating areas were negotiated for use as air-to-ground training ranges, which were important so that aircrews could maintain weapons delivery proficiency and check aircraft release systems. Efforts were made to ensure that all crews had expended live munitions and thoroughly understood safe escape and weapons effects before Desert Storm. Hq USCENTAF/RSAF exercises provided a vehicle for multinational composite force training and basic proficiency for crews with alert commitments.

---

[15](S/NF) Starr.

[16]This problem also existed in the continental United States, where civilian aviation competes for utilization of all air and ground ranges. Only ranges in restricted airspace such as the Red Flag ranges were conducive to medium-altitude tactics.

In September, CENTAF instituted weekly package training exercises to promote interoperability and integrated training. The objectives of these exercises were to familiarize pilots and controllers with local terrain and meteorological conditions in possible combat areas and to demonstrate to Coalition land forces that air support could be used safely close to their positions.

Exercises increased in size and complexity as Desert Shield progressed. Exercise emphasis shifted early from supporting the defensive D-Day plan to supporting the evolving offensive air campaign plan, with deception playing a major role. Exercise Imminent Thunder, conducted in November 1990, promoted joint and combined training and interoperability. It included an amphibious operation and considerable air play. The training focus had moved from a defensive reaction to an Iraqi attack, and finally to an offensive scenario that included the liberation of Kuwait. The objectives for the air forces included exercising a D-Day alert package and the command and control process for close air support, air interdiction, and offensive counterair in a coordinated manner. Imminent Thunder involved over 2,300 total sorties, including 1,300 close air support missions.

At the same time, the overall planning focus was changing. The "Black Hole" strategic planning cell in Riyadh was developing an offensive plan in accordance with Central Command's desire that the first phase of war against Iraq be composed entirely of air attacks on Iraq and Kuwait. As this plan was fleshed out and targets identified, training was modified to prepare for the offensive air war.

With the new focus on the central area of Iraq, a study of the dense antiaircraft artillery concentrations in Iraq's air defense network prompted some units to emphasize training for medium-altitude (5,000-25,000 feet) ingress and attacks. Training missions took on new emphasis; some tactics, others timing and coordination, and others dress rehearsals of actual missions.

Exercises tested the procedures for these new offensive plans. The Tanker/Air Space Control Exercise, for example, manned all the AWACS orbits, then cycled a large number of fighters through air refueling from a tanker in a short time. Similarly, the Border Air Refueling and Intercept Exercise developed air combat readiness and increased fighter/ AWACS proficiency. As 17 January approached, these exercises also served to lull the Iraqis into a false sense of security because they became accustomed to seeing a periodic high level of night operations.[17] The deception would serve well on the first night of the war.

This section focused on the mainstream air training conducted in Saudi Arabia. Appendix E to this Report presents a compilation of all Desert Shield exercises. All airpower forces brought particular capabilities to Desert Storm. Discussions of their training are available in the following appendices: B-52s, Appendix G; SOF, Appendix H; and Navy/Marine Corps, Appendix I.

Desert Storm Training Lessons Learned

Desert Storm provided the crucible for testing the previous training of Coalition units. The intent of the exercises during Desert Shield had been to prepare units for the anticipated conflict but, as with all wars, the conflict did not develop exactly as expected. As the war progressed, shortcomings in training were noted, procedures corrected, and lessons passed to other units.

Perhaps the most crucial question in the initial stage of the war was whether to continue to fly low–the focus of most Desert Shield and preconflict training–or to move to medium altitudes in the face of Iraqi antiaircraft artillery. During Desert Shield, some units analyzed the Iraqi opposition and transitioned to medium-altitude ingress and attacks. Others, however, continued training at low level. The argument was summed up by a Royal Air Force Jaguar pilot at a postconflict NATO tactics symposium.

> The major decision that we had to make was which tactics to employ, low-level or high-level. The arguments in favor of employing low-level tactics included the following; the aircraft itself and its weapons system have been optimized for low-level operations; our weapons stocks consisted predominantly of cluster and retarded bombs which could only be delivered from low-level; and the pilots have been specifically trained over the years to operate in the low-level regime and this was where we initially thought we would be the most comfortable and indeed the most effective. We were therefore leaning towards the opinion that you should 'fight the way you train' and that we should stay at low-level. This was in fact the way that we planned and the way that we intended to execute our pre-planned 'D' day targets, should they have been tasked.[18]

---

[17](S) Large border exercises were frequently scheduled for Wednesday nights, and the air campaign started on a Wednesday night.

[18]Extracted from discussions with personnel from Hq AAFCE on 30 Apr 1992.

Some units did "fight the way they trained." In the early days of the war, B-52s, F-111s, EF-111s, RAF Tornados, and some Navy units conducted their attacks from low level. However, the intensity of the antiaircraft artillery encountered and the inability of the Iraqi Air Force, along with the reduction of the surface-to-air missile threat due to Coalition suppression of enemy air defenses, convinced these units to conduct operations at medium-altitude. This tactics change, for which training had not been emphasized, led to other problems.

For example, the issue of F-16 weapons employment caused difficulties during the initial days of the war. A postconflict analysis states,

> Initial mission effectiveness, in terms of "bombs off on first pass," was less than desired. There are multiple reasons why this happened, to include the confusion of the first days of combat, and the defensive maneuvers required for survival. However, another reason was the low knowledge level of medium- and high-altitude delivery constraints. Due to the previous low-altitude training emphasis or lack of medium-altitude releases, few pilots were exposed to some of the associated problems, such as extremely high crosswinds and high G releases due to delay cues. It should be noted that even though there was a training deficiency, the learning curve was steep.[19]

It is important to note that aircrew training quickly overcame the problems.

[DELETED]

[DELETED].[20]

Other errors affecting impact points could be caused by early or late bomb release due to target anticipation, aircraft buffeting due to winds, or cross wind errors. The bottom line was, the farther away from the target a nonguided munition is released, the more uncertainty as to its exact impact. [DELETED].[21] [DELETED].

[DELETED]

---

[19](S/NF/WN/NC) *Tactical Analysis Bulletin*, Vol 91-2, Jul 1991, p 4-13.

[20](S/NF/WN/NC) *Ibid*, p 4-13.

[21](S/NF/WN/NC) *Ibid*.

[DELETED].[22]

[DELETED].

Problems were not limited to those of the Coalition: As U.S. F-15Es exited Iraqi airspace after attacking Scud-associated targets in Northwest Iraq on the first night of the air war, they observed a MIG-29 pilot shoot down his wingman, and then fly into the ground.[23]

Peacetime preparation has always been an optimization between cost and value gained. Training involves munitions, aircraft, aircrews and support personnel, training ranges, and airspace. Air-to-air training in particular requires large amounts of airspace, since maneuvers in both the horizontal and vertical planes are involved. Frequently, air traffic control puts restrictions on the airspace boundaries, forcing training engagements to be flat and artificial. Air-to-ground units having difficulty scheduling weapons delivery ranges and the associated airspace can only practice high-altitude weapons deliveries with advanced coordination with the Federal Aviation Administration. The A-10 Wing Weapons Officer at King Fahd Airport reported the following problems due to peacetime practices:

> Restrictions on chaff and flare usage in the United Kingdom meant that the chaff and flare systems of the jets were rarely fully used prior to deployment. The squadron's jets required much trouble shooting of their chaff and flare dispensing systems while preparing for combat. During the war, it became apparent that pilots were unsure or unaware of procedures for rehoming the Triple Ejector Rack (TER) after bombs were unloaded during Integrated Combat Turns. Rehoming the TER is a maintenance function which could have been avoided, had we not just simulated reloading weapons during peacetime exercises. These are just two examples of problems

---

[22](S/NF/WN/NC) *Ibid*, F-16 working group, pp 4-14 - 4-15. (Although both techniques were identified as training habit patterns, they are not limited to flying aircraft.)

[23](S/NF/WN/NC) *Ibid*. The same incident was described in *Aviation Week and Space Technology*, 18 Feb 1991. It said that an Iraqi MIG-29 shot down his partner aircraft, then crashed in an early Desert Storm mission. [DELETED]

caused by a lack of usage of weapon systems during our training prior to deployment for Desert Shield.[24]

In conclusion, the story of training for Desert Storm was a success story, one that began long before the Iraqi invasion of Kuwait. Training adjustments made in Desert Shield convincingly demonstrated the inherent flexibility that training conferred. The force that defeated Iraq was decades in the making and emphasized realistic, combat-oriented training from the beginning. Realistic training was stressed as a constant theme through the development of not only the individual but also the Coalition force. The factors and practices enabling the development of this force, and training of the aircrews that flew missions, prepared them for this war. Red Flag was a constant theme mentioned by pilots and aircrews as instrumental in their training. Desert Shield training took this common ground as a building block for the evolving air campaign. For example, newer tactics grew out of a recognition that aircrews needed to release weapons at medium- to high-altitude, and Desert Shield training exercises provided opportunities to sharpen that skill.

Aircrews did not come to the Arabian Peninsula during Desert Shield to train for a war; they came prepared to fight a war. This was the result of years of U.S. air training effort as well as the recurring overseas exercise deployments to the Southwest Asia region. The investment in training over the decades between the Vietnam War and the Gulf War reaped dividends in terms of U.S. lives saved in combat, a truly meaningful measure of merit. The training of the personnel had indeed matched the quality of the weapons systems and tactics, and the combination of the three overwhelmed the enemy.

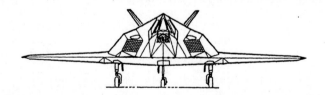

---

[24]Report given by Captain Meir, Wing Weapons Officer, A-10, King Fahd Airport, to AAFCE Gulf War Conference. Note that this was as much a maintenance and peacetime procedures problem as a training problem. Source: HQ AAFCE TLP Gulf War Conference Report.

6

Conclusions

Addressed within the operational and strategic context established by the other reports in the Survey, the preceding discussion suggests a number of conclusions. The most obvious is that the weapons, tactics, and training brought to bear in aerial combat played a major role in establishing the tempo, driving the conduct, and determining the outcome of the Gulf War.

Iraqi Capabilities

Saddam Hussein's forces clearly had the capacity to inflict considerably greater losses on Coalition forces than they did. Iraq's air force, while outnumbered and outclassed, nevertheless possessed significant numbers of capable systems, notably the Mirage F-1 and the MIG-29. If aggressively and competently used, these aircraft could have caused serious problems for the Coalition. Iraq also possessed significant numbers of highly capable SAMs, backed by a large antiaircraft artillery force, all linked to capable early-warning radars through the KARI air defense system. While the system lacked the capacity to counter the full weight of Coalition air power, it could, if operated as advertised, have enabled Iraqi commanders to coordinate defensive efforts far more effectively than they did. It is important to note that not all Iraqi forces displayed a lack of tactical skill and initiative; the Scud mobile missile force is an obvious case in point.

Coalition attacks on command and control targets reduced the Iraqi air defenses almost immediately to uncoordinated local efforts. An analysis of the effectiveness of the suppression of enemy air defense (SEAD) missions on radar-directed defensive systems shows a clear correlation between high-speed antiradiation missile (HARM) shots, and the reduction in Iraqi radar emissions. Also, HARM use led to a rapid and dramatic decline in guided, as opposed to unguided, firings of Iraqi radar missiles and in Coalition aircraft losses to radar missiles.[1] At the same time, Iraqi SAM and antiaircraft artillery gunners did not exhibit any great degree of cleverness or initiative. In the absence of Iraqi records, the lackluster performance supported by EPW interviews suggests deficiencies in leadership, training, or both, but the sharp decline in radar missile effectiveness–a decline not noted in infrared missile or antiaircraft artillery effectiveness– testifies positively as to the effectiveness of Coalition tactics.[2]

One Iraqi tactical success story was the handling of the Scud mobile missile force. The Iraqi mobile missile force exhibited impressive competence in camouflage, concealment, and communications security. Although a definitive assessment is not possible, it is apparent that at a minimum, the Iraqis were able to employ, and at the same time largely preserve, their mobile intermediate-range ballistic missile capability despite a major commitment of U.S. and Coalition resources to the anti-Scud campaign.

Weapons Systems

Among U.S. and Coalition aerial weapons systems, the outstanding successes were the F-117 stealth fighter, the Tomahawk cruise missile, laser-guided bombs (LGBs) used in combination with night-capable target acquisition and designator systems, and the HARM. The F-117 and Tomahawk, both examples of sophisticated, highly complex and expensive weapons systems, performed as advertised, demonstrating unprecedented tactical capabilities with important operational and strategic ramifications. These two systems enabled U.S. air power to penetrate a dense and sophisticated air defense net and attack directly at the heart of enemy power without preliminary suppressive attacks and without aircrew losses. The combination of LGBs and night-capable target acquisition and designator systems deprived Iraqi forces the cover of darkness to a degree unprecedented in aerial warfare. There were, however, significant limitations to the Coalition's ability to exploit this capability; most Coalition aircraft were unable to both drop and guide LGBs, and a very

---

[1](S/NF/WN/NC) For more information see the *Effects and Effectiveness* report.

[2]Losses and Damage inflicted by radar SAMs drop precipitously, but once Coalition aircraft abandoned low altitude tactics on day three, losses and damage inflicted by IR SAMs and AAA remain essentially constant.

360

high proportion of LGBs were dropped by a relatively small number of platforms, specifically, F-111Fs, F-117s, F-15Es, and A-6Es. As did the F-117 and Tomahawk, HARM performed as advertised, making a major contribution to the SEAD effort.

The heavy Air Force investment in aerial refueling platforms, with a strength of 694 tankers, was another success story.[3] Air refueling gave U.S. and Coalition air power enormous tactical flexibility, and Air Force tankers supported Coalition, Navy, and to a lesser extent Marine as well as Air Force sorties. The KC-10 and the KC-135R made disproportionate contributions to the refueling effort, the former because of its large fuel offload and ability to reconfigure from flying boom to probe and drogue configuration in flight and the latter because of the increased tactical flexibility bestowed by its highly fuel-efficient turbofan engines. Although Marine, Navy, and Royal Air Force tankers also made significant contributions, they were responsible for a considerably smaller share of refueling sorties and pounds of fuel transferred than were Air Force tankers. Since the vast majority of U.S. and Coalition tactical platforms had relatively short combat radiuses, air refueling became a tactical necessity. Among major Coalition strike platforms, only B-52s conducting operations from Saudi Arabia could strike targets anywhere in Iraq without air refueling. F-111s and A-6s could strike some targets in Iraq and the KTO without air refueling, and forward-based A-10s and AV-8s generally operated without tanker support; as a practical reality all other strikes required air refueling.[4] All F-117 sorties were air refueled, and F-4G "Wild Weasels" with their fuel-inefficient J-79 engines were particularly dependent on tanker support.

Weapon systems were not devoid of deficiencies. Perhaps the most dramatic was the inability of Coalition aircraft to acquire and attack Iraqi

---

[3](S) The USAF tanker fleet consisted of 59 KC-10s and 635 KC-135s, including 269 KC-135Rs; information from Air Force Air Staff, Mobility Forces/XOFM, Maj Collins, 16 Dec 1992, Air Force Association *Almanac* for 1991. Of these, 29 KC-10s and 193 KC-135s (65 of them KC-135Rs), were deployed in the AOR at the peak of the Desert Storm and another 17 KC-10s and 69 KC-135s (26 of them KC-135Rs), were operating in direct support from outside the AOR. For more information on the USAF Tanker Fleet, see the (S/NF/WN/NC) *Logistics* report.

[4](S) The above statement summarizes a complex set of relationships and ignores the fact that aerial refueling was used as much for operational flexibility as for simple range extension.

mobile missile systems using onboard sensors with any degree of consistency. The switch from low- to medium-altitude bombing deliveries highlighted tactics and training problems and exposed hardware and software deficiencies. Neither DOD nor the Air Force had adequately anticipated the need for a conventional deep-penetrating "bunker-busting" munition like the GBU-28.

Combat search and rescue in Desert Storm had significant problems. The Air Force MH-53J was the only Coalition combat rescue platform capable of operating in a high-threat environment. But the crews, though well trained in their primary special operations mission, were not trained in combat search and rescue tactics. Equally important, the one MH-53J squadron in theater had a primary special operations mission. Additionally, command and control relationships were complex, not clearly defined, and contributed to the loss of an Army CH-47 committed to a rescue mission.

Tactics

Flexibility was a dominant tactical characteristic of U.S. air power in Desert Storm. Though not all the Coalition air forces possessed equivalent hardware resources and most were not as thoroughly trained in large composite force tactics–the Royal Air Force was an exception–Coalition air forces did share this advantage in flexibility to varying degrees. Examples of this inherent tactical flexibility, a product of hard, realistic training and a tactical culture which demands and rewards initiative, are imbedded in the preceding chapters of this report. Here, two examples will suffice: the first was the ability of U.S. aircrews to improvise refuelings and find their way to their targets despite unforecasted adverse weather and other unplanned obstacles.[5] The second was the successful use of B-52 bombing to create psychological effects on Iraqi forces. Procedures for the bombings were devised and implemented by relatively junior SAC officers in Saudi Arabia in response to Central Command's desire to place the Republican Guards and other Iraqi ground forces under constant pressure.

---

[5](S) Comment by Col Bobby Bufkin, USAF, Commander of Red Flag, to Dr. John Guilmartin, GWAPS, 30 Jan 1992. As Red Flag commander, Col Bufkin had dealt with elements of all the major participating Coalition air forces in an intense training environment and was familiar with their equipment and training methods.

362

Electronic warfare played a larger role in Desert Shield and Desert Storm than in any previous conflict. U.S. air forces dominated in this arena. The United States fielded a wider array of specialized electronic warfare platforms than any other nation could have done and applied them to good effect in a tactically coordinated manner. The success of the SEAD campaign was largely a reflection of the ability of the Coalition to dominate the electromagnetic high ground. The Constant Source network for collecting and disseminating information about enemy electronic threats made important contributions to this struggle and represents a significant success story in its own right.

The SEAD campaign itself represents a tactical success of considerable magnitude. The successful tactical integration of a wide range of diverse assets, including EF-111 and EA-6 jammers and F-4G Wild Weasels, provides a prime example of the flexibility already noted.

Training

It is axiomatic that superior weapons systems can be rendered ineffective by poor or poorly executed tactics. It is equally axiomatic that hard, realistic training is the bedrock requirement for the development of sound tactics and for good tactical execution. The accuracy of both of these observations was richly demonstrated in the Gulf War, positively by Coalition forces and negatively by Iraqi forces. The negative case is most apparent in the utter lack of tactical success achieved by the Iraqis with aircraft well up to world standards—the MIG-29 and Mirage F-1—and the mediocre results they obtained with excellent surface-to-air missile and gun systems, notably the Roland, SA-6, SA-8, and ZSU 23-4.[6] Paradoxically, the positive case is harder to make because the high training standards of Coalition and—particularly—U.S. air forces made the tactically difficult look easy. In short, the intensive, realistic, combat-oriented training paid off.

---

[6] The argument that overwhelming numbers of generally superior Coalition aircraft denied the Iraqi Air Force the chance to demonstrate its tactical capabilities does not hold up historically. Two examples from World War II make the point: In 1939, the Polish Air Force, surprised, outnumbered, and flying obsolete aircraft, outscored the Luftwaffe in air-to-air kills. The number of highly trained Japanese pilots were depleted in 1942-43 and by 1945 were faced by overwhelming numbers of U.S. aircraft, almost all of them technically superior. The Japanese did, however, field a small number of state-of-the-art fighters in the final months of the war, and in the hands of some of the few surviving capable pilots, these achieved dramatic, if isolated, successes.

The millions of dollars and thousands of hours spent to support training, especially in a series of exercises such as Red Flag conducted at Nellis AFB in Nevada, the National Military Training Center at Fort Irwin in California, the Marine Corps training areas at Twentynine Palms in California and at Yuma in Arizona, the Navy ranges at NAS Fallon in Nevada, and in a host of other exercises throughout the world, proved their worth.

**While planes were being readied pilots were briefed
for the first daylight attack.**

Appendix A

Definition of Aerial Missions

Definitions of Tactical Air Missions and Tasks Flown in Operation Desert Storm[1]

Counter Air: missions conducted to attain and maintain a specified degree of air superiority by destroying, neutralizing, or disrupting enemy air power. Counter air involves both offensive and defensive operations as well as the suppression of enemy air defenses. The ultimate goal is total air superiority.

Offensive Counter Air (OCA): missions normally conducted throughout enemy airspace and designed to destroy or neutralize enemy air power close to the source. This may be accomplished through an air-to-air engagement or an air-to-surface attack of an enemy airfield and its facilities. Friendly forces have the initiative to conduct OCA at a time and place of their choice.

Defensive Counter Air (DCA): missions operations normally conducted over friendly territory in reaction to enemy initiative. There are two types of active air defense: area defense and point defense.

1. Area defense is more flexible but requires a high degree of discipline and coordination to avoid missing an inbound enemy. The air component commander (ACC) is normally designated the area air defense commander. His assets include antiaircraft weapons systems of the land component commander and the naval component commander as well as his fighter units.

2. Point defense protects high-value assets and key points along lines of communications.

---

[1](S/NF/WN/NC) Abstracted from *MCM 3-1*, Volume I, Tactical Employment, 4 Jul 89, pp 2-1 thru 2-4.

Suppression of Enemy Air Defenses (SEAD): missions conducted to increase the survival and effectiveness of friendly operations. SEAD assets seek out and destroy or disrupt enemy surface-to-air defenses or integrated air defense systems (IADS).

Air Interdiction (AI): missions to delay, divert, disrupt, or destroy the enemy's military potential. Once identified and prioritized by component commanders and approved by the joint force commander, all air interdiction targets are included in missions executed by the ACC.

Close Air Support (CAS): missions requested by a ground commander for support of friendly forces. Because of the proximity of friendlies, each CAS mission requires detailed coordination and integration with the organic fire and movement of friendly troops.

Tactical Surveillance and Reconnaissance: missions to provide commanders with timely information before and during tactical operations. Surveillance and reconnaissance have four applications: prediction of enemy intent, reporting enemy status, threat warning, and targeting.

Specialized tasks: actions that enhance the execution and successful completion of the above missions. Tactical air forces perform the following specialized tasks:

1. Electronic Combat (EC): actions undertaken to control selected parts of the electromagnetic spectrum in support of strategic and tactical operations. EC strategy employs electronic warfare; elements of command, control, and communications countermeasures (C^{3}CM); and SEAD to exploit weaknesses in an enemy's ability to wage war and to apply force against his offensive, defensive, and supporting capabilities. The purpose is to enhance the ability of U.S. war fighting systems to achieve military objectives.

2. Special Operations: [DELETED].

3. Combat Search and Rescue (CSAR): missions or operations conducted to support the rescue of downed combat aircrews. These actions preserve and return to duty critical combat resources, deny the enemy a possible source of intelligence, and contribute to morale and motivation of combat aircrews.

Methods of Employment

A single tactical mission may require several employment methods and a variety of considerations. For example, OCA may include several methods of employment during one composite force operation. Detailed operating considerations differ among types of aircraft; broad categories are presented below:

1. Sweep. Sweep aircraft establish air superiority in a designated area for a specified time period by seeking out and destroying enemy aircraft in the air. Autonomous sweep operations may be conducted by using only on-board fire-control and identification systems. However, in today's all-aspect threat arena, maximum effectiveness is realized by using ground-controlled intercept (GCI), airborne warning and control systems (AWACSs), and other sources of real-time intelligence to increase ability to employ beyond visual range (BVR) and to heighten overall battle situation awareness.

2. Combat Air Patrol (CAP). Two types of CAP are point CAP and screen or barrier CAP (BARCAP). Point CAP falls under the concept of active air defense—protecting high-value assets (i.e., airfields; command, control and communications facilities; storage facilities; or lines of communication). BARCAP, or screen, is used to prevent the enemy from reaching an asset and is established at some forward point between the enemy and that asset. For example, BARCAP is used to protect AWACS and Compass Call, or may be used to establish a screen well forward of an airfield or friendly troop concentration.

3. Escort. Escort is normally used to protect a composite force operation. It may take the form of close escort—when fighters fly in close proximity to attack force or other asset; or it may be performed as detached escort—when escort fighters do not fly close to the asset being protected.

4. Air-to-Surface Attacks Against Specified Targets. Attacks against specified targets may be conducted either in AI, OCA, or CAS. The types of targets and the threat will normally dictate the choice of weapons. The possibility of mission diverts (AI to CAS, for example) makes it mandatory for aircrews to be totally familiar with the effects of the weapons carried aboard their aircraft.

5. <u>Air-to-Surface Attacks Using Specialized Weapons</u>. Weapons requiring detailed employment planning (i.e., precision-guided munitions) may be employed to accomplish a variety of missions.

6. <u>Armed Reconnaissance</u>. Armed reconnaissance locates and destroys targets of opportunity.

Appendix B

Coalition PSYOPS Leaflets and Handbills

Above:
Translation:

'Desert Storm is coming to your area. Flee Immediately!'

Below:

"'Iraqi citizens, Saddam's military has placed your lives in danger. The Coalition Forces are coming. We will be striking this area soon. We do not wish to harm innocent citizens. Evacuate this area immediately and head north. Civilian areas in Baghdad will not be targeted. Flee immediately!'

ايها المواطنون العراقيون

قد عرضتكم قوات صدام العسكرية الى الخطر الشديد .

ان القوات المتحالفة تتقدم نحوكم بسرعة هائلة و سنبدا

بقصف هذا الموقع قريبا و لا نريد اصابة المدنيين الابرياء .

اخلوا هذه منطقة واتجهوا الى الشمال . ان الاحياء السكنية

في مدينة بغداد لن تتعرض للقصف .

اهربوا فورا !!!!

Below:

'The United States abides by the rules of the Geneva Convention. Ceasing fire will
provide you the following:
- Humane Treatment
- Food and Water
- Medical Treatment
- Shelter
- Return to your homes after hostilities '

تلتزم الولايات المتحدة الاميركية بقوانين و بنود ميثاق جنيف.
إن توقفك عن القتال يؤمن لك التالي:

• المعاملة الانسانية

• الطعام و الماء

• العناية الطبية

• المأوى

• العودة الى منازلكم بعد انتهاء الحرب

Above:

'TOO LATE!'

'The PSYOP campaign told soldiers to leave their vehicles to avoid injury... It proved what President Bush said about not fighting the Iraqi people...'

-A Senior Iraqi Officer

Below:

'This location is subject to bombardment. Escape now and save yourselves.'

FRONT

Iran's growing air force...?

لقد بادر 'صدام في اعادة شط العرب لايران والان.....

يقدم لهم سلاحكم الجوي

لكن هناك خطوة افضل بامكانكم اتخاذها وهي الذهاب الى المملكة العربيه السعودية.

اعلنوا بواسطة اجهزة الارسال عن رغبتكم بالالتجاء الى اخوانكم العرب. اقترب بطائرتك

بشكل انفرادي، انزل عجلات الهبوط وسلط كافة انوار الطائرة، عندها اطرح جميع

الذخائر الموجودة على متنها واقفل اجهزة تصويب الاهداف ثم تابع التحليق

بسرعة لا تتجاوز ٢٥٠ الى ٣٠٠ عقدة في الساعة.

أنك ستحصل على معاملة انسانية، وعند انتهاء الازمة سيسمح

لك بالعودة الى وطنك لاعادة بنانه من جديد.

First, Saddam gave away the Shat-Al-Arab, and now... He's giving them your Air Force! A better alternative would be to fly to Saudi Arabia. Radio your intentions to seek refuge with your Arab brothers, come as a single plane, have landing gear down and all lights on, jettison all ordinance and turn off targeting emitters, fly at 250-350 knots per hour. You will be allowed to return home to help rebuild your homeland.

Above:

'This is your first and last warning! Tomorrow, the 16th Infantry Division will be bombed!! Flee this location now!'

Below:

'The 16th Infantry Division will be bombed tomorrow. The bombing will be heavy. If you want to save yourselves leave your location and do not allow anyone to stop you. Save yourselves and head toward the Saudi border, where you will be welcomed as a brother '

غدا سوف تضرب فرقة المشاة السادسة عشر وسيكون
القصف شديد ، إذا أردت النجاة أترك مكانك ، ولا تسمح
لأحد ان يمنعك. أنقذ نفسك وتوجه الى الحدود
السعودية وسوف تجد من يستقبلك كأخ.

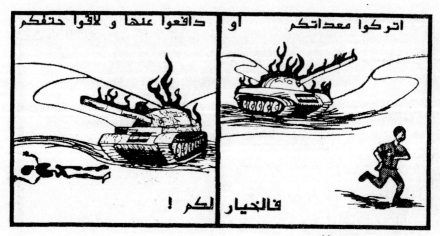

Above:
'Leave your equipment or defend it and die!'
'The choice is yours!'

Left:
'Warning!
This location will be shelled. Leave your equipment and save yourselves.
Warning!'

'The PSYOP effort was focused on breaking the Iraqi will to resist, and on increasing the fears of the Iraqi soldiers, while pointing out that the Coalition was opposed not to the Iraqi people, but only to Iraqi's national policy.'
Conduct of the Persian Gulf War, An Interim Report to Congress, Department of Defense, 1991

Above:

'Cease resistance. You are cut off.'

Below:

'Use the following procedure to cease resistance:
Remove magazine from your weapon.
Place weapon over your left shoulder with the muzzle down.
Place your hands over your head and proceed slowly.
Wave a white cloth to signal your peaceful intent or hold up this leaflet.
All armies of the Multi-National Forces understand that this pass shows your honorable commitment to peace.'

اتبعوا الاساليب التالية للتوقف عن المقاومة :

اسحب مخزن الذخيرة من سلاحك.

احمل السلاح على كتفك الايسر مع توجيه الماسورة الى الاسفل.

ارفع يديك فوق رأسك واقترب ببطء.

لوح بقماشة او منديل ابيض للدلالة عن رغبتك المسالمة، او ارفع هذا المنشور.

ان جميع الجيوش المنتمية الى القوات

المتعددة الجنسيات على علم بتلك المبادرة التي تبرز فيها عن رغبتك في السلام.

375

Above:

'Saddam is against Peace. Save Iraq, Stop Saddam. No more war, Peace Now. Save Iraq. Iraq is against Saddam.'

Below:

"'Iraqi people, Peace. Saddam is the cause of the war and its sorrows. He must be stopped. Join with your brothers and demonstrate rejection of Saddam's brutal policies. There will be no peace with Saddam.'

ايها المواطنون العراقيون

السلام عليكم

صدام هو المتسبب في الحرب وتتائجها لكم هي ـ ارامل

وايتام ومعوقون ومشوهون ولكم الخيار انتم لا احد غيركم بوضع

حد له وانتم القادرون انضموا الى اخوانكم واظهروا رفضكم

لسياسته المدمرة لكم ولوطنكم لن يكين هناك سلام بوجود صدام.

Iraqi PSYOP Leaflets and Handbills

LIBERTY STADIUM CRIES FOR HELP BECAUSE OF YOUR AGGRESSION AND KILLING CIVILIANS, INNOCENT KIDS, MOTHERS AND OLDS.

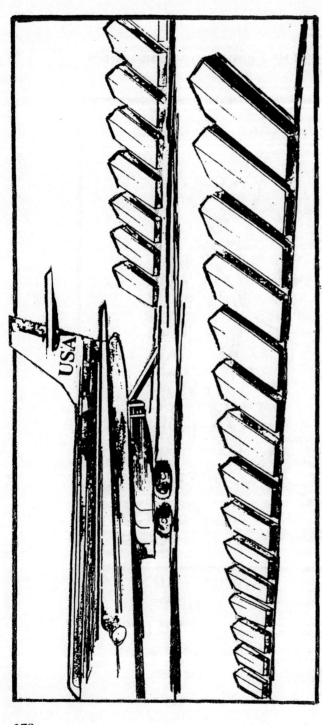

DEAR SOLDIERS :

YOUR COMMANDERS HAVE SAID THAT THE WAR WILL TAKE FEW DAYS WERE THEY CORRECT ? AND CONVINCED YOU THAT LOSES WILL BE MINIMUM IN THE GROUND COMBAT WE ASSURE THAT THEY WON'T BE CORRECT

379

(U) *"Our holy things, our land, and our honor are in safe hands."*
US troops cavorting with alcohol and women in Saudi Arabia, while King
Fahd expresses his approval. Note Star of David around neck of US
soldier.

Alif Ba' (Baghdad)

Mr Bush's hobby: increasing the budget

Appendix C

The Aeronautical Rating

It would be difficult to understand how airpower was applied in the Gulf War without understanding the significance of the military aeronautical rating and–directly to the point at hand–without understanding the training required to achieve that rating. The role in Desert Shield and Desert Storm of rated aircrew members–that is, pilots, weapons system operators (WSOs), electronic warfare officers (EWOs), navigators or other Service equivalents–was pivotal. The basis of that importance was aviation training. The aeronautical rating thus represents a common core of professional skill and knowledge that was brought to bear tactically in the Gulf War. This appendix will provide the reader with a sense of that core in a brief discussion of undergraduate flight training.

The aeronautical rating was regarded differently by the various air forces with which we are concerned, but the reader should bear in mind that the common core of professional and technical skills and knowledge that the aeronautical rating represents was more basic and important. Simply put, the Coalition air forces shared an international language of airpower, one acquired as an essential part of military aviation training. At the most basic level that language is English, the international language of aviation. Pilots trained to fly, according to the ICAO (International Commercial Aviation Organization) standards that govern international air traffic, must speak English to function within the system.[1] Outside of China and the nations of the former Soviet bloc, the vast majority of military aviation training worldwide is conducted in English.

---

[1]International Civil Aviation Organization, *International Standards, Recommended Practices and Procedures for Air Navigation Services, Aeronautical Telecommunications*, Annex 10, Vol. II (*Communication Procedures*), 4th ed (April 1985), chap 5 "Aeronautical Mobile Service": para 5.2.1.1.2 under para 5.2.1.1 "Language to be used" reads as follows: "Recommendation–Pending the development and adoption of a more suitable form of speech for universal use in aeronautical radiotelephony communications, the English language should be available, on request from any aircraft station unable to comply with 5.2.1.1.1 [stating that in general air to ground communications should be conducted in the language of the station on the ground] at all stations on the ground serving designated airports and routes used by international services."

The hard core of this common heritage is reflected in close relations and shared professional standards among the U.S. air forces and those of the English-speaking nations of the British Commonwealth. Standards of training and airmanship are high in all of these forces, and pilots routinely exchange assignments among them with minimal friction. A U.S. Air Force or Navy fighter pilot or weapons system operator experiences no more difficulty settling into a Royal Air Force, Canadian Air Force, or Royal Australian Air Force squadron than in moving to a new squadron within his own Service. Significantly, the Royal Saudi Air Force was able to interface far more easily and quickly with its Coalition counterparts than were the Saudi naval or ground forces. The proximate cause was that all Saudi pilots speak English, but the common language went beyond the spoken idiom: the Royal Saudi Air Force prides itself on having taken the best of each, in training, philosophy, and equipment, from the U.S. Air Force and the Royal Air Force.[2]

Basic Flying Training

The following discussion focuses on undergraduate pilot training, but the same basic points apply to the training of all rated officers. The U.S. military pilots who flew in Desert Shield/Desert Storm were enrolled in pilot training through a number of mediums. All were volunteers. Almost without exception, Air Force, Navy/Marine, and Army officer pilots were college graduates when they entered flight training. Army warrant officer pilots tended to be educated beyond the high school level. All were required to pass a stringent flight physical emphasizing eye sight (vision correctable to 20/20 or better was required), good general health, and a stable psychological makeup. Other screening mechanisms included administration of the AFOQT (Air Force Officer Qualifying Test) or the Navy or Army equivalent, Service academy graduation, and recommendations by ROTC officials.

The paths through undergraduate pilot training to operational flying assignments of the pilots who flew in Desert Storm are summarized in the three figures below. All U.S. military undergraduate pilot training programs are based on a combination of rigorous classroom instruction, dual flight instruction, and solo flight practice. The Air Force and Navy/Marine programs last approximately a year. The Army undergraduate helicopter program is somewhat shorter.

---

[2]Comment to Lt Col Mark Tarpley, USAF, by a senior RSAF officer.

U.S. Air Force Pilot Training

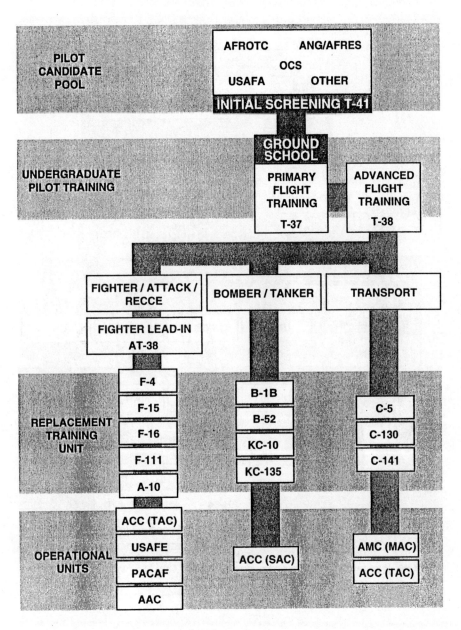

(Note: The Parentheses indicate the USAF organization at time of Desert Storm)

U.S. Army Pilot Training

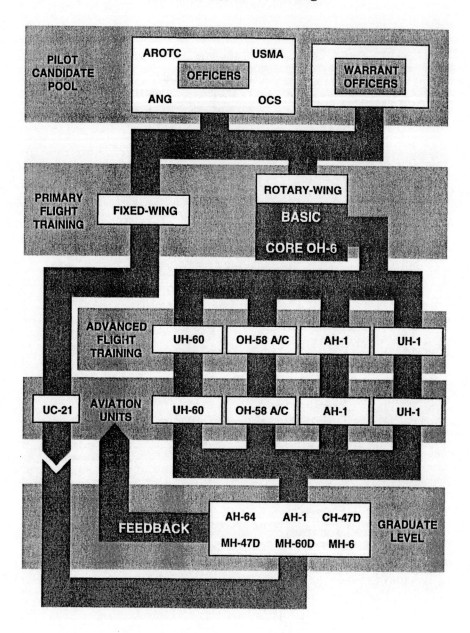

U.S. Navy Pilot Training

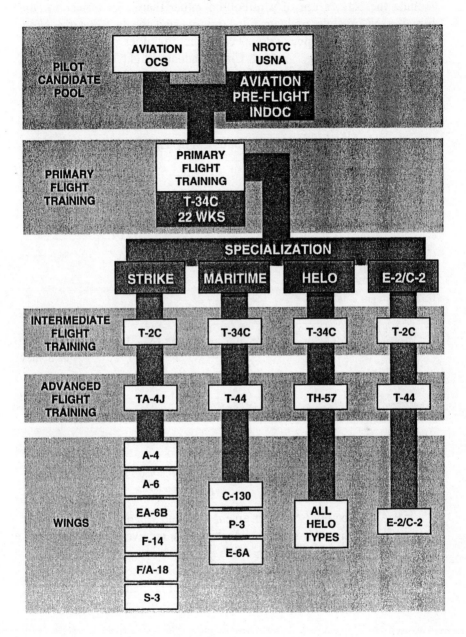

Salient differences between the Air Force and Navy programs include the Navy's use of a turboprop rather than a jet trainer for the initial stage of undergraduate pilot training and the fact that the Navy separates its pilot trainees into specialist communities prior to award of the aeronautical rating. A USAF Undergraduate Flight Training Table is included to give an idea of program content, time spent, flying hours required, and cost using Air Force undergraduate pilot training as an example. Navy figures are broadly similar.

USAF Undergraduate Flight Training[3]

Ground Phase:	17 days	$4,300		
Academics			56.0 hours	
T-37 Training:	90 days	$8,300		
Academics			84.5 hours	
Flying			80.9 hours	62 Sorties
Simulators			27.3 hours	
T-38 Training:	120 days	$162,000		
Academics			81.5 hours	
Flying			109.8 hours	86 sorties
Simulators			29.6 hours	

All Air Force pilots are instrument qualified when they receive their aeronautical rating. Air Force helicopter pilots receive their initial flight instruction in helicopters within the Army training system and are assigned to helicopter units until they receive fixed-wing transition training, normally at the Captain to Major point in their careers. As with the Air Force, all Navy pilots are commissioned officers and instrument

---

[3]Headquarters, Air Training Command, Director of Operations provided these figures to the authors via facsimile transmission on 29 Jun 1992.

qualified. Navy helicopter pilots receive their initial flight training in fixed-wing aircraft and are trained entirely by the Navy.

Marine Corps aviators receive their basic flight instruction within the Navy training system. The training and tactical philosophies of the aviation branches of the Navy and Marine Corps closely parallel one another, though the Marines emphasize direct support of troops in contact. As with the Air Force and Navy, Marine officer aviators rotate between flying and staff assignments. All Marine officers are line officers; support functions such as logistics and medical are provided by the Navy. Rated Marine aviators are commissioned officers.

The U.S. Army approach to aviation differs from those of the Air Force and Navy. This approach reflects the reality that Army aviation units support the operations of maneuver divisions and corps and fall directly under the appropriate ground unit commander. All Army pilots receive their initial training in helicopters, and the vast majority are assigned to helicopter units. In contrast to the Air Force and Navy, Army pilots do not receive an instrument rating as part of their initial pilot training. The Army has no requirement for aerial navigators, although enlisted and warrant officer reconnaissance systems operators perform similar functions. The bulk of Army pilots are warrant officers, specialist aviators who spend almost all of their careers in the cockpit and cannot command. Officer pilots rotate into and out of flying assignments in much the same way as their Air Force or Navy counterparts.

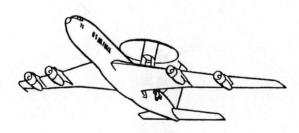

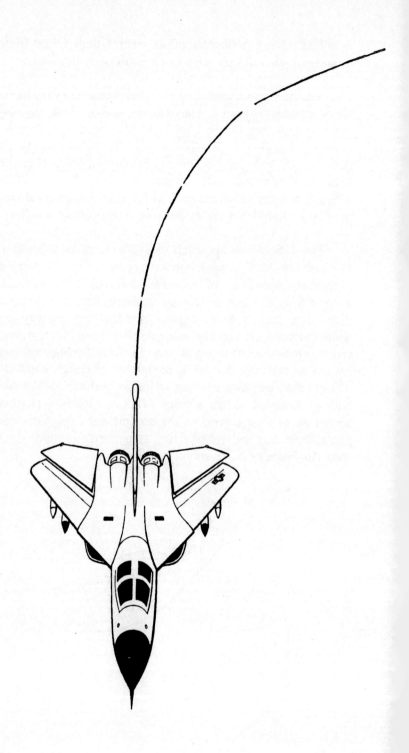

Appendix D

Historical USCENTAF Exercises 1985 - 1990

Date	Name
Jul-Aug 85	Bright Star 85
Jul-Aug 85	Inferno Creek 85*
Apr-May 86	Accurate Test 86
Jul-Aug 87	Bright Star 87
Jul-Aug 87	Shadow Hawk 87*
Jul-Aug 87	Inferno Creek 87*
Sep-Dec 89	Bright Star 90
Oct-Nov 89	Shadow Hawk 90*
Oct-Nov 89	Inferno Creek 90*

* Part of overall Bright Star Exercise

Exercise Bright Star 85

1. **Exercise Description:** Bright Star 85 (BS-85) was a JCS-coordinated, USCENTCOM-scheduled joint/combined Field Training Exercise conducted during 13 July - 31 August 1985. [DELETED].[1]

2. **Exercise Objectives:**[2]

   a. Conduct joint/combined interdiction, close air support, and counterair operations.

---

[1](S) USCENTAF Exercise Bright Star 85 After Action Report, 31 Oct 1985, p 1-1.

[2](S) *Ibid.*

b. Integrate U.S. and Egyptian air defense forces.

c. Conduct electronic warfare (EW) operations against Soviet-built air defense systems.

d. Exercise joint/regional communications connectivity.

3. **Participating Forces and Units:**[3]

Force	Unit
8 x F-4G	37th Tactical Fighter Wing
8 x F-4E	347th Tactical Fighter Wing
2 x E-3	552d Air Warning and Control Wing
2 x EC-130	7th Airborne C^2 Squadron
10 x C-130	Military Airlift Command
3 x B-52	28th Bombardment Wing
4 x KC-135	126th Air Refueling Wing

4. **Sequence of Events:**[4]

Deployment	13 July - 2 August 1985
Employment	3 - 10 August 1985
Redeployment	10 - 31 August 1985

5. **Major Milestones and Accomplishments:**[5]

a. Despite the usual flight clearance problems at the outset, the flying operations were the most extensive and productive exercised in SWA to date. Missions under the control of AWACS and ABCCC included low-level navigation, airfield at-

---

[3](S) *Ibid*, p 1-2.

[4](S) *Ibid*, p 1-3.

[5](S) *Ibid*, Attch 2.

tacks, airfield defense, interdiction, close air support (CAS), dissimilar air combat training (DACT), attacks against a simulated carrier battle group, a live firepower demonstration, air refueling, intratheater airlift, and tactical and strategic airdrops of troops and equipment.

b. The combination of AWACS and ABCCC proved invaluable in the safe, organized, and effective execution of the wide variety of missions. Egyptian participation on both of these aircraft significantly enhanced the Egyptian Air Force's air defense command and control throughout the exercise.

c. F-4G Wild Weasel aircraft were deployed to SWA for the first time and demonstrated their value as an extremely effective defense suppression asset. [DELETED].

d. The increased quantity and quality of CAS (compared to Bright Star 83) provided to USARCENT and the Egyptian ground forces caused the Egyptians to initiate a concerted effort to improve their own CAS training program.

e. The use of multiple drop zones and airfields throughout the exercise area provided realistic challenges to the airlift aircrews as well as the Combat Control Teams (CCTs) and the Airlift Control Center (ALCC).

f. The integration of bomber and tanker forces into CENTAF air operations was excellent.

6. **Lessons Learned (Relearned):**[6]

a. Initial command and control of early arriving forces was a problem because the forces arrived before bare base facilities on the airfields were prepared to receive them. Consequently, personnel were billeted in civilian hotels with no communications links to the airbase. Future deployments should include communications equipment to establish links between person-

---

[6](S) *Ibid.*

nel billeted in civilian hotels and the Tactical Air Control Center for emergencies and/or changes in the flying schedule.

b. U.S. Liaison Officers in the Egyptian Air Operations Center, Cairo Approach Control, Cairo West Tower, and at the American Embassy performed a crucial role in coordinating a myriad of activities essential for smooth air and ground operations throughout the exercise.

c. Although the opportunities for electronic combat (EC) training were excellent, U.S. personnel were denied access to Egyptian surface-to-air missile and ground-controlled intercept sites. Denying access to these sites prevented both U.S. and Egyptian air defense personnel from receiving valuable EC training, which should be given higher priority in future exercise planning.

d. The installation of a mobile ground-controlled approach (GCA) facility at Cairo West was highly successful and helped U.S. and Egyptian air traffic controllers provide positive control to more than 2,000 sorties. As the only air traffic control radar control facility in Egypt, the GCA provided safe separation to both arriving and departing aircraft.

Exercise Inferno Creek 85

1. Exercise Description: Inferno Creek 85 (IC-85) was a JCS-directed, CENTCOM-scheduled joint/combined Field Training Exercise conducted from 31 July 1985 to 24 August 1985.[DELETED].[7]

2. Exercise Objectives:[8]

a. Maximize regional involvement in pursuit of improved security and defense capabilities.

---

[7](S) USCENTCOM Bright Star 85 After Action Report, 24 Mar 1986, p 2-6.

[8](S) USCENTAF Exercise Inferno Creek 85 After Action Report, 2 Dec 1985, p 1-1.

b. Conduct joint/combined air operations with the SOAF and U.S. Navy.

c. Exercise portions of real-world contingency plans that center on air defense activities in the region.

d. Demonstrate rapid deployment and sustainment activities in a bare base environment.

3. **Participating Forces and Units:**[9]

Force	Unit
8 x F-15	1st Tactical Fighter Wing
2 x E-3	552d Air Warning and Control Wing
2 x KC-10	2d Bombardment Wing

4. **Sequence of Events:**[10]

Deployment	31 July - 11 August 1985
Employment	12 - 18 August 1985
Redeployment	20 - 24 August 1985

5. **Major Milestones and Accomplishments:**[11]

a. Employment operations consisted of three phases, as follows:

(1) Attacks against a Carrier Battle Group. KC-10s refueled fighters from both sides.

(2) Fleet defense

(3) Defending airbases

---

[9](S) *Ibid*, p 1-2.

[10](S) *Ibid*, p 1-3.

[11](S) *Ibid*.

6. **Lessons Learned (or Relearned):**[12]

    a. There was no combined operations center to control and coordinate flying operations; future exercises should establish such a center with unit representatives available during periods of intensive flying operations.

    b. As in previous exercises, the training environment was excellent. This, along with the professionalism and flying expertise of host aircrews, offered an outstanding training experience for deployed units.

Exercise Accurate Test 86

1. **Exercise Description:** Accurate Test 86 (AT-86) was a JCS-directed, CENTCOM-scheduled joint/combined Field Training Exercise conducted in Oman during 17 April to 8 May 1986. [DELETED].[13]

2. **Exercise Objectives:**[14]

    a. Develop a strategic deployment/redeployment plan to optimize available airlift resources.

    b. Demonstrate strategic deployment capabilities and combat readiness of selected CENTAF forces.

    c. Conduct combined air defense operations with the SOAF.

    d. Exercise long-haul joint communications among Thumrait, the U.S. Embassy in Muscat, and Headquarters CENTCOM and CENTAF in the United States.

    e. Exercise sustainment under field conditions in a desert environment using minimum combat and communications support.

---

[12](S) *Ibid*, Annex A.

[13](S) USCENTAF Exercise Accurate Test 86 EXORD, 31 Jan 1986, p 1.

[14](S) *Ibid*, p v.

3. **Participating Forces and Units:**[15]

Force	Unit
12 x F-16	388th Tactical Fighter Wing
2 x E-3	552d Air Warning and Control
1 x RC-135 (Rivet Joint)	55th Strategic Reconnaissance Wing

4. **Sequence of Events:**[16]

Deployment	17 - 26 April 1986
Employment	25 April - 2 May 1986
Redeployment	2 - 8 May 1986

5. **Major Milestones and Accomplishments:**[17]

    a. This was the first deployment of F-16 and RC-135 to area.

    b. The exercise again demonstrated that AWACS could operate effectively from a bare base location. [DELETED].

    c. The combined CENTAF, Strategic Air Command (SAC), and SOAF flying missions provided excellent training for the aircrews, as had previous exercises in Oman.

    d. [DELETED]. The E-3 had the unique opportunity to control day VFR (no radar) fighters in an offensive role.

---

[15](S) *Ibid*, p vi.

[16](S) *Ibid*, p 5.

[17](S) USCENTAF Exercise Accurate Test 86 After Action Report, 31 Jul 1986, pp 1-4, 1-8.

6. **Lessons Learned (or Relearned):**[18]

    a. The SOAF, once again, stated its desire for air refueling by U.S. KC-10s or KC-135s. The SOAF did not understand why the U.S. Navy provided air refueling to them during Beacon Flash exercises while the Air Force would not without a foreign military sales case.

    b. The number of F-16 engine problems (3 compressor stalls and 1 stall/stagnation) was significantly higher than normal, given the sortie rates and numbers of aircraft involved. Fuels at Thumrait Air Base were tested and found to be of high quality, and foreign object damage was ruled out as a possible cause.

Exercise Bright Star 87[19]

1. **Exercise Description**: Bright Star 87 (BS-87) was a. JCS-directed, CENTCOM-scheduled, joint/combined Field Training Exercise. [DELETED].

2. **Exercise Objectives:**[20]

    a. Conduct joint/combined interdiction, close air support, and counterair operations with Egyptian armed forces and the U.S. Navy, Marines, and Army Central Command.

    b. Conduct Electronic Warfare (EW) operations against Soviet-designed air defense systems.

    c. Exercise combined/joint integrated air defense command, control, and communications with host nation air defense forces.

    d. Exercise joint regional communications connectivity.

---

[18](S) *Ibid*, Section 2.

[19](S) USCENTAF Exercise Bright Star 87 EXORD, 1 Jun 1987, p iv.

[20](S) *Ibid*, p 1-2.

e. Exercise sustainment, under field conditions, in a Southwest Asia (SWA) environment.

3. **Participating Forces and Units:**[21]

Force	Unit
8 x F-15	1st Tactical Fighter Wing
8 x F-4G	37th Tactical Fighter Wing
5 x B-52	5th Bomb Wing
4 x KC-135	190th Air Refueling Group
2 x E-3	552d Air Warning and Control Wing
2 x EC-130	41st Electronic Combat Squadron
5 x C-130	314th Tactical Airlift Wing

4. **Sequence of Events:**[22]

Deployment	1 July - 12 August 1987
Employment	12 - 20 August 1987
Redeployment	20 August - 6 September 1987

5. **Major Milestones and Accomplishments:**[23]

a. Ninety-two percent of the CENTAF scheduled sorties were flown, and ninety-nine percent of the sorties flown were effective, resulting in the most productive combined training exercise in SWA to date. Missions under the control of AWACS included low-level navigation, airfield attack, airfield defense, interdiction, dissimilar air combat training (DACT), attacks against a U.S. Navy Surface Action Group, a live firepower demonstration, air refueling, and tactical and strategic airdrops of troops and equipment.

---

[21](S) *Ibid*, p A-1.

[22](S) *Ibid*, p v.

[23](S) USCENTAF Exercise Bright Star 87 After Action Report, 30 Oct 1987, pp 1-3, 1-5.

b. This was the second time for the F-4G in SWA, and its performance demonstrated its value as a defense suppression asset. The training opportunities provided by attacks on Soviet-built air defense sites were invaluable. In addition, F-4G operations in conjunction with Egyptian F-16s and Marine F-18s provided valuable interdiction and joint maritime training in a realistic environment.

c. Electronic combat training was outstanding. [DELETED].

d. Airlift forces received valuable training in that many tons of cargo and approximately 450 troops were either airdropped or airlanded.

6. **Lessons Learned (or Relearned):**[24]

a. Coordination of air operations with the Egyptian Air Defense Command is a slow and cumbersome process and caused some mission cancellations and delays until the Tactical Air Control Center personnel understood the EAF coordination process and Egyptian personnel understood the Bright Star concept of operations.

b. Conduct of air operations and training with the host nation would be greatly facilitated if knowledgeable Liaison Officers were provided at the Tactical Air Control Center to assist in coordinating flight clearances, training, use of ranges, and many other areas that must be relearned by both U.S. and host nation units during each exercise.

Exercise Shadow Hawk 87

1. **Exercise Description:** Shadow Hawk 87 (SH-87) was a joint/combined exercise designed to increase regional involvement

---

[24](S) *Ibid*, Attch 2.

in pursuit of improved security and defense. The exercise was conducted in conjunction with Bright Star 87. [DELETED].[25]

2. **Exercise Objectives:**[26]

    a. Integrate Jordanian and U.S. planning efforts to improve combined employment of both air forces.

    b. Conduct combined tactical air operations to include offensive counterair, interdiction, and close air support.

    c. Plan and execute combined airlift operations of RJAF personnel and equipment.

    d. Exercise joint regional communications connectivity.

3. **[DELETED]**

4. **Sequence of Events:**[27]

Deployment	15 - 23 July 1987
Employment	24 - 30 July 1987
Redeployment	31 July - 3 August 1987

5. **Major Milestones and Accomplishments:**[28]

    a. A total of thirty-six Jordanians received orientation flights; fourteen in the F-16 and twenty-two in the E-3.

    b. The Rapidly Deployable Integrated Command and Control (RADIC) system was deployed to Jordan for the first time. RADIC is a lightweight system that provides the E-3 AWACS air picture to air defense staffs for use in air employment opera-

---

[25](S) USCENTAF Exercise Bright Star 87, 1 Jun 1987, p 1.

[26](S) USCENTAF Exercise Shadow Hawk 87 After Action Report, 1 Sep 1987, p 1-2.

[27](S) *Ibid*, p 1-2.

[28](S) *Ibid*, pp 1-3, 1-4.

tions. The Jordanians were impressed with RADIC and wanted it back during future exercises.

c. The F-16s provided opposition air for the RJAF F-1s, and, once again, the RJAF aircrews demonstrated a high level of proficiency in all aspects of air operations.

6. **Lessons Learned (or Relearned):**[29]

a. CENTAF headquarters was formed as a part of the combined joint headquarters, but the air war was prosecuted from the Air Defense Operations Center (ADOC) at another location. As a result, CENTAF was not able to effectively interface with their Jordanian counterparts and had little control of the air war. One lesson learned was that future exercises should consider deployment of a Tactical Air Control Center and collocation of CENTAF with the RJAF ADOC.

b. The RADIC was not operational during three of the six exercise employment days due to a lack of spare parts and inadequate time for system setup and checkout. The recommendation followed that future exercises should include earlier deployment of RADIC and more spares to ensure that it is fully operational for the entire exercise period.

c. Problems were encountered with distribution of the Air Tasking Order (ATO). The plan was to distribute the ATO via host nation facsimile systems, but the ATOs were transmitted at too low a priority and U.S. personnel did not know where the facsimile systems were located. Future exercises were recommended to continue with the facsimile system for ATO distribution.

Exercise Bright Star 90

1. **Exercise Description:** Bright Star 90 (BS-90) was a JCS-directed, CENTCOM-scheduled, joint/combined Field Training Exercise. [DELETED].[30]

---

[29](S) *Ibid*, Section 2.

[30](S) USCENTAF Bright Star 90 Exercise Plan, 31 Jul 1989, p ii.

2. **Exercise Objectives:**[31]

   a. Conduct joint/combined counterair and EW air operations
       with U.S. Navy, Marine, and Army forces and the Egyptian
       armed forces (EAF).

   b. Conduct EW operations against Soviet-made Egyptian air
       defense systems.

   c. Exercise joint regional communications connectivity.

   d. Exercise sustainment under field conditions in a SWA envi-
       ronment, using minimum combat and support equipment.

3. **Exercise Forces:**[32]

Force	Unit
8 x F-15	1st Tactical Fighter Wing
7 x F-4G	35th Tactical Fighter Wing
4 x EF-111	366th Tactical Fighter Wing
2 x EC-130	41st Electronic Combat Squadron
3 x KC-135	340th Air Refueling Wing
2 x B-52	379th Bombardment Wing
2 x E-3	552d Air Warning and Control Wing
5 x C-130	Military Airlift Command

4. **Sequence of Events:**[33]

Deployment	15 September - 9 November 1989
Employment	11 - 16 November 1989
Redeployment	17 November - 12 December 1989

---

[31](S) *Ibid*, p 1-2.

[32](S) *Ibid*, p A-1-1.

[33](S) *Ibid*, p ii.

5. **Major Milestones and Accomplishments:**[34]

   a. Bright Star 90 continued emphasis on EW operating in an environment that included Soviet-made air defense systems.

   b. EF-111 aircraft participated for the first time, and integrated employment operations were flown using the capabilities of both the EF-111 and the F-4G Wild Weasel.

   c. EC-130 (Compass Call) aircraft participated for the first time. Communications jamming parameters were restricted by the host nation, and this degraded training effectiveness for both U.S. and Egyptian forces, an unfortunate but necessary precaution.

   d. AWACS proved invaluable in the safe, organized, and effective execution of a wide variety of missions. Egyptian participation on board AWACS enhanced combined air defense operations throughout the exercise.

   e. EW training was also excellent. F-4Gs employed self-protection countermeasures by integrating flying tactics with chaff dispensers and electronic countermeasure (ECM) pods against Egyptian air defense radars, resulting in a realistic wartime environment. B-52s conducted active ECM against the Egyptian threat systems and also received excellent training.

   f. Airlift forces airdropped or airlanded over 450 personnel and many tons of cargo. A combined airdrop by 18 Egyptian and U.S. C-130s demonstrated a high level of aircrew proficiency.

6. **Lessons Learned (or Relearned):**[35]

   a. As in previous exercises, the coordination and integration of flying activities continued to be a problem. [DELETED].

---

[34](S) Information taken from USCENTAF inputs to the joint universal lessons learned system (JULLS) for Exercise Bright Star 90, USCENTAF Exercise data files, and unit after action reports on file in the 9th Combat Plans Squadron at Shaw AFB, SC.

[35](S) *Ibid.*

b. After the startup coordination problems were resolved, integration with the EAF went better than in previous Bright Star exercises. Perhaps the most significant "lesson learned" for CENTAF was an awareness of the EAF coordination process and the need to make sure that exercise scenarios include time to smooth out disconnects during initial air operations.

Exercise Shadow Hawk 90

1. **Exercise Description:** Shadow Hawk 90 (SH-90) was a joint/combined exercise designed to increase regional security and defense capabilities. The exercise was conducted in conjunction with Bright Star 90. [DELETED].[36]

2. **Exercise Objectives:**[37]

    a. Conduct combined/joint training of staff officers in preparing, planning, and executing joint operations.

    b. Plan and conduct combined/joint training operations related to tactical air operations and tactical airlift.

    c. Exercise communications and air defense systems in an electronic warfare (EW) environment.

    d. Conduct training in crisis resupply operations.

3. **Participating Forces and Units:**[38]

Force	Unit
12 x F-4	122d Tactical Fighter Wing (ANG)
6 x F-16	363d Tactical Fighter Wing
2 x E-3	552d Air Warning and Control Wing
3 x C-141	438th Military Airlift Wing

---

[36](S) USARCENT Joint Task Force Alpha Shadow Hawk 90, 31 Aug 1990, p 1.

[37](S) *Ibid.*

[38](S) *Ibid.*

4. **Sequence of Events:**[39]

Deployment	17 September - 29 October 1989
Employment	29 October - 3 November 1989
Redeployment	3 - 15 November 1989

5. **Major Milestones and Accomplishments:**[40]

   a. A mix of tactical, AWACS, and airlift sorties were flown to include counterair and interdiction by F-16s along with two airborne assaults of Jordanian personnel and equipment by the airlift forces.

   b. Four days of scenario activities: two days of offensive action by the Jafr-based F-16s and RJAF F-5s aided by AWACS, and two days of defensive activities with opposition provided by RJAF F-1s and F-5s. AWACS was netted with Jordanian ground radar sites for a combined air defense system.

   c. Electronic combat was exercised with F-16s. [DELETED].

6. **Lessons Learned (or Relearned):**[41]

   a. Pilots reported that the opportunity to work together was a valuable experience and trained them to accomplish their mission better.

   b. Although the AWACS successfully controlled all required air-to-air events, the exercise would have gone more smoothly had AWACS deployed earlier and had the exercise familiarization (FAM) period included two FAM days instead of one.

---

[39](S) *Ibid.*

[40]CENTAF inputs to JULLS, USCENTAF Exercise data files, and unit After Action Reports.

[41]*Ibid.*

Exercise Inferno Creek 90

1. **Exercise Description:** Inferno Creek 90 (IC-90) was a JCS-directed, CENTCOM-scheduled joint/combined Field Training Exercise conducted from 24 October to 18 November 1989. This exercise was conducted in conjunction with Bright Star 90. [DELETED].[42]

2. **Exercise Objectives:**[43]

    a. Conduct and evaluate combined operations.

    b. Integrate Oman/U.S. combined planning.

    c. Enhance integrated air/ground close air support (CAS) operations.

    d. Maximize use of prepositioned assets.

3. **Participating Forces and Units:**[44]

Force	Unit
6 x F-16	363d Tactical Fighter Wing
2 x E-3	552d Air Warning and Control Wing

4. **Sequence of Events:**[45]

Deployment	24 October - 2 November 1989
Employment	3 - 8 November 1989
Redeployment	10 November - 12 December 1989

---

[42](S) USCENTAF Joint Task Force Charlie Inferno Creek 90 Exercise plan, 1 May 1987, p 1.

[43](S) *Ibid*, p iv.

[44](S) *Ibid*, p A-1-1.

[45](S) *Ibid*, p v.

5. **Major Milestones and Accomplishments:**[46]

   a. The return of the AWACS with the RADIC System significantly improved airfield defense capability and provided valuable training benefits to both CENTAF and SOAF air defense controllers and staff officers.

   b. The airfield attack and airfield defense scenarios offered high-quality training.

6. **Lessons Learned (or Relearned):**

   a. The Inferno Creek/Accurate Test exercises provide high-quality training. [DELETED].[47]

---

[46]CENTAF inputs to JULLS, CENTAF Exercise data files, and unit After Action Reports.

[47]*Ibid.*

Appendix E

Desert Shield Exercises[1]

Unique and Recurring Training Exercises

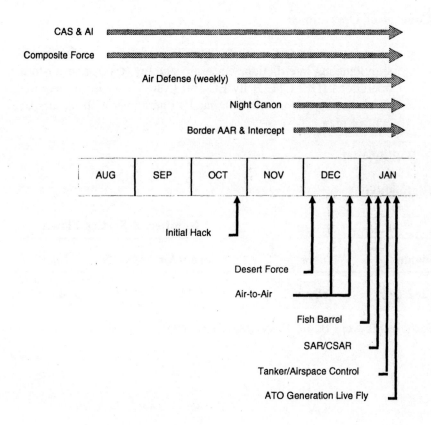

[1]All information was extracted .om a MFR written by Lt Col Robert S Coombs, USCENTAF, *Desert Shield Training and Exercises*, 20 Mar 1991.

Exercise Initial Hack 24 - 26 Oct 1990

Objectives:

• Increase operations tempo, C^3, two carrier simultaneous operations, joint/combined planning, and tanker operations in multiple, simultaneous refueling tracks.

• Expose participants to conditions duplicating actual scenarios, continuous operations, and air/ground staff operations.

Concept of Operations:

• Exercise tanker and receiver flows to planned orbits and tracks; simultaneous interdiction, close air support (CAS), and air-to-air operations [DELETED] fly EC-130 (ABCCC) sorties as required; conduct forty-eight hour continuous operations with an airspace control plan.

[DELETED].

Highlights:

		Number of Sorties Flown		
Fighter	Tanker	Air-to-Air	AWACS	Total
282	88	48	13	431

Participants were USAF, Navy, RSAF, RAF, CAF.

Exercise Imminent Thunder   15 - 20 Nov 1990

CENTCOM **Objectives:**

- Joint/combined training and interoperability of friendly forces, enhance coordination and communication capabilities, improve joint/combined air operations, enhance Naval surface operations, exercise combined link-up and reinforcement operations, conduct amphibious operations, and conduct carrier battlegroup operations in support of amphibious operations.

CENTAF/RSAF **Objectives:**

- Exercise D-Day alert interdiction package; execute mission commander's operations order; exercise CAS C^3 process and conduct CAS/offensive counterair (OCA)/air interdiction (AI) missions in a coordinated manner; support amphibious operations; and coordinate search and rescue/combat search and rescue (SAR/CSAR).

Concept of Operations:

Phase 1

Offensive Air Operations:

- Perform alert notice and simulate aircraft/crew generation; simulate D-Day. [DELETED].

CAS/AI

- Exercise the Tactical Air Control System (TACS) C^2 in a limited jamming environment, integrate CAS/kill zones, and fly integrated AC-130/A-10 night antiarmor operations. [DELETED].

Phases 2 through 5

Amphibious Operations, Reinforcement, Redeployment

- Establish amphibious operating area and support Navy and Marine operations; missions included DCA (ground alert), CAS, air-to-air CAPs, and air refueling.

SAR/CSAR

- SOCCENT/CENTAF exercised Helos and A-10s with two preplanned pick ups and an immediate launch. [DELETED].

Highlights:

Phase 1

A total of 2,300 sorties were flown, with thirty composite force packages and 1,300 CAS sorties. D-Day (dress rehearsal) involved: twelve composite force packages, 273 sorties, and six airfield attacks. The mission commander operations order was exercised.

Phases 2 through 5

A total of 550 sorties were flown, with CAS/Navy AOA support: 88 USAF and FAF CAS sorties and 35 tanker sorties.

Exercise Desert Force   5 - 7 Dec 1990

Objectives:

- Conduct two carrier simultaneous operations, coordinate command and control, airspace management plans, CSAR, and tanker and receiver flows to planned orbit and tracks.

- Fly composite force integrated training with Coalition forces.

Concept of Operations:

- Fly a dress rehearsal of actual D-Day [DELETED].

Highlights:

A total of 430 sorties were flown by the following Coalition forces: USAF, FAF, CAF, RSAF, USN, and RAF.

Air-To-Air Training Exercises   East 17 - 19 Dec 1990
                                             West 22 - 23 Dec 1990
Objectives:

- Practice air combat maneuvering (ACM) and improve AWACS Weapons Director (WD) proficiency.

- Exercise High Value Airborne Asset (HVAA) protection and F-1 dissimilar air combat training.

Concept of Operations:

East: ACM–two versus two aircraft [DELETED].

West: ACM–two versus two and two versus four aircraft [DELETED].

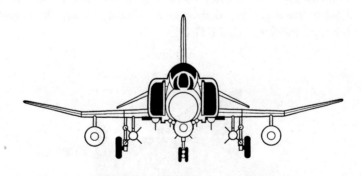

Highlights:

More than 200 sorties were flown with the following participants:

> HVAA:
> AWACS   Tankers
> Compass Call   ABCCC
>
> Blue Air:
> USAF–F-15,   RSAF–F-15
> RAF–Tornado F-3   FAF–M-2000
>
> Red Air:
> USAF–F-16,   CAF–CF-18
> USMC–F/A-18   IAF–Tornado
> KAF–F-1

Exercise Fish Barrel   7 - 9 Jan 1991

Objectives:

- Evaluate the C^2 procedures. [DELETED]. Exercise procedures for attacking armor both in day and night, and practice CAS sortie distribution.

Concept of Operations:

- Perform CAS and AI using friendly ground forces; incorporate Night Canon training. Fly dedicated AWACS/ opposing air; concentrate package training [DELETED].

Highlights:

There were 360 daytime and 216 nightime CAS/AI sorties flown with the following participants:

CAS/AI Training
USAF	A-10, OA-10, AC-130, F-16, F-15E, F-111F
USN	A-6
USMC	F/A-18, AV-8B, A-6
USA	AH-64, OH-58D, AH-1
KAF	A-4
RSAF	F-5
RAF	Jaguar
FAF	Jaguar

Package Training
USAF	F-16, F-4G, B-52, F-15E, F-15, EF-111, F-111F
CAF	CF-18
RAF	Tornado F-3, GR-1
RSAF	F-15, Tornado
FAF	Jaguar, M-2000, F-1CR

Navy Package Training
USN	A-6E, A-7, F-18, F-14, EA-6B, KA-6D
USAF	EF-111, F-4G
RSAF	Tornado IDS
RAF	Tornado GR-1

Joint SAR/CSAR Exercise   11 Jan 1991

Objectives:

- Exercise assets and C^3.

Concept of Operations:

- Conduct three rescue missions (2 SAR and 1 CSAR), two night and one day extraction, and operate C^3 through AWACS to the Joint Rescue Coordination Center.

Highlights:

The participants were: RSAF–Bell-212, USN–HH-60, and SOCCENT–MH-53, MH-60.

Tanker/Airspace Control Exercise   6, 13 Jan 1991

Objectives:

- Fly tankers at D-Day-level sortie requirements, utilize AWACS for tanker control, and test air traffic control procedures in saturated airspace conditions.

Concept of Operations:

- Fly the maximum number of tankers and fighters for short periods of time, activate air refueling tracks not used during training, and man all AWACS orbits.

Highlights:

The participants and number of refueling tracks were:

	6 Jan	13 Jan
Tankers	57	72
Air Refueling Tracks	19	20
Receivers	105	136

ATO Generation Exercise   12, 16 Jan 1991

Objectives:

- Exercise full ATO cycle.

416

Concept of Operations:

- Strictly a "paper" exercise that started with initial planning and target nomination in the Guidance, Apportionment, and Targeting cell to the production and distribution of the D+2 ATO in the ATO Division.

Highlights:

Both days were required to smooth out the process, and difficulties were experienced processing the ATO into the Computer Assisted Force Management System.

Recurring Training and Exercises

Air Defense Exercise Weekly Nov/Dec 1990

Objectives:

- Exercise C^3, practice detection, identification, and reaction.

Concept of Operations:

- Scheduled every week [DELETED].

Highlights:

There were 178 sorties over 14 vulnerability periods. The participants were:

Fakers	
USMC	F/A-18, A-6, AV-8B
USAF	F-15E, EF-111, F-111F, F-4G, F-16
USN	A-6, A-7
RAF	Tornado GR-1
FAF	Jaguar

Defensive Counterair

USAF	F-15
USMC	F/A-18
USN	F-14
RSAF	F-15, Tornado ADV
CAF	CF-18
RAF	Tornado F-3

Package Training   Weekly Sep 1990 - Jan 1991

Objectives:

- Promote interoperability of friendly forces, conduct integrated training, and exercise actual operations and procedures, planning, tactics, and C^3.

Concept of Operations:

- Enhance unit training programs by formally establishing two days a week (afternoon and night) for flights, designate mission commanders for each package.

Highlights:

Over 4,000 sorties were estimated flown, and all aspects of the integrated air campaign were exercised.

CAS/AI Training   Weekly Sep 1990 - Jan 1991

Objectives:

- Exercise elements of TACS that support CAS and AI missions, i.e., fighters, WOC, TACC/Combat Ops, CAS Director, and ABCCC, ASOC, TACP, AFAC, GTAC, ANGLCO [Air and Naval Gunfire Liaison Company (USMC)] Team.

- Develop and exercise C^2 procedures; familiarize pilots and controllers with terrain, landmarks, and meteorological conditions.

- [DELETED].

418

Concept of Operations:

- Fly CAS with different controlling agencies. [DELETED].

- The priorities were: CAS–support controllers with field exercises; AI–target areas near anticipated war operations.

Highlights:

A maximum of 110 sorties per day with the following participants:

CAS

USAF	A-10, OA-10, F-16, AC-130, C-130
USA	AH-64, AH-1, OH-58
USMC	AV-8B, F/A-18
FAF	Jaguar

AI

USAF	A-10, F-16, ABCCC
USMC	AV-8B, F/A-18, A-6
USN	A-6
RSAF	F-5
KAF	A-4
FAF	Jaguar
RAF	Jaguar

Night canon: Weekly Dec 1990 - Jan 1991

Objectives:

- Develop best tactics, C^2 methods, and BDA capability using tasked mission aircraft; and practice airspace deconfliction.

Concept of Operations:

- Conduct night antiarmor attacks.

Highlights:

A maximum of 48 sorties were flown at night.

419

**Border Air Refueling   Daily 17 Dec 1990 - 9 Jan 1991
and Intercept Exercise**

Objectives:

- Demonstrate air combat readiness/capability, reduce predictability, and increase fighter/AWACS proficiency.

Concept of Operations:

- Give Iraq a look, increase border presence (visible).

- [DELETED].

Highlights:

Sorties averaged 24 to 32 per day.

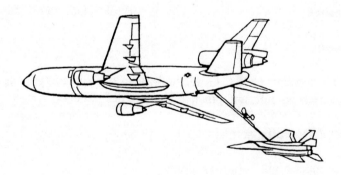

Appendix F

Flag Exercises

Red Flag

Red Flag had its roots in Vietnam. Spurred in part by relatively low exchange rates against North Vietnamese MIGs, Air Force officials returned to the institutional memory that roughly ninety percent of the aircrew losses occurred within the first ten combat sorties. Military leaders believed that combat losses could be reduced if aircrews were "seasoned" in a controlled environment similar to combat. Several proposals were made that optimized the mix of units participating against associated costs. In 1975 General Dixon, Commander of Tactical Air Command, declared that the first Red Flag exercise would provide the highest sense of realism in an enemy threat environment that peacetime training could offer.

Lessons learned from Vietnam became the guiding light for Red Flag exercises. This exercise is not a forum for checking out new people or developing new tactics but rather for evaluating approved tactics, gaining confidence in flight skills, and learning to orchestrate the efforts of a composite force. Safety is a paramount consideration for the 10 sorties that each aircrew flies. The tempo of realism increases gradually throughout these 10 days. Tactical Air Command's goal for Red Flag participation is once every 15-18 months per aircrew. The exercise lasts approximately 6 weeks and is subdivided into 3 two-week periods. Units rotate crews in for each two-week period to allow maximum participation. Red Flag is scheduled approximately 3 times a year and costs roughly $1.5 million per exercise, excluding costs for infrastructure support and range. The overall exercise objective is to provide a safe, simulated combat environment that allows participants to employ composite force tactics against strategic and tactical targets defended by a challenging, integrated air defense system. The following tables identify statistics about all flag exercises from their inception to the Gulf War.

Flag Exercises[1]

Year	Red	Green	Maple	Sorties	Hours	# Aircrews
1975	1			552	671	unknown
1976	9			9535	15363	2827
1977	10			16596	27645	6975
1978	9		2	19350	32164	6958
1979	7		2	19440	33930	9240
1980	3		2	10185	17718	6084
1981	3	1	2	17878	3022	7982
1982	3	1	2	15753	25821	6758
1983	3	1	2	16043	27033	6334
1984	4	1	2	19781	34248	7167
1985	3	2	2	22561	40893	8440
1986	3	1	2	16678	30734	6309
1987	4	1	2	20095	37252	6431
1988	3	1	1	16641	28630	4434
1989	4	1	1	19135	34530	4816
1990	3	1	1	14522	25489	4465

Flag Exercises[2] (continued)

Coalition Participants in Red Flag Exercises[3]

Year:	76	77	78	79	80	81	82	83	84	85	86	87	88	89	90	91
Britain	X		X	X	X	X	X	X	X	X	X	X	X	X	X	
Canada		X	X		X	X	X	X	X	X	X	X	X	X	X	
Egypt					X				X							
France					X	X		X	X		X		X	X		
Italy														X		
Saudi Arabia																

---

[1]414 CTS FAX, Fiscal Year Summary, 19 Mar 1992.

[2]*Ibid.*

[3]Capt Vic Wager, HQ ACC/DOTS Database, 16 Sep 1992.

422

Flag Exercises[4] (continued)

Canada	Egypt	France	Britain	Italy	Saudi Arabia
CF-5	F-16	Jaguar	Buccaneer	C-130	F-5E
CF-147	F-5E	C-160	C-130K	Tornado	
CC-30		F-1	Jaguar		
CF-18		C-130	Harrier		
CF-104			Tornado		
CH-136			Vulcan		
			C-130R		
			F-106		
			F-4M		
			VC-10		
			Victor		

Flag Exercises[5] (continued)

Other Foreign Participants in Red Flag Exercises

Year:	76	77	78	79	80	81	82	83	84	85	86	87	88	89	90	91
Australia				x			x				x			x		x
Belgium								x			x		x			x
Denmark								x								x
Germany	x			x	x	x		x		x					x	x
Greece					x		x							x		
Israel				x									x			
Jordan					x		x		x				x			
Korea		x	x					x							x	
Netherlands							x	x		x				x		
Norway										x			x			x
Singapore						x	x			x				x		
Thailand					x											
Turkey				x												

---

[4] 414 CTS FAX, Fiscal Year Summary, 19 Mar 1992.

[5] Ibid.

Red Flag exercises require a geographical space large enough to accommodate large composite force packages: interdiction sorties that may stretch tens of miles enroute to targets; air defense fighter tactics that may at times begin intercepts beyond visual range (30-50 nm) and take another 20 miles horizontally and 30,000 feet vertically to complete their engagement; several hundred aircraft without supersonic restrictions; air-to-ground targets (airbases, bridges, tanks, etc.) the same size and composition as wartime targets; and an airbase that can handle the launch, recovery, and emergency landings of all the airplanes. The enormity of the task and requirements for the training environment pointed toward federal land in the Nevada desert, depicted on the following map.

Each scenario pits a blue force, whose objective is to attack red interdiction and close air support targets, against a red force whose objective is to defend its resources. The mock war is controlled by range procedures, participant training objectives, a red force cadre that exercises control of the intensity and tempo of air combat consistent with training objectives, and range safety personnel. The Nellis AFB "aggressors" are the cadre of red fighters, that emulate enemy fighter tactics. Other air defense fighter units that are evaluating their combat air patrol (CAP) and air base defense tactics augment the aggressors. Ground-based area and point defenses form the other half of the enemy integrated air defense system (IADS). Manned and unmanned threat emitters run by civilian contractors and the Red Flag staff simulate Soviet-style ground threats such as the SA-2, 3, 4, 6, 8 and ZSU 23-4, providing realistic acquisition, track, and launch indications to blue force aircraft. The underlying Red Flag objective is to train the blue forces by creating an environment in which blue forces have to be vigilant and execute tactics that ensure mission success while minimizing simulated losses.[6] The following table listing red force units from Green Flag 90-4 was conducted August 1990, and is typical of all flag exercises.

---

[6]COMTAC Exercise Plan 80, Red Flag, 1 Feb 1992. Additional information on general Red Flag overview provided by HQ USAF/XOFC and ACC/DOXET.

424

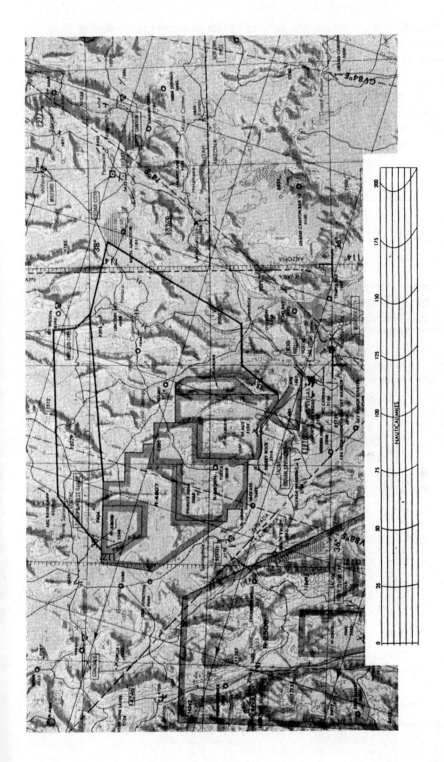

425

Blue forces constitute the largest group of participants during Flag exercises and are composed primarily of fighter forces. Over the years increasingly more participants have come from Strategic Air Command (SAC), Military Airlift Command (MAC), the Navy, the Marines, the Army, and the foreign nations. The following table listing blue force participants from Green Flag 90-4 is representative of the types and quantities of aircraft in each flag exercise.

Summary of Red Forces in Green Flag 90-4[7]

Unit	Aircraft (Number)	Home Base	Number of Sorties	Flight Hours
56 TTW	F-16 (8)	MacDill AFB, FL	AD-213	414.1
57 FWW	F-16 (6)	Nellis AFB, NV	AD-281	388.8
58 TTW	F-16 (6)	Luke AFB, AZ	AD-94	153.2
388 TFW	F-16 (6)	Hill AFB, UT	AD-63	137.4
VMFA-235	F/A-18 (6)	MCAS Kaneohe Bay, HI	AD-54	62.5
41 ECS	EC-130H (1)	Davis-Monthan AFB, AZ	C3CM-8	44.5
RTTF	KC-135 (3)	March AFB, CA	AAR-46	200.8
		Total	**759**	**1,401.3**

[7] *USAF Tactical Air Warfare Center Green Flag 90-4 Final Report*, Nov 1990, p 1-9.

Summary of Blue Forces in Green Flag 90-4[8]

Unit	Aircraft Number	Home Base	Type/Number of Sorties	Flight Hours
36 TFW	F-15 (8)	Bitburg AB, GE	AD-183	274.5
422 TES	F-15 (2)	Nellis AFB, NV	AD-7	6.8
32 TFS	F-15 (8)	Soesterburg AB, NL	AD-69	101.6
33 TFW	F-15 (10)	Eglin AFB, FL	AD-366	599.5
121 TFW	A-7D (6)	Rickenbacker ANGB, OH	AI-114	126.2
27 TFW	F-111D (8)	Cannon AFB, NM	AI-146	191.0
366 TFW*	F-111A (6)	Mt Home AFB, ID	AI-50	58.9
388 TFW	F-16 (10)	Hill AFB, UT	AI-304	467.5
VMFA-235	F/A-18	MCAS Kaneohe Bay, HI	SEAD-101	150.9
VMAQ-4	EA-6A (3)	NAS Whidbey Island, WA	SEAD-25	37.6
67 TRW	RF-4C (6)	Bergstrom AFB, TX	RECCE-177	345.1
52 TFW	F-4G/F-16 (4)	Spangdahlem AB GE	SEAD-90	156.3
35 TFW	F-4G (10)	George AFB, CA	SEAD-183	272.4
4443 TEG	F-4G (3)	George AFB, CA	SEAD-18	26.7
43 ECS	EC-130H (2)	Sembach AB GE	C3CM-15	35.4
41 ECS	EC-130H (2)	Davis-Monthan AFB, AZ	C3CM-37	97.2
42 ECS	EF-111 (3)	RAF Upper Heyford UK	EW, C3CM-79	142.1
390 ECS	EF-111 (3)	Mt. Home AFB, ID	EW, C3CM-90	151.7
552 AWACW	E-3 (2)	Tinker AFB, OK	C3-49	179.1
55 SRW	RC-135 (2)	Offutt AFB, NE	C3I-30	210.3
42 BMW	B-52G (2)	Loring AFB, ME	AI-41	217.9
379 BMW	B-52G (2)	Wurtsmith AFB, MI	AI-44	180.9
416 BMW	B-52G (2)	Griffiss AFB, NY	AI-33	176.0
RTTF	KC-135 (7)	March AFB, CA	AAR-153	644.0
63 MAW	C-141 (3)	Norton AFB, CA	25	57.1
317/435 TAW	C-130 (4)	Pope AFB, NC	25	53.4
		Total	2,454	4,960.1

*Core Unit

---

[8]*Ibid*, p-13.

Well in advance of any Flag exercise, objectives are defined and a scenario is written. Planning staffs and mission directors are assigned by the numbered Air Forces to orchestrate the efforts of everyone participating. Units, with agreement from their higher headquarters, volunteer, based on their training requirements, availability, and funds remaining. The complex logistical problems are worked out during various predeployment conferences and form a basis for contingency deployment planning.

Specific flag training begins several months in advance of the deployment. Squadron weapons and training officers develop specific unit training requirements and a plan to meet the objectives. Aircrews are identified based on their needs, availability, experience, and squadron positions (flight lead, instructor, etc.). Ground training is a mixture of self-paced and class academics covering three main categories: flight/weapons safety and range orientation, equipment, and tactics. If the unit objective is the live drop of a particular kind of ordnance, detailed ground academics provide a thorough refresher about the weapon, flight restrictions, preflight, delivery parameters, and safe escape. Other equipment items covered will be electronic countermeasure (ECM) pods, radar, Have Quick, LANTIRN or other lasing devices, and survival equipment, to name a few. The unit weapons shop develops a number of weapons delivery tactics consistent with training objectives and the flag scenario. Tactics discussions are a refresher of unit tactics and an overview of other unit procedures and tactics, including the enemy's. Emphasis is placed on flying the flag crews together to the maximum extent possible, and special flying programs were initiated to ensure each participant is fully qualified and proficient in all aspects of his mission.

Planning staffs normally deploy to Nellis several days in advance of the exercise participants. Their function is to review the scenario and act as a higher headquarters planning staff. Academics may or may not be given to the mission directors and their planning staffs, depending on their requests. All aircraft arrive on a Saturday, and maintenance prepares for operations on Monday. Sunday the aircrews receive ground academics and are given their first Air Tasking Order (ATO). As mentioned earlier, the two-week exercises gradually increase in complexity and tempo. An example of a typical training schedule and scenario follows.[9]

---

[9]440th TFT6, Red Flag 92-2, After Action Rpt.

Typical Schedule

RED FLAG BLUE TRAINING SCENARIO
92-2, Period 2

Updated: 13 Jan 92	DAY 1	DAY 2	DAY 3	DAY 4	DAY 5
DAY Air-to-Air RATIO NIGHT	H O L I D A Y	FAM DAY	8 V 8 / 4 V 4	8 V 8 / 4 V 4	8 V 8 / 4 V 4
BVR CRITERIA		FAM DAY	OCA Intial Sweep - NCTR and/or AWACS declaring Hostile OCA Against Flow - NCTR or AWACS		OCA Initial Sweep - NTRC & AWACs Declaring Hostile••OCA Against Flow - NCTR or AWACs Declaring Hostile & Lack of Mode 1, Mode 4. OCA - Lack of Friendly Mode 1
TOT BLOCK TIME		FAM DAY	YES	YES	YES
Wounded Bird EXERCISE		FAM DAY	YES	YES	YES
Safe Passage procedures		FAM DAY	YES	YES	YES
Medium Alt Tactics		FAM DAY	NO	YES	OPTION
Low Alt Step Down *		FAM 500'	500'	300'	300'**

* See SPINS for additional restrictions   ** See SPINS, Chapter 4, Paragraph 6g(1)(h);

	DAY 6	DAY 7	DAY 8	DAY 9	DAY 10
DAY Air-to-Air RATIO NIGHT	8 V 8 / 4 V 4	8 V 8 / 4 V 4	8 V 8 / 4 V 4	8 V 8 / 4 V 4	8 V 8 / 4 V 4
BVR CRITERIA	OCA Initial Sweep - NCTR & AWACs Declaring Hostile OCA Against Flow - NCTR or AWACs Declaring Hostile & Lack of Mode 1, Mode 4.				
TOT BLOCK TIME	YES	YES	YES	YES	YES
Wounded Bird EXERCISE	YES	YES	YES	YES	YES
Safe Passage procedures	YES	YES	YES	YES	YES
Medium Alt Tactics	NO	NO	YES	OPTION	OPTION
Low Alt Step Down *	500'	300'**	300'**	300'**	300'**

* See SPINS for additional restrictions   ** See SPINS, Chapter 4, Paragraph 6g(1)(h); RF/CC approval below 300' (min 100')

Typical Schedule-continued

RED FORCE SCENARIO
RED FLAG 92-2, Period 2

	DAY 1	DAY 2	DAY 3	DAY 4	DAY 5	DAY 6	DAY 7	DAY 8	DAY 9	DAY 10
Targets for Interdiction Aircraft	H	FAM	Ranges 75 & 76	Ranges 71 & 75	Ranges 75 & 76	Ranges 71 & 75	→	Ranges 71 & 76		→
• Augmentees • AT - Day • AT - Night Replicating:	O	FAM	•4 F-14 / 4 MIG-29 / 4SU-27(A) / (Level 2)	•4 F-14 / 4 MIG-29 / 4SU-27(A) / (Level 3)	•4 F-14 / 4 MIG-29 / 4SU-27(C) / (Level 4)	•4 F-14 / 4 MIG-29 / 4SU-27(A) / (Level 2)	•4 F-14 / 4 MIG-29 / 4SU-27(A) / (Level 3)	•4 F-14 / 4 MIG-29 / 4SU-27(A) / (Level 3)	•4 F-14 / 4 MIG-29 / 4SU-27(C) / (Level 4)	•4 F-14 / 4 MIG-29 / (Level 4)
Free Fire Zone	L	FAM	SAM Zone 1	SAM Zone 3	SAM Zone 4	SAM Zone 1	SAM Zone 1	SAM Zone 3	SAM Zone 4	→
SAM Threats: • Interdiction	I	FAM	All SAMs Up	EC West SAMs Only	TPEC SAMs Only	All SAMs Up	→	EC West SAMs Only	TPEC SAMs Only	→
AAA (All)	D A	FAM	All AAA Up	5000' AAA Kill Zone Around Targets		All AAA Up	→	5000' AAA Kill Zone Around Targets		
Comm Jamming	Y	Auto Jam Demo	ICD Only	Manual Only	→	ICD Only	Manual Only			→
Radar Jamming		None	None	None at Night	→	None	None at Night	→		NONE
Passive Detection		PM Only	→	Yes	→	PM Only	→	Yes	→	None
Airspace Restrictions		FAM	Separate MEZ & FEZ No Initial CAPs		JEZ	Separate MEZ & FEZ No Initial CAPs East of Worthington			JEZ	JEZ
Kill Removal		FAM	Kill Regeneration for A/A Only		Permanent Kill Removal A/A & A/O Day Only	Kill Regeneration for A/A Only			Permanent Kill Removal A/A & A/G (Day only)	

The first missions are flown for range orientation. A mission commander is assigned for the day's operations; he integrates the efforts of package commanders who plan and coordinate each of three successive waves. Package commanders are responsible for coordinating and deconflicting the tactics for their "gorilla" packages. Additionally they discuss air and SAM defense tactics with their air and EW support. All the elements of a composite force, including the launch sequence, refueling, formations, and ingress and egress, are practiced in a benign environment.

430

The ATO is disseminated to all units. Flight leads identify which packages they are assigned along with their targets and support assets. The mission commander holds a meeting of all flight leads to discuss tactics and a general game plan. Flight leads discuss the best way their aircraft can support the mission. After the meeting, flight leads get together with the aircrews of their flight and tasks are delegated. For the F-16, assuming a flight of four aircraft, the lead and number three aircraft may determine target area tactics and deconflict with other flights in the area. The number two aircraft may be assigned to plan the route and number four to get the intelligence assessment and weapons data. The details of subordinating tasks are left to flight lead discretion. Every area of the mission, which includes mission data, ground procedures, departure, refueling, ingress, target area, egress, and landing, is planned.

After the mission has been planned in detail, a mass briefing with all participants is held to brief the overall operations. These details include the day's objectives, weather/notice to airmen (NOTAMS)/timehack (synchronized time check), intel scenario, red force operating instructions and special instructions, blue force operations, and safety. Immediately after the mass brief, participants go to individual flight briefs where the details of flight operations are enumerated. Every aspect of the mission and areas of potential impact are discussed.

Probably the greatest learning tool available at Red Flag is the ability to accurately reconstruct the mission. Every training situation can be broken into three components: planning, execution, and evaluation. Participants learn in each of the three phases, and because the process is experiential rather than intellectual, events can be measured and remembered. The Red Flag facility is an excellent environment for all stages. During the planning stage, all participants have the opportunity to interact and exchange information. It becomes more than rote memory; it becomes an application of the aggregate of learning experiences of the forces throughout the years. The addition of foreign participants and sister Services has broadened the learning environment, enabling the Coalition to fight as a single air force.

The actual mission can be monitored from select briefing rooms using the Red Flag Measurement Debriefing System (RFMDS). The RFMDS is an advanced training system that records and displays the activities and results of simulated tactical air combat missions flown on the Nellis range complex. The aircraft flying with the RFMDS pods allow Red Flag missions to be monitored live and replayed for postmission analysis. Each aircraft is monitored electronically, and a computer-enhanced display provides real-time depiction of the battle, across the full spectrum of operations for the entire Red Flag training area. Commanders, planning staffs, and crews who are not flying can monitor the battle as it unfolds in the Red Flag facility.

The day's operations are debriefed in a similar manner. After landing, crews debrief and record results and significant lessons or factors affecting their package. Pertinent information for the flight includes conduct of the flight, strengths and weaknesses of the tactics, and hits and misses of the weapons. Shots taken or observations about other members of the gorilla are recorded and passed to the mission commander. He debriefs all members of the package using the RFMDS to illustrate valuable points, areas of contention, or positive learning situations. After the mission commanders (both Blue and Red) have debriefed, a final mass debrief is held to discuss lessons learned, the conduct of the day's operations, and safety factors. Finally, aircrews pick up the ATO for the next day and begin planning.

The RFMDS provides feedback and is an important learning tool available on the Nellis ranges. The following examples depict a sample RFMDS mission with high-activity (aircraft graphic) and low-activity (triangle) aircraft tracks. When tracking in high-activity mode, the RFMDS can depict an aircraft in time and three-dimensional space, provide performance data on that aircraft, and show positional relationships with other high-activity aircraft, surface threats, or ground targets. An aircraft must be equipped with an Aircraft Instrumentation Subsystem (AIS) for tracking as high activity. The RFMDS is designed to permit low-altitude tracking of aircraft in specified operating areas. The system depicts low-activity aircraft in time and two-dimensional space. The aircraft must be transmitting its scheduled identification, friend or foe (IFF) Mode III squawk to be tracked as low activity. The major limitations of the system are that a maximum of thirty-six high-activity aircraft can be displayed at one time, and most C-130 and all C-141 aircraft lack interface capability for high-activity tracking. An example of a RFMDS high/low activity display is provided.

The RFMDS can also display the event time and type of weapons delivery: air-to-air, air-to-surface, and surface-to-air. Aircraft weapons

FMDS High/Low Activity and RFMDS Simulation Results

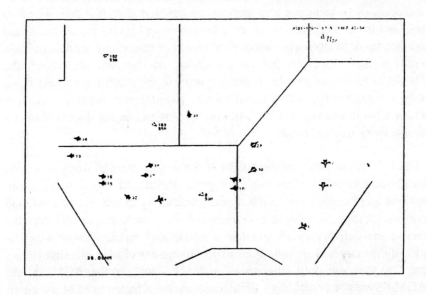

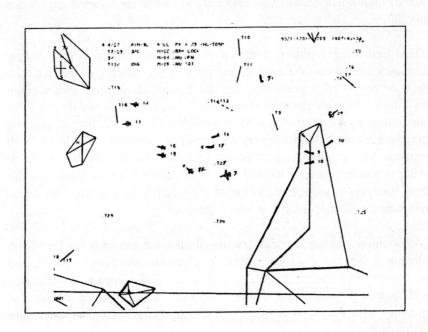

433

systems must interface directly with the AIS to be displayed, and the aircraft must be tracking in the high-activity mode. For air-to-air and surface-to-air weapons, the system can also identify the targeted aircraft if that aircraft is tracking in the high-activity mode (see following Figures for air-to-air and surface-to-air RFMDS depictions). Several major limitations degrade mission reconstruction; although the system knows who is shooting whom, the fly-out of air-to- air missiles is not determined; the system is not interfaced with the high-speed antiradiation missile (HARM) and therefore does not know what it was targeted against; and the system can not display shots on low-activity tracked targets.

The RFMDS can simulate the results of the employment of many air-to-air, air-to-surface, and surface-to-air weapons. Results of the simulation can include graphic depiction of the fly-out, probability of kill, kill or miss, and reasons for miss. To achieve a weapons delivery simulation, the RFMDS must record the delivery event and for air-to-air and surface- to-air weapons identify the targeted aircraft. Four major limitations of weapons simulations are: a) they are only simulations and not actual, b) the AGM-65 and AGM-88 are not available, c) simulations are not affected by ECM and chaff, and d) high-fidelity simulations are only available for selected targets and aircraft.

The Red Flag building contains six separate consoles for aircrew feedback. Each console permits independent monitoring of the live mission or replay of a previously recorded mission on three independent monitors. Four of the consoles provide large dual-screen displays for utilization by large groups. Two consoles can record one display on standard 3/4-inch tape for replay on a separate video cassette player. Each console has a color printer for printing a snapshot of the mission. Aircrews may schedule the use of a console for individual mission debrief/analysis or request recording of the mission on videotape for documentation and later review at home station.

An additional resource available to the aircrew for debrief is the Television Ordnance Scoring System (TOSS), a precision electronic camera and computer measurement system. Cameras record the impact of munitions, and computers measure the impact points that can be displayed as videos or graphics with measured results. Not all targets on the Nellis ranges are instrumented.

434

RFMDS Shot Pairing, Centroid View
and RFMDS Shot Pairing, Pilot View

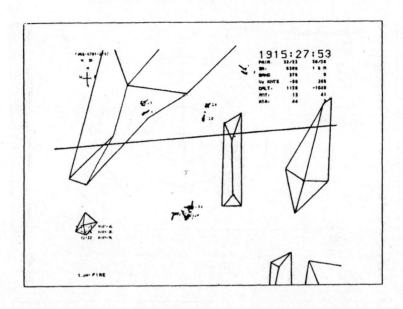

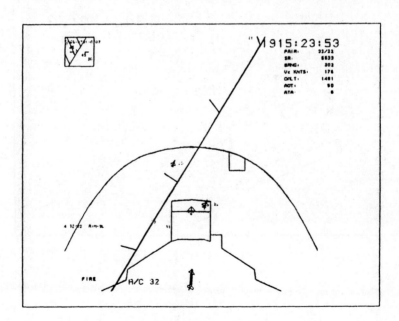

RFMDS Shot Pairing, Threat Boresight View
and RFMDS Point Target

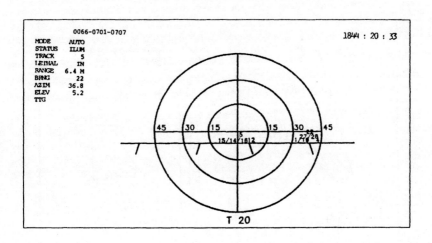

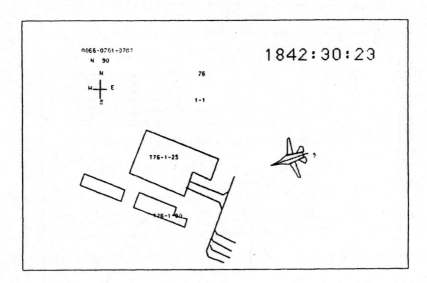

Appendix G

B-52 Training—The Diego Garcia Problem

Between 9 August and 16 August 1990, Strategic Air Command (SAC) deployed twenty B-52s to Diego Garcia, a small island in the Indian Ocean. Diego Garcia became the first bomber operations base supporting U.S. Central Command (USCENTCOM) in Desert Shield. It has a tropical climate, a factor that posed many training problems in the ensuing months.

[DELETED]. Crews and maintainers were experienced at conventional operations from deployed locations but lacked specific expertise in Southwest Asia (SWA), since the bulk of their previous training focused on a conventional war in Europe.[1] This necessitated a training program to expose the crews to SWA tactics. The program had to be conducted on a remote tropical island over 3,000 nautical miles from the Kuwaiti Theater of Operations.

The forces deployed to Diego Garcia were faced with a training task unique to Desert Shield. To train for the developing conflict properly required access to the Arabian Peninsula and integration into the U.S. Air Force, Central Command (USCENTAF) Desert Shield airspace management system. The Kingdom of Saudi Arabia, allowed B-52 training on 20 August 1990. These late August missions provided opportunities for aircrews to gain a basic orientation of the terrain characteristics and regional communication procedures, including communicating with the AWACS.[2]

[DELETED].

The training program that evolved on Diego Garcia involved a low number of sorties per month, mandated by the long duration of the missions and the scarcity of the resources at the remote base. To maxi-

---

[1](S/NF/WN/RD) *History of the Strategic Air Command*, Vol I, (1 Jan - 31 Dec 1990), Office of the Historian, Headquarters Strategic Air Command Offutt AFB, NE, pp 93-194.

[2](S/NF/WN/RD) *Ibid*, p 211.

mize efficiency, mission profiles and routes were developed to provide navigation and packaged fighter operations. [DELETED].[3]

Gradually, adequate training profiles were developed, coordinated with CENTAF, and flown. Two distinct training profiles soon emerged, one over the Arabian Peninsula and the other to a local island. Peninsula missions provided the most realistic combat training and combined the following: night water augmentation takeoff (water augmentation for increased engine thrust procedures were unique to the B-52G), cell departure, emission control procedures, secure and AWACS communications procedures, heavyweight air refueling, low-level training, timing control, bombing, multiple axis of attack, ECM training, and limited pilot instrument approach training. This robust profile offered training opportunities to all pilot, navigator, and electronic crew positions.

The island profile was much shorter in duration and provided training for events that required more frequency or were simply unavailable on the peninsula. The island training profile featured cell take-off, departure and join-up, simulated bombing runs, ECM procedures, and pilot proficiency items such as touch and go landings.[4]

The formalization of this effort developed into an Initial Mission Qualification Training (IMQT) program. [DELETED]. With this formalized training program, the commander was able to monitor the wing's training program and its combat readiness.[5]

The bomber force at Diego Garcia quickly amassed a sizable number of flying hours, and sustaining the fleet required the establishment of an Intermediate Level Maintenance Center (ILMC) at Andersen AFB, Guam. [DELETED].[6] [DELETED].

[DELETED].[7]

---

[3](S/NF/WN/RD) *Ibid*, pp 212-214.

[4](S) Headquarters Strategic Air Command, Operations Desert Shield and Desert Storm, "The Bomber Story," p 27.

[5](S) *Ibid*, p 26.

[6](S/NF/WN/RD) *History of the Strategic Air Command*, p 458.

[7](S/NF/WN/RD) *Ibid*, p 215.

The training program produced effective crew preparation under extreme geographical constraints. But General Chain, SAC Commander in Chief, expressed a desire to increase the frequency of training missions into the Arabian Peninsula for Diego-based crews. In November 1990, the SAC Director of Operations directed that the tempo of training be increased into the peninsula for each bomber crew. This new emphasis generated a fresh look at the realism and efficiency of training programs. [DELETED]. The resultant training enhancements resulted from diligent efforts to arrange and refine more challenging training profiles.[8]

The challenge of training for a war 3,000 miles away in a geographical setting that was a complete opposite from the operating base represented a unique training experience. [DELETED]. By December and early January, the increases in frequency and realism were paying off just as the deadline for Iraq to withdraw began to approach. On 15 January 1991, in response to STRATFOR (Director of SAC operation under CENTAF) guidance, all training missions were stopped. Training had ceased; the time for war had come.[9]

The effectiveness of the training program for the B-52 crews certainly was limited by many circumstances. The outcomes of their missions can be analyzed for months to come with varying results. However, this much may be said: when surveyed by Hq SAC with the question "Did the SAC training program prepare you for combat?", eighty percent of the B-52 aircrew members responded yes.[10] This, combined with the fact that no B-52s were lost in the war as a result of combat, reflects that the difficult training problems were resolved and proved successful to the effective employment of the B-52.

Training for CONUS SAC B-52 Crews

Hq SAC and the 15th Air Force recognized early on that because of forward basing constraints, the training for the CONUS B-52 units would be difficult. In October 1990, the 15th Air Force proposed a series of exercises so that B-52 crews could simulate the situations they would

---

[8](S/NF/WN/RD) *Ibid*, pp 233-234.

[9](S/NF/WN/RD) *Ibid*, pp 234-235.

[10](S) HQ Strategic Air Command, Postwar Bomber Training Conference, 25-26 Apr 1991, After Action Rpt. Extracted from briefing slide used during the conference.

likely encounter in combat missions in a war against Iraq. Through a revision of the Red Flag schedule for SAC units, Desert Warrior was developed. Desert Warrior was aimed at giving the crews exposure to the CENTAF ATO procedures and tactics. [DELETED].

[DELETED].

Some significant benefits were derived from this exercise series. Eight Air Force units participated in the exercise and also flew in Desert Storm. They described Desert Warrior as a crash course that helped familiarize them with tactics that were used in Southwest Asia. However, all participants recognized this as a stop-gap measure that did not replace the training taking place in-theater. [DELETED].[11]

---

[11](S/NF/WN/RD) *History of the Strategic Air Command*, pp 236-237.

Appendix H

Special Operations Forces (SOF) Training Considerations

Before Desert Shield, SOF trained exclusively to conduct clandestine special operations missions under cover of darkness. For the helicopter crews this required extremely low-altitude penetrations of enemy airspace, landings, and egress, all completely blacked out. The prolonged deployment made it difficult to maintain currency in primary aircrew skills, a problem applying to both MH-53J and MC-130 crews. To compound the problem, they were tasked with the Combat Search and Rescue (CSAR) role in which they were not trained.[1] Both aircraft depend on terrain-following radar for low-altitude penetration, and crews quickly found that the fine sand characteristic of the Arabian peninsula was partially transparent to their radars, leading to less than anticipated obstacle clearance.[2] Poor visibility caused by the extremely find sand, kept suspended in the air by relatively light winds, was a particular problem for helicopter crews.[3] This phenomenon was responsible for the loss of several U.S. Army helicopters at night during Desert Shield, prompting the imposition of minimum altitude and illumination restrictions. The MH-53J-equipped 20th Special Operations Squadron (SOS) was the only helicopter unit exempted from these restrictions due to their FLIR, radar, and hover coupler capability.[4] Night landings were, by far, the most demanding event and required the development of specialized techniques

---

[1]Aerospace Rescue and Recovery Service, the Air Force component responsible for CSAR, was disestablished in 1983 and its component units either disbanded or absorbed by SOC and its first-line equipment (notably the MH-53Js and HC-130 tankers) transferred to SOF. Air Rescue Service was reestablished in 1989 but had no combat-capable, long-range helicopter units during Desert Shield/Desert Storm.

[2](S) Intvw, J. Guilmartin and Col F. Goldstein, GWAPS, of Lt Col Richard Comer, USAF, commander of the MH-53J-equipped 20th Special Operations Squadron, 1 Sep 1992.

[3](S) Lt Col Comer, *History of Desert Shield/Desert Storm*, p 8.

[4](S) Intvw, Lt Col Comer.

techniques included the use of small chemical lights as hover points, use of the MH-53's infrared searchlight, and making fully coupled approaches.[5] For daylight CSAR missions, helicopter crews recognized the need for close escort, and A-10 support was provided. Escort tactics relearned from Vietnam proved effective.[6]

Fixed-wing SOF crews were generally well prepared for the war. They suffered the same problems associated with poor visibility from blowing sand. There were initial problems acquiring munitions and Saudi training range support for the AC-130 gunships. Ranges and equipment for high-speed airdrops had to be resolved for MC-130 Combat Talon crews to maintain proficiency. Initially, few Talon crews were qualified to drop the BLU-82 bomb. Overall, Air Force SOF credited good training with helping to keep losses low, a point on which the 20th SOS commander was particularly emphatic.[7]

[5](S) Lt Col Comer, *History of Desert Shield/Desert Storm*, pp 8-9. The problem was particularly acute on moonless nights.

[6]Intvw, Guilmartin and Goldstein, GWAPS, of Col George Gray.

[7](S) Intvw, Lt Col Comer.

Appendix I

Navy/Marine Corps Desert Shield/
Desert Storm Training

U.S. Navy

Navy training for air units occurs at various levels but revolves around the basic unit of the carrier air wing and its attendant aircraft carrier deployment cycle. The training accomplished by the various units in preparation for the Gulf War thus varied according to their assignments as the Desert Shield and Desert Storm scenario unfolded. This section will discuss that training. It begins with an overview of the normal training done by a squadron and a wing preparing for a deployment. The various differences in the predeployment preparation of the eight carrier air wings that operated in Desert Shield and in Desert Storm will next be developed. Finally, in-theater training for Desert Storm will be discussed.

Squadron and Carrier Air Wing Training

A Navy carrier air wing contains all of the elements that allow it to accomplish almost any application of air power in the pursuit of national interests. Assigned to a particular aircraft carrier, it normally consists of nine squadrons with a mix of different aircraft. The generic air wing consists of two squadrons of F-14 fighters, two squadrons of F/A-18 strike fighters, and one squadron each of A-6E long-range attack aircraft; and EA-6B electronic countermeasure aircraft, S3 antisubmarine aircraft, E-2 airborne early warning aircraft, and SH3 or SH60 antisubmarine helicopters. Training revolved about a cycle consisting of time at home stations, on predeployment work-up, and on deployments to overseas locations for six to eight months' duration.

While in the United States, all aircraft of a particular type were based at the same naval air station. Here they accomplished squadron training supported by their local functional wing commander. Individual aircrews and squadrons had to maintain proficiency in a program called Liberty Elite. This program assigned requirements that aircrews must complete to maintain readiness in their aircraft types. The qualifications of each aircrew member and the squadron overall were continuously updated. The Liberty Elite data were reported on the SORTS system, and if a squadron failed to meet these Liberty Elite goals, it had to report in at reduced readiness status.[1]

Each home station has facilities nearby to accommodate the training for that particular aircraft. These facilities include operating areas for air-to-air training, bombing ranges, low-level training routes, overwater scored mining ranges, and a radar bombing scoring unit that can evaluate simulated radar bomb drops.

Though the squadron is supported at its home station by the local functional wing commander, its operational commander remains its carrier air wing commander. Approximately six months before a scheduled deployment of their aircraft carrier, all the squadrons of the carrier air wing go to Naval Air Station (NAS), Fallon, to begin preparing for the upcoming cruise. Supported by Fallon's Naval Strike Warfare Center ("Strike U"), the wing goes through a series of exercises designed to build proficiency as an air wing. Multiple squadron events such as air combat, air-to-air refueling, and intercept training along with large-scale bombing strikes are accomplished. The final exercise is a large-scale operation in support of a simulated scenario that the wing might expect to encounter on its upcoming deployment. Air wings deploying to the Mediterranean theater used a different scenario than those going to the western Pacific or Indian Ocean. The Mediterranean scenario exercises involved the full range of possible threats—"enemy" aggressor aircraft, modern surface-to-air missiles, and antiaircraft artillery—and targets that were as realistic as possible, such as simulated airfields. Real ordnance was delivered, and the planning procedures for the strikes were prepared by one of the wing mission planning teams. Besides the air wing deployment to Fallon, F-14 and F/A-18 squadrons deployed there for a week of intense air combat maneuvering (ACM) training, called the Fleet Fighter ACM Readiness Program and Strike Fighter Readiness Program.

After completing the Fallon detachment, the air carrier wing joined its parent aircraft carrier and continued predeployment training. This was normally in three phases: carrier refresher training, wherein the squadrons

---

[1](S) For more information on the SORTS ratings, see the Center for Naval Analyses (CNA), Desert Storm Reconstruction Rpt, Vol XIII, Training, pp 3-10 - 3-16.

return to the procedures of operating off the ship; basic exercises; and advanced exercises. The exercises conducted from the carrier ran the gamut of possible fleet operations such as large-scale strikes ashore involving all squadrons, strikes against other naval forces, practice nuclear contingency missions, support for amphibious operations, and defense of the battle group from large-scale enemy raids. Types of operations range from cyclic operations of twelve hours operating/twelve hours off to flex deck operations in which the carrier operates for twenty-four hours a day for several days. The last portion of the advanced exercise period was the Operational Readiness Exercise, the "final exam" for the air wing and the battle group team. Deployment followed shortly thereafter.

Desert Storm Preparations

The carrier deployment figure below shows the schedule of the carrier battle groups that participated in Desert Shield and Desert Storm. USS *John F. Kennedy*, USS *Saratoga*, and USS *Midway* had relatively long periods in the theater, while USS *Roosevelt*, USS *Ranger*, and USS *America* arrived just at the commencement of hostilities.

Carrier Deployment and Southwest Asia (SWA) In-Chop Timelines[2]

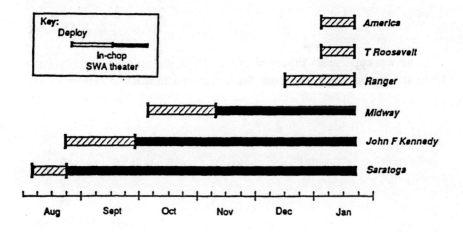

---

[2](S) CNA, Vol XIII, p 2-2.

Workup Cycles for CONUS Desert Storm Carrier Battle Groups[3]

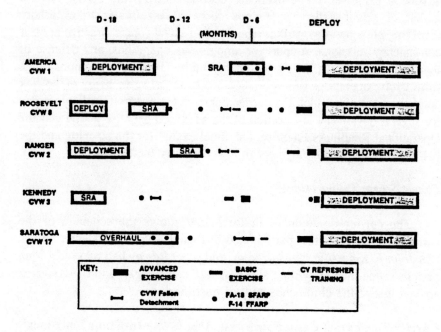

The workup cycles Figure above portrays the training cycles for the five carriers that deployed from the U.S. to participate in Desert Storm.

---

[3](S) *Ibid.*

It shows that four of the five had completed their air wing detachments at Fallon prior to the invasion of Kuwait. The scenarios presented at Fallon consisted of two major assignments from the National Command Authority. In the first, the wing had to conduct a one-time strike on the "enemy" country to demonstrate U.S. power, basically a Libya-style operation. The second scenario presented the wing with two days (and nights) to achieve damage against certain targets in the country. The intent of the second exercise was to conduct a campaign, gain control of the air by defeating the Air Force and Air Defense Net, and finally to conduct operations against designated targets. In most cases low-level ingress and attack tactics were employed.[4] Only one air wing aboard the USS *America* was able to tailor its Fallon deployment towards the Kuwait scenario. Its detachment focused more on close air support, special warfare operations, and combat search and rescue than did prewar air wing Fallon operations.[5] [DELETED].[6]

Training in Theater

The three carriers that deployed to Southwest Asia early in Desert Shield participated in a series of exercises and training evolutions that were in many ways like the advanced exercises of their training cycles. The Major Desert Shield Exercise table displays the types and frequency of those exercises.[7]

---

[4]Intvw, RADM Mike Luecke, OPNAV 73, Aug 1992.

[5](S) CNA Rpt, Vol XIII, p 1-2.

[6](S) *Ibid*, p A-5.

[7](S) *Ibid*, p 3-2.

FIGURE DELETED

FIGURE DELETED

In the theater, training conducted by the carriers in the Red Sea (USS *John F. Kennedy*, USS *Saratoga*) differed from that conducted by the USS *Midway* in the North Arabian Sea. The Red Sea carriers conducted most of their exercises in Saudi Arabia and thus dealt much more closely with the JFACC. They became very accustomed to working with the ATO process. As the Master Attack Plan developed, they conducted "mirror image" strikes towards the Iraqi border that included joint tasking evolutions.[8] The USS *Midway*, on the other hand, conducted most of its operations in the Gulf of Oman because of sensitivities about operating in the Persian Gulf.[9]

---

[8]Debrief, CDR Smith, Navy Black Hole Representative, GWAPS files.

[9]Intvw, Capt James Burin, Commander, Carrier Air Wing Five, Aug 1992.

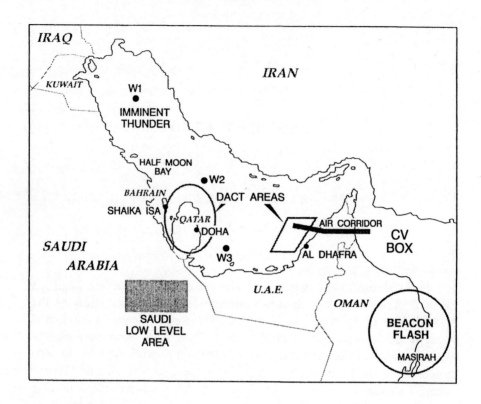

CVW Training Areas graphics is a graphic from a brief by the Commander of Carrier Air Wing Five detailing his Desert Shield training.[10] These exercises included: support for an amphibious operation in Saudi Arabia (Imminent Thunder); a Beacon Flash exercise with the Omanis, which included strikes ashore and air-to-air combat; and Defensive Air Combat Maneuvering training with Al Dhafra of the United Arab Emirates (against Mirage 2000) and Qatar (against F-1s). Except for a short period when supporting Imminent Thunder, the USS *Midway* operated mostly in the Gulf of Oman, where it also conducted

---

[10]Briefing slides "Carrier Air Wing Five Desert Shield/Desert Storm" received from Capt Burin, Aug 1992, GWAPS files.

mirror image strikes. The Commander of the Air Wing on the USS *Midway* fully expected that he would conduct his operations from the Gulf of Oman should hostilities occur.[11] As such, the USS *Midway* never developed the rapport with the Joint Force Air Component Commander and the ATO process that the Red Sea carriers did.

As the on-station carriers participated in these exercises, COMUSNAVCENT and his subordinate commanders published their training objectives. The carriers that were preparing to deploy were able to tailor their predeployment exercises to the situation expected in Desert Storm; based in some respects on these training objectives. A Southwest Asia scenario was used for the advanced phase battle group exercise for USS *John F. Kennedy*, USS *Ranger*, USS *Roosevelt*, and USS *America*.[12]

The Center for Naval Analyses (CNA) conducted the reconstruction program for the Navy's effort in Desert Storm. Their study of training identified numerous issues for further consideration. These issues were broken into two types, those that were not normally considered in training syllabi before Desert Storm and those that were.

The training issues in the weapons, tactics, and training arena that were not normally covered or stressed by training syllabi included:

- ATO process;

- Joint theater-wide connectivity;

- [DELETED]

- Air Force tanking of strike packages;

- [DELETED]

- [DELETED]

- [DELETED]

---

[11]Intvw, Capt Burin.

[12](S) CNA Rpt, Vol XIII, p 2-4.

- High-altitude weapons delivery; and

- [DELETED].

CNA concluded that although these issues arose in a unique scenario, they might be relevant to future conflicts.

The training issues that they identified as normally covered in training syllabi included:

- Force and aircraft training in rules of engagement (ROE);

- [DELETED]

- Carrier operations.

[DELETED].[13]

U.S. Marine Corps

Before 2 August 1990, individual Marine Corps aircrew training centered on Naval Air Training and Operating Procedures Standardization (NATOPS) and Training and Readiness (T&R) Manual qualifications. Much of the aviation training was not geographically oriented. While Marine units routinely trained for conditions such as cold weather, mountain and desert terrain, and shipboard operations, the training was not always aimed at a particular country or region. Iraq's invasion of Kuwait changed the status quo and served to focus portions of Marine Corps aviation training on Southwest Asia.

Beginning on 2 August, Marine Aviation Weapons and Tactics Squadron One (MAWTS-1), based at MCAS Yuma, Arizona, took the lead in orienting Marine aviation to a possible war against Iraq. Between 2 August and 5 September 1990, forty instructors from MAWTS-1 traveled and briefed Marine Corps units on Iraqi military capabilities, equipment, tactics, and lessons learned from the Iran-Iraq war. Included in these discussions were recommendations on how to employ Marine aviation assets against the anticipated Iraqi threat. At the same time, twenty-three

---

[13](S) *Ibid*, p 1-3.

MAWTS-1 instructors were augmenting aviation and Marine Air Command and Control System units already in SWA. During this time, MAWTS-1 developed the Southwest Asia Integrated Contingency Training package.

From 1 October to 5 November 1990, 26 squadrons (136 fixed-wing and 54 rotary-wing aircraft), a Hawk battery, a Stinger battery, and a Direct Air Support Squadron underwent customized instruction tailored to individual readiness levels. Included in the instruction were an academic syllabus, individual work-ups, and a series of integrated exercises incorporating the requirements to operate in the Southwest Asia environment.

A second package was conducted 26 November to 19 December 1990, with an additional fourteen squadrons being trained. On 20 December, MAWTS-1, Detachment A, with forty-four personnel ashore and twenty-six afloat, was formed to support the Marines in Southwest Asia. When the war started, MAWTS-1 had seventy instructors in SWA supporting the 1st Marine Expeditionary Force Headquarters, 1st and 2nd Marine Divisions and 3d Marine Aircraft Wing ashore, and the 4th and 5th Marine Expeditionary Brigades afloat.

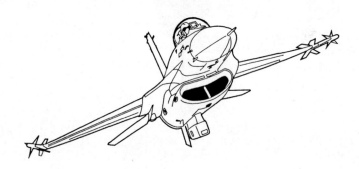

Index

460

MCM 13-15, 23, 25, 142, 143, 152, 155, 156, 159, 161, 190, 365
McPeak, Merrill 276
McSwain, Donald 172
medical 301, 310, 389
medical support 310
MEF 215, 236, 237
meteorology 148, 155
MH-53 120, 173, 300, 302, 303, 310, 416, 442
MH-60 119, 121, 300, 301, 310, 416
Mig-17 19, 20
Mig-19 24
Mig-21 19-21, 24
Mig-23 19-21
Mig-25 19-21, 24
Mig-29 1, 19-22, 28, 197, 198, 357, 359, 363
Military Airlift Command 300, 309, 392, 403, 426
Ministry of Defense 2
Mirage 2000 20, 109, 450
Mirage F-1 19, 20, 24, 359, 363
missile 1, 6, 8-10, 14, 15, 17, 24, 25, 27, 28, 30-36, 45, 48-51, 54, 56, 57, 59, 61-64, 66, 71, 77-81, 85, 89, 91, 93, 95, 97, 102-105, 107-113, 115-117, 118, 122, 123, 125, 137, 140-142, 143, 164, 168, 169, 170, 171, 173, 185, 188, 190, 196-198, 201, 203, 213, 222, 223, 224, 227, 228, 232, 237, 238, 242, 243, 245, 248-253, 264, 268-271, 275, 276, 278, 280, 282, 284, 290, 292, 293, 295, 306, 307, 311, 326, 329, 331, 332, 351, 356, 359, 360, 361, 363, 394, 434, 444
MK-20 45, 47, 57, 60, 74, 88, 222, 224, 227, 237, 253
MK-36 68, 69
MK-36/40 68
MK-77 84
MK-82 68-71, 76, 122, 222, 253, 259, 260
MK-84 69-71, 75, 76, 83, 86, 176, 212, 259, 260
MLRS 215
mobility 281, 287, 361
mobilization 299

Moore, Royal N. 216
moving target indicator 227
Mubarak, President 35
munition 28, 31, 39, 43, 44, 45, 47-51, 55, 60, 64, 66, 67, 69, 73, 79, 80, 82-90, 92, 121, 122, 135, 139-141, 148, 153, 158, 160, 161, 170, 174, 179, 203, 204, 222, 225, 226, 229, 249, 230, 242, 252, 257, 259, 261, 263, 270, 279, 290, 291, 306, 348, 353, 356, 357, 361, 367, 434, 442
Nassau 60
National Guard Bureau 299
NATO 87, 98, 355
naval 57, 61, 62, 69, 83, 94, 97, 104, 108, 182, 186, 190, 202, 215-217, 232, 237, 238, 250, 255, 267, 296, 298, 312, 327, 344, 365, 384, 411, 418, 443, 444, 445, 451, 452
NAVCENT 190, 237, 296
navigation 42, 45, 46, 59, 78, 86, 96, 111, 116, 118, 119-121, 127, 131, 137, 141, 148, 152, 153, 155, 160, 161, 194, 224, 225, 226, 248, 254, 266, 269, 271, 348, 349, 353, 383, 392, 399, 438
Navy 2, 3, 36, 56-60, 65, 69, 73, 74, 76, 78-81, 83, 89, 94, 98, 99, 103, 104, 106-108, 118, 137, 186, 188, 190, 215, 230, 231, 234, 237, 238, 248, 271, 275, 296, 298, 301, 302, 308, 311-315, 318, 327, 330, 344, 355, 356, 361, 364, 384, 387-389, 395, 398, 399, 403, 410, 412, 415, 426, 443, 449, 451
NBC 45, 47, 170, 174, 175, 178
Nellis AFB, NV 244, 282, 346, 349, 364, 424, 426-428, 431, 432, 434
Netherlands 423
network 3, 6, 26, 30, 32, 41, 98, 174, 287, 354, 362
New York Times 247, 291
Night Canon 414, 419
Nighthawk track 320
North Vietnam 333
North Vietnamese 421
Norton AFB, CA 427
Norway 423

Part II

Space Operations

Part II

Spacc Operations

Task Force Chief

Mr. Richard A. Gunkel

Principal Authors

Maj. Teresa R. Clark
Mr. Richard A. Gunkel
Mr. Lawrence L. Lausten
Capt. Barbara A. Phillips
Lt. Col. Mitchell P. Slate

Principal Contributors

Lt. Col. Stephen P. Hoffhines
Mr. Andrew G. Landrus
Capt. Thomas R. McCabe
Col. Eugene O'Neil

Report Acknowledgements

The survey and analysis of the performance of space systems were assigned to the Logistics, Support, and Space Task Force directed by Mr. Richard A. Gunkel. Maj. Theresa R. Clark and Lt. Col. Mitchell P. Slate of HQ USAF/XO managed the research and writing of the Space study. Capt. Barbara A. Phillips was key to the research and writing of chapters six and seven. Mr. Lawrence R. Lausten wrote chapters four and five. Colonel Slate and Major Clark wrote the remaining chapters. Ms. CeCe French managed keyboarding manuscripts; she was keeper of the files and able administrator.

This task force also produced an annex that covered the role and performance of National Systems during Desert Shield and Desert Storm. The research and writing of this annex was sponsored by the National Reconnaissance Office and accomplished by Mr. Andrew G. Landrus. Col. Eugene O'Neill and Lt. Col. Stephen P. Hoffhines served as NRO managers. Colonel Slate served as the integrator and technical editor of both volumes.

Precis of the Space Report

As all reports of the Gulf War Air Power Survey, the report on Space Operations has been submitted to a security and policy review board for general publication. Not surprisingly, the bulk of information in this area could not be released without compromising national security. Accordingly, the following is a precis of the report compiled by this task force.

The purpose of the Space study was to comprehensively survey the space systems used during the Gulf War. Of five major themes in this report, this task force first examined *planning and training for the use of space systems*, including space awareness among American forces sent to the Gulf, within the context of a subtheme common to many Survey volumes: the importance of the five and a half months of Desert Shield.

From the outset, Central Command planners and the space community built space linkages to warfighters. Many annexes to Operations Plan 1002-90 prepared for the U.S. Commander in Chief, Central Command, drew on space systems; ample documentation exists, for example, in procedures for establishing satellite communications links. On the other hand, weaknesses in other areas were difficult to fit into prewar training scenarios as well as exercises, such as bomb damage assessment and other intelligence functions. It was therefore no surprise that the degree of planning and training for the use of space correlates closely with the results. With respect to those areas where space capabilities had not yet been fully integrated with warfighting doctrine and tactics, Coalition forces derived maximum advantage from experience during the five and a half months of Desert Shield to familiarize themselves and train with space capabilities.

The second issue to emerge from the Space study was *space mobilization*, which included the mobilization of ground "user" equipment to the Persian Gulf and also maintenance of spacecraft in orbit and the launching of new systems. In some cases, the space capability was immediately available because the receiver equipment was already in place and the satellite system was functioning in its peacetime (or wartime) role, as in the case of F-16s equipped with Global Positioning

System receivers. The rate at which space capabilities were mobilized depended on a number of factors: the availability and heft of ground equipment and satellites, launch windows, and processing action required to launch a spacecraft into orbit; the time required to check out a newly launched satellite; the time required to reposition satellites for better coverage of the theater; and, finally, the coordination of placing trained personnel.

The third issue concerns the determinants of the *military utility of space systems*. This issue involved the contribution of space systems to communications, navigation, weather, imaging, and intelligence. In some cases it was necessary to cross functional boundaries and depart from the pure "space story." The detection of Scuds by the Defense Support Program, for example, warranted a discussion of Coalition success in destroying mobile targets. Nevertheless, the true value of space support must be measured in terms of concrete warfighting results.

The fourth theme deals with the *command and control of space systems*, highlighting the difficulty of a complex and in some respects highly guarded space community that had oriented its support toward more "strategic" customers such as the National Command Authority and various intelligence agencies. In the Gulf War, this set of space providers was thrust into a tactical environment that demanded time-responsive, geographically oriented, and widest-dissemination support. Many of the key intelligence-related assets, however, were not controlled by the theater commander.

The fifth and final theme covers the *role of commercial space systems and receiver equipment*. Some commercial satellite systems, such as LANDSAT and INTELSAT, were passed on to the Coalition military establishment. The procurement and use of "channels" by commercial satellite systems also augmented the needed communications capacity. Conversely, some military systems, such as the Global Positioning System were shared with commercial customers, while Coalition forces were able to procure commercial receivers to augment the military ground equipment. This theme was also important in examining Iraqi access to space support. Coalition members cooperated to deny Iraq access to commercial satellite imagery products by halting the flow of SPOT images from France. At the same time, Iraq "used" Cable News Network (CNN) worldwide coverage to some advantage.

Several issues that created an impact during the research and analysis of this study deserve mention. Research did not focus on the providers of space support but rather on the "space product" itself and its operational impact. Researchers, therefore, relied on primary data generated in the theater, where they faced a number of obstacles. In many cases, the users were not familiar with space capabilities. For example, how communications satellites influenced combat operations was not documented because *what was said over the phone* in hundreds of thousands of conversations was not recorded *and not documented*. Many users, moreover, were not aware that they were talking via satellite.

Glossary

AAA	Antiaircraft Artillery
AAAM	Advanced Air-to-Air Missile
AADC	Area Air Defense Commander
AAI	Air-to-Air Interrogator Set
AAV	Amphibious Assault Vehicle
AAR	After Action Report
AASLT Div	Air Assault Division (US)
AB	Air Base
ABCCC	Airborne Battlefield Command and Control Center
ABDR	Aircraft Battle Damage Repair
ABF	Advanced Bomb Family
ABFDS	Aerial Bulk Fuel Delivery System
Abn Corps	Airborne Corps (US)
AC	Active Component
ACA	Airspace Control Authority or Airlift Clearance Authorities
ACAS	Air Combat Assessment Summary
ACC	Air Component Commander or Airspace Coordination Center or Arab Cooperation Council
ACCS	Airborne Command and Control Squadron
ACE	Airborne Command Element (USAF) or Aviation Combat Element (USMC) or Air Combat Element (NATO) or Armored Combat Earthmover (US Army)
ACM	Air Combat Maneuvers

ACO	Airspace Coordination Order or Airspace Control Order
ACR	Armored Cavalry Regiment
ACV	Armored Combat Vehicle (US Army) or Air Cushion Vehicle (USN)
AD	Air Division
ADA	Air Defense Artillery
A/DACG	Arrival/Departure Airfield Control Group
ADOC	Air Defense Operations Center
ADX	Air Defense Exercise
AECC	Aeromedical Evacuation Control Center
Aegis	Ship based long-range air defense system.
AELT	Aeromedical Evacuation Liaison Team
AES	Aeromedical Evacuation Squadron
AEW	Airborne Early Warning
AFB	Air Force Base
AFCOMAC	Air Force Combat Ammunition Center
AFDIGS	Air Force Digital Graphics System
AFEWC	Air Force Electronic Warfare Center
AFGWC	Air Force Global Weather Center
AFHRA	Air Force Historical Research Agency
AFLC	Air Force Logistics Command
AFLIF	Air Force Logistics Information File
AFLMC	Air Force Logistics Management Center
AFMSS	Air Force Mission Support System
AFR	Air Force Reserve

AFSC	Air Force Systems Command or Air Force Specialty Code
AFSOC	Air Force Special Operations Command
AFSOUTH	Allied Forces, South (NATO)
AFWMPRT	Air Force Wartime Manpower and Personnel Readiness Team
AGE	Aerospace Ground Equipment
AGL	Above Ground Level
AI	Air Interdiction
AIF	Automated Installation File
AIR	Air Inflatable Retarder
AIWS	Advanced Interdiction Weapons System
ALARM	Air-Launched Anti-Radiation Missile
ALC	Air Logistics Center
ALCC	Airlift Control Center
ALCE	Airlift Control Element
ALCM	Air-Launched Cruise Missile
ALMSNSCD	Airlift Mission Schedule
ALO	Air Liaison Officer
AMI	Aeronautical Militare Italiana
AMRAAM	Advanced Medium-Range Air-to-Air Missile
AMU	Aircraft Maintenance Unit
ANG	Air National Guard
ANGLCO	Air and Naval Gunfire Liaison Company (USMC)
AO	Area of Operation
AOB	Air Order of Battle
AOR	Area of Responsibility
APC	Armored Personnel Carrier

APCC	Aerial Port Control Center
APOD	Aerial Port of Debarkation
APS	Afloat Prepositioning Ship
ARBS	Angle Rate Bombing Set (USMC)
ARC	Air Reserve Components
ARCENT	U.S. Army Forces, Central Command
AREFS	Air Refueling Squadron
ARM	Antiradiation Missiles
ARNG	U.S. Army National Guard
ARS	Air Rescue Service
ARW	Air Rescue Wing
ASARS	Advanced Synthetic Aperture Radar System
ASD(PA)	Assistant Secretary of Defense (Public Affairs)
ASD(SO-LIC)	Assistant Secretary of Defense (Special Operations and Low Intensity Conflict)
ASM	Air-to-Surface Missile
ASMA	Air Staff Management Aide (UK and Iraq)
ASOC	Air Support Operations Center (Army/USAF)
ASUWC	Anti-to-Surface Unit Warfare Commander (USN)
ATACMS	Army Tactical Missile System
ATAF	Allied Tactical Air Force (NATO)
ATC	Air Training Command (USAF)
ATGM	Anti-Tank Guided Munition
ATO	Air Tasking Order
ATTG	Automated Tactical Target Graphic

AUTODIN	Automatic Digital Network
AVCAL	Aviation Coordinated Allowance List (USN)
AVLB	Armored Vehicle-Launched Bridge
Avn Bde	Aviation Brigade (US)
AWACS	Airborne Warning and Control System
AWN	Automated Weather Network
AWS	Airborne Warning System
BAAF	Bahrain Amiri Air Force
BAI	Battlefield Air Interdiction
BARCAP	Barrier Combat Air Patrol
BAS	Basic Allowance for Subsistence
BBBG	Battleship Battle Group
BCE	Battlefield Coordination Element
BDA	Bomb Damage Assessment
Bde	Brigade (US)
BDU	Battle Dress Uniform
BE or BEN	Basic Encyclopedia (number)
BEEF	Base Engineer Emergency Force
BLT	Battalion Landing Team (USMC)
BMP	Soviet armored personnel carrier
BMS	Bombardment Squadron
BMW	Bombardment Wing
B/N	Bombardier/Navigator
BND	German Federal Intelligence Service
BTG	Basic Target Graphic
BVR	Beyond Visual Range
BW	Biological Warfare

C-Day	Deployment Day
C3	Command, Control, and Communications
C3CM	Command, Control, Communications Countermeasures
C3I	Command, Control, Communications, and Intelligence
C3IC	Coordination, Control, Communications, and Intelligence Center
C4	Command, Control, Communications, and Computers
CA	Civil Affairs
CADOB	Consolidated Air Defense Order of Battle
CAF	Canadian Air Force
CAFMS	Computer Aided Force Management System
CAFT	Center for Anti-Fratricide Technology
CALCM	Conventional Air Launched Cruise Missile
CAMS	Core Automated Maintenance System
CAP	Combat Air Patrol
CAS	Close Air Support or Combat Ammunition System
CASSUM	Close Air Support Summary
CAT	Crisis Action Team
CB	Chemical/Biological
CBU	Cluster Bomb Unit
CBW	Chemical/Biological Weapons
CCD	Camouflage, Concealment and Deception

CCIP	Continuously Computed Impact Point
CCRC	Combined Control and Reporting Center
CEM	Combined Effects Munition
CEMIRT	Civil Engineering Maintenance, Inspection, Repair, and Training
CENTAF	U.S. Air Force, Central Command
CENTCOM	U.S. Central Command
CEP	Circular Error Probable
CES	Civil Engineering Squadron
CEV	Combat Engineer Vehicle
CFT	Conformal Fuel Tank
CI	Civilian Internees
CIA	Central Intelligence Agency
CIFS	Close-In Fire Support (USMC)
CINC	Commander-in-Chief
CINCCENT	Commander-in-Chief U.S. Central Command
CINCMAC	Commander-in-Chief, Military Airlift Command
CINCSPACE	Commander-in-Chief U.S. Space Command
CINCTRANS	Commander-in-Chief, U.S. Transportation
CINCTRANSCOM	Commander-in-Chief U.S. Transportation Command
CJCS	Chairman, Joint Chiefs of Staff
CMMS	Congressionally Mandated Mobility Study
CNN	Cable News Network

COCOM	Combatant Command (Command Authority)
COMALF	Commander, Airlift Forces
COMAO	Composite Air Operation
COMMZ	Communications Zone
COMPES	Contingency Operations Mobility Planning and Execution System
COMSEC	Communications Security
COMTAC	Commander of Tactical Air Command
COMUSCENTAF	Commander, U.S. Air Force, Central Command
COMUSCENTCOM	Commander, U.S. Central Command
CNA	Center for Naval Analysis
CNO	Chief of Naval Operations
COMINT	Communications Intelligence
COMSAT	Communications Satellite
CONUS	Continental United States
COSCOM	Corps Support Command (US Army)
CPX	Command Post Exercise
CRAF	Civil Reserve Air Fleet
CRC	Control and Reporting Center
CS	Combat Support
CSAR	Combat Search and Rescue
CSG	Contingency Support Graphic
CSS	Combat Service Support
CSSA	CENTAF Supply Support Agency or Combat Service Support Area
CT	Counterterrorism
CTJTF	Counterterrorism Joint Task Force
CVBG	Aircraft Carrier Battle Group (USN)

CW	Chemical Warfare
CWEP	Conventional Weapons Enhanced Penetration
CWP	Contingency Weather Package
D&D	Decoy and Deception
DACT	Dissimilar Aerial Combat Tactics
DARPA	Defense Advanced Research Projects Agency
DAS	Deep Air Support (USMC)
DASC	Direct Air Support Center (USMC)
DCA	Defense Communications Agency
DCI	Director of Central Intelligence
D-Day	Unnamed day on which an operations begins
DDN	Defense Data Network
DF	Direction Fired or Direction Finding
DFR/ME	Defense Fuel Region, Middle East
DFSC	Defense Fuel Supply Center
DFSP	Defense Fuel Supply Point
DIA	Defense Intelligence Agency
DIS	Daily Intelligence Summary
DISA	Defense Information Systems Agency
Div	Division
DLA	Defense Logistics Agency
DLIR	Downward Looking Infrared
DMA	Defense Mapping Agency
DMDC	Defense Manpower Data Center
DMI	Directorate of Military Intelligence (Israel, Iraq, Egypt)

DMSP	Defense Meteorological Satellite Program
DMPI	Desired Mean Point of Impact
DNA	Defense Nuclear Agency
DOC	Designed Operational Capability
DOD	Department of Defense
DOE	Department of Energy
DOPMA	Defense Officer Personnel Management Act
DOS	Department of State
DOT	Department of Transportation
DOWSR	Directorate of Weather for Strategic Reconnaissance
DPA	Defense Production Act
DPG	Defense Planning Guidance
DSB	Defense Science Board
DSCS	Defense Satellite Communication System
DSFU	Desert Storm Forecast Unit
DSMAC	Digitized Scene Mapping and Correlation
DSP	Defense Support Program
EAC	Echelon Above Corps or Eastern Area Command
ECM	Electronic Countermeasures
ECS	Electronic Combat Squadron
EDS	European Distribution System
EDT	Eastern Daylight Time
ELINT	Electronic Intelligence
EMIS	Electro-Magnetic Isotope Separation

EOB	Electronic Order of Battle
EOD	Explosive Ordnance Disposal
EOGB	Electro-Optically Guided Bomb
EOTDAS	Electro-Optical Tactical Decision Aid Software
EPW	Enemy Prisoner of War
ESA	European Space Agency
EST	Eastern Standard Time
ETTF	European Tanker Task Force
EUCOM	European Command
EW	Electronic Warfare
EWO	Electronic Warfare Officer
EWWS	Electronic Warfare Warning System or Set
FAC	Forward Air Control
FAE	Fuel Air Explosive
FAF	French Air Force
FAPES	Force Augmentation Planning and Execution System
FEBA	Forward Edge of the Battle Area
FEWS	Follow-on Early Warning System
FHTV	Family of Heavy Tactical Vehicles
FID	Foreign Internal Defense
FLIR	Forward-Looking Infrared
FLOGEN	Flow Generation computer model
FLOT	Forward Line of Own Troops
FMC	Fully Mission Capable
FMF	Fleet Marine Force
FMS	Foreign Military Sales

FMSE	Fuels Management Support Equipment
FMTV	Family of Medium Tactical Vehicles
FNOC	Fleet Numerical Oceanography Center (USN)
FOL	Forward Operating Location
FORSCOM	U.S. Army Forces Command
FOSK	Follow-on Spares Kits
FOV	Field of View
FROG	Free Rocket Over Ground
FSCL	Fire Support Coordination Line
FSS	Fast Sealift Support
FTX	Field Training Exercise
G-Day	Day the ground war began
GAO	General Accounting Office
GC	Geneva Convention
GCC	Gulf Cooperation Committee
GCI	Ground Control Intercept
GCU	Guidance and Control Unit
GDSS	Global Decision Support System
GENA	Ground Air Navigation Aids radar (U.K./Saudi)
GHQ	General Headquarters (usually theater level)
GLO	Ground Liaison Officer
GMT	Greenwich Mean Time
GNA	Goldwater-Nichols DOD Reorganization Act
GOB	Ground Order of Battle
GOK	Government of Kuwait
GOSC	General Officer Steering Committee

GP	General Purpose bomb
GPS	Global Positioning System or Satellite
H-Hour	Specific time at which operations commence
HA	Heavy Armor
HARM	High Speed Antiradiation Missile
HAB	Hardened Aircraft Bunker
HAS	Hardened Aircraft Shelter
HEMTT	Heavy Expanded Mobility Tactical Truck
HET	Heavy Equipment Transporter
HF	High Frequency
HIDACZ	High Density Airspace Control Zone
HMMWV	High Mobility Multipurpose Wheeled Vehicle
HNS	Host-nation Support
HTPM	Hard Target Penetrator Munitions
HUD	Heads-Up Display
HUMINT	Human Resources Intelligence
HVAA	High Value Airborne Assets
I&W	Indications and Warnings
IAADF	Iraqi Air and Air Defense Forces
IADF	Iraqi Air Defense Forces
IADS	Integrated Air Defense System
IAEC	International Atomic Energy Commission
IAF	Italian Air Force
ICAO	International Commercial Aviation Organization

ICRC	International Committee of the Red Cross
IDF	Israel Defense Force
IFF	Identification Friend or Foe
IFR	Instrument Flight Reference
IFV	Infantry Fighting Vehicle
IIR	Intelligence Information Report or Imaging Infrared
ILM	Intermediate-Level Maintenance
ILMC	Intermediate-Level Maintenance Center
IMA	Individual Mobilization Augmentee
IMET	International Military Education and Training
IMINT	Imagery Intelligence
IMQT	Initial Mission Qualification Training
INS	Inertial Navigation System
IOC	Intercept Operations Center or Integrated Operations Center
IOT&E	Initial Operational Test and Evaluation
IP	Initial Point
IPDS	Inland Petroleum Distribution System (US Army)
IR	Infrared
IRR	Individual Ready Reserve
ISW	Integrated Strike Warfare
ITAC	Intelligence and Threat Analysis Center (US Army)
ITF	Intelligence Task Force (DIA)
IZAF	Iraqi Air Force
J-1	Manpower & Personnel Directorate (Joint)

J-2	Intelligence Directorate (Joint)
J-3	Operations Directorate (Joint)
J-4	Logistics Directorate (Joint)
J-5	Strategic Plans & Policy Directorate (Joint)
J-6	Command, Control & Communications Systems Directorate (Joint)
J-7	Operational Plans & Interoperability Directorate (Joint)
J-8	Force Structure Resource & Assessment Directorate (Joint)
JAAT	Joint Air Attack Team
JAG	Judge Advocate General
JAIC	Joint Atomic Intelligence Committee
Jaguar	Land-based ground attack aircraft
JAMPS	Joint Automated Message Program
JCEOI	Joint Communications Electronics Operations Instructions
JCMEC	Joint Captured Material Exploitation Center
JCS	Joint Chiefs of Staff
JCSE	Joint Communications Support Element
JDOP	Joint U.S./Saudi Directorate of Planning
JDS	Joint Deployment System
JFACC	Joint Force Air Component Commander.
JFC	Joint Forces Commander
JFC-E	Joint Forces Command East
JFC-N	Joint Forces Command North

JFLCC	Joint Forces Land Component Commander
JFMCC	Joint Forces Maritime Component Commander
JFSOCC	Joint Forces Special Operations Component Commander
JIB	Joint Information Bureau
JIC	Joint Intelligence Center
JIPC	Joint Imagery Production Center
JIST	Joint Intelligence Survey Team
JMCC	Joint Movement Control Center
JMEM	Joint Munitions Effectiveness Manual
JOPES	Joint Operations Planning and Execution System
JPEC	Joint Planning and Execution Community
JPTS	Jet Propellant Thermally Stable
JRC	Joint Reconnaissance Center
JRCC	Joint Rescue Coordination Center
JS	Joint Staff
JSCP	Joint Strategic Capabilities Plan
JSEAD	Joint Suppression of Enemy Air Defenses
JSIPS	Joint Service Imagery Processing System
JSOTF	Joint Special Operations Task Force
JSPS	Joint Strategic Planning System
JSTARS	Joint Surveillance Target Attack Radar System (E-8)
JTACMS	Joint Tactical Missile System
JTCB	Joint Target Coordination Board

JTF	Joint Task Force
JTFME	Joint Task Force Middle East
JTIDS	Joint Tactical Information Distribution System
JTTP	Joint Tactics, Techniques and Procedures
JULL	Joint Uniform Lessons Learned
KAF	Kuwaiti Air Force
KCATF	Kuwait Civil Affairs Task Force
KHZ	Kilohertz
KKMC	King Khalid Military City
KIA	Killed In Action
KTO	Kuwait Theater of Operations
LAMPS	Light Airborne Multi-Purpose System (USN)
LANDSAT	Land Satellite, NASA/NOAA Satellite Program
LANTCOM	Atlantic Command
LANTIRN	Low Altitude Navigation and Targeting Infrared System for Night
LAV	Light Armored Vehicle
LCAC	Air Cushioned Landing Craft
LCC	Land Component Commander
LDGP	Low Drag General Purpose bomb
LENSCE	Limited Enemy Situation/Correlation Equipment
LG	Logistics
LGB	Laser Guided Bomb
LGGAIR	Logistics Airlift
LIATE	LANTIRIN Intermediate Automatic Test Equipment

LOC	Lines of Communication
LOS	Line of Sight
LOTS	Logistics Over the Shore
LRC	Logistics Readiness Center (USAF)
LRI	Long Range International
LVS	Logistics Vehicle System
MAC	Military Airlift Command
MACCS	Marine Air Command and Control System
MACG	Marine Air Control Group
MAG	Marine Airlift Group
MAGTF	Marine Air Ground Task Force
MAIRS	Military Airlift Integrated Reporting System
MAJCOMS	Major Commands
MAP	Master Attack Plan
MARCENT	U.S. Marine Corps, Central Command
MARDIV	Marine Division
MASF	Mobile Aeromedical Staging Facility
MASS	MICAP Asset Sourcing System
MAW	Marine Aircraft Wing
MCI	Ministry of Culture and Information (Iraq)
MCM	Mine Countermeasures or Multi-Command Manual
MEB	Marine Expeditionary Brigade
Mech Div	Mechanized Infantry Division
MEF	Marine Expeditionary Force
MEL	Mobile Erector-Launcher used for mobile missiles

METS	Mobile Electronic Test Set
METSAT	Meteorological Satellite
MEU	Marine Expeditionary Unit
MHE	Materiel Handling Equipment
MIA	Missing In Action
MIF	Maritime Interdiction Force
MICAP	Mission Critical Parts or Mission Capable or Mission Capability Limiting
MILCON	Military Construction
MILSATCOM	Military Satellite Communications
MILSTAR	Military Strategic and Tactical Relay System
MIO	Maritime Intercept Operations
MIPE	Mobile Intelligence Processing Element
MIS	Military Intelligence Study
MISREP	Mission Report
MLRS	Multiple Launch Rocket System
MLV	Memory Loader Verifier
MOBREP	Manpower Mobilization and Accession Status Report
MOD	Ministry of Defense
MODA	Ministry of Defense and Aviation (Saudi Arabia)
MOPP	Mission Oriented Protective Posture
MPES	Medical Planning and Execution System
MPF	Maritime Prepositioning Force
MPS	Maritime Prepositioning Ships
MRE	Meals Ready to Eat

MRR	Minimum Risk Route
MRS	Mobility Requirements Study
MSC	Military Sealift Command
MSE	Mobile Subscriber Equipment
MSI	Multi-Spectral Imagery
MSK	Mission Support Kits
MTACC	Marine Tactical Air Command Center
MTI	Moving Target Indicator
MTL	Master Target List
MTMC	Military Traffic Management Command
NAC	Northern Area Command
NALE	Naval Amphibious Liaison Element
NATO	North Atlantic Treaty Organization
NAVCENT	U.S. Navy, Central Command
NAVEUR	Naval Forces, Europe
NAVSTAR	Navigational Satellite Timing and Ranging
NBC	Nuclear, Biological, and Chemical
NCA	National Command Authorities
NCTR	Noncooperative Target Recognition
NDRF	National Defense Reserve Fleet
NDS	NPIC Data Systems
NF or NOFORN	Not Releasable to Foreign Nationals
NGB	National Guard Bureau
NGFS	Naval Gunfire Support
NIE	National Intelligence Estimate
NMAC	Near Mid-Air Collision
NMCS	Not Mission Capable Supplies

NMCM	Not Mission Capable Maintenance
NMIC	National Military Intelligence Center
NMIST	National Military Intelligence Support Teams
NOAA	National Oceanographic and Atmospheric Administration
NOB	Naval Order of Battle
NODDS	Naval Oceanographic Data Dissemination System
NPIC	National Photo Interpretation Center
NSA	National Security Agency
NSC	National Security Council
NTC	Night Targeting Cell (in GAT)
NVG	Night Vision Goggles
O&M	Operations and Maintenance
OAS	Offensive Avionics System
OASD/(DR&E)	Office of the Assistant Secretary of Defense (Defense Research & Engineering)
OASD/(SO/LIC)	Office of the Assistant Secretary of Defense (Special Operations/Low Intensity Conflict)
OB	Order of Battle
OCA	Offensive Counter Air
OCP	Observation Command Post
OICC	Operational Intelligence Crisis Center
OP	Observation Post
OPAIR	Opposing Air
OPCON	Operational Control
OPDS	Offshore Petroleum Distribution System (USN)

OPEC	Organization of Petroleum Exporting Countries
OPLAN	Operation Plan
OPORD	Operation Order
OPSEC	Operational Security
OSD	Office of the Secretary of Defense
OSI	Office of Special Investigations (USAF)
OSP	Operational Support Package
PACOM	Pacific Command
PA	Public Affairs
PAO	Public Affairs Officer
PCITF	Positive Combat Identification Task Force
PGM	Precision Guided Munitions
PIN	Primary Identification Number
PLO	Palestine Liberation Organization
PLS	Palletized Loading System
PLV	Program Loader Verifier
PMC	Partially Mission Capable
PMEL	Precision Measurement Equipment Laboratory
PMT	Pastoral Ministry Team
PNVS	Pilot Night Vision System
POG	Psychological Operations Group
POL	Petroleum, Oils and Lubricants
POMCUS	Pre-positioning of Material Configured to Unit Sets
POW	Prisoner of War
PREPO	Pre-positioned

PSYOP	Psychological Operation
PSYOPS	Psychological Operations
PTAS	Provisional Tactical Airlift Squadron
QEAF	Qatari Emiri Air Force
QRCT	Quick Reaction Communications Terminal
R&D	Research and Development
R&M	Reliability and Maintainability
RADIC	Rapidly Deployable Integrated Command and Control system
RAF	Royal Air Force (U.K.)
RAFVR	Royal Air Force Voluntary Reserve
RAM	Radar Absorptive Material
RC	Reserve Component
RCAF	Royal Canadian Air Force
RCC	Rescue Coordination Center or Revolutionary Command Council (Iraq)
RDAF	Royal Dutch Air Force
RDF	Rapid Deployment Force or Radio Direction Finding
RDIT	Rapid Deployment Imagery Terminal
RDJTF	Rapid Deployment Joint Task Force
Red Horse	Rapid Engineer Deployable, Heavy Operational Repair Squadron, Engineer
REMIS	Reliability and Maintainability Information System
RFI	Request for Information
RFMD	RED FLAG Measurement Debriefing
RGFC	Republican Guard Force Command (Iraq)
RIBS	Readiness in Base Services

RJAF	Royal Jordanian Air Force
RLT	Regimental Landing Team (USMC)
RO/RO	Roll On/Roll Off
ROE	Rules of Engagement
ROTHR	Relocatable Over-The-Horizon Radar
RPV	Remotely Piloted Vehicle
RRF	Ready Reserve Force or Ready Reserve Fleet
RSADF	Royal Saudi Air Defense Force
RSAF	Royal Saudi Air Force
RSLF	Royal Saudi Land Force
RTNEPH	Real-Time Nephanalysis
RW	Reconnaissance Wing
RWR	Radar Warning Receiver
S&TI	Scientific and Technical Intelligence
SA	Selective Availability
SAAF	Saudi Arabian Armed Forces
SAC	Strategic Air Command
SAG	Saudi Arabian Government or Surface Action Group (USN)
SAM	Surface-to-Air Missile
SAMAREC	Saudi Arabian Marketing and Refining Company
SANG	Saudi Arabian National Guard
SAR	Search and Rescue
SAS	Special Air Service (U.K.)
SATCOM	Satellite Communications
SBS	Special Boat Service (U.K.)
SBSS	Standard Base Supply System

SCUD	Soviet surface-to-surface missile
SCI	Sensitive Compartmented Information
SCIF	Sensitive Compartmented Information Facility
SEAD	Suppression of Enemy Air Defenses
SEAL	Sea Air Land
SECDEF	Secretary of Defense
SFG	Special Forces Group
SFW	Sensor Fuzed Weapon
SHAPE	Supreme Headquarters, Allied Powers, Europe
SHF	Super High Frequency
SIDS	Secondary Imagery Dissemination System
SIGINT	Signals Intelligence
SINCGARS	Single Channel Ground/Airborne Radio Subsystem
SIOP	Single Integrated Operations Plan
SITREP	Situation Report
SLAM	Standoff Land Attack Missile
SLAR	Side-Looking Airborne Radar
SLOC	Sea Lines of Communications
SMESA	Special Middle East Shipping Agreement
SNIE	Special National Intelligence Estimate
SOAF	Sultanate of Oman Air Force
SOC	Sector Operations Center (Air Defense) or Special Operations Command
SOCCENT	Special Operations Command, Central Command

SOCOM	Special Operations Command
SOF	Special Operations Forces
SOFA	Status of Forces Agreement
SOG	Special Operations Group
SOS	Special Operations Squadron
SOW	Special Operations Wing
SPACC	U.S. SPACECOM Space Control Center
SPEAR	Strike Projection Evaluation and Anti-Air Warfare Research (USN)
SPINS	Special Instructions
SPOT	French Satellite Probatoire d'Observation de la Terre
SRBM	Short-range Ballistic Missile
SRP	Sealift Readiness Program
SRW	Surveillance and Reconnaissance Wing
SSA	Selective Service Act
SSM	Surface-to-Surface Missile
STAMP	Standard Air Munitions Package
STGP	Special Tactics Group (USAF)
STON	Short Ton (2,000 pounds or 0.9 metric tons)
STPJ	Special Tactic Paramedics (USAF)
STRAPP	Standard Tank, Rack, Adapter, and Pylon Package
STRATFOR	Strategic Forces Advisors
STU	Secure Telephone Unit
SURVIAC	Survivability and Vulnerability Information Analysis Center
SWA	Southwest Asia

SYERS	Senior Year Electro-Optical Reconnaissance System
TAC	Tactical Air Command
TACAIR	Tactical Air
TACC	Tactical Air Control Center
TACON	Tactical Control
TACP	Tactical Air Control Party
TACS	Tactical Air Control System
TACSAT	Tactical Satellite
TADIL	Tactical Digital Information Link or Tactical Data Interface Link
TAF	Tactical Aircraft Forces
TAG	Tactical Airlift Group
TAIRCW	Tactical Air Control Wing
TALD	Tactical Air-Launched Decoy
TALO	Theater Airlift Liaison Officer
TANKREP	Tank Killer Report
TAOC	Tactical Air Operations Center (USMC)
TARCAP	Target Combat Air Patrol
TARPS	Tactical Air Reconnaissance Pod System
TAW	Tactical Airlift Wing
TAWC	Tactical Air Warfare Center
TBM	Tactical Ballistic Missile
TCN	Transportation Control Number
TDA	Tactical Decision Aid
TEL	Transporter-Erector-Launcher
TEMPER	Tent Expendable Modular Personnel
TER	Triple Ejector Rack

TERCOM	Terrain Contour Matching
TFS	Tactical Fighter Squadron
TFW	Tactical Fighter Wing
TIALD	Thermal Imaging and Laser Designating
TIARA	Tactical Intelligence and Related Activities
TIBS	Tactical Information Broadcast System (USAF)
TIROS	Television and Infrared Observation Satellites
TIS	Tactical Intelligence Squadron
TLAM	Tomahawk Land-Attack Missile
TMD	Tactical Ballistic Missile Defense
TO	Technical Order
TO&E	Table of Organization and Equipment
TOAF	Tactical Operations Area Forecast
TOT	Time Over Target
TPFDD	Time-Phased Force Deployment Data
TPFDL	Time-Phased Force Deployment List
TR	Theater Reserves
TRADOC	Training and Doctrine Command (US Army)
TRAM	Target Recognition and Acquisition Multisensor (USN)
TRANSCOM	U.S. Transportation Command
TRAP	Tanks, Racks, Adapters, and Pylons
TRG	Tactical Reconnaissance Group
TTF	Tanker Task Force
TTM	Tactical Target Material

TTP	Tactics, Techniques, and Procedures
UAE	United Arab Emirates
UAEAF	United Arab Emirates Air Force
UAV	Unmanned Aerial Vehicle
UAWS	USAREUR Automated Weather System
UCMJ	Uniform Code of Military Justice
UHF	Ultra High Frequency
UK	United Kingdom
ULN	Unit Line Number
UMMIPS	Uniform Military Management and Movement Indicator System
UN	United Nations
UND	Urgency of Need Designator
UNSC	United Nations Security Council
USACE	U.S. Army Corps of Engineers
USAF	United States Air Force
USAFE	U.S. Air Force Europe
USAFR	United States Air Force Reserve
USAR	U.S. Army Reserve
USC	United States Code
USCENTCOM	Central Command
USCG	U. S. Coast Guard
USCINCCENT	Commander-in-Chief U.S. Central Command
USCINCCENT	U.S. Commander-in-Chief, Central Command
USDAO	U.S. Defense Attache Office
USEUCOM	U.S. European Command
USG	United States Government

USIA	U.S. Information Agency
USMC	U.S. Marine Corps
USN	U.S. Navy
USNAVCENT	U.S. Navy, U.S. Central Command
USNR	U.S. Navy Reserve
USPACCOM	U.S. Pacific Command
USSOCOM	U.S. Special Operations Command
USSOUTHCOM	U.S. Southern Command
USSPACECOM	U.S. Space Command
USTRANSCOM	U.S. Transportation Command
UTC	Unit Type Code
UTE	Utilization Rate
VA	Department of Veteran's Affairs
VCJCS	Vice Chairman, Joint Chiefs of Staff
VFR	Visual Flight Reference
WAM	Wide Area Mine
WATCHCON	Watch Condition
WCDC	War Crimes Documentation Center
WFOV	Wide Field of View
WHNS	Wartime Host-Nation Support
WIA	Wounded in Action
WIN	Worldwide Military Command and Control System Intercomputer Network
WN or WNINTEL	Warning Notice: Intelligence Sources and Methods Involved
WOC	Wing Operations Center
WRM	War Reserve Material
WRSK	War Readiness Spares Kits
WSO	Weapons System Operator

WWIMS	Worldwide Indicators and Monitoring System
WWMCCS	Worldwide Military Command and Control System
WXG	Weather Group

ISBN 0-16-042927-7

9 780160 429279

90000